XML
in Plain English

XML
in Plain English

Sandra E. Eddy

IDG Books Worldwide, Inc.
An International Data Group Company

Foster City, CA • Chicago, IL • Indianapolis, IN • New York, NY

XML in Plain English

Published by
M&T Books
An imprint of IDG Books Worldwide, Inc.
919 E. Hillsdale Blvd., Suite 400
Foster City, CA 94404
www.idgbooks.com (IDG Books Worldwide Web site)

Library of Congress Catalog Card Number: 98-73785

ISBN: 0-7645-7006-4

Printed in the United States of America

10 9 8 7 6 5 4 3 2

1P/RT/RQ/ZY/FC

Distributed in the United States by IDG Books Worldwide, Inc.

Distributed by Macmillan Canada for Canada; by Transworld Publishers Limited in the United Kingdom; by IDG Norge Books for Norway; by IDG Sweden Books for Sweden; by Woodslane Pty. Ltd. for Australia; by Woodslane (NZ) Ltd. for New Zealand; by Addison Wesley Longman Singapore Pte Ltd. for Singapore, Malaysia, Thailand, Indonesia, and Korea; by Norma Comunicaciones S.A. for Colombia; by Intersoft for South Africa; by International Thomson Publishing for Germany, Austria, and Switzerland; by Toppan Company Ltd. for Japan; by Distribuidora Cuspide for Argentina; by Livraria Cultura for Brazil; by Ediciencia S.A. for Ecuador; by Ediciones ZETA S.C.R. Ltda. for Peru; by WS Computer Publishing Corporation, Inc., for the Philippines; by Unalis Corporation for Taiwan; by Contemporanea de Ediciones for Venezuela; by Computer Book & Magazine Store for Puerto Rico; by Express Computer Distributors for the Caribbean and West Indies. Authorized Sales Agent: Anthony Rudkin Associates for the Middle East and North Africa.

For general information on IDG Books Worldwide's books in the U.S., please call our Consumer Customer Service department at 800-762-2974. For reseller information, including discounts and premium sales, please call our Reseller Customer Service department at 800-434-3422.

For information on where to purchase IDG Books Worldwide's books outside the U.S., please contact our International Sales department at 650-655-3200 or fax 650-655-3297.

For information on foreign language translations, please contact our Foreign & Subsidiary Rights department at 650-655-3021 or fax 650-655-3281.

For sales inquiries and special prices for bulk quantities, please contact our Sales department at 650-655-3200 or write to the address above.

For information on using IDG Books Worldwide's books in the classroom or for ordering examination copies, please contact our Educational Sales department at 800-434-2086 or fax 317-596-5499.

For press review copies, author interviews, or other publicity information, please contact our Public Relations department at 650-655-3000 or fax 650-655-3299.

For authorization to photocopy items for corporate, personal, or educational use, please contact Copyright Clearance Center, 222 Rosewood Drive, Danvers, MA 01923, or fax 978-750-4470.

 is a trademark under exclusive license to IDG Books Worldwide, Inc., from International Data Group, Inc.

 is a trademark of IDG Books Worldwide, Inc.

ABOUT IDG BOOKS WORLDWIDE

Welcome to the world of IDG Books Worldwide.

IDG Books Worldwide, Inc., is a subsidiary of International Data Group, the world's largest publisher of computer-related information and the leading global provider of information services on information technology. IDG was founded more than 25 years ago and now employs more than 8,500 people worldwide. IDG publishes more than 275 computer publications in over 75 countries (see listing below). More than 90 million people read one or more IDG publications each month.

Launched in 1990, IDG Books Worldwide is today the #1 publisher of best-selling computer books in the United States. We are proud to have received eight awards from the Computer Press Association in recognition of editorial excellence and three from *Computer Currents'* First Annual Readers' Choice Awards. Our best-selling *...For Dummies®* series has more than 50 million copies in print with translations in 38 languages. IDG Books Worldwide, through a joint venture with IDG's Hi-Tech Beijing, became the first U.S. publisher to publish a computer book in the People's Republic of China. In record time, IDG Books Worldwide has become the first choice for millions of readers around the world who want to learn how to better manage their businesses.

Our mission is simple: Every one of our books is designed to bring extra value and skill-building instructions to the reader. Our books are written by experts who understand and care about our readers. The knowledge base of our editorial staff comes from years of experience in publishing, education, and journalism — experience we use to produce books for the '90s. In short, we care about books, so we attract the best people. We devote special attention to details such as audience, interior design, use of icons, and illustrations. And because we use an efficient process of authoring, editing, and desktop publishing our books electronically, we can spend more time ensuring superior content and spend less time on the technicalities of making books.

You can count on our commitment to deliver high-quality books at competitive prices on topics you want to read about. At IDG Books Worldwide, we continue in the IDG tradition of delivering quality for more than 25 years. You'll find no better book on a subject than one from IDG Books Worldwide.

IDG
BOOKS
WORLDWIDE

John Kilcullen
John Kilcullen
CEO
IDG Books Worldwide, Inc.

Steven Berkowitz
Steven Berkowitz
President and Publisher
IDG Books Worldwide, Inc.

IDG Books Worldwide, Inc., is a subsidiary of International Data Group, the world's largest publisher of computer-related information and the leading global provider of information services on information technology. International Data Group publishes over 275 computer publications in over 75 countries. More than 90 million people read one or more International Data Group publications each month. International Data Group's publications include: ARGENTINA: Buyer's Guide, Computerworld Argentina, PC World Argentina; AUSTRALIA: Australian Macworld, Australian PC World, Australian Reseller News, Computerworld, IT Casebook, Network World, Publish, Webmaster; AUSTRIA: Computerwelt Österreich, Networks Austria, PC Tip Austria; BANGLADESH: PC World Bangladesh; BELARUS: PC World Belarus; BELGIUM: Data News; BRAZIL: Annuário de Informática, Computerworld, Connections, Macworld, PC Player, PC World, Publish, Reseller News, Supergamepower; BULGARIA: Computerworld Bulgaria, Network World Bulgaria, PC & MacWorld Bulgaria; CANADA: CIO Canada, Client/Server World, ComputerWorld Canada, InfoWorld Canada, NetworkWorld Canada, WebWorld; CHILE: Computerworld Chile, PC World Chile; COLOMBIA: Computerworld Colombia, PC World Colombia; COSTA RICA: PC World Centro America; THE CZECH AND SLOVAK REPUBLICS: Computerworld Czechoslovakia, Macworld Czech Republic, PC World Czechoslovakia; DENMARK: Communications World Danmark, Computerworld Danmark, Macworld Danmark, PC World Danmark, Techworld Denmark; DOMINICAN REPUBLIC: PC World Republica Dominicana; ECUADOR: PC World Ecuador; EGYPT: Computerworld Middle East, PC World Middle East; EL SALVADOR: PC World Centro America; FINLAND: MikroPC, Tietoverkko, Tietoviikko; FRANCE: Distributique, Hebdo, Info PC, Le Monde Informatique, Macworld, Reseaux & Telecoms, WebMaster France; GERMANY: Computer Partner, Computerwoche, Computerwoche Extra, Computerwoche FOCUS, Global Online, Macwelt, PC Welt; GREECE: Amiga Computing, GamePro Greece, Multimedia World; GUATEMALA: PC World Centro America; HONDURAS: PC World Centro America; HONG KONG: Computerworld Hong Kong, PC World Hong Kong, Publish in Asia; HUNGARY: ABCD CD-ROM, Computerworld Szamitastechnika, Internetto online Magazine, PC World Hungary, PC-X Magazin Hungary; ICELAND: Tolvuheimur PC World Island; INDIA: Information Communications World, Information Systems Computerworld, PC World India, Publish in Asia; INDONESIA: InfoKomputer PC World, Komputek Computerworld, Publish in Asia; IRELAND: ComputerScope, PC Live!; ISRAEL: Macworld Israel, People & Computers/Computerworld; ITALY: Computerworld Italia, Macworld Italia, Networking Italia, PC World Italia; JAPAN: DTP World, Macworld Japan, Nikkei Personal Computing, OS/2 World Japan, SunWorld Japan, Windows NT World, Windows World Japan; KENYA: PC World East African; KOREA: Hi-Tech Information, Macworld Korea, PC World Korea; MACEDONIA: PC World Macedonia; MALAYSIA: Computerworld Malaysia, PC World Malaysia, Publish in Asia; MALTA: PC World Malta; MEXICO: Computerworld Mexico, PC World Mexico; MYANMAR: PC World Myanmar; NETHERLANDS: Computer! Totaal, LAN Internetworking Magazine, LAN World Buyers Guide, Macworld Netherlands, Net, WebWereld; NEW ZEALAND: Absolute Beginners Guide and Plain & Simple Series, Computer Buyer, Computer Industry Directory, Computerworld New Zealand, MTB, Network World, PC World New Zealand; NICARAGUA: PC World Centro America; NORWAY: Computerworld Norge, CW Rapport, Datamagasinet, Financial Rapport, Kursguide Norge, Macworld Norge, Multimediaworld Norge, PC World Ekspress Norge, PC World Nettverk, PC World Norge, PC World ProduktGuide Norge; PAKISTAN: Computerworld Pakistan; PANAMA: PC World Panama; PEOPLE'S REPUBLIC OF CHINA: China Computer Users, China Computerworld, China InfoWorld, China Telecom World Weekly, Computer & Communication, Electronic Design China, Electronics Today, Electronics Weekly, Game Software, PC World China, Popular Computer Week, Software Weekly, Software World, Telecom World; PERU: Computerworld Peru, PC World Profesional Peru, PC World SoHo Peru; PHILIPPINES: Click!, Computerworld Philippines, PC World Philippines, Publish in Asia; POLAND: Computerworld Poland, Computerworld Special Report Poland, Cyber, Macworld Poland, Networld Poland, PC World Komputer; PORTUGAL: Cerebro/PC World, Computerworld/Correio Informatico, Dealer World Portugal, Mac*In/PC*In Portugal, Multimedia World; PUERTO RICO: PC World Puerto Rico; ROMANIA: Computerworld Romania, PC World Romania, Telecom Romania; RUSSIA: Computerworld Russia, Mir PK, Publish, Seti; SINGAPORE: Computerworld Singapore, PC World Singapore, Publish in Asia; SLOVENIA: Monitor; SOUTH AFRICA: Computing SA, Network World SA, Software World SA; SPAIN: Communicaciones World España, Computerworld España, Dealer World España, Macworld España, PC World España; SRI LANKA: Infolink PC World; SWEDEN: CAP&Design, Computer Sweden, Corporate Computing Sweden, Internetworld Sweden, it.branschen, Macworld Sweden, MaxiData Sweden, MikroDatorn, Natverk & Kommunikation, PC World Sweden, PCaktiv, Windows World Sweden; SWITZERLAND: Computerworld Schweiz, Macworld Schweiz, PCtip; TAIWAN: Computerworld Taiwan, Macworld Taiwan, NEW VISiON/Publish, PC World Taiwan, Windows World Taiwan; THAILAND: Publish in Asia, Thai Computerworld; TURKEY: Computerworld Turkiye, Macworld Turkiye, Network World Turkiye, PC World Turkiye; UKRAINE: Computerworld Kiev, Multimedia World Ukraine, PC World Ukraine; UNITED KINGDOM: Acorn User UK, Amiga Action UK, Amiga Computing UK, Apple Talk UK, Computing, Macworld, Parents and Computers UK, PC Advisor, PC Home, PSX Pro, The WEB; UNITED STATES: Cable in the Classroom, CIO Magazine, Computerworld, DOS World, Federal Computer Week, GamePro Magazine, InfoWorld, I-Way, Macworld, Network World, PC Games, PC World, Publish, Video Event, THE WEB Magazine, and WebMaster; online webzines: JavaWorld, NetscapeWorld, and SunWorld Online; URUGUAY: InfoWorld Uruguay; VENEZUELA: Computerworld Venezuela, PC World Venezuela; and VIETNAM: PC World Vietnam.

5/7/98

Credits

Acquisitions Editor
Laura Lewin

Development Editor
Matthew E. Lusher

Technical Editor
Simon St. Laurent

Copy Editors
Bill McManus
Nicole Fountain

Project Coordinator
Susan Parini

Cover Coordinator
Cyndra Robbins

Book Designer
London Road Design

Graphics and Production Specialists
Linda Marousek
Hector Mendoza
Dina F Quan
E. A. Pauw

Quality Control Specialists
Mick Arellano
Mark Schumann

Proofreader
Jennifer K. Overmyer

Indexer
Ty Koontz

About the Author

Sandra E. Eddy, who writes both how-to and reference books about the Internet, Windows, and Windows applications, has been involved in computing since 1980. She is the author of well over one dozen books, including two editions of the comprehensive reference handbook, *HTML in Plain English*, and the easy-to-use how-to book on animating GIFs, *The GIF Animator's Guide* (both published by IDG Books Worldwide, Inc.). Until she became a full-time freelance writer in 1993, Ms. Eddy was a documentation manager and technical writer for a major software company. For over nine years, she wrote and edited documents ranging from the most complex reference guides for mainframe-computer operators to user manuals for PC-based applications to presentations for conferences. Ms. Eddy, who graduated from the Pennsylvania State University, is listed in *Who's Who in the East*. She lives with her husband and two golden retrievers in upstate New York.

In loving memory of Bart,
a golden friend who left us too soon.

Preface

Welcome to *XML in Plain English*. This reference handbook is designed to provide you with quick yet comprehensive information about the Extensible Markup Language (XML), which enables you to create custom markup languages; and the XLink Language and the XPointer Language, with which you can create sophisticated XML documents. In addition, two chapters are devoted to the cascading style sheet (CSS) and Document Style Semantics and Specification Language-Online (DSSSL-O) standards and an appendix covers Universal Character Set (UCS), or Unicode 2.0, and the supported character sets. Also included are many examples that you can use as both learning tools and templates for coding documents.

This handbook cuts to the heart of XML. When you want to create a new element, you don't need to learn about the background of XML; all you need is the name of the *production* (that is, XML instructions or components comprising instructions) and purpose, its syntax, attributes, and practical examples. Although *XML in Plain English* does not cover Web programming and scripting, it leads you right up to those levels and, through the Webliography, points you to online resources and much other XML information. This book is for all levels of XML developers — from first-time users to those most advanced.

XML in Plain English is the one essential XML reference that should have a special place next to your personal computer.

How This Book Is Organized

XML in Plain English is designed to be easy to use, regardless of your level of experience. *XML in Plain English* is organized as follows:

- **Chapter 1: *Overview*.** If you want to learn more about the origins of XML and find out how to create, post, and test XML documents, read through this part of the book.

- ***XML in Plain English*.** If you know what you want to do but can't remember the production or attribute name, view this thumbnail list of plain-English tasks and related XML productions and attributes.

- ***XML A to Z*.** If you know the name of the production or attribute you want to use, scan this alphabetically arranged list to find out the chapters in which the productions and attributes are located.

- **Chapter 2: *XML Syntax*.** If you know the production or attribute name but want to learn more about it or how to use it, browse through these pages. In this chapter, you find each production or attribute, its *production number* (the superscript number that often appears on the right side of a production name is a cross-reference to the XML specification), its purpose, its complete syntax and components, usage notes, related productions, and numerous examples.

- **Chapter 3: *XLink Language*.** If you want to learn about the productions with which you add both simple links and extended links to a document, look through this chapter.

- **Chapter 4: *XPointer Language*.** If you want to know about the productions with which you add extended pointers to an extended link, read the pages in this chapter.

- **Chapter 5: *Cascading Style Sheets*.** Throughout most of personal-computing history, individuals creating word processor documents have set standard paragraph formats using style sheets. Then, they have applied individual properties, or styles, from the style sheets to paragraphs in both new and old documents. You are now witnessing the beginning of the style-sheet era for electronic documents. This chapter provides an introduction and overview of cascading style sheets. You find each property along with its purpose, its complete syntax, usage notes, related styles, and examples.

- **Chapter 6: *DSSSL-O*.** XML also supports Document Style Semantics and Specification Language-Online (DSSSL-O), which provides an alternate and a more full-featured (but more difficult) way to style documents. In this chapter, you find each property along with its purpose, complete syntax, and usage notes, related styles, and selected examples.

- **Appendix A: *Unicode Characters and Character Sets*.** XML emphasizes *internationalization*, the use of many languages in documents. When you create documents using multiple languages, you use different alphabets and symbols, all of which should be supported. This appendix provides illustrated tables of characters and character sets (especially those commonly used by English-speaking people) and specifies non-English characters and character sets.

- **Appendix B: *XML Editors and Utilities*.** You can use a constantly growing group of XML editors and utilities to create and edit XML documents easily and efficiently on many computer platforms. This appendix lists editors and utilities along with the names of the developers and the URLs at which you can learn more about the programs.

- **Glossary.** XML, its parent SGML, style sheets, and the Internet have their own unique vocabularies. If you have never seen a particular term or you want a clarification, browse through this glossary of XML, SGML, style sheet, and Internet terms.

- **Webliography.** If you want to learn more about any of the information covered or mentioned in this book, look in the extensive Webliography (a Web bibliography) of XML and XML-related resources. The headings in the Webliography follow those in the rest of the book. The entry for each resource provides an Internet address and a brief description.

The Syntax Used in This Book

The two types of syntax provided with each production is Extended Backus-Naur Form (EBNF) notation and standard programming syntax.

Extended Backus-Naur Form (EBNF) Notation

EBNF syntax is the "official" standard used by those developing XML-based markup languages and for those learning about the productions and components that make up markup languages such as XML, its parent SGML, and its close relative HTML. EBNF uses the following conventions:

`Symbol│symbol ::= expression`	Each statement, which is known as a *rule*, defines one production, or *symbol*, in the XML syntax, or *grammar*. XML is case-sensitive; symbols having initial uppercase characters indicate a *regular expression* (that is, a way of grouping characters or options) and all other symbols are all lowercase characters. Note: When inserting an XML rule in a document, do not enter the symbol or ::=; enter the expression only.
`#xN`	Enter #x and N, a hexadecimal integer matching any UCS-4 code value in ISO/IEC 10646. For more information about Unicode characters, see Chapter 1, *Overview*, Appendix A, *Unicode Characters and Character Sets*, and the Webliography.
`[a-zA-Z], [#xN-#xN]`	Enter one of the characters within the range A-Z, or #xN to #xN. In this book, brackets ([ ]) appear in a larger point size to standardize the appearance of other characters that enclose parts of expressions.
`[^a-z], [^#xN-#xN]`	Do **not** enter any of the characters within the range adjacent to the **NOT** character.

`[^abc]`, `[^#xN#xN#xN]`	Do **not** enter any of the characters adjacent to the **NOT** character.
`"string"`	Enter the literal string enclosed within the quotation marks. Do **not** mix quotation marks and single quote marks in an expression.
`'string'`	Enter the literal string enclosed within the single quote marks. Do **not** mix quotation marks and single quote marks in an expression.
`(expression)`	Enter an expression comprised of a combination of the previously listed parts of XML syntax and using the following syntax, where A represents an expression:

`A?`	An expression followed by a question mark indicates that the expression is optional.
`A B`	One expression followed by another must be matched exactly. Note: A range (for example, A-B) contains no spaces, but the minus sign indicating an absent expression (A - B) is both preceded and succeeded by a space.
`A|B`	Expressions separated by pipe symbols indicate ORs (that is, you may use one or the other). In other words, just choose one. In this book, pipes appear in a larger point size to differentiate them from pipe characters within productions.
`A - B`	The first expression must be present, and the expression following the minus sign must be absent.
`A+`	The expression **must** appear one or more times.
`A*`	The expression **may** appear one or more times. Note: In this book, the parentheses enclosing a range are in a larger point size to standardize the appearance of other characters that enclose parts of expressions.

Standard Programming Syntax

Standard programming syntax uses the following conventions:

{ }   You must choose one of the attributes, values, characters, or punctuation within the braces. In this book, braces appear in a larger point size. In general, required attributes are listed before optional attributes. In this book, braces appear in a larger point size to standardize the appearance of other characters that enclose parts of expressions.

[ ]   You may choose one or more of the attributes, values, characters, or punctuation within the brackets. In this book, brackets appear in a larger point size to differentiate them from bracket characters within productions and to standardize the appearance of other characters that enclose parts of expressions.

| A pipe symbol indicates an OR. Choose one attribute or value OR another. In other words, just choose one. In this book, pipes appear in a larger point size to differentiate them from pipe characters within productions.

^   Do **not** choose any of the characters or range of characters adjacent to the **NOT** character.

. . .   An ellipsis indicates an unlimited continuation of the preceding attribute and that the next attribute is the end of the series.

Italics   Italicized text represents a variable (such as a folder/directory, file name, path, character, number, URI, and so on) that you enter. Most times, enclose a variable within quotation marks (" ") or single quote marks (' '), making sure to use the standard syntax as a guide; never mix quotation marks and single quote marks in a production.

default   If an attribute or value is underlined, it is the default. In other words, if you do not use the attribute, your browser will automatically use the default attribute or value.

Conventions Used in This Book

Throughout this book, each production's description uses the same general format. The heading includes the name of the production, its superscripted production number within brackets (for XML, XLink, and XPointer only), and a very brief description. Following that are a longer description, two types of syntax (for XML, XLink, and XPointer only), information about components and other attributes comprising the syntax, notes about using the production, one or more examples, and a list of related productions.

●—NOTE

A production number (for example, [84]) is useful when referring to the XML specification or working draft at the World Wide Web Consortium (W3C). In the W3C document, productions are arranged in production-number order and with related productions or components used to form XML documents.

A few attributes warrant their own entries in Chapter 2, *XML Syntax*, and Chapter 3, *XLink Language*. Attributes, which do not have production numbers, follow the same format as that for productions.

The conventions used in *XML in Plain English* are as follows:

- XML, XLink, and XPointer are case-sensitive, so you must type the exact combination of uppercase and lowercase characters.

- Productions, attributes, and entities that are to be typed into an XML document are displayed in a monospaced typeface.

- *Italicized* text represents both new terms and variables (such as a file name, number, or URL) that you name and enter. When you see italicized text, substitute the file name, number, or URL for the italicized text.

- In the XML, XLink, and XPointer chapters, examples are composed of both normal and boldface text. Boldface text highlights the part of the example affected by the current production or attribute.

- Default values, which are automatically supplied when you do not use a particular attribute, are underlined.

How to Reach the Author

I would like to hear from you — especially if you can furnish tips, shortcuts, and tricks that you have used to create innovative and praiseworthy XML documents. If I have missed an aspect of XML or an important example , be sure to let me know. My e-mail address is eddygrp@sover.net.

Acknowledgments

There's no getting around it — the author whose name is on the cover of a computer or Internet book is only one of many people responsible for the birth of a book and its development into a finished product. Without the support of editors and experts, the author would be up the creek without a paddle, completely at sea, and well over her head — to recoin a few nautical clichés. And there's nothing like the encouragement of family and friends to build the spirits — especially when deadlines loom and attempting to comprehend technical standard is the last thing the author wants to do. In this section I'd like to thank all those whose support has been so important.

A special thank you to acquisitions editor Laura Lewin and senior development editor Matt Lusher. Without your support, this book would not have possible.

Thanks also to the other people at IDG Books for making this a rewarding experience. Thanks to the copy-editing team of Bill McManus and Nicole Fountain; and thanks very much to the project coordinator, Susan Parini.

For his XML (and other technical) expertise and attention to detail, an enthusiastic thank you to the technical editor, Simon St. Laurent, who is the author of *XML: A Primer* and *Dynamic HTML: A Primer*, also published by IDG Books Worldwide, Inc.

A special thank you for the patience and persistence of my agent, Matt Wagner of Waterside Productions.

For their continued encouragement, thanks to my family and friends.

For their special and continuing contributions — Toni and Eli. And in loving memory of Indy.

Finally, thanks to the readers of *XML in Plain English*. I hope that you'll let me know what you think of the book and how I can make the next edition even better.

Sandra E. Eddy
eddygrp@sover.net

Brief Contents

Contents

Overview

1

A s the introduction to this book explains, the Extensible Markup Language (XML) enables you to create custom markup languages. For example, if you work in a particular industry, you can incorporate particular technical terms into your new language. If you create most of your documents by using the Standard Generalized Markup Language (SGML), you have a head start; because XML is a subset of SGML, you can convert those documents to XML. Then, you can use the XLink Language and the XPointer Language to add simple and extended hypertext links, and post your documents to the World Wide Web (*WWW* or the *Web*).

In the introduction, you found out about *Extended Backus-Naur Form* (EBNF) notation. EBNF is the standard syntax used to define the elements and attributes that make up a custom language. Before you start your first XML document (or read through an existing custom-language definition), you should take the time to learn EBNF. For more

1

information about EBNF, see the "Extended Backus-Naur Form" section in the Webliography.

XML in Plain English explains XML at the most basic level; the book is tailor-made for those who create custom markup languages and for those who "code" XML documents by using text editors and word processors. However, those who use XML editors, such as those listed in Appendix B, *XML Editors and Utilities*, should know that underneath the documents shown on their desktops are the same XML statements and attributes that the custom-language developers see.

All custom languages developed using XML syntax, and many XML documents using those languages, must be edited at the element-and-attribute level. For example, to tailor an XML document for a particular output, a person writing XML pages might find that adding XML statements directly to the document is faster and easier than working through menu commands and dialog boxes in an XML editor. Or, a writer who wants to search through a document for all second-level headings and replace them with third-level headings could use a full-featured word processor to perform a one-step search-and-replace-all operation, rather than using an XML editor, which might allow only a search-and-replace for text shown onscreen. The decision to use a word processor, text editor, or XML editor depends on what you want to accomplish and the features of the chosen application. Remember that XML is a very new language, so most applications that will help you write and edit XML documents are still being developed.

In addition to covering the basics of XML, custom-language development, and document creation, this chapter provides the background and history of XML and its relatives SGML and HTML, information about page validation, the steps used to register a domain name, and an overview of the process of uploading a page to a server. The following are the sections in this chapter:

- *The History of Hypertext*, which briefly describes SGML, the Web, HTML, XML, and the history of each.

- *XML Basics*, which discusses the building blocks of XML, including elements, tags, attributes, and content.

- *Well-Formed and Valid XML Documents,* which introduces and describes the two types of XML documents: well-formed and valid.

- *XML Document Structure,* which discusses the main parts of an XML document: the document prolog and the document instance.

- *Creating a DTD,* which shows you to create a document type definition (DTD), to define XML elements and their attributes as well as other components of XML document.

- *Adding Links to an XML Document,* which summarizes how you can write simple and extended links and use extended pointers (XPointers) to further refine a link.

- *HTML and XML Together,* which discusses how to keep using your HTML documents under XML.

- *Testing a Document,* which discusses well-formed and valid documents, their differences and similarities, and summarizes how to test or parse an XML document.

- *Making XML Documents Available to the World,* which provides the step-by-step processes of choosing and registering a domain name and uploading a document to a server.

The History of Hypertext

The interest in hypertext is a relatively recent development, due to the introduction and rapidly increasing popularity of the Web and its current language, HTML. *Hypertext* enables a user to connect disconnected chunks of text and multimedia — graphics, animation, audio, and video — into an informal network of information. In essence, the user builds a temporary document that is tailored to his or her own needs.

The concept of hypertext is over 50 years old. In July 1945, Vannevar Bush wrote an article titled "As We May Think" for *Atlantic Monthly,* in which he described a machine for "...browsing and making notes in an extensive online text and graphics system."

Theodor (Ted) Holm Nelson coined the terms *hypertext* and *hypermedia* (which encompass both text and multimedia) in 1960. He wrote the book *Computer Lib/Dream Machines* (originally published by Mindful Press in 1974 and republished in 1987 by Microsoft Press), which influenced the introduction of the Web. In the late 1970s, Nelson introduced Project Xanadu, which produced digital library and hypertext publishing systems — another pioneering effort that unfortunately did not reach fruition.

Although universities and other institutions experimented with hypertext during the '60s and '70s, it generally faded into the background until Apple introduced Hypercard in 1987 and Apple and Microsoft developed their Mac and Windows Help systems, respectively, with which users can click hypertext terms to jump from one topic to another or open a description box.

SGML

Standard Generalized Markup Language (SGML) was made an International Standardization Organization (ISO) standard in 1986. Because SGML is a standard, commercial organizations worldwide use it for document publishing and distribution, and for custom markup-language creation. For example, HTML is SGML's most famous creation. SGML documents can contain text and multimedia elements, as well as headings of all levels, paragraphs, and a few formatted elements. Unlike HTML documents, those written in SGML do not contain formats or enhancements, such as boldface, center alignment, and so on. Each SGML document has an associated document type definition (DTD), which defines rules for document contents. DTDs can stand by themselves; for example, each version of HTML has been defined in a DTD.

The World Wide Web

The World Wide Web demonstrates the true and best nature of hypertext. You can link to most pages on the Web by clicking hyperlinks on Web pages or by typing in their *Uniform Resource Locators* (URLs), or addresses, regardless of the server on which they reside — anywhere in the world. For example, you can start a session on the Web by viewing a document in California, and then click a link to jump to a Web site in Australia or Japan, go to the next site in France or Sweden, and so on, until you find your way around the world several times in just minutes. Hypertext differentiates the Web from all other Internet resources, as it provides you with an alternative to the traditional way of reading printed or online pages (sequentially, line by line, from top to bottom, and page by page, until you reach the end of the document or the end of your attention span, whichever happens first).

The Web is a relatively new part of the Internet. In the late 1980s, researchers at the European Laboratory for Particle Physics (CERN) in Switzerland developed the Web to make jobs easier; they wanted easy access to research documents that were networked at their laboratory. By 1990, they introduced a text-only browser and developed HTML. In 1991, they implemented the Web at CERN; and in 1992 they introduced the Web to the Internet community. Note that Hypertext Transport Protocol (http) is the protocol for *Web browsing*, the process of linking to specific addresses (URLs) on the Web.

HTML

HTML, Hypertext Markup Language, has been designed to handle the Web's hypermedia functionality. Within a simple text document, an HTML writer inserts an *element*, or command, that links one site on the Internet to another; describes the document to browsers, search indexes, computers, networks, and people; or defines the look of the document. Several HTML standards have developed since HTML's inception; HTML 4.0 is the current standard.

HTML elements enable you to define, format, or enhance pages for the Web, including the following:

- Select text and change its typeface or font size, or enhance it with boldface, italics, underlines, or strikethroughs.

- Insert links to other sections of the current document, documents at other sites, audio files, and video files.

- Decorate a document with graphics of all shapes and sizes, or use them as image maps that a user can click to link to other pages. You can also embed *GIF animations*, which are series of several graphic files incorporated into a single file.

1

- Create tables, which allow you to have more control over a document's formats and arrange data in easy-to-understand columns.

- Specify background colors for an HTML document, an entire table, a table row, or even a particular table cell.

- Use *frames*, which are multiple panes, each of which can display its own HTML document, instead of using single pages onscreen. For example, you can use two small static frames to display a site title and a table of contents that links to individual pages, respectively. Then, you can use a larger third frame to display the individual pages as the user clicks the links in the table of contents.

- Construct fill-out forms, simple or complex, that enable users to send mail to you, answer questionnaires, and even order from your catalog.

- Use programming and scripts to create dynamic pages that change as a visitor moves his or her mouse, presses keys on the keyboard, and so on.

Currently, the World Wide Web Consortium (W3C), which is responsible for setting HTML standards, is planning the next HTML version, which will be based on a set of XML tags. For more information about present and future HTML versions, periodically go to W3C's HTML Activity page (`http://www.w3.org/MarkUp/Activity/`).

XML

Extensible markup language (XML) is a subset of SGML: XML is comprised of many SGML productions, but is much less complex than SGML. Like SGML, you use XML to develop a markup language, with elements and attributes customized for your business or industry. After a language is created, you can use XML — in the same way that you use HTML — to create documents.

Both XML and HTML support the Unicode Consortium's Universal Character Set (UCS). This set not only includes special characters, including punctuation and mathematical symbols, but also adds foreign-language characters and alphabets, to make XML an international standard.

XML and HTML support the use of *style sheets*, which help you to define the structure and appearance of an entire large, complex document. However, whereas HTML styles its own output in many ways, XML requires styles for formatted and enhanced output. In addition, XML goes beyond HTML by supporting the full version of Document Style Semantics and Specification Language (DSSSL) and Cascading Style Sheets 2 (CSS2). The future style sheet standard for XML will be XML Stylesheet Language (XSL), which is based on DSSSL Online, a subset of DSSSL created specifically for electronic documents.

●—**NOTE** ─────────────────────────────

DSSSL works with any SGML document. Because XML is a subset of SGML, XML also works with DSSSL. However, because XML is a subset, some XML productions may not work with older DSSSL processors that have not been updated to process both SGML and XML documents.

You can display XML data within an HTML document and use the HTML standard within an XML document. However, because XML is new, the rules for doing this haven't yet been finalized.

Other XML features and functions include the following:

- XML allows various types of document displays, not only for many computer platforms, but also for many other devices. Programmers can use any programming or scripting language to define documents.

- XML supports but does not require DTDs. If you use a DTD, you can define specific document types for both browsers and users.

- XML's supporting standards (XLink and XPointer) enable linking that is more sophisticated than in HTML. In HTML and XML, you can link to a single URL. However, XML's supporting standards allow the use of several links simultaneously, as well as groups of links.

- XML's supporting standards support printed and electronic documents and other output files in which the content and appearance are customized for different users.

- XML permits processing on either the client or the server computers. This allows developers to distribute and, optionally, save resources.

●—**NOTE**————————————————————————

Currently, the XML 1.0 specification is set. However, the XLink and XPointer languages are still being developed and will probably change.

XML Basics

If you know about HTML elements, attributes, and tags, you are well on your way to understanding XML. However, for those of you who are not familiar with HTML, you must note that elements and tags are *not* the same thing. An element begins with a *start tag* (the less-than [<] character, the element name, and the greater-than [>] character) and ends with an *end tag*, which adds the slash (/) to the less-than and greater-than characters. Within the start tag and end tag are the element name, optional attributes, and other content. For example:

```
<text>This is an element.</text>
```

●—**TIP**————————————————————————

In HTML, some elements allow you to omit the end tag. However, in XML, the end tag is *always* present. If you currently work with HTML documents but plan to convert to XML in the future, adding both required and optional end tags to your HTML documents is a good idea—for future compatibility with XML. XML also provides *empty-element tags*, which are elements that have no current content. An empty-element tag refers to an object, such as an image or a line break, that will be added to a document when it is output. However, browsers that have not been updated recently do not recognize empty-element tags.

Attributes let you define values for elements; for example, you can start a numbered list with a particular value or incorporate color, boldface, and so on for text controlled by a particular element type. Or, you can add an identifier to a graphic so that you can find it in a document — for linking purposes or to specify the start (or end) of an area to be formatted or enhanced. Elements with attributes look something like this:

```
<element option1="value1" option2="value2">
</element>
```

Notice that the start tag, within the less-than and greater-than symbols, includes all the attributes; for example:

```
<box border width="70" height="50"></box>
```

where:

- < marks the beginning of the start tag.
- box is the element name.
- border is an attribute that turns on a border.
- width=70 is an attribute that sets the box width to 70 pixels.
- height=50 is an attribute that sets the box height to 50 pixels.
- > marks the completion of the start tag.
- < marks the beginning of the end tag.
- / is the important signal that differentiates this end tag from the start tag.
- box is the element name.
- > marks the completion of the end tag.

●—NOTE ——————————————————————————

If you use both XML and HTML in your documents, the common practice is to make XML elements all lowercase and HTML elements all uppercase.

You can nest XML elements within other elements, depending on how you define the elements; for example:

```
<text size="12"><bold><ital>Watch this space!
</ital></bold></text>
```

The text element attribute size changes the size of the text to 12 points. The start and end bold (boldface) elements are nested within the text elements, and the ital (italics) elements are embedded within the bold elements. Notice that the nesting is completely symmetrical and does not overlap:

```
<text>              </text>
   <bold>          </bold>
      <ital>   <ital>
```

When creating an XML document, one of the few rules you can violate is overlapping nested elements. Using the previous example, if you change the elements' layout to this:

```
<text size="12"><bold><ital>Watch this space!
</text></bold></ital>
```

and overlap nested elements:

```
<text>              </ital>
   <bold>           </bold>
      <ital>  </text>
```

processing of your document ends prematurely. For more information about the integrity of XML documents, read on.

Well-Formed and Valid XML Documents

XML supports two types of documents: well-formed and valid. Both types of documents produce appropriate XML output.

Well-formed documents

Well-formed documents must contain at least one root element:

```
<saying>Money is the root of all evil.</saying>
```

Thus, the following is not a well-formed document:

```
Money is the root of all evil.
```

Well-formed documents must nest child elements within the root element; for example:

```
<sayinglist>
<saying>Money is the root of all evil.</saying>
<saying>Money talks.</saying>
</sayinglist>
```

So, the following is not well-formed (because of the missing root element):

```
<saying>Money is the root of all evil.</saying>
<saying>Money talks.</saying>
```

nor is the following (because of a missing start tag and improper end tag):

```
<sayinglist>
<saying>Money is the root of all evil.</saying>
Money talks.</saying>
<sayinglist>
```

Well-formed documents can use almost any XML production except element and attribute declarations. These declarations belong in DTDs, which are associated with valid documents (see the following section).

● NOTE

As you read through the XML productions in Chapter 2, *XML Syntax*, be sure to review the notes about well-formed documents.

Valid documents

Valid documents meet all the criteria for being well-formed. In addition, valid documents always have an associated DTD. As you have already learned, a DTD defines rules for document contents; that is, the elements and attributes of the markup language with which the document is created. Because all the well-formed examples in the previous section have no associated DTD, none are valid.

During processing, a validating XML processor creates a hierarchy of elements, with the root element, all its child and sibling elements, and the child, ancestor, and sibling elements of those child elements. Two XML features take advantage of this hierarchy, as follows:

- When you add extended links (XLinks) and extended pointers (XPointers) to a document, you can jump to particular generations of elements.

- When you style an XML document, style sheets use this hierarchy of elements to set styles for elements and their child elements.

DTDs also allow a company or department to set standards that control the content and look of each document. This way individual document creators don't have to develop or edit a particular style — it's already in the DTD.

●—NOTE

XML element and attribute declarations belong in DTDs *only*. If a particular XML production is limited to DTDs, you'll find a note to that effect in Chapter 2, *XML Syntax*.

XML Document Structure

Early versions of HTML required an <HTML> element at the top and bottom of an HTML document. Within that were nested <HEAD> and <BODY> elements that defined the two main sections of the document. (In later HTML versions, these elements became optional.) XML documents follow the same general two-section format: The document *prolog* is at the head of the document, and the *instance* is the body. (Some XML developers say that the instance is the entire document, including the prolog.)

The document prolog

The prolog, which must precede any element but can be completely empty, can contain identifying information about an XML document. This includes an XML declaration (and the current XML standard) and document type declaration; for example:

```
<?xml version="1.0"?>
<!DOCTYPE sampdoc[>
```

The preceding example could be the prolog for a well-formed document.

The following example refers to an external DTD:

```
<?xml version="1.0"?>
<!DOCTYPE sampdoc SYSTEM "sample.dtd">
```

The prolog can also contain comments and other *processing instructions*, which tell the XML processor how to handle the statement enclosed within the <? and ?> delimiters.

The XML declaration can also include an *encoding declaration* (typically encoding="UTF-8"), which states the form of the Unicode characters, and a *standalone declaration*, which indicates whether the document is a standalone document (standalone= "yes") or is associated with an external document (standalone="no"). Other encoding declarations are possible. The following XML declaration includes an encoding declaration and a standalone declaration:

```
<?xml version="1.0" encoding="UTF-8" standalone="yes"?>
```

The document instance

The document instance includes the remaining part of the XML document; that is, everything but the prolog. (However, some XML developers say that the instance includes the entire document.) The instance contains definitions of elements and attributes, as well as entities and content. As you learn about DTDs in the following sections, you'll find out more about what makes up a document instance in *DTDs*, XML documents in which you set all the rules about elements and attributes. In other XML documents, the instance contains the actual contents of the document — the characters, paragraphs, pages, graphics, and white space that will make up the XML output.

Creating a DTD

This section shows you how to create a DTD, step by step. Suppose that you want to create a restaurant guide database that contains several identification fields: the required restaurant name and some optional information, such as the street address, city, state, ZIP code, one or more voice and fax telephone numbers, one or more categories of cuisines, and fields that log record-creation and record-editing information.

Inserting the prolog

The prolog starts any XML document, as follows:

```
<?xml version="1.0"?>
<!DOCTYPE restaurant [
]>
```

Defining the root element and listing top-level elements

Use the element declaration to list the root element and its first generation of child elements. Generations of elements are similar to generations of human families: They include parents (that is, roots), ancestors (all elements above the parents), descendants (all elements below the parents), and children. In fact, several generations of child elements can exist. For example, the first generation of child elements are immediately under the root, the second generation (analogous to grandchildren) of child elements are under the first generation of child elements, the third generation (analogous to great-grandchildren) of child elements are under the second generation, and so on. The following example shows the definition of the root element, restaurant, and its children (all within the parentheses).

```
<!ELEMENT restaurant (name, address, city, state, zip,
   tel_voice, tel_fax, info, rating_icon, record_info)>
```

The element declaration starts with the uppercase keyword !ELEMENT, and each top-level element is separated from the next with a comma. The comma separator indicates that each element *must* appear in the order in which it was defined in the element declaration. However, you can separate all or some elements with pipe (|) symbols, which allow more latitude: each element may occur one or more times and can appear in any order. You can use a combination of commas and pipes to control strictly the use of some elements and allow relaxation in the use of others. You can also place lists of elements, separated by pipes or commas, within parentheses. As the preceding declaration demonstrates, parentheses group like elements; in this case, all the first-generation child elements of the restaurant element.

Specifying element occurrences

After you define the root element and list the top-level elements, you can use the following EBNF symbols to control the number of times that an element can appear in a record:

- ? indicates that an element can occur up to one time but does not have to occur at all.

- * indicates that an element (such as multiple telephone numbers) can occur an unlimited number of times.
- + indicates that an element (such as the restaurant name) *must* occur one or more times.

Now, the element declaration looks like this:

```
<!ELEMENT restaurant (name+, address, city, state, zip,
tel_voice*, tel_fax*, info*, rating_icon,
record_info?)>
```

Remember that using commas in an element declaration indicates that data must be entered in the exact order in which the elements appear. To allow some data to be entered in any order, change the commas to pipe symbols (|):

```
<!ELEMENT restaurant (name+, address, city, state, zip,
(tel_voice|tel_fax)*,info*, rating_icon,
record_info?)>
```

This now enables you to enter telephone numbers in any order.

Defining the top-level elements and listing child elements

After you specify the element occurrences, you can specify the contents of the elements immediately under the root element and list child elements, where necessary:

```
<!ELEMENT name        (#PCDATA)>
<!ELEMENT address     (#PCDATA)>
<!ELEMENT city        (#PCDATA)>
<!ELEMENT state       (#PCDATA)>
<!ELEMENT zip         (#PCDATA)>
<!ELEMENT tel_voice   (#PCDATA)>
<!ELEMENT tel_fax     (#PCDATA)>
<!ELEMENT info        (#PCDATA)>
<!ELEMENT rating_icon EMPTY>
<!ELEMENT record_info (create_date, edit_date, editor)
```

1

#PCDATA represents *parsed character data,* which indicates non-markup data; that is, simply text.

● **NOTE** ─────────────────────────────────

#PCDATA can contain both elements and character data. All parsed character data eventually is parsed, and some may be modified by the parser.

The EMPTY element specifies an element with no current content. No end tag exists; the start tag is simply a marker for future content, such as a graphic.

The record_info element contains three child elements: create_date, the date on which the record was created; edit_date, the last date on which the record was edited; and editor, the name of the last person who edited the record.

● **NOTE** ─────────────────────────────────

You can align markup elements any way that you want to in an XML document. For example, the preceding lines align the element names and types in a columnar format.

Continue defining elements and listing child elements until you have completed all the elements in the DTD.

Defining the attributes of elements

You can define attributes to restrict or require input for an element. For example, for your restaurant guide, restricting the categories of meals and cuisines is a good idea, to make the database easier to sort for future output. (Remember that you can always edit the DTD to include additional options.) Also, listing opening and closing hours for each entry might be important to those perusing the restaurant guide, so input in one set of hours fields is required (#IMPLIED). (The second set is optional (#REQUIRED), because not all restaurants close in the middle of their business days.) The following example lists attributes for the info element.

```
<!ATTLIST info
        meals           (breakfast|brunch|lunch
                        |snacks|dinner|late)        #IMPLIED
        cuisine         (american|bar|chinese
                        |french|german|gourmet
```

```
                |italian|pizza|vegetarian)   #IMPLIED
    start_hours_1                            #REQUIRED
    end_hours_1                              #REQUIRED
    start_hours_2                            #IMPLIED
    end_hours_2                              #IMPLIED
  >
```

Declaring entities

An entity is an all-purpose term meaning a special character, specific text, or even a file such as a graphic. XML supports several types of entities: parsed and unparsed, external and internal, and general and parameter in various combinations.

A *parsed entity* contains named replacement data that has been called by an entity reference and run through an XML parser. At the end of processing, the parsed data replaces the current contents of the entity. In contrast, an *unparsed entity* is not processed. It has a named *notation* (set of characters), which the XML processor sends to the target application.

As you might have guessed, the content of an *internal entity* is stored completely within the DTD; an internal entity is always parsed. An *external entity* has its content stored in a separate file, completely outside the XML document; an external entity is parsed or unparsed.

A *general entity* is a variable that is named within document instance text. A general entity is preceded by an ampersand symbol (&) and other optional characters and is succeeded by a semicolon (;). Valid general entities can be internal parsed, external parsed, and external unparsed. General entities are comprised of the following subcategories:

- *Parsed general entities*, which start with the & character.
- *Decimal character references*, which start with the &# characters.
- *Hexadecimal character references*, which start with the &#x characters.

A *parameter entity* (PE) is a parsed variable, named within document markup, in the document prolog or document instance. A parameter entity is preceded by a percent symbol (%) and ended with a semicolon (;).

Declaring parsed general entities

A parsed general entity contains replacement text that has been processed by an XML parser. The following example shows a general entity declaration:

```
<!ENTITY copyright "This document is copyrighted
by The Eddy Group, Inc.">
```

Then, when you specify the &copyright; entity within a document, the XML processor replaces the entity with the text defined within the entity declaration.

XML reserves the general entities shown in Table 1.1. In the table, the first column lists the reserved characters and the second column shows the entity that replaces the character in well-formed documents.

Table 1-1   *Reserved XML Entities for Well-Formed Documents*

To produce this character:	Insert this entity:
ampersand (&)	&amp;
apostrophe (')	&apos;
greater-than (>)	&gt;
less-than (<)	&lt;
quotation mark (")	&quot;

Under some circumstances, you can declare an external entity; for example, if you work with lengthy documents (such as online books) you can "modularize" by declaring external pages, or even sections or chapters. Your home or index page can be a list of external entities that call individual documents. Then, when you edit pages at your site, you can simply replace one version of a page with a newer one. For example, the following entities are all stored on your local area network (LAN):

```
<!ELEMENT bigbook (#PCDATA)
<!ENTITY intro PUBLIC "intro.rtf">
<!ENTITY chap1 PUBLIC "chap1-001.rtf">
```

```
<!ENTITY chap2 PUBLIC "chap2-001.rtf">
<!ENTITY chap3 PUBLIC "chap3-001.rtf">
<!ENTITY chap4 PUBLIC "chap4-001.rtf">
```

which you can change to

```
<!ELEMENT bigbook (#PCDATA)
<!ENTITY intro PUBLIC "intro.rtf">
<!ENTITY chap1 PUBLIC "chap1-002.rtf">
<!ENTITY chap2 PUBLIC "chap2-001.rtf">
<!ENTITY chap3 PUBLIC "chap3-001.rtf">
<!ENTITY chap4 PUBLIC "chap4-001.rtf">
```

If the external entity is stored outside of your LAN, replace PUBLIC with SYSTEM:

```
<!ELEMENT introduction (#PCDATA)
<!ENTITY introdoc SYSTEM "introdoc.rtf">
```

Declaring character and hexadecimal references

You can declare character and hexadecimal references from the XML-supported characters in the ISO/IEC 10646 character set. (The IEC is the *International Electrotechnical Commission*.) To declare a character reference, use the following syntax:

```
&#{0-9[0-9[...0-9]};
```

Thus, you precede a character reference with the &# characters and follow it with a semicolon. The character reference itself is composed of a combination of the digits ranging from 0 to 9.

To declare a hexadecimal reference in the ISO/IEC 10646 character set, use the following syntax:

```
&#x{0-9|a-f|A-F[0-9|a-f|A-F[...0-9|a-f|A-F]]};
```

This time, the hexadecimal reference is preceded by the &#x characters. The character reference is composed of the digits ranging from 0 to 9 and the case-insensitive letters ranging from A to F.

Declaring parameter entities

As you have learned, a parameter entity is a parsed variable named within declarations. A parameter entity, which is preceded by a percent symbol (%) and ended with a semicolon (;), works in about the same way that a general parsed entity does: it can be a shortcut for a longer string of markup contents. For example:

```
<!ENTITY % HTMLlat1 PUBLIC
"-//W3C//ENTITIES Full Latin 1//EN//HTML">
%HTMLlat1;
```

The preceding example shows an external parameter entity for the Full Latin 1 character entity set and the related general entity.

A parameter entity can group like elements together, as the following examples show:

```
<!ENTITY % InputType
"(TEXT | PASSWORD | CHECKBOX |
  RADIO | SUBMIT | RESET |
  FILE | HIDDEN | IMAGE | BUTTON)"
>
```

or

```
<!ENTITY % list "(UL | OL | DIR | MENU)">
```

Both examples show parameter entities used in the HTML standard. The first example groups input elements under the name InputType, and the second example groups list elements under the name list. Then, you can declare grouped child elements rather than a possibly lengthy list of individual elements.

An earlier example in this chapter defined a child element with children of its own:

```
<!ELEMENT record_info (create_date, edit_date, editor)
```

You can also group the date elements in this way:

```
<!ENTITY % dates " (create_date | edit_date) "
```

and define the elements as follows:

```
<!ELEMENT record_info (%dates, editor)
```

Adding Links to an XML Document

The XLink standard contains elements that enable you to write extended links, which in conjunction with XPointers (extended pointers) establish hyperlinks in XML documents. XML documents can include the following two types of links:

- *Simple links*, which are analogous to the A element in HTML. Simple links allow you to jump from a location in the current document to a destination in the current document or in another document. Simple links always move in one direction.

- *Extended links*, which enable you to define many links. Using extended links, you can jump from any link to any other link. You can identify the content associated with a particular link, so that if the content changes but the identifier remains the same, you can still access the link.

To learn how to use links in XML documents, see the "Specifying a Simple Link in a DTD" and "Specifying an Extended Link in a DTD" sections at the beginning of Chapter 3.

HTML and XML Together

Every HTML document can be a well-formed XML document. First, change the top of an HTML document from the following:

```
<!DOCTYPE HTML PUBLIC "-//W3C//DTD HTML 4.0//EN">
```

to this:

```
<?xml version="1.0"?>
```

Then, go through each line of the document, checking for the following:

- Every start tag must have a matching end tag.
- All attribute values are enclosed within quotation marks or single quotes.
- All empty tags (elements used as placeholders for future contents) use the following syntax:
 (note the space

1

between the element name and the slash) or `<img src="image.gif"/>` (note that no space is between the attribute value and the slash).

If you decide to migrate from HTML to XML, consider creating valid documents. This means that you must associate a DTD with each document. Obviously, using one DTD for all of your documents is much easier than creating several DTDs. A side benefit is having one standard and the same types of output for all of your XML documents. To keep up-to-date with the activities of both XML and HTML development, periodically go to the HTML Activity page (`http://www.w3.org/MarkUp/Activity/`).

Ultimately, you could write a new XML language, combining the best HTML elements and attributes and your own custom elements and attributes.

Testing a Document

When you create an HTML document, you use either the HTML editor or the browser to test the document for appropriate syntax, supported HTML elements and attributes, and properly named URLs for links and graphics. You also check how your page looks under various browsers. When you create an XML document, you test the document in about the same way. Then, instead of using an online HTML validator, you run your XML document through an XML parser; some parsers are used to test well-formed documents and others are used to test valid documents. XML parsers check syntax, elements, and URLs by using programmed criteria. An XML parser evaluates each line of a document and creates a tree of elements, sometimes creating a diagram of the root element, its child elements, and their children.

●—**NOTE**————————————————————————

Some XML parsers require that you have some form of Java installed on your computer. For a list of XML parsers and the site from which you can download Java, see Appendix B, *XML Editors and Utilities*.

Note that a validating XML parser must test a document against its DTD.

Making XML Documents Available to the World

When you start writing your first XML document, you probably intend to post it to the Web and make it available to an audience of millions around the world. Weeks or months before you start developing the document, you should consider the following important factors:

- Do you want to create a unique presence on the Web? This might mean registering a domain name for you or your company.

- Are you prepared to set up a Web site? First, contact your Internet service provider (ISP) and find out how much space is available for your future documents and how people can contact your company. For example, are you limited to e-mail contact, or can your documents include forms that your visitors can fill in? How do you post XML documents to an ISP server?

This last section of the chapter covers registering a domain name and posting an XML document.

Registering a domain name

Many businesses and individuals want to use their own domain name rather than their ISP's name. You could have this address, which includes your ISP's name:

```
http://www.provider.net/~example/
```

or this address, which includes your own unique domain name:

```
http://www.example.com/
```

You can register a domain name by following these steps:

1. Choose one or two acceptable names.
2. At the InterNIC site (`http://rs.internic.net/rs-internic.html`), check to see whether one of the chosen names is available.

3. If the domain name is already in use, repeat steps 1 and 2 until you identify a unique name.

4. Complete a registration template and select a payment type. You can even use a credit card.

5. Wait up to three weeks for the InterNIC to process your application.

●─NOTE

Many Internet service providers (ISPs) can register your domain name at no cost (beyond the annual fee for registration) or for a nominal charge.

Posting a document

Internet providers have different procedures for uploading an XML (or an HTML) document and its associated files to a server. You may need to establish a telnet connection, enter UNIX commands, use an FTP utility, or a terminal emulator, or a combination of two or three of these. However, all uploads follow these basic steps:

1. From the Web or via e-mail or fax, obtain and read your ISP's instructions for uploading. (This may also include directions for specifying *permissions*, whether you will allow others to read or even edit your XML files.)

2. Place the XML document and all files associated with it — graphics, audio, and video — in a single directory or folder on your computer.

3. On your computer, open the XML document and change the directory, folder, filenames, and URLs to the names of the assigned folders or directories on your ISP's server.

4. On your computer, save the edited XML document. If you have created an XML document, you may have to change the extension to .xml, depending on your ISP's instructions.

5. If necessary, install on your computer any utilities that your ISP requires to upload files.

6. Using your ISP's instructions, log on to the assigned server and create one or more folders or directories.

7. Upload the XML document and associated files into the newly created folders or directories. You may have to rename the XML document and other files to conform with the ISP's standards.

XML in Plain English

This reference is for those of you who know what you want to do in an XML document but may not remember the name of a particular production or attribute. The left column lists tasks that you may want to perform, arranged alphabetically by *italicized* keywords; the right column contains the name of the production or attribute with which you accomplish your goal. Then, for a complete description of the production or attribute, its syntax, attributes, and more, you can go to the chapter where that production or attribute is described. The *XML Elements A to Z* section can help you locate the chapter.

If you want to...	Use this production or attribute
specify an *absolute location term*	`AbsTerm`
actuate link traversal with or without a request	`actuate`
instruct the XML processor to use the following *alternate style sheet*	`xml:alternate style sheet`
pass *arguments* to a keyword about the relative location of an element to be selected	`Arguments`
define an *attribute*	`AttDef`
name an *attribute* to control the selection of an element	`Attr`
provide *attribute information*	`Attribute`
declare an element's *attribute list*	`AttlistDecl`
map user-chosen *attribute names* for a linking element	`xml:attributes`
specify an *attribute type*	`AttType`
define an *attribute-match location term*	`AttrTerm`
state an *attribute's value*	`AttValue`
specify a *base character*	`BaseChar`
specify detailed link *behavior*	`behavior`
specify one *character* in a name	`NameChar`
specify one legal *character*	`Char`
define *character data* within a character data section	`CData`
create a *character data section*	`CDSect`
mark the end of a *character data section*	`CDEnd`
mark the start of a *character data section*	`CDStart`
name a legal *character referred* to in the ISO/IEC character set	`CharRef`
define *child*-element content	`children`
specify a *choice list* of content particles	`choice`
specify a *combining character*	`CombiningChar`
add a *comment* to an XML document	`Comment`
name a *conditional section*	`conditionalSect`

If you want to...	**Use this production or attribute**
enter a *connector* symbol to indicate how a link is retrieved from its containing resource	Connector
specify a *content particle* grammar	cp
specify an element's *content type*	contentspec
declare whether a *default value* is required or optional	DefaultDecl
specify a *digit*	Digit
create an XML *document*	document
specify an XML *document type declaration*	doctypedecl
specify an XML *element*	element
create *element content* within the tags	content
constrain element content using an *element type declaration*	elementdecl
identify an *empty element tag*	EmptyElemTag
define an *encoding declaration*	EncodingDecl
specify an *encoding name*	EncName
define an *end tag* for a nonempty element	ETag
define an *entity declaration*	EntityDecl
identify an *entity reference*, a named general entity's content	EntityRef
enumerate a list of name tokens	Enumeration
specify one or more *enumerated* notation names or name tokens	EnumeratedType
add an *equal* sign to an expression	Eq
insert an *extender* symbol	Extender
specify a well-formed *external general parsed entity*	ExtParsedEnt
specify a well-formed *external parameter entity*	ExtPE
provide information about an *external parsed entity*	TextDecl
identify an *external subset*	extSubset
declare *external subset markup and conditions*	extSubsetDecl

If you want to...	**Use this production or attribute**
specify a valid XML *general entity* attribute	`ENTITY`
specify a list of valid XML *general entity* attributes	`ENTITIES`
define a *general entity*	`EntityDef`
identify a *general entity declaration*	`GEDecl`
specify an absolute *HTML address*	`HTMLAddr`
name an *IANA language code*	`IanaCode`
specify a valid XML *identifier* attribute	`ID`
specify a valid XML *identifier cross-reference* attribute	`IDREF`
specify a list of valid XML *identifier cross-reference* attributes	`IDREFS`
identify an element by a particular *identifier*	`IdLoc`
specify an *ideographic* symbol or glyph	`Ideographic`
mark an included section nested within an *ignored* section	`Ignore`
name a conditionally *ignored section*	`ignoreSect`
define an *ignored section's contents*	`ignoreSect-Contents`
indicate an *included section*	`includeSect`
identify an *inline or out-of-line link*	`inline`
select all or one *instance* of an element's location	`InstanceOrAll`
insert an *instance number*	`Instance`
specify an *internal entity value*	`EntityValue`
assign an *ISO639 language code*	`ISO639Code`
name a *keyword* indicating the relative location of an element to be selected	`Keyword`
instruct XML to process the following *XML language code*	`xml:lang`
specify a *language code* or identifier	`Langcode`
name a *language identifier*	`LanguageID`
specify a *letter* of the current alphabet	`Letter`
name a type of *location term*	`OtherTerm`

If you want to...	Use this production or attribute
aim a *locator* at a link resource	Locator
declare *markup* of elements, attributes, entities, or notation in parameter entities	markupdecl
insert *miscellaneous information* in a prolog	Misc
define *mixed* element content of character data and child elements	Mixed
specify a valid XML *name*, starting with a letter or underscore	Name
specify a valid XML *name token*, starting with any character	Nmtoken
specify one or more valid XML *name tokens*, starting with any character	Nmtokens
specify one or more valid XML names, starting with a letter	Names
indicate *nonmarkup character data*	CharData
identify a *node type*	NodeType
insert a *notation declaration*	NotationDecl
declare a list of *notation names*	NotationType
set the *number of characters* in a string	Length
specify an *offset* number to start a string match	Position
list one or more *other location terms*	OtherTerms
declare a *parameter entity*	PEDecl
define a *parameter entity*	PEDef
identify a *parameter entity reference*	PEReference
identify a *parsed external entity*	ExternalID
name a *processing instruction's target* application	PITarget
instruct an XML *processor*	PI
specify a *public identifier character*	PubidChar
name a *public identifier literal*	PubidLiteral
query to find an XPointer	Query
name an entity or parameter entity *reference*	Reference

If you want to...	Use this production or attribute
specify a *relative location term*	`RelTerm`
name a *remote resource locator*	`href`
specify the *role of a local link resource*	`content-role`
specify the *role of a remote link resource*	`role`
specify a content-particles *sequence list*	`seq`
show whether a link resource is displayed or processed	`show`
find a *spanning subresource location term*	`SpanTerm`
declare a *standalone document*	`SDDecl`
define a *start tag* for a nonempty or empty XML element	`STag`
specify the number of *steps* that extended link group processing continues to other groups	`steps`
specify a character data *string*	`StringType`
define a *string-match location term*	`StringTerm`
instruct the XML processor to use the following *style sheet*	`xml:style sheet`
specify a language or country *subcode*	`Subcode`
resolve an external identifier into a *system identifier*	`PublicID`
specify a *system identifier URI*	`SystemLiteral`
specify the *title of a local link resource*	`content-title`
specify the *title of a remote link resource*	`title`
state that an element attribute is a *tokenized set*	`TokenizedType`
name a *Uniform Resource Identifier*	`URI`
declare an *unparsed external entity*	`NDataDecl`
identify a *user-assigned language*	`UserCode`
indicate an attribute *value* on which to base an element selection	`Val`
specify XML *version information*	`VersionInfo`
insert an XML *version number*	`VersionNum`
insert *whitespace* in an XML document	`S`

If you want to...	Use this production or attribute
preserve the *whitespace* in an XML document	`xml:space`
describe an *XML document*	`prolog`
identify an *XML document as such*	`XMLDecl`
process the following one or more XLink *linking elements*	`xml:link`
name one or two *XPointers*	`XPointer`

XML A to Z

This reference is a table of the productions and attributes covered comprehensively in Chapter 2, *XML Syntax*, Chapter 3, *XLink Language*, and Chapter 4, *XPointer Language*. Here, you find an alphabetically arranged master list of XML productions and attributes and the chapters in which they are located.

Production/Attribute	Chapter
AbsTerm	XPointer (Ch. 4)
actuate	XLink (Ch. 3)
Arguments	XPointer (Ch. 4)
AttDef	Syntax (Ch. 2)
AttlistDecl	Syntax (Ch. 2)
Attr	XPointer (Ch. 4)
Attribute	Syntax (Ch. 2)
AttrTerm	XPointer (Ch. 4)
AttType	Syntax (Ch. 2)
AttValue	Syntax (Ch. 2)
BaseChar	Syntax (Ch. 2)
behavior	XLink (Ch. 3)
CData	Syntax (Ch. 2)
CDEnd	Syntax (Ch. 2)
CDSect	Syntax (Ch. 2)
CDStart	Syntax (Ch. 2)
Char	Syntax (Ch. 2)
CharData	Syntax (Ch. 2)
CharRef	Syntax (Ch. 2)
children	Syntax (Ch. 2)
choice	Syntax (Ch. 2)
CombiningChar	Syntax (Ch. 2)
Comment	Syntax (Ch. 2)
conditionalSect	Syntax (Ch. 2)
Connector	XLink (Ch. 3)
content	Syntax (Ch. 2)
content-role	XLink (Ch. 3)
contentspec	Syntax (Ch. 2)
content-title	XLink (Ch. 3)
cp	Syntax (Ch. 2)
DefaultDecl	Syntax (Ch. 2)
Digit	Syntax (Ch. 2)
doctypedecl	Syntax (Ch. 2)
document	Syntax (Ch. 2)
element	Syntax (Ch. 2)
elementdecl	Syntax (Ch. 2)

Production/Attribute

Chapter

Production/Attribute   Chapter

Production/Attribute	Chapter
seq	Syntax (Ch. 2)
show	XLink (Ch. 3)
SpanTerm	XPointer (Ch. 4)
STag	Syntax (Ch. 2)
steps	XLink (Ch. 3)
StringTerm	XPointer (Ch. 4)
StringType	Syntax (Ch. 2)
Subcode	Syntax (Ch. 2)
SystemLiteral	Syntax (Ch. 2)
TextDecl	Syntax (Ch. 2)
title	XLink (Ch. 3)
TokenizedType	Syntax (Ch. 2)
URI	XLink (Ch. 3)
UserCode	Syntax (Ch. 2)
Val	XPointer (Ch. 4)
VersionInfo	Syntax (Ch. 2)
VersionNum	Syntax (Ch. 2)
xml:alternate style sheet	Syntax (Ch. 2)
xml:attributes	XLink (Ch. 3)
XMLDecl	Syntax (Ch. 2)
xml:lang	Syntax (Ch. 2)
xml:link	XLink (Ch. 3)
xml:space	Syntax (Ch. 2)
xml:style sheet	Syntax (Ch. 2)
XPointer	XPointer (Ch. 4)

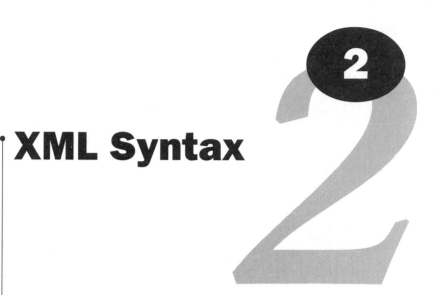

XML Syntax

This chapter is the cornerstone of this book; here, you will find detailed information about XML syntax, which is used to define custom markup languages.

AttDef [53]	Attribute Definition

Purpose
Defines a particular attribute, including its name, data type, and default value.

EBNF Syntax
```
AttDef ::= S Name S AttType S DefaultDecl
```

Standard Syntax
```
[ ... ]Name [ ... ]AttType[ ... ]DefaultDecl
```

Where

- S represents one or more whitespace characters: spaces, carriage returns, line feeds, or tabs. (See the S production.) Syntax:
  `{[#x20|#x9|#xD|#xA][#x20|#x9|#xD|#xA]...[#x20|#x9|#xD|#xA]}`

- Name specifies a valid XML name, starting with a letter or underscore character, for an attribute. (See the Name production.) Syntax:
  `#xnnnn [#xnnnn][_][:][#xnnnn]|[0|`
  `1|2|3|4|5|6|7|8|9][.]|[-][#xnnnn]`
  `[#xnnnn]...[#xnnnn]`

- AttType specifies an attribute type. (See the AttType production.) Syntax:
  `StringType|TokenizedType|EnumeratedType`

- DefaultDecl declares whether a default value is required or optional. (See the DefaultDecl production.) Syntax:
  `#REQUIRED|#IMPLIED|[[#FIXED[ ... ]]AttValue]`

Notes

AttDef is a component of the AttlistDecl production.

Attributes are included within start tags and empty-element tags, not end tags.

Each attribute contains two components: a name and a value. Each name-value pair is known as an *attribute specification*.

An attribute value fine-tunes the production. For example, you can use a value to align content in a particular way, enhance it, or change its appearance in other ways.

For an XML document to be well-formed, each attribute under a production — regardless of whether it has content — must be unique. However, the value of an attribute does not have to be unique.

For an XML document to be valid, each of its element types must have been declared.

For an XML document to be valid, each of its elements' attributes must have been declared and must match the declared type.

For an XML document to be well-formed, its attribute values must be within the internal subset (the part of the DTD that is located within the source document) and not refer to external entities.

Use the `AttlistDecl` production to fine-tune an element, its attributes, and its child elements.

If you declare more than one attribute list for a particular element type, an XML processor merges them and may issue a warning message.

●—**NOTE**————————————————————————

A *warning* message indicates that processing continues; an *error* message usually results in the end of processing.

If you declare more than one definition for a particular attribute, an XML processor recognizes the first definition, disregards the rest, and may issue a warning message.

Examples

The following example shows the three attributes defined for the ENHANCE element:

```
<!ATTLIST ENHANCE
          id      ID      #REQUIRED
          name    CDATA   #IMPLIED
          type    (bold|italics|underline)
>
```

The following example shows the method attribute of the HTML FORM element:

```
          method   (GET|POST)   GET
```

Related Productions

AttlistDecl, AttType, DefaultDecl, markupdecl, Name, S

AttlistDecl [52]   Attribute List Declaration

Purpose

Declares an element type's attribute list, including attribute names, data types, and default values.

EBNF Syntax

```
AttlistDecl ::= '<!ATTLIST' S Name AttDef* S? '>'
```

Standard Syntax

2

```
<!ATTLIST [ ... ]Name [AttDef[AttDef
    [...AttDef]]][ ... ]>
```

Where

- <!ATTLIST is an uppercase-only reserved keyword that indicates the start of an attribute list.

- S represents one or more whitespace characters: spaces, carriage returns, line feeds, or tabs. (See the S production.) Syntax:
  {[#x20|#x9|#xD|#xA][#x20|#x9|#xD|#xA]...
  [#x20|#x9|#xD|#xA]}

- Name specifies a valid XML name, starting with a letter or underscore character, for an element type. (See the Name production.) Syntax:
  #xnnnn [#xnnnn][_][:][#xnnnn]|[0
  |1|2|3|4|5|6|7|8|9][.]|[-][#xnnnn]
  [#xnnnn]...[#xnnnn]

- AttDef writes an attribute definition. (See the AttDef production.) Syntax:
  [...]Name [...]AttType[...]DefaultDecl

- > indicates the end of an attribute list.

Notes

AttlistDecl is a component of the markupdecl production.

AttlistDecl is a representation of an attribute within a document type definition (DTD).

Attributes are included within start tags and empty-element tags, not end tags.

Each attribute contains two components: a name and a value. Each name-value pair is known as an *attribute specification*.

An attribute value fine-tunes the element. For example, you can use a value to align content in a particular way, enhance it, or change its appearance in other ways.

For an XML document to be valid, each of its element types must have been declared.

For an XML document to be valid, each of its elements' attributes must have been declared and must match the declared type.

Use the `AttlistDecl` production to fine-tune an element, its attributes, and its child elements.

If you declare more than one attribute list for a particular element type, an XML processor merges them and may issue a warning message.

If you declare more than one definition for a particular attribute, an XML processor recognizes the first definition, disregards the rest, and may issue a warning message.

● NOTE

A *warning* message indicates that processing continues; an *error* message usually results in the end of processing.

Because the greater-than symbol (>) is used to indicate the end of the attribute list, you should specify a greater-than symbol within character data by using the entity `&gt;`.

Example

The following example shows the attribute list for the ENHANCE element:

```
<!ATTLIST ENHANCE
        id    ID     #REQUIRED
        name  CDATA  #IMPLIED
        type  (bold|italics|underline)
>
```

Related Productions

AttDef, AttType, DefaultDecl, markupdecl, Name, S

Attribute [41]   Attribute

Purpose

Provides further information about an attribute.

EBNF Syntax

```
Attribute ::= Name Eq AttValue
```

Standard Syntax

> `Name[ ... ]=[ ... ]AttValue`

Where

- `Name` specifies a valid XML name, starting with a letter or underscore character. (See the `Name` production.) Syntax: `#xnnnn [#xnnnn][_][:][#xnnnn]|[0 |1|2|3|4|5|6|7|8|9][.]|[-][#xnnnn] [#xnnnn]...[#xnnnn]`

- `Eq` represents an equal sign (=) preceded and succeeded by one or more spaces. (See the `Eq` production.) Syntax: =

- `AttValue` states the value of an attribute. (See the `AttValue` production.) Syntax: `{"[^<&"]]|'[^<&']]}|[Reference[Reference [ ...Reference]]]{"|'}`

Notes

`Attribute` is a component of the `EmptyElemTag` and `STag` productions.

Attributes are included within start tags and empty-element tags, not end tags.

Each attribute contains two components: a name and a value. Each name-value pair is known as an *attribute specification*.

An attribute value fine-tunes the element. For example, you can use a value to align content in a particular way, enhance it, or change its appearance in other ways.

For an XML document to be well-formed, each attribute under an element — regardless of whether it has content — must be unique. However, the value of an attribute does not have to be unique.

For an XML document to be valid, each of its element types must have been declared.

For an XML document to be valid, each of its elements' attributes must have been declared and must match the declared type.

For an XML document to be well-formed, its attribute values must be within the internal subset (the part of the DTD that is located within the source document) and not refer to external entities.

Use the `AttlistDecl` element to fine-tune an element, its attributes, and its child elements.

The ampersand (&) and less-than symbol (<) are reserved; they indicate the start or end of markup, among other things. To specify an ampersand or less-than symbol within character data, use the entities & or <, respectively.

Example

The following example is a start tag with two attributes:

```
<HITHERE ALIGN="left" ID="abc">
```

Related Productions

content, element, EmptyElement, Eq, ETag, STag

AttType [54]   Attribute Type

Purpose

Specifies a type for a declared attribute.

EBNF Syntax

```
AttType ::= StringType | TokenizedType
               | EnumeratedType
```

Standard Syntax

```
StringType | TokenizedType | EnumeratedType
```

Where

- StringType specifies a character data string without constraints. (See the StringType production.) Syntax: CDATA

- TokenizedType states that an element attribute is a *tokenized set*, a character data string with some constraints. (See the TokenizedType production.) Syntax: ID | IDREF | IDREFS | ENTITY | ENTITIES | NMTOKEN | NMTOKENS

- EnumeratedType specifies one or more enumerated notation names or name tokens. (See the EnumeratedType production.) Syntax: *NotationType | Enumeration*

2

Notes

`AttType` is a component of the `AttDef` production.

Use the `AttType` production only within document type definitions (DTDs).

An attribute type allows you to ensure that proper and valid data is entered in an XML document.

Attributes are included within start tags and empty-element tags, not end tags.

Well-formed parsers ignore attribute types.

For an XML document to be valid, each of its elements' attributes must have been declared and its content must match the declared type.

Example

The following example shows two attribute types — a tokenized type and string type, respectively:

```
id      ID      #REQUIRED
name    CDATA   #IMPLIED
```

Related Productions

`EnumeratedType, StringType, TokenizedType`

AttValue [10]   Attribute Value

Purpose

States the value of an attribute.

EBNF Syntax

```
AttValue ::= '"' (^<&"] | Reference)* '"'
           | "'" (^<&'] | Reference)* "'"
```

Standard Syntax

```
{"[^<&"]]|'[^<&']]}|[Reference[Reference
   [ ...Reference]]]{"|'}
```

Where

- <, &, ", ', and] are characters *not* to be included in the production.
- Reference names an entity or parameter-entity reference. (See the Reference production.) Syntax: &*Name*; | &#*dec_nums*; | &#x*hex_nums*;

Notes

AttValue is a component of the Attribute and DefaultDecl productions.

Simply put, the *attribute value* is the value of an element's attribute.

A literal, such as AttValue, replaces the current value of an entity or attribute.

AttValue supports entity references, which must be preceded by a # symbol. Each entity reference replaces one character.

The attribute value must follow the rules and constraints of the attribute type. For example, if the type is a decimal number, the value must also be a decimal number. And if the type is a string, the string must be enclosed within single quote marks or quotation marks.

The ampersand (&) and less-than symbol (<) are reserved; they indicate the start or end of markup, among other things. To specify an ampersand or less-than symbol within character data, use the entities & or <, respectively.

If you enclose a production, string, element, or other object within single quote marks, do not use single quote marks within the production, string, element, or other object; if you enclose a production, string, element, or other object within quotation marks, do not use quotation marks within the production, string, element, or other object. Within character data, you can use the apostrophe (') or quotation mark (") characters.

If a quotation mark is included in a string, consider enclosing the string within single quote marks; if a single quote mark is included in a string, consider enclosing the string within quotation marks.

Do not mix single quote marks and quotation marks; quote marks at the beginning and end of a production, string, element, or other object must match.

Example

The following example shows a start tag, its two attributes, and their values:

```
<HITHERE ALIGN="left" ID="abc">
```

The following example shows an attribute list with its element, choices, and default value:

```
<!ATTLIST PRE_TYPE   xml:space   (default|preserve)
    'preserve'>
```

Related Productions

Attribute, DefaultDecl, EntityDef, EntityValue, PEDef, PEReference, PubidChar, PubidLiteral, Reference, SystemLiteral

---

BaseChar [85]   Base Character

Purpose

Specifies a base character.

EBNF Syntax

```
BaseChar ::= [#x0041-#x005A] | [#x0061-#x007A]
           | [#x00C0-#x00D6] | [#x00D8-#x00F6]
           | [#x00F8-#x00FF] | [#x0100-#x0131]
           | [#x0134-#x013E] | [#x0141-#x0148]
           | [#x014A-#x017E]
```

Standard Syntax

```
#xnnnn
```

● **NOTE** ───────────────────────────────────────

For a list of supported base characters, see the preceding EBNF syntax.

Where

- #x*nnnn* represents an alphabetic character supported by the Unicode Organization. For a complete list of supported base characters, see Appendix A, *Unicode Characters and Character Sets*. For more information about Unicode characters, see Chapter 1, *Overview*, and the *Webliography*.

2

Note

BaseChar is a component of the Letter production.

Related Productions

Char, CharRef, CombiningChar, Digit, EntityRef, Extender, Ideographic, Letter, Name, PEReference, Reference

CData [20]   Character Data

Purpose

Defines character data within a character data section.

EBNF Syntax

CData ::= (Char* - (Char* ']]>' Char*))

Standard Syntax

[[*Char*[*Char*[...*Char*]]]]

Where

- Char specifies one legal character. (See the Char production.) Syntax: #*xnnnn*[*n*[*n*]]

Notes

CData is a component of the CDSect production.

A CDATA section cannot contain working elements. In other words, you can include markup, such as tags, but an XML processor treats it strictly as character data.

Do not confuse the CData production with a CDATA section. (Notice the difference in case.)

Character data sections identify text blocks that are not XML markup but that may be confused with markup. You can use CDATA sections to organize a DTD.

Mark the start of a CDATA section with the string <![CDATA[and the end with the string]]>. So, do not use the <, [, and] characters within the section.

Within a CDATA section, you can use the ampersand (&) and less-than symbol (<), because these symbols are not reserved for any use within the section.

Because the greater-than symbol (>) is reserved as an end indicator, you should specify a greater-than symbol within character data by using the entity >.

You cannot nest CDATA sections.

The CDATA type for attributes is related to the CDATA section; many of the same rules apply to both.

Example

You could consider this CDATA section example as a reaction to the typical greeting "Hello, world!":

```
<![CDATA[<text>Goodbye, cruel world!</text>]]>
```

Related Productions

CDEnd, CDSect, CDStart, Char

CDEnd [21]   Character Data
                                        Section End

Purpose

Indicates the end of a block of character data.

EBNF Syntax

```
CDEnd ::= ']]>'
```

Standard Syntax

```
]]>
```

Where

]]> marks the end of the character data section.

Notes

CDEnd is a component of the CDSect production.

Mark the start of a CDATA section with the string <![CDATA[and the end with the string]]>. So, do not use the <, [, and] characters within the section.

Within a CDATA section, you can use the ampersand (&) and less-than symbol (<), because these symbols are not reserved for any use within the section.

Because the greater-than symbol (>) is reserved as an end indicator, you should specify a greater-than symbol within character data by using the entity >.

You cannot nest CDATA sections.

Example

You could consider this CDATA section example as a reaction to the typical greeting "Hello, world!":

```
<![CDATA[<text>Goodbye, cruel world!</text>]]>
```

Related Productions

CData, CDSect, CDStart

CDSect [18]   Character Data Section

Purpose

Creates a character data section: the beginning, contents, and end.

EBNF Syntax

```
CDSect ::= CDStart CData CDEnd
```

Standard Syntax

```
CDStart CData CDEnd
```

2

Where

- CDStart indicates the beginning of a character data section. (See the CDStart production.) Syntax: <![CDATA[
- CData defines character data within a character data section. (See the CData production.) Syntax: [[Char[Char [...Char]]]
- CDEnd indicates the end of a block of character data. (See the CDEnd production.) Syntax:]]>

Notes

CDSect is a component of the content production.

You can place a CDATA section wherever you would insert other character data.

A CDATA section cannot contain working elements. In other words, you can include markup, such as tags, but an XML processor treats it strictly as character data.

Do not confuse the CData production with a CDATA section. (Notice the difference in case.)

Character data sections identify text blocks that are not XML markup but that may be confused with markup. You can use CDATA sections to organize a DTD.

Mark the start of a CDATA section with the string <![CDATA[and the end with the string]]>. So, do not use the <, [, and] characters within the section.

Within a CDATA section, you can use the ampersand (&) and less-than symbol (<), because these symbols are not reserved for any use within the section.

Because the greater-than symbol (>) is reserved as an end indicator, you should specify a greater-than symbol within character data by using the entity >.

You cannot nest CDATA sections.

Example

You could consider this CDATA section example as a reaction to the typical greeting "Hello, world!":

```
<![CDATA[<text>Goodbye, cruel world!</text>]]>
```

Related Productions

CData, CDEnd, CDStart

CDStart [19]   Character Data Start

Purpose

Indicates the beginning of a character data section.

EBNF Syntax

```
CDStart ::= '<![CDATA['
```

Standard Syntax

```
<![CDATA[
```

Where

- `<[!CDATA[` marks the start of a character data section.

Notes

CDStart is a component of the CDSect production.

Indicate the start of a CDATA section with the string `<![CDATA[` and the end with the string `]]>`. So, do not use the `<`, `[`, and `]` characters within the section.

For additional notes, see the CDSect production.

Example

You could consider this CDATA section example as a reaction to the typical greeting "Hello, world!":

```
<![CDATA[<text>Goodbye, cruel world!</text>]]>
```

Related Productions

CData, CDEnd, CDSect

Char [2]   Character

Purpose

Specifies one legal character.

EBNF Syntax

```
Char ::= #x9 | #xA | #xD | [#x20-#xD7FF]
       | [#xE000-#xFFFD]
       | [#x10000-#x10FFFF]
```

Standard Syntax

#x0009|#x000A|#x000D|[#x0020-#xD7FF]|[#xE000-#xFFFD]
|[#x10000-#x10FFFF]

Where

- #x9 (Unicode code #x0009) inserts a tab (HT). This control character moves the cursor to the next tab stop.

- #xA (Unicode code #x000A) inserts a line feed (LF). This control character moves the cursor to the next line below its present position.

- #xD (Unicode code #x000D) inserts a carriage return (CR). This control character moves the cursor to the beginning of the next line.

- #x20-#xD7FF, #xE000-#xFFFD, and #x10000-#x10FFFF are other characters defined by the Unicode Organization. For more information about Unicode characters, see Chapter 1, *Overview*, Appendix A, *Unicode Characters and Character Sets*, and the *Webliography*.

Notes

Char is a component of the CData, Comment, Ignore, and PI productions.

Valid characters include letters, digits, and other characters.

XML requires that processors support the UTF-8 (the default) and UTF-16 character codes. Processors can also support additional character codes.

UTF-8 includes ASCII as a subset.

For a list of character-class productions (that is, BaseChar, CombiningChar, Digit, Extender, Ideographic, and Letter), see Appendix A, *Unicode Characters and Character Sets*. For more information about Unicode characters, see Chapter 1, *Overview*, and the *Webliography*.

Related Productions

CData, Comment, Ignore, PI

CharData [14]	Character Data

Purpose

Indicates any nonmarkup character data.

EBNF Syntax

CharData ::= [^<&]* - ([^<&]* ']]>' [^<&]*)

Standard Syntax

[[^<&][^<&]...[^<&]]]

Where

- < and & are characters *not* to be included in the production.

Notes

CharData is a component of the content production.

Character data is one component of text; the other is markup. Character data is all text that is not markup.

Do not use the]]> combination of characters as character data in a CDATA section; this combination is reserved and marks the end of the character data section. (See the CData, CDEnd, CDSect, and CDStart productions.)

The ampersand (&) and less-than symbol (<) are reserved; they indicate the start or end of markup, among other things. To specify an ampersand or less-than symbol within character data, use the entities & or <, respectively.

Because the greater-than symbol (>) is reserved as an end indicator, you should specify a greater-than symbol within character data by using the entity >.

Example

The following example is an entire self-contained XML document with one line of character data:

```
<?xml version="1.0"?>
<!DOCTYPE endstate[
<!ELEMENT endstate (#PCDATA)>
]>
<endstate>Goodbye, cruel world!</endstate>
```

Related Production

content

CharRef [66]   Character Reference

Purpose

Names a legal character referred to in the ISO/IEC 10646 character set.

EBNF Syntax

```
CharRef ::= '&#' [0-9]+ ';'
          | '&#x' [0-9a-fA-F]+ ';'
```

Standard Syntax

```
&#{0-9[0-9[...0-9]}; |&#x{0-9|a-f|A-F[0-9|a-f|A-F
   [...0-9|a-f|A-F]]};
```

Where

- &# marks the start of a *hexadecimal* code. Valid values range from 0 to 9 and from case-insensitive A to F.
- &#x marks the start of a *decimal* code. Valid values range from 0 to 9.
- 0-9 are decimal or hexadecimal numbers from 0 to 9.
- a-f and A-F represent lowercase or uppercase hexadecimal numbers a, b, c, d, e, and f.
- ; terminates the character.

Notes

CharRef is a component of the Reference production.

A character reference is also known as a *nonprinting* or *nonkeyboard* character, although you can find some of these characters on some computer keyboards.

An entity always has content, and most entities have a name.

Character references and entities begin with a variety of characters, but all end with a semicolon (;):

- Decimal character references start with the &# characters.
- Hexadecimal character references start with the &#x characters.
- Parsed general entities start with an ampersand (&).
- Parameter-entity references start with a percent sign (%).

The ASCII character set is supported by the UTF-8 version of Unicode. For a complete list of supported Unicode characters, see Chapter 1, *Overview*, Appendix A, *Unicode Characters and Character Sets*, and the *Webliography*.

For an XML document to be well-formed, its legal characters must conform to the rules set for the Char production. (See the Char production.)

For an XML document to be well-formed, all elements must be nested properly: All tags, elements, comments, processing instructions, character references, and entity references must be completely enclosed within one entity.

The ampersand (&) and less-than symbol (<) are reserved; they indicate the start or end of markup, among other things. To specify an ampersand or less-than symbol within character data, use the entities & or <, respectively.

Example

The following are examples of character references:

```
&#251;
&#x628;&#x631;&#x627;&#x64a;
```

Related Productions

BaseChar, Char, CombiningChar, Digit, EntityRef, Extender, Ideographic, Letter, Name, PEReference, Reference

children [47]   Child Element Content

Purpose
Defines child element content.

EBNF Syntax
```
children ::= (choice | seq) ('?' | '*' | '+' )?
```

Standard Syntax
```
{choice|seq}[?|*|+]
```

Where
- choice specifies a choice list of content particles. (See the choice production.) Syntax: ([...]cp[[...] |[...]cp[[...]|[...]cp[[...] |[...]cp]]][...]
- seq specifies a content-particles sequence list. (See the seq production.) Syntax: ([...]cp[[...], [...]cp][[...],[...]cp]...[[...], [...]cp][...])
- ? is a character indicating that a production or content particle can occur up to one time.
- * is a character indicating that a production or content particle can occur an unlimited number of times.
- + is a character indicating that a production or content particle *must* occur one or more times.

Notes
children is a component of the contentspec production.

Use the children production only within document type definitions (DTDs).

If the ?, *, or + character is not present, the element or content particle occurs once.

For more information, see the Notes sections of the elementdecl and contentspec productions.

Examples

The following example declares the longdoc element, which includes three elements:

```
<!ELEMENT longdoc (intro, body, index)>
```

The following example declares the mixedtext element, which can contain both data and another element:

```
<!ELEMENT mixedtext (#PCDATA|ital>
```

Related Productions

choice, contentspec, cp, Name, S, seq

---

choice [49]   Choice List

Purpose

Specifies a choice list of content particles.

EBNF Syntax

choice ::= '(' S? cp (S? '|' S? cp)* S?

Standard Syntax

```
([ ... ]cp[[ ... ]|[ ... ]cp[[ ... ]|[ ... ]cp
[[ ... ]  |[ ... ]cp]]][ ... ]
```

Where

- S represents one or more whitespace characters: spaces, carriage returns, line feeds, or tabs. (See the S production.) Syntax: {[#x20|#x9|#xD|#xA][#x20|#x9|#xD|#xA]... [#x20|#x9|#xD|#xA]}
- cp includes a content particle grammar. (See the cp production.) Syntax: {Name|choice|seq}[?|*|+]

Notes

choice is a component of the children and cp productions.

Content models consist of *content particles* (CPs), which are names of child element types, as well as choice lists and sequence lists, which are, in turn, other content particles. This allows you to write very complex element-type declarations, which must be matched exactly during processing. Of course, the more complex a declaration, the more chances exist for errors in processing an XML document.

For an XML document to be valid, any PEReference replacement text must be nested completely within its content particle in a choice, Mixed, or seq production.

For an XML document to be valid, any PEReference replacement text cannot be empty and its first or last nonblank characters should not be a pipe (|) or ,) character combination.

For more information, see the Notes section under the elementdecl and contentspec productions.

Examples

The following example declares the mixedtext element, which can contain both data and another element:

```
<!ELEMENT mixedtext (#PCDATA|ital)>
```

The following example shows an attribute list with its element, choices, and default value:

```
<!ATTLIST PRE_TYPE    xml:space    (default|preserve)
     'preserve'>
```

Related Productions

children, contentspec, cp, Name, S, seq

CombiningChar [87]   Combining Character

Purpose

Specifies a character that combines with letters of the alphabet and other characters to denote special pronunciation or meaning.

EBNF Syntax

```
CombiningChar ::= [#x0300-#x0345] | [#x0360-#x0361]
    | [#x0483-#x0486] | [#x0591-#x05A1]
  | [#x05A3-#x05B9]
    | [#x05BB-#x05BD] | #x05BF | [#x05C1-#x05C2]
  | #x05C4
    | [#x064B-#x0652] | #x0670 | #x06D6-#x06DC]
    | [#x06DD-#x06DF] | [#x06E0-#x06E4]
  | [#x06E7-#x06E8]
    | [#x06EA-#x06ED] | [#x0901-#x0903] | #x093C
    | [#x093E-#x094C] | #x094D | [#x0951-#x0954]
    | #x0962-#x0963] | [#x0981-#x0983] | #x09BC
  | #x09BE
    | #x09BF | [#x09C0-#x09C4] | [#x09C7-#x09C8]
    | #x09CB-#x09CD] | #x09D7 | [#x09E2-#x09E3]
  | #x0A02
    | #x0A3C | #x0A3E | #x0A3F | [#x0A40-#x0A42]
    | [#x0A47-#x0A48] | [#x0A4B-#x0A4D]
  | [#x0A70-#x0A71]
    | [#x0A81-#x0A83] | #x0ABC | [#x0ABE-#x0AC5]
    | [#x0AC7-#x0AC9] | [#x0ACB-#x0ACD]
  | [#x0B01-#x0B03]
    | #x0B3C | [#x0B3E-#x0B43] | [#x0B47-#x0B48]
    | [#x0B4B-#x0B4D] | [#x0B56-#x0B57]
  | [#x0B82-#x0B83]
    | [#x0BBE-#x0BC2] | [#x0BC6-#x0BC8]
  | [#x0BCA-#x0BCD]
    | #x0BD7 | [#x0C01-#x0C03] | [#x0C3E-#x0C44]
    | [#x0C46-#x0C48] | #x0C4A-#x0C4D]
  | [#x0C55-#x0C56]
    | [#x0C82-#x0C83] | [#x0CBE-#x0CC4]
  | [#x0CC6-#x0CC8]
    | [#x0CCA-#x0CCD] | [#x0CD5-#x0CD6]
  | [#x0D02-#x0D03]
```

```
    |   [#x0D3E-#x0D43]  |  [#x0D46-#x0D48]
|  [#x0D4A-#x0D4D]
    |  #x0D57  |  #x0E31  |  [#x0E34-#x0E3A]
|  [#x0E47-#x0E4E]
    |  #x0EB1  |  [#x0EB4-#x0EB9]  |  [#x0EBB-#x0EBC]
    |  [#x0EC8-#x0ECD]  |  [#x0F18-#x0F19]  |  #x0F35
|  #x0F37
    |  #x0F39  |  #x0F3E  |  #x0F3F  |  [#x0F71-#x0F84]
    |  [#x0F86-#x0F8B]  |  [#x0F90-#x0F95]  |  #x0F97
    |  [#x0F99-#x0FAD]  |  [#x0FB1-#x0FB7]  |  #x0FB9
    |  [#x20D0-#x20DC]  |  #x20E1  |  [#x302A-#x302F]
|  #x3099
    |  #x309A
```

Standard Syntax

#x*nnnn*

● **NOTE** ──────────────────────────────────

For a list of supported base characters, see the preceding EBNF syntax.

Where

- #x*nnnn* represents a combining character supported by the Unicode Organization. For a complete list of supported combining characters, see Appendix A, *Unicode Characters and Character Sets*. For more information about Unicode characters, see Chapter 1, *Overview*, and the *Webliography*.

Note

CombiningChar is a component of the NameChar production.

Related Productions

BaseChar, Char, CharRef, Digit, EntityRef, Extender, Ideographic, Letter, Name, PEReference, Reference

Comment [15]

Comment

Purpose

Inserts a nonprinting, nonparsed comment in the XML document.

EBNF Syntax

```
Comment ::= '<!--' ((Char - '-')
   | ('-' (Char - '-')))* '-->'
```

Standard Syntax

```
<!--[[Char]|[-Char][[Char]|[-Char]]...[[Char]
   |[-Char]]]-->
```

Where

- `<!--` marks the beginning of the comment.
- `Char` specifies one legal character. (See the `Char` production.) Syntax: #*xnnnn*[*n*[*n*]]
- `-->` marks the end of the comment.

Notes

`Comment` is a component of the `content`, `markupdecl`, and `Misc` productions.

Do not include one hyphen(-) or two hyphens in a comment; the hyphen is reserved for the start and end of the comment.

Comments describe markup, do not affect processing, and do not appear in printed output.

Do not include comments within a `CDATA` section or within markup.

An XML comment is much more restricted than an SGML comment. SGML comments can appear within declarations; XML comments cannot. However, declarations can appear within XML comments in the form of comments.

For an XML document to be well-formed, all components must be nested properly: All tags, elements, comments, processing instructions, character references, and entity references must be completely enclosed within one entity.

XML applications do not have to be able to read comments, although some do. Use processing instructions (PIs) to instruct an application. For more information, see the PI production.

The Comment production is the counterpart to ! in HTML.

2

Example

The following example marks the start of an element definition:

```
<!-- defining <para> paragraph element -->
```

conditionalSect [61]   Conditional Section

Purpose

Names a conditional section that is either included or ignored during processing.

EBNF Syntax

```
conditionalSect ::= includeSect | ignoreSect
```

Standard Syntax

```
includeSect|ignoreSect
```

Where

- includeSect names an included section. (See the includeSect production.) Syntax: <![[...] INCLUDE[...][[*extSubsetDecl;*] [*extSubsetDecl;*]...[*extSubsetDecl;*]]]>
- ignoreSect names a conditionally ignored section. (See the ignoreSect production.) Syntax: <![[...]IGNORE [...][[*ignoreSectContents*] [*ignoreSectContents*] ...[*ignoreSectContents*]]]>

Notes

conditionalSect is a component of the extSubsetDecl production.

Use the conditionalSect production only within document type definitions (DTDs).

A conditional section can include declarations, comments, processing instructions, whitespace, and other conditional sections.

SGML and XML developers use conditional sections when they program validating parsers and when they develop sets of complex DTDs. The standard DTD writer does not need to use conditional sections.

If you are an accomplished XML developer, you can use PEReferences to identify and process particular conditional sections, instead of using the conditionalSect element and its components.

Only INCLUDEd conditional sections are an "official" part of a DTD; IGNOREd sections, including INCLUDEd sections nested within them, are not considered part of a DTD.

Properly programmed XML processors should process both INCLUDEd and IGNOREd sections.

If a conditional section's keyword is a PEReference, an XML processor should replace its content before including or ignoring particular conditional sections.

You can use conditional sections within external subsets (the part of a DTD that is stored in a separate document, completely outside the source document) but not within internal subsets (the part of the DTD that is located within the source document).

Examples

The following example shows the reference to an external subset, quotes.dtd, in the source document, and some additional lines:

```
<?xml version="1.0"?>
<!DOCTYPE test SYSTEM "quotes.dtd">
<saying>
<para>
A stitch in time saves nine.
</para>
<para>
A fool and his money are soon parted.
</para>
```

and two elements defined within the quotes.dtd document:

```
<!ELEMENT saying (para*)>
<!ELEMENT para (#PCDATA)>
```

The following is a segment of an external subset with conditional sections:

```
<!ENTITY  %  hello    'INCLUDE' >
<!ENTITY  %  goodbye 'IGNORE'  >

<![%hello; [
<!ELEMENT histate (#PCDATA)>
]]>

<![%goodbye; [
<!ELEMENT byestate (#PCDATA)>
]]>
```

Related Productions

extSubsetDecl, Ignore, ignoreSect, ignoreSectContents, includeSect, S

---

content [43]   Element Content

Purpose

Defines element content within the start and end tags.

EBNF Syntax

```
content ::= (element | CharData | Reference | CDSect
    | PI | Comment)*
```

Standard Syntax

[*element* | *CharData* | *Reference* | *CDSect* | *PI* | *Comment*]
[*element* | *CharData* | *Reference* | *CDSect* | *PI* | *Comment*]
... [*element* | *CharData* | *Reference* | *CDSect* | *PI* | *Comment*]

Where

- element defines an XML element, with or without content. (See the element production.) Syntax: *EmptyElemTag* | *STag content ETag*

- CharData indicates the character data that does not include markup characters. (See the CharData production.) Syntax: [[^<&][^<&]...[^<&]]

- Reference names an entity or parameter-entity reference. (See the Reference production.) Syntax: &Name; | &#dec_nums; | &#xhex_nums;

- CDSect creates a character data section: the beginning, contents, and end. (See the CDSect production.) Syntax: CDStart CData CDEnd

- PI writes processing instructions. (See the PI production.) Syntax: <?PITarget [[...][Char[Char]...[Char]]?>

- Comment inserts a nonprinting, nonparsed comment in the XML document. (See the Comment production.) Syntax: <!--[[Char]|[-Char][[Char]|[-Char]]... [[Char]|[-Char]]]-->

Notes

content is a component of the element and extParsedEnt productions.

All the text and child elements between the start tag and end tag of a nonempty element are its content.

An internal general parsed entity is well-formed if it is identical to its associated content production.

An external general parsed entity is well-formed if it is identical to its associated extParsedEnt production.

The ampersand (&) and less-than symbol (<) are reserved; they indicate the start or end of markup, among other things. To specify an ampersand or less-than symbol within character data, use the entities & or <, respectively.

Because the greater-than symbol (>) is reserved as an end indicator, you should specify a greater-than symbol within character data by using the entity >.

Use the contentspec production to fine-tune element content.

Examples

The following example is an entire self-contained XML document with character data content within the start tag and end tag:

```
<?xml version="1.0"?>
<!DOCTYPE endstate[
<!ELEMENT endstate (#PCDATA)>
]>
<endstate>Goodbye, cruel world!</endstate>
```

Related Productions

Attribute, content, element, EmptyElement, Eq, ETag, STag

contentspec [46]	Content Type Specification

Purpose

Specifies an element's content type.

EBNF Syntax

```
contentspec ::= 'EMPTY' | 'ANY' | Mixed | children
```

Standard Syntax

EMPTY | ANY | *Mixed* | *children*

Where

- EMPTY is an uppercase-only reserved keyword that specifies an element with no content. No end tag exists; the start tag is simply a marker.
- ANY is an uppercase-only reserved keyword indicating that the current element can contain any of the other defined elements, including itself.
- Mixed is a reserved keyword element indicating that the current element can contain both character data and child elements. (See the Mixed production.) Syntax: ([...] #PCDATA[[...] | [...] *Name*] [...]]|

[...]*Name*]...[[...]|[...]*Name*]]
[...])*|([...]#PCDATA[...])

- children is a reserved keyword element that defines child element content. (See the children production.) Syntax: {*choice*|*seq*}[?|*|+]

Notes

contentspec is a component of the elementdecl production.

Use the contentspec production only within document type definitions (DTDs).

Simply put, *element content* is one or more child elements in the content of a particular element type. Element content does not include any character data. If an element contains only child elements, you can control the order in which the child elements appear. When you declare element content, you are implicitly following a *content model*, which sets valid child element types and the order in which they appear in the element content. The productions in the XML content-model category are children, cp, choice, and seq.

Mixed content defines the content of an element as both element content and character data.

ANY allows any content, as long as it abides by XML rules and constraints. ANY is a good way to bring old SGML and HTML documents into conformance with XML rules. To create a DTD quickly for one of these documents (that is, to enable a well-formed document to become a valid document), define all the element types in the document and declare each of their content as ANY. Then, at your convenience, you can edit each element type and content further.

For an XML document to be valid, a DTD containing element declarations must exist. Then, for each element type:

- If the element declaration contains the EMPTY keyword, the element is empty.
- If the element declaration contains the ANY keyword, at least one child element, and possibly the current element, have been declared.
- If the element declaration contains the Mixed keyword, the element can contain both character data and child elements.
- If the element declaration contains the children keyword, at least one child element has been declared.

For an XML document to be valid, any PEReference replacement text must be nested completely within its content particle in a choice, Mixed, or seq production.

For an XML document to be valid, any PEReference replacement text cannot be empty and its first or last nonblank characters should not be a pipe (|) or ,) character combination.

You cannot declare the same element type more than once in an XML document. However, you can declare attributes and entities more than once.

Examples

The following example is an entire self-contained XML document with one declared element:

```
<?xml version="1.0"?>
<!DOCTYPE endstate[
<!ELEMENT endstate (#PCDATA)>
]>
<endstate>Goodbye, cruel world!</endstate>
```

The following example declares the longdoc element, which includes three elements:

```
<!ELEMENT longdoc (intro, body, index)>
```

The following example declares the empty image element:

```
<!ELEMENT image EMPTY>
```

The following ksink element can contain any contents:

```
<!ELEMENT ksink ANY>
```

The following example declares the mixedtext element, which can contain both data and another element:

```
<!ELEMENT mixedtext (#PCDATA|ital>
```

Related Productions

children, choice, contentspec, cp, elementdecl, Mixed, Name, S, seq

cp [48]   Content Particle Grammar

Purpose
Specifies a content particle grammar in element content.

EBNF Syntax

```
cp ::= (Name | choice | seq) ('?' | '*' | '+')?
```

Standard Syntax

{Name|choice|seq}[?|*|+]

Where

- Name specifies a valid XML name, starting with a letter or underscore character. (See the Name production.)
  Syntax: #xnnnn [#xnnnn][_][:][#xnnnn]|[0|1|2|3
  |4|5|6|7|8|9][.]|[-][#xnnnn][#xnnnn]...
  [#xnnnn]
- choice specifies a choice list of content particles. (See the choice production.) Syntax: ([...]cp[[...]|
  [...]cp[[...]|[...]cp[[...]|
  [...]cp]]][...]
- seq specifies a content-particles sequence list. (See the seq production.) Syntax: ([...]cp[[...],
  [...]cp][[...],[...]cp]...[[...],
  [...]cp][...])
- ? is a character indicating that a production or content particle can occur up to one time.
- * is a character indicating that a production or content particle can occur an unlimited number of times.
- + is a character indicating that a production or content particle *must* occur one or more times.

Notes

cp is a component of the choice and seq productions.

If the ?, *, or + character is not present, the production or content particle occurs once.

Content models consist of content particles (CPs), which are names of child element types, as well as choice lists and sequence lists, which are, in turn, other content particles. This enables you to write very complex element-type declarations, which must be matched exactly during processing. Of course, the more complex a declaration, the more chances that exist for errors in processing an XML document.

For more information, see the Notes section under the elementdecl and contentspec productions.

Examples

The following example is an entire self-contained XML document with one declared element:

```
<?xml version="1.0"?>
<!DOCTYPE endstate[
<!ELEMENT endstate (#PCDATA)>
]>
<endstate>Goodbye, cruel world!</endstate>
```

The following example declares the longdoc element, which includes three elements:

```
<!ELEMENT longdoc (intro, body, index)>
```

The following example declares the mixedtext element, which can contain both data and another element:

```
<!ELEMENT mixedtext (#PCDATA|ital>
```

The following example shows an attribute list with its element, choices, and default value:

```
<!ATTLIST PRE_TYPE   xml:space   (default|preserve)
    'preserve'>
```

Related Productions

children, choice, contentspec, Name, S, seq

DefaultDecl [60]	**Default Value Declaration**

Purpose

Declares whether a particular attribute is required or optional.

EBNF Syntax

```
DefaultDecl ::= '#REQUIRED' | '#IMPLIED'
    | (('#FIXED' S)? AttValue)
```

Standard Syntax

#REQUIRED | #IMPLIED | [[#FIXED[...]]*AttValue*]

Where

- #REQUIRED is an uppercase-only reserved keyword indicating that the defined attribute *must* be supplied.

- #IMPLIED is an uppercase-only reserved keyword indicating that the defined attribute *may* be supplied.

- #FIXED is an uppercase-only reserved keyword indicating that the defined attribute *must* always have the default attribute value.

- S represents one or more whitespace characters: spaces, carriage returns, line feeds, or tabs. (See the S production.) Syntax: {[#x20|#x9|#xD|#xA][#x20|#x9|#xD|#xA]... [#x20|#x9|#xD|#xA]}

- AttValue states the value of an attribute. (See the AttValue production.) Syntax: {"[^<&"]]|'[^<&']]}|[*Reference*[*Reference* [...*Reference*]]]{"|'}

Notes

DefaultDecl is a component of the AttDef production.

In previous XML drafts, DefaultDecl was known as Default.

Because they start with a #, you cannot confuse the #REQUIRED, #IMPLIED, and #FIXED keywords with a valid XML name.

Attributes are included within start tags and empty-element tags, not end tags.

Each attribute contains two components: a name and a value. Each name-value pair is known as an *attribute specification*.

An attribute value fine-tunes the element. For example, you can use a value to align content in a particular way, enhance it, or change its appearance in other ways.

A #FIXED attribute value declared for a particular element type means that you do not have to restate the value every time that you specify the element type in an XML document.

For an XML document to be well-formed, each attribute under an element, regardless of whether it has content, must be unique. However, the value of an attribute does not have to be unique.

For an XML document to be valid, each of its element types must have been declared.

For an XML document to be valid, each of its elements' attributes must have been declared and must match the declared type.

For an XML document to be valid, whenever an element type with a #REQUIRED attribute appears, the attribute and an attribute value must be present.

For an XML document to be valid, whenever an element type with an #IMPLIED attribute appears and does not have a value, the XML processor must report the missing value and continue processing.

For an XML document to be valid, whenever an element type is not #REQUIRED or #IMPLIED, the attribute value is the assigned default value.

For an XML document to be valid, whenever an element type with a #FIXED attribute appears with a value that is not the assigned default value, the XML processor issues a fatal-error message.

For an XML document to be valid, whenever an element type with a #FIXED attribute appears without a value, the XML processor supplies the assigned default value.

An XML processor normalizes the attribute value in the following ways before sending it to the target application:

- It replaces or appends the #20 space character to line-end characters, normalized whitespace (S) characters, external parsed entities, and internal parsed entities.
- It replaces each entity reference with its replacement text.
- It appends other characters to normalized attribute values.
- It removes leading and trailing #x20 characters and removes instances of two or more succeeding #x20 characters.

Nonvalidating XML processors treat nondeclared attributes as if they have a CDATA value.

The ampersand (&) and less-than symbol (<) are reserved; they indicate the start or end of markup, among other things. To specify an ampersand or less-than symbol within character data, use the entities & or <, respectively.

2

Examples

The following example shows two attribute defaults:

```
id      ID      #REQUIRED
name    CDATA   #IMPLIED
```

The following example shows the method attribute of the HTML FORM element:

```
method  (GET|POST)  GET
```

Related Productions

AttDef, AttValue, S

Digit [88]   Digit

Purpose

Specifies a digit.

EBNF Syntax

```
Digit ::= [#x0030-#x0039] | [#x0660-#x0669]
    | [#x06F0-#x06F9] | [#x0966-#x096F] |
[#x09E6-#x09EF]
    | [#x0A66-#x0A6F] | [#x0AE6-#x0AEF] |
[#x0B66-#x0B6F]
    | [#x0BE7-#x0BEF] | [#x0C66-#x0C6F] |
[#x0CE6-#x0CEF]
    | [#x0D66-#x0D6F] | [#x0E50-#x0E59] |
[#x0ED0-#x0ED9]
    | [#x0F20-#x0F29]
```

Standard Syntax

```
#xnnnn
```

●—NOTE

For a list of supported base characters, see the preceding EBNF syntax.

Where

- #x*nnnn* represents a digit supported by the Unicode Organization. For a complete list of supported digits, see Appendix A, *Unicode Characters and Character Sets*. For more information about Unicode characters, see Chapter 1, *Overview*, and the *Webliography*.

Note

Digit is a component of the Instance, Length, NameChar, and Position productions.

Related Productions

BaseChar, Char, CharRef, CombiningChar, EntityRef, Extender, Ideographic, Letter, Name, PEReference, Reference

---

doctypedecl [28]   Document Type Declaration

Purpose

Specifies an XML document type (or *doctype*) declaration, which contains a document type definition (DTD).

EBNF Syntax

```
doctypedecl ::= '<!DOCTYPE' S Name (S ExternalID)? S?
    ('[' (markupdecl | PEReference | S)* ']' S?)? '>'
```

Standard Syntax

```
<!DOCTYPE[ ... ]Name[[ ... ]ExternalID][ ...]
    [[markupdecl|PEReference|[ ... ][[markupdecl
    |PEReference|[ ... ]...[[markupdecl|PEReference
    |[ ... ]][ ... ]>
```

Where

- `<!DOCTYPE` is an uppercase-only reserved keyword that indicates the start of a document type declaration.

- `S` represents one or more whitespace characters: spaces, carriage returns, line feeds, or tabs. (See the `S` production.) Syntax: `{[#x20|#x9|#xD|#xA][#x20|#x9|#xD|#xA]...` `[#x20|#x9|#xD|#xA]}`

- `Name` specifies a valid XML name, starting with a letter or underscore character. (See the `Name` production.) Syntax: `#xnnnn [#xnnnn][_][:][#xnnnn]|[0|1|2` `|3|4|5|6|7|8|9][.]|[-][#xnnnn][#xnnnn]...` `[#xnnnn]`

- `ExternalID` names a parsed external entity. (See the `ExternalID` production.) Syntax: `SYSTEM[ ... ]` *`SystemLiteral`*`|PUBLIC[ ... ]`*`PubidLiteral`* `[ ... ]`*`SystemLiteral`*

- `[` indicates the beginning of a markup declaration or parameter-entity reference.

- `markupdecl` declares markup of elements, attributes, entities, or notation. (See the `markupdecl` production.) Syntax: *`elementdecl`*`|`*`AttlistDecl`*`|`*`EntityDecl`* `|`*`NotationDecl`*`|`*`PI`*`|`*`Comment`*

- `PEReference` identifies a parameter-entity reference. (See the `PEReference` production.) Syntax: `%`*`Name`*`;`

- `]` indicates the end of a markup declaration or parameter-entity reference.

- `>` indicates the end of a document type declaration.

Notes

`doctypedecl` is a component of the `prolog` production.

The document type declaration must precede any start tags in an XML document.

A `<!DOCTYPE` declaration is required for an XML document to be valid; otherwise, the best the document can do is be well-formed.

A document type declaration can point to both an *external subset* (an external parsed entity, the part of a DTD that is stored in a separate document, completely outside the source document) and an *internal subset* (the part of the DTD that is located within the source document), either or both of which may contain markup declarations that define an XML grammar, its attributes, and its constraints, for one or more documents, including the current one. This grammar is known as the document type definition (DTD). Note that document type *declarations* are *never* referred to as DTDs.

For an XML document to be valid, every element type in the document must have been declared in the DTD.

A DTD can be located in the internal subset (the part of the DTD that is located within the source document). In this case, the DTD is local. However, storing the DTD separately in an external subset (the part of a DTD that is stored in a separate document, completely outside the source document) is preferable, so that it can serve several documents.

Parameter entities are processed first, resulting in replacement text being placed in the markup declarations.

If an XML document is associated with a DTD, it does not necessarily have to be valid. For example, you can use a *nonvalidating* XML processor on the document, which doesn't validate the document and isn't required to read the external subset (the part of a DTD that is stored in a separate document, completely outside the source document).

For an XML document to be valid, the name in the doctype declaration must be identical to the name of the root element being defined.

Because the greater-than symbol (>) is reserved as an end indicator, you should specify a greater-than symbol within character data by using the entity >.

Examples

The following example specifies an internal subset:

```
<?xml version="1.0"?>
<!DOCTYPE endstate[
<!ELEMENT endstate (#PCDATA)>
]>
<endstate>Goodbye, cruel world!</endstate>
```

The following example specifies an external subset, `goodbye.dtd`:

```
<?xml version="1.0"?>
<!DOCTYPE endstate SYSTEM "goodbye.dtd">
<endstate>Goodbye, cruel world!</endstate>
```

Related Productions

document, ExternalID, markupdecl, Name, PEReference, prolog, S

---

document [1]   Document Name

Purpose

Creates the current document.

EBNF Syntax

document ::= prolog element Misc*

Standard Syntax

prolog element [Misc[Misc[...Misc]]]

Where

- prolog generally describes an XML document. (See the prolog production.) Syntax:
  [XMLDecl][[Misc][Misc]...[Misc]][doctypedecl[[Misc][Misc]...[Misc]]]

- element defines an XML element, with or without content. (See the element production.) Syntax: *EmptyElemTag|STag content ETag*

- Misc inserts miscellaneous information in a prolog. (See the Misc production.) Syntax: *Comment|PI|[...]*

Notes

This element identifies the current document, including the version of XML that was used to create it.

Although Misc enables you to add comments, processing instructions, and whitespace to the document production, use good syntax. Being careful helps links to work properly and XML processors to interpret XML statements correctly.

An XML document must contain at least one element, the root or document element, which is the parent of all other elements in the document.

The *document entity* is the entire XML document as it will be read by a nonvalidating XML processor. This is in contrast to a *document module*, which is a part of the document distributed over a network.

For an XML document to be well-formed, the document entity must be identical to the document production.

Examples

The following example is an entire self-contained XML document:

```
<?xml version="1.0"?>
<!DOCTYPE endstate[
<!ELEMENT endstate (#PCDATA)>
]>
<endstate>Goodbye, cruel world!</endstate>
```

The following example is an XML document with an external DTD:

```
<?xml version="1.0"?>
<!DOCTYPE endstate SYSTEM "goodbye.dtd">
<endstate>Goodbye, cruel world!</endstate>
```

Related Productions

Misc, prolog, VersionInfo, XMLDecl

---

element [39]   Element

Purpose

Specifies an XML element, with or without content.

EBNF Syntax

element ::= EmptyElemTag | STag content ETag

Standard Syntax

EmptyElemTag|STag content ETag

Where

- EmptyElemTag identifies an empty-element tag. (See the EmptyElemTag production.) Syntax: {<*Name* [[...] *Attribute*][[...]*Attribute*]...[[...] *Attribute*]]}[...]{/>}

- STag defines a start tag for an XML element. (See the STag production.) Syntax: <*Name*[[[...] *Attribute*][[...]*Attribute*]...[[...] *Attribute*]]][...]>

- content creates element content within the start and end tags. (See the content production.) Syntax: [element|CharData|Reference|CDSect|PI |Comment][element|CharData|Reference|*CDSect* |*PI*|*Comment*]...[*element*|*CharData*|*Reference* |*CDSect*|*PI*|*Comment*]

- ETag defines an end tag for an element. (See the ETag production.) Syntax: </*Name*[...]>

Notes

element is a component of the content and document productions. An XML document must contain at least one element.

An element includes a start tag, an end tag, and the content within the tags.

An *element type*, or generic identifier (GI), is the name in the start tag and end tag. For example, in the tags <speech> and </speech>, speech is the element type. The following HTML list

    <UL>
    <LI>Beatles</LI>
    <LI>Rolling Stones</LI>
    <LI>Elvis</LI>
    </UL>

includes five elements (every occurrence of <UL>, <LI>, and </UL>, </LI>) and two element types (<UL>/</UL> and <LI>/</LI>).

Element types with content have start tags (see the STag element) and end tags (see the ETag production); empty elements have empty-element tags (see the EmptyElemTag production).

For an XML document to be well-formed, the name of a particular element type must be the same for both the start tag and end tag.

For an XML document to be well-formed, all elements must be nested properly: All tags, elements, comments, processing instructions, character references, and entity references must be completely enclosed within one entity.

For an XML document to be valid, every element type in the document must have been declared in the DTD.

For an XML document to be valid, there must be an element declaration and:

- If the element declaration contains the EMPTY keyword, the element is empty. (See the contentspec production.)

- If the element declaration contains the ANY keyword, at least one child element, and possibly the current element, has been declared. (See the contentspec production.)

- If the element declaration contains the Mixed keyword, the element can contain both character data and child elements. (See the contentspec and Mixed productions.)

- If the element declaration contains the children keyword, at least one child element has been declared. (See the contentspec and children productions.)

Because the greater-than symbol (>) is reserved as an end indicator, you should specify a greater-than symbol within character data by using the entity >.

Use the elementdecl production to fine-tune an element, its attributes, and its child elements.

Examples

The following example is an entire self-contained XML document with one declared element:

```
<?xml version="1.0"?>
<!DOCTYPE endstate[
<!ELEMENT endstate (#PCDATA)>
]>
<endstate>Goodbye, cruel world!</endstate>
```

The following examples show some empty elements:

```
<IMG align="left" id="bighome"
src="bighouse.GIF"></IMG>


<br></br>
</br>
```

Related Productions

content, document, EmptyElemTag, Eq, ETag, STag

---

elementdecl [45]   Element Type Declaration

Purpose

Constrains element content by using an element type declaration.

EBNF Syntax

```
elementdecl ::= '<!ELEMENT' S Name S contentspec S? '>'
```

Standard Syntax

```
{<!ELEMENT[ ... ]Name[ ... ]contentspec}[ ... ]{>}
```

Where

- <!ELEMENT is an uppercase-only reserved keyword that marks the start of the element type declaration.
- S represents one or more whitespace characters: spaces, carriage returns, line feeds, or tabs. (See the S production.) Syntax:
  {[#x20|#x9|#xD|#xA][#x20|#x9|#xD|#xA]...[#x20|#x9|#xD|#xA]}
- Name specifies a valid XML name, starting with a letter or underscore character. (See the Name production.) Syntax:
  #xnnnn [#xnnnn][_][:][#xnnnn]|[0|1|2|3|4|5|6|7|8|9][.]|[-][#xnnnn][#xnnnn]...[#xnnnn]

- contentspec specifies an element's content type. (See the contentspec production.) Syntax:
  EMPTY|ANY|*Mixed*|*children*

- > marks the end of the element type declaration.

2

Notes

elementdecl is a component of the markupdecl production.

Use the elementdecl production only within document type definitions (DTDs).

Using an element declaration, you can fine-tune the definition and behavior of an element, its attributes, and its child elements.

Simply put, *element content* is one or more child elements in the content of a particular element type. Element content does not include any character data. If an element contains only child elements, you can control the order in which the child elements appear. When you declare element content, you are implicitly following a *content model*, which sets valid child element types and the order in which they appear in the element content. The productions in the XML content-model category are children, cp, choice, and seq.

Mixed content defines the content of an element as both element content and character data.

You cannot declare the same element type more than once in an XML document. However, you can declare attributes and entities more than once.

Because the greater-than symbol (>) is reserved as an end indicator, you should specify a greater-than symbol within character data by using the entity >.

Examples

The following example is an entire self-contained XML document with one declared element:

```
<?xml version="1.0"?>
<!DOCTYPE endstate[
<!ELEMENT endstate (#PCDATA)>
]>
<endstate>Goodbye, cruel world!</endstate>
```

The following example declares the longdoc element, which includes a sequence of three elements:

```
<!ELEMENT longdoc (intro, body, index)>
```

The following example declares the longdoc element, which includes a choice of three elements:

```
<!ELEMENT longdoc (intro|body|index)>
```

The following example declares the empty image element:

```
<!ELEMENT image EMPTY>
```

The following ksink element can contain any contents:

```
<!ELEMENT ksink ANY>
```

The following example declares the mixedtext element, which can contain both data and another element:

```
<!ELEMENT mixedtext (#PCDATA|ital)>
```

The following example declares the mixedtext element, which can contain both data and two parameter-entity references:

```
<!ELEMENT mixedtext (#PCDATA|%typeface;|%pointsize;)>
```

The following example from the Math Markup Language declares the EQ empty element:

```
<!ELEMENT EQ          EMPTY       >
```

Related Productions

children, choice, contentspec, cp, Mixed, Name, S, seq

EmptyElemTag [44]   Empty-Element Tag

Purpose

Identifies an empty element.

EBNF Syntax

```
EmptyElemTag ::= '<' Name (S Attribute)* S? '/>'
```

Standard Syntax

```
{<Name [[ ... ]Attribute][[ ... ]Attribute]
...[[ ... ]Attribute]]}[ ... ]{/>}
```

Where

- < marks the start of the empty-element tag.

- Name specifies a valid XML name, starting with a letter or underscore character. (See the Name production.) Syntax: #xnnnn [#xnnnn][_][:][#xnnnn]|[0|1|2|3|4|5|6 |7|8|9][.]|[-][#xnnnn][#xnnnn]...[#xnnnn]

- S represents one or more whitespace characters: spaces, carriage returns, line feeds, or tabs. (See the S production.) Syntax: {[#x20|#x9|#xD|#xA][#x20|#x9|#xD|#xA]...[#x20|#x9 |#xD|#xA]}

- Attribute names an attribute used to select an element. (See the Attribute production.) Syntax: Name[...] =[...]AttValue

- /> marks the end of the empty-element tag.

Notes

EmptyElemTag is a component of the element production.

In previous XML drafts, EmptyElemTag was known as EmptyElement.

An empty-element tag marks the future location of an object, such as a graphic or line break, in document output. In contrast, a nonempty element contains content that will be part of the document output.

You can mark an empty element in the following ways:

- In a document, insert a start tag immediately followed by an end tag.

- Declare it by using the EmptyElemTag production.

- Declare any element EMPTY by using the contentspec production.

If you want your XML documents to work properly under a variety of computer platforms, use the EmptyElemTag production for all elements that you declare to be EMPTY.

For an XML document to be well-formed, each attribute under an element, regardless of whether it has content, must be unique. However, the value of an attribute does not have to be unique.

For an XML document to be well-formed, all elements must be nested properly: All tags, elements, comments, processing instructions, character references, and entity references must be completely enclosed within one entity.

For an XML document to be valid, each of its element types must have been declared.

For an XML document to be valid, each of its elements' attributes must have been declared and must match the declared type.

For an XML document to be well-formed, its attribute values must be within the internal subset (the part of the DTD that is located within the source document) and not refer to external entities.

A less-than symbol (<) is reserved; it indicates the start of markup, among other things. To specify a less-than symbol within character data, use the entity <.

Because the greater-than symbol (>) is reserved as an end indicator, you should specify a greater-than symbol within character data by using the entity >.

Examples

These examples show some empty elements:

```
<IMG align="left" id="bighome"
src="bighouse.GIF"></IMG>

<br></br>
</br>
```

Related Productions

Attribute, content, element, EmptyElement, ETag, Eq, STag

EncName [81]	Encoding Name

Purpose

Specifies an encoding name.

EBNF Syntax

```
EncName ::= [A-Za-z] ([A-Za-z0-9._] | '-')*
```

Standard Syntax

{[A-Z|a-z]}[[A-Z|a-z|0-9|.|_]|-][[A-Z|a-z|0-9
|.|_]|-]
...[[A-Z|a-z|0-9|.|_]|-]

Where

- a-z and A-Z represent lowercase and uppercase letters of the current alphabet.
- 0-9 are numbers from 0 to 9.
- ., _, and - are supported characters.

Notes

EncName is a component of the EncodingDecl production.
Valid EncNames include:

- UTF-8, UTF-16, ISO-10646-UCS-2, and ISO-106046-UCS-4 for Unicode and ISO/IEC 10646.
- ISO-8859-1, ISO-8859-2, ISO-8859-3, ISO-8859-4, ISO-8859-5, ISO-8859-6, ISO-8859-7, ISO-8859-8, and ISO-8859-9 for ISO8859.
- ISO-2022-P, Shift_JIS, and EUC-P for JIS X-0208-1997.
- Encodings that are registered with the Internet Assigned Numbers Authority (IANA) at http://www.iana.org.

IANA-registered names are case-insensitive.
For more information about encoding declarations, see the Notes section under the EncodingDecl production.

Example

The example shows a declaration for the ISO-8859-1 (Latin-1) encoding:

```
<?xml version="1.0" encoding="ISO-8859-1"?>
```

Related Productions

EncodingDecl, Eq, S, TextDecl, XMLDecl

EncodingDecl [80]   Encoding Declaration

Purpose

Declares an encoding name.

EBNF Syntax

```
EncodingDecl ::= S 'encoding' Eq ('"' EncName '"'
  | "'" EncName "'" )
```

Standard Syntax

```
[ ... ]encoding = {"|'}EncName{"|'}
```

Where

- S represents one or more whitespace characters: spaces, carriage returns, line feeds, or tabs. (See the S production.) Syntax:
  {[#x20|#x9|#xD|#xA][#x20|#x9|#xD|#xA]...[#x20|#x9|#xD|#xA]}

- encoding is a reserved keyword indicating that an encoding name follows.

- Eq represents an equal sign (=) preceded and succeeded by one or more spaces. (See the Eq production.) Syntax: =

- EncName specifies an encoding name. (See the EncName production.) Syntax: {[A-Z|a-z]}[[A-Z|a-z|0-9|.|_]|-]
  [[A-Z|a-z|0-9|.|_]|-]...[[A-Z|a-z|0-9|.|_]|-]

Notes

EncodingDecl is a component of the TextDecl and XMLDecl productions.

XML requires that processors support the UTF-8 (the default) and UTF-16 character codes. Processors can also support additional character codes.

UTF-8 includes ASCII as a subset.

Entities encoded with UTF-16 must start with the Byte Order Mark #xFEFF, which is the ZERO WIDTH NO-BREAK SPACE character, to distinguish them from entities encoded with UTF-8.

Each external parsed entity can use its own unique encoding.

If an external parsed entity uses an encoding that is *not* UTF-8 or UTF-16, it must contain an opening `TextDecl` that includes an `EncodingDecl`.

XML requires that processors support the UTF-8 (the default) and UTF-16 character codes. Processors can also support additional character codes.

UTF-8 includes ASCII as a subset.

Valid `EncNames` include:

- `UTF-8`, `UTF-16`, `ISO-10646-UCS-2`, and `ISO-106046-UCS-4` for Unicode and ISO/IEC 10646.

- `ISO-8859-1`, `ISO-8859-2`, `ISO-8859-3`, `ISO-8859-4`, `ISO-8859-5`, `ISO-8859-6`, `ISO-8859-7`, `ISO-8859-8`, and `ISO-8859-9` for ISO8859.

- `ISO-2022-P`, `Shift_JIS`, and `EUC-P` for JIS X-0208-1997.

- Encodings that are registered with the Internet Assigned Numbers Authority (IANA) at `http://www.iana.org`.

IANA-registered names are case-insensitive.

Each external parsed entity in an XML document that includes an `EncodingDecl` must use that declared encoding. If the encoding is different from the declared encoding, processing ends with a fatal error.

If an external parsed entity does not include an `EncodingDecl` or the Byte Order Mark, it must use UTF-8. Otherwise, a fatal error occurs.

XML requires that processors support the UTF-8 (the default) and UTF-16 character codes. Processors can also support additional character codes.

UTF-8 includes ASCII as a subset.

If an `EncodingDecl` is not located in the proper location, at the beginning of its external parsed entity, a fatal error occurs.

If an XML processor does not recognize an encoding, declared or not, a fatal error occurs.

If you enclose a production, string, element, or other object within single quote marks, do not use single quote marks within the production, string, element, or other object; if you enclose a production, string, element, or other object within quotation marks, do not use quotation marks within the production, string, element, or other object.

Do not mix single quote marks and quotation marks; quotes at the beginning and end of a production, string, element, or other object must match.

Example

The example shows a declaration for the ISO-8859-1 (Latin-1) encoding:

```
<?xml version="1.0" encoding="ISO-8859-1"?>
```

Related Productions

EncName, Eq, S, TextDecl, XMLDecl

ENTITIES
General Entity Attribute List

Purpose

Specifies a list of valid XML general entities.

EBNF Syntax

See the TokenizedType production.

Standard Syntax

See the TokenizedType production.

Notes

ENTITIES is an uppercase-only reserved keyword indicating that a list of ENTITYs follows.

For an XML document to be valid, the ENTITIES attribute must conform to the Names production.

For more information, see the Notes section under the TokenizedType production. TokenizedType is a component of the AttType production.

Related Attributes

ENTITY, ID, IDREF, IDREFS, NMTOKEN, NMTOKENS

Related Productions

Name, Names, Nmtoken, Nmtokens, TokenizedType

2

ENTITY	General Entity Attribute

Purpose

Specifies a valid XML general entity.

EBNF Syntax

See the TokenizedType production.

Standard Syntax

See the TokenizedType production.

Notes

ENTITY is an uppercase-only reserved keyword indicating that the defined attribute is an entity.

For an XML document to be valid, the ENTITY attribute must conform to the Name production.

For an XML document to be valid, each ENTITY must be an unparsed entity declared in the DTD.

For more information, see the Notes section under the TokenizedType production. TokenizedType is a component of the AttType production.

Related Attributes

ENTITIES, ID, IDREF, IDREFS, NMTOKEN, NMTOKENS

Related Productions

Name, Names, Nmtoken, Nmtokens, TokenizedType

EntityDecl [70]   Entity Declaration

Purpose

Declares an entity.

EBNF Syntax

```
EntityDecl ::= GEDecl | PEDecl
```

Standard Syntax

```
GEDecl | PEDecl
```

Where

- GEDecl writes a general entity declaration. (See the GEDecl production.) Syntax: <!ENTITY[...]*Name* [...]*EntityDef*[...]>
- PEDecl writes a parameter-entity declaration. (See the PEDecl production.) Syntax: <!ENTITY[...] %[...]*Name*[...]*PEDef*[...]>

Notes

EntityDecl is a component of the markupdecl production.

Use the EntityDecl production only within DTDs.

An *unparsed entity* contains unparsed data, which may or may not be valid and has not been processed through an XML parser. An unparsed entity has a named notation, which the XML processor sends to the target application.

A *parsed entity* contains parsed data, which is replacement text and which has been processed through an XML parser. A parsed entity has a name and is called by an entity reference.

An *internal entity* has its content stored completely within the DTD. An internal entity is a parsed EntityValue. Its content is declared within the current XML document. Any other entity is an external entity.

An *external entity* has its content stored in a separate file that is completely outside the XML document. An unparsed external entity has an NDataDecl declaration. All other external entities are parsed.

According to the XML specification, processors that check whether a document is well-formed do not have to collect and expand external entities.

A *general entity* is a variable named within the text of the document instance. In contrast, a *parameter entity* is a variable named within markup. A general entity is preceded by an ampersand symbol (&) and succeeded by a semicolon (;). Valid general-entity categories are internal parsed general, external parsed general, and external unparsed general.

An internal general parsed entity is well-formed if it is identical to its associated content production.

An external general parsed entity is well-formed if it is identical to its associated extParsedEnt production.

A *parameter entity* (PE) is a variable that is named within markup in the prolog of a document, document type definition (DTD), or the document instance. A parameter entity is parsed, is preceded by a percent symbol (%), and is ended with a semicolon (;).Valid parameter-entity categories are internal parsed parameter and external parsed parameter. In other words, no unparsed parameter entities exist.

For an XML document to be well-formed, all elements must be nested properly: All tags, elements, comments, processing instructions, character references, and entity references must be completely enclosed within one entity. In addition, internal parsed parameter entities must be syntactically correct; external parameter entities must be syntactically correct and identical to their associated extPE productions.

Examples

The following example shows a general entity declaration:

```
<!ENTITY copyright "This document is copyrighted by
    the Eddy Group, Inc.">
```

The following example shows the parameter-entity declaration within the HTML INPUT element:

```
<!ENTITY % InputType
"(TEXT | PASSWORD | CHECKBOX |
    RADIO | SUBMIT | RESET |
    FILE | HIDDEN | IMAGE | BUTTON)"
>
```

The following example shows an external parameter entity for the Full Latin 1 character entity set and the related general entity:

```
<!ENTITY % HTMLlat1 PUBLIC
"-//W3C//ENTITIES Full Latin 1//EN//HTML">
%HTMLlat1;
```

Related Productions

EntityDef, EntityValue, ExternalID, GEDecl, markupdecl, Name, NDataDecl, PEDecl, PEDef, S

EntityDef [73]   Entity Definition

Purpose

Defines a general entity.

EBNF Syntax

EntityDef ::= EntityValue | (ExternalID NDataDecl?)

Standard Syntax

EntityValue|[*ExternalID*[*NDataDecl*]]

Where

- EntityValue specifies an internal entity value. (See the EntityValue production.) Syntax:
  {"[^%&"]|'[^%&']}[|*PEReference*|*Reference*] [|*PEReference*|*Reference*]...[|*PEReference* |*Reference*]{"|'}

- ExternalID names a parsed external entity. (See the ExternalID production.) Syntax: SYSTEM[...] *SystemLiteral*|PUBLIC[...]*PubidLiteral* [...]*SystemLiteral*

- NDataDecl declares an unparsed external entity. (See the NDataDecl production.) Syntax: [...]NDATA [...]*Name*

Notes

EntityDef is a component of the GEDecl production.

An *unparsed entity* contains unparsed data, which may or may not be valid and has not been processed through an XML parser. An unparsed entity has a named notation, which the XML processor sends to the target application.

A *parsed entity* contains parsed data, which is replacement text and which has been processed through an XML parser. A parsed entity has a name and is called by an entity reference.

An *internal entity* has its content stored completely within the DTD. An internal entity is a parsed EntityValue. Its content is declared within the current XML document. Any other entity is an external entity.

An *external entity* has its content stored in a separate file that is completely outside the XML document. An unparsed external entity has an NDataDecl declaration. All other external entities are parsed. Well-formedness checkers do not need to collect external entities.

A *general entity* is a variable named within the text of the document instance. In contrast, a parameter entity is a variable named within markup. A general entity is preceded by an ampersand symbol (&) and succeeded by a semicolon (;). Valid general entity categories are internal parsed general, external parsed general, and external unparsed general.

For a document to be well-formed, its internal general parsed entities must be identical to their associated content productions and its external general parsed entities must be identical to their associated extParsedEnt productions.

The ampersand (&) and less-than symbol (<) are reserved; they indicate the start or end of markup, among other things. To specify an ampersand or less-than symbol within character data, use the entities & or <, respectively.

Example

The following example shows a general entity declaration, including an entity definition:

```
<!ENTITY copyright "This document is copyrighted by
    the Eddy Group, Inc.">
```

Related Productions

EntityDecl, EntityValue, ExternalID, GEDecl, markupdecl, Name, NDataDecl, PEDecl, PEDef, S

EntityRef [68]   Entity Reference

Purpose

Identifies an entity reference, a named general entity's content.

EBNF Syntax

EntityRef ::= '&' Name ';'

Standard Syntax

&Name;

Where

- & marks the beginning of the entity reference.
- Name specifies a valid XML name, starting with a letter or underscore character. (See the Name production.) Syntax:
  #xnnnn [#xnnnn][_][:][#xnnnn]
  |[0|1|2|3|4|5|6|7|8|9][.]|[-][#xnnnn]
  [#xnnnn]...[#xnnnn]
- ; marks the end of the entity reference.

Notes

EntityRef is a component of the Reference production.

An entity always has content, and most entities have a name.

Character references and entities begin with a variety of characters, but all end with a semicolon (;):

- Decimal character references start with the &# characters.
- Hexadecimal character references start with the &#x characters.
- Parsed general entities start with an ampersand (&).
- Parameter-entity references start with a percent sign (%).

For an XML document without a DTD to be well-formed, the entity reference name must match the same name in an entity declaration, but a well-formed document doesn't need to declare amp, lt, gt, apos, or quo before it is referred to.

For an XML document to be well-formed, if it has an internal DTD subset without any occurrence of the PEReference element, the entity reference name must match the same name in an entity declaration. In addition, a well-formed document does not need to declare amp, lt, gt, apos, or quot. You must declare the entity before you refer to it.

For a standalone XML document to be well-formed, the entity reference name must match the same name in an entity declaration, but a well-formed document doesn't need to declare amp, lt, gt, apos, or quot. Furthermore, the entity must be declared before it is referred to.

For an XML document to be well-formed, an entity reference must not have an unparsed entity name in its contents. Instead, refer to unparsed entities in ENTITY or ENTITIES attribute values. (See the ENTITY and ENTITIES entries in this chapter.)

For an XML document to be well-formed, its parsed entities must not have any recursive reference in their contents.

For an XML document to be well-formed, all elements must be nested properly: All tags, elements, comments, processing instructions, character references, and entity references must be completely enclosed within one entity.

For a nonstandalone XML document with an external subset (the part of a DTD that is stored in a separate document, completely outside the source document) or external parameter entities to be valid, the entity reference name must match the same name in an entity declaration.

For a nonstandalone XML document with an external subset (the part of a DTD that is stored in a separate document, completely outside the source document) or external parameter entities to be compatible with SGML, it should declare amp with the && character reference, lt with &<, gt with >, apos with ', or quot with ".

Example

The following are examples of entity references:

```
&copyright;
&editdate;
```

Related Productions

AttValue, BaseChar, Char, CharRef, CombiningChar, content, Digit, EntityValue, Extender, Ideographic, Letter, Name, PEReference, Reference

EntityValue [9]   Internal Entity Value

Purpose

Specifies an internal entity value.

EBNF Syntax

```
EntityValue ::= '"' ([^%&"] | PEReference
    | Reference)* '"' | "'" ([^%&'] | PEReference
    | Reference)* "'"
```

Standard Syntax

{ " [^%& "] | ' [^%& '] } [| *PEReference* | *Reference*]
   [| *PEReference* | *Reference*]
... [| *PEReference* | *Reference*] { " | ' }

Where

- %, &, ", and ' are characters *not* to be included in the production.
- PEReference identifies a parameter-entity reference. (See the PEReference production.) Syntax: %*Name*;
- Reference names an entity or parameter-entity reference. (See the Reference production.) Syntax:
  &*Name*;
  | &#*dec_nums*; | &#x*hex_nums*;

Notes

EntityValue is a component of the EntityDef and PEDef productions.

A literal such as EntityValue replaces the current value of an entity or attribute.

EntityValue supports entity references, which must be preceded by a # symbol. Each entity reference replaces one character.

For an XML document to be well-formed, each internal general parsed entity must be identical to its associated content production.

If you enclose a production, string, element, or other object within single quote marks, do not use single quote marks within the production, string, element, or other object; if you enclose a production, string, element, or other object within quotation marks, do not use quotation marks within the production, string, element, or other object.

Within character data, you can use the apostrophe (`&apos;`) or quotation mark (`&quot;`) characters.

Do not mix single quote marks and quotation marks; quotes at the beginning and end of a production, string, element, or other object must match.

The ampersand (`&`) is reserved; to specify an ampersand within character data, use the entity `&amp;`.

Example

The following example shows a declared parameter entity from the Math Markup Language:

```
<!ENTITY % att-base          'base CDATA     "10"' >
```

Related Productions

AttValue, EntityDef, PEDef, PEReference, PubidChar, PubidLiteral, Reference, SystemLiteral

EnumeratedType [57]	**Enumerated Name/ Name Token**

Purpose

Specifies one or more enumerated notation names or name tokens.

EBNF Syntax

```
EnumeratedType ::= NotationType | Enumeration
```

Standard Syntax

NotationType|Enumeration

Where

- NotationType lists all the possible names of a notation type. (See the NotationType production.) Syntax: NOTATION[...]([...]Name[[...]|[...] Name][[...]|[...]Name]...[[...] |[...]Name]][...])

- Enumeration lists all the possible name tokens for an attribute. (See the Enumeration production.) Syntax: ([...]Nmtoken [[...]|[...]Nmtoken] [[...]|[...]Nmtoken]...[[...] |[...]Nmtoken][...])

Notes

EnumeratedType is a component of the AttType production.

Notation defines the elements of a body of knowledge by using a formalized set of symbols or an alphabet. Braille, musical notes, and even computer file formats are types of notation. In XML, a notation names the format of an unparsed entity or an element that contains a notation attribute, or names the target application of a processing instruction.

An *enumeration* is a list of possible values.

A notation name is always associated with a URI (Uniform Resource Identifier).

For an XML document to be valid, each notation attribute type must match a declared notation name.

For an XML document to be valid, each enumeration type must match a declared Nmtoken token. (See the Nmtoken production.)

For an XML document to be valid and compatible with SGML, each Nmtoken token in a particular element type should be unique.

Examples

The following example presents a list of notation names:

NOTATION   (CGM | TIF | JPG | GIF)

The following example is an enumerated list of name tokens:

(1st | 2nd | 3rd | 4th)

Related Productions

Enumeration, Etoks, NotationType, Ntoks

Enumeration [59]   Enumeration

Purpose

Lists all the possible name tokens for an attribute.

EBNF Syntax

```
Enumeration ::= '(' S? Nmtoken (S? '|'
    S? Nmtoken)* S? ')'
```

Standard Syntax

```
([ ... ]Nmtoken [[ ... ]|[ ... ]Nmtoken][[ ... ]
|[ ... ]Nmtoken]...[[ ... ]|[ ... ]Nmtoken][ ... ])
```

Where

- (marks the start of the names on the list.
- S represents one or more whitespace characters: spaces, carriage returns, line feeds, or tabs. (See the S production.) Syntax: {[#x20|#x9|#xD|#xA][#x20|#x9|#xD |#xA]...[#x20|#x9|#xD|#xA]}
- Nmtoken specifies a valid XML name token, starting with any character. (See the Nmtoken production.) Syntax: NameChar[[NameChar]...[NameChar]]
- | is a character that separates one name from the next.
-) marks the end of the names on the list.

Notes

Enumeration is a component of the EnumeratedType production.

An *enumeration* is a list of possible values for an attribute type.

For an XML document to be valid, each enumeration type must match a declared Nmtoken token. (See the Nmtoken production.)

For an XML document to be valid and compatible with SGML, each Nmtoken token in a particular element type should be unique.

Example

The following example is an enumerated list of name tokens:

(1st | 2nd | 3rd | 4th)

Related Productions

EnumeratedType, Nmtoken, S

Eq [25]   Equal Sign

Purpose

Adds an equal sign to an expression.

EBNF Syntax

Eq ::= S? '=' S?

Standard Syntax

[...]=[...]

Where

- S represents one or more whitespace characters: spaces, carriage returns, line feeds, or tabs. (See the S production.) Syntax: {[#x20|#x9|#xD|#xA][#x20|#x9|#xD |#xA]...[#x20|#x9|#xD|#xA]}
- = is an equal sign.

Notes

Eq is a component of the Attribute, EncodingDecl, SDDecl, and VersionInfo productions.

The Eq production is a part of the XML specification. Do not use Eq in DTDs and XML documents. Instead, use the equal sign (=).

Example

The following example declares a standalone document:

```
<?xml version="1.0" standalone="yes"?>
```

Related Productions

Attribute, Comment, doctypedecl, document, EncodingDecl, Misc, PI, prolog, S, SDDecl, VersionInfo, VersionNum, XMLDecl

---

ETag [42]   End Tag

Purpose

Defines an end tag for a nonempty element.

EBNF Syntax

```
ETag ::= '</' Name S? '>'
```

Standard Syntax

```
</Name[ ... ]>
```

Where

- </ marks the start of the end tag.
- Name specifies a valid XML name, starting with a letter or underscore character, of the element type. (See the Name production.) Syntax: #x*nnnn* [#x*nnnn*][_][:][#x*nnnn*] |[0|1|2|3|4|5|6|7|8|9][.]|[-][#x*nnnn*] [#x*nnnn*]...[#x*nnnn*]
- S represents one or more whitespace characters: spaces, carriage returns, line feeds, or tabs. (See the S production.) Syntax: {[#x20|#x9|#xD|#xA][#x20|#x9|#xD |#xA]...[#x20|#x9|#xD|#xA]}
- > marks the end of the end tag.

Notes

ETag is a component of the element production.

An end tag indicates the end of element content.

The element type name for the start tag must match that for the end tag.

Every XML element with a start tag must also have an end tag. This is different from HTML, in which some end tags are optional and some are omitted altogether.

For an XML document to be well-formed, all elements must be nested properly: All tags, elements, comments, processing instructions, character references, and entity references must be completely enclosed within one entity.

Because the greater-than symbol (>) is reserved as an end indicator, you should specify a greater-than symbol within character data by using the entity >.

Example

The following example is an entire self-contained XML document with one end tag:

```
<?xml version="1.0"?>
<!DOCTYPE endstate[
<!ELEMENT endstate (#PCDATA)>
]>
<endstate>Goodbye, cruel world!</endstate>
```

Related Productions

Attribute, content, element, EmptyElement, Eq, STag

Extender [89]   Extender Symbol

Purpose

Inserts an extender symbol.

EBNF Syntax

```
Extender ::= #x00B7  |  #x02D0  |  #x02D1  |  #x0387
  | #x0640
     | #x0E46 |#x0EC6  | #x3005  | [#x3031-#x3035]
     | [#x309D-#x309E]  | [#x30FC-#x30FE]
```

Standard Syntax

```
#xnnnn
```

2

● **NOTE** ─────────────────────────────────────

For a list of supported base characters, see the preceding EBNF syntax.

Where

- #xnnnn represents an extender character supported by the Unicode Organization. For a complete list of supported extender characters, see Appendix A, *Unicode Characters and Character Sets*. For more information about Unicode characters, see Chapter 1, *Overview*, and the *Webliography*.

Note

Extender is a component of the NameChar production.

Related Productions

BaseChar, Char, CharRef, CombiningChar, Digit, EntityRef, Extender, Ideographic, Letter, Name, NameChar, PEReference, Reference

ExternalID [75]   Parsed External Entity

Purpose

Identifies a parsed external entity.

EBNF Syntax

```
ExternalID ::= 'SYSTEM' S SystemLiteral
             | 'PUBLIC' S PubidLiteral S
             SystemLiteral
```

Standard Syntax

```
SYSTEM[ ... ]SystemLiteral
      |PUBLIC[ ... ]PubidLiteral[ ... ]SystemLiteral
```

Where

- `SYSTEM` is an uppercase-only reserved keyword indicating that a system identifier follows.

- `S` represents one or more whitespace characters: spaces, carriage returns, line feeds, or tabs. (See the `S` production.) Syntax:
  `{[#x20|#x9|#xD|#xA][#x20|#x9|#xD|#xA]...[#x20|#x9|#xD|#xA]}`

- `SystemLiteral` is a URI identifying external entity content. (See the `SystemLiteral` production.) Syntax: `{"|'}URI{"|'}`

- `PUBLIC` is an uppercase-only reserved keyword indicating that a public identifier follows.

- `PubidLiteral` names a public identifier. (See the `PubidLiteral` production.) Syntax: `{"|'}[[PubidChar] [PubidChar]...[PubidChar]]{"|'}`

Notes

`ExternalID` is a component of the `doctypedecl`, `EntityDef`, `NotationDecl`, and `PEDef` productions.

All system identifiers are URIs.

A *parsed entity* contains parsed data, which is replacement text and which has been processed through an XML parser. A parsed entity has a name and is called by an entity reference.

An *external entity* has its content stored in a separate file that is completely outside the XML document. An unparsed external entity has an `NDataDecl` declaration. All other external entities are parsed.

A *parameter entity* (PE) is a variable that is named within markup in the prolog of a document, document type definition (DTD), or the document instance. A parameter entity is parsed, is preceded by a percent symbol (%), and is ended with a semicolon (;). Valid parameter-entity categories are internal parsed parameter and external parsed parameter. In other words, no unparsed parameter entities exist.

For an XML document to be well-formed, internal parsed parameter entities must be syntactically correct; external parame-

2

ter entities must be syntactically correct and identical to their associated `extPE` productions. For an XML document to be valid, a # and associated fragment identifier cannot be part of the system identifier URI.

For an XML document to be valid, a relative system identifier URI must relate back to the document resource in which the entity declaration resides; that is, the document entity, the external DTD subset entity, or an external parameter entity.

For an XML document to be valid, the XML processor converts non-ASCII characters (such as nonkeyboard characters) in a system identifier URI to UTF-8 and then to hexadecimal.

Example

The following example shows two external IDs:

```
<!ENTITY copyright SYSTEM "copyright.txt">
<!ENTITY copyright SYSTEM
    "http://www.myfiles.com/copyright.txt">
```

Related Productions

doctypedecl, EntityDef, NotationDecl, PEDef, S, SystemLiteral

extParsedEnt [78]	**External Parsed Entity**

Purpose

Specifies a well-formed external general parsed entity.

EBNF Syntax

extParsedEnt ::= TextDecl? content

Standard Syntax

[*TextDecl*] *content*

Where

- `TextDecl` inserts a text declaration. (See the `TextDecl` production.)
  Syntax: <?xml[*VersionInfo*] *EncodingDecl*
  [...]?>

- content creates element content within the start and end
  tags. (See the content production.) Syntax: [element
  |CharData|Reference|CDSect|PI|Comment]
  [element|CharData|Reference|*CDSect*|*PI*
  |*Comment*]...[*element*|*CharData*|*Reference*
  |*CDSect*|*PI*|*Comment*]

Notes

For an XML document to be well-formed, all elements must be
nested properly: All tags, elements, comments, processing instructions, character references, and entity references must be completely enclosed within one entity.

A *parsed entity* contains parsed data, which is replacement text
and which has been processed through an XML parser. A parsed
entity has a name and is called by an entity reference.

An *external entity* has its content stored in a separate file that
is completely outside the XML document. An unparsed external
entity has an NDataDecl declaration. All other external entities are
parsed.

A *general entity* is a variable named within the text of the document instance. In contrast, a *parameter entity* is a variable named
within markup. A general entity is preceded by an ampersand
symbol (&) and succeeded by a semicolon (;). Valid general entity
categories are internal parsed general, external parsed general,
and external unparsed general.

An external general parsed entity is well-formed if it is identical to its associated extParsedEnt production.

Example

The following example could be a very small external parsed entity:

```
<?xml version="1.0" encoding="UTF-8"?>
<!DOCTYPE endstate[
<!ELEMENT endstate (#PCDATA)>
]>
<endstate>Goodbye, cruel world!</endstate>
```

If the preceding example is an external parsed entity, the current XML document must include an internal subset, such as:

```
<?xml version="1.0"?>
<!DOCTYPE endstate SYSTEM "endstate.dtd">
```

Related Productions

content, extPE, extSubsetDecl, TextDecl

2

extPE [79]   External Parameter Entity

Purpose

Specifies a well-formed external parameter entity.

EBNF Syntax

extPE ::= TextDecl? extSubsetDecl

Standard Syntax

[*TextDecl*] *extSubsetDecl*

Where

- TextDecl inserts a text declaration. (See the TextDecl production.) Syntax: <?xml[*VersionInfo*] *EncodingDecl*[...
  ]?>
- extSubsetDecl declares external subset (the part of a DTD
  that is stored in a separate document, completely
  outside the source document) markup and conditions. (See
  the extSubsetDecl production.) Syntax:
  [*markupdecl*|*conditionalSect*|*PEReference*
  |[...]][*markupdecl*|*conditionalSect*
  |*PEReference*|[...]]...[*markupdecl*
  |*conditionalSect*|*PEReference*|[...]]

Notes

The extPE and extSubset productions have the same syntax.

A *parsed entity* contains parsed data, which is replacement text
and which has been processed through an XML parser. A parsed
entity has a name and is called by an entity reference.

An *external entity* has its content stored in a separate file that
is completely outside the XML document. An unparsed external

entity has an NDataDecl declaration. All other external entities are parsed.

A *parameter entity* (PE) is a variable that is named within markup in the prolog of a document, document type definition (DTD), or the document instance. A parameter entity is parsed, is preceded by a percent symbol (%), and is ended with a semicolon (;). Valid parameter-entity categories are internal parsed parameter and external parsed parameter. In other words, no unparsed parameter entities exist.

An external parameter entity is well-formed if it is identical to its associated extPE production.

Example

The following example is a well-formed external parameter entity:

```
<?xml version="1.0" encoding="UTF-8"?>
<!DOCTYPE endstate[
<!ELEMENT endstate (#PCDATA)>
]>
<endstate>Goodbye, cruel world!</endstate>
```

Related Productions

content, extParsedEnt, extSubsetDecl, TextDecl

extSubset [30]   External Subset

Purpose

Identifies an external subset.

EBNF Syntax

extSubset ::= TextDecl? extSubsetDecl

Standard Syntax

[*TextDecl*] *extSubsetDecl*

2

Where

- TextDecl inserts a text declaration. (See the TextDecl production.) Syntax: <?xml[*VersionInfo*] *EncodingDecl*[...]?>

- extSubsetDecl declares external subset markup and conditions. (See the extSubsetDecl production.) Syntax: [*markupdecl*|*conditionalSect*|*PEReference* |[...]][*markupdecl*|*conditionalSect* |*PEReference*|[...]]...[*markupdecl* |*conditionalSect*|*PEReference*|[...]]

Notes

The external subset is an external parsed entity and the part of a DTD that is stored in a separate document, completely outside the source document.

Note that the extPE and extSubset productions have the same syntax.

An external subset can include a text declaration, which helps when the subset uses a particular Unicode encoding.

PEReferences are allowed within markup declarations in external subsets and external parameter entities.

Internal subsets (the part of the DTD that is located within the source document) are higher in precedence than external subsets.

You can use conditional sections within external subsets but not within internal subsets.

Example

The following example is a well-formed external parameter entity (remember to refer to the external entity within the source document):

```
<!ENTITY % HTMLlat1 PUBLIC
"-//W3C//ENTITIES Full Latin 1//EN//HTML">
```

Related Productions

conditionalSect, extSubsetDecl, markupdecl, PEReference, S, TextDecl

extSubsetDecl [31]

External Subset Declaration

2

Purpose

Declares external subset markup and conditions.

EBNF Syntax

```
extSubsetDecl ::= ( markupdecl | conditionalSect
    | PEReference | S )*
```

Standard Syntax

```
[markupdecl|conditionalSect|PEReference|[ ... ]]
[markupdecl|conditionalSect|PEReference|[ ... ]]
...[markupdecl|conditionalSect|PEReference|[ ... ]]
```

Where

- markupdecl declares markup of elements, attributes, entities, or notation. (See the markupdecl production.) Syntax: *elementdecl|AttlistDecl|EntityDecl |NotationDecl|PI|Comment*

- conditionalSect names a conditional section. (See the conditionalSect production.) Syntax: *includeSect |ignoreSect*

- PEReference identifies a parameter-entity reference. (See the PEReference production.) Syntax: %*Name*;

- S represents one or more whitespace characters: spaces, carriage returns, line feeds, or tabs. (See the S production.) Syntax: {[#x20|#x9|#xD|#xA][#x20|#x9|#xD|#xA]... [#x20|#x9|#xD|#xA]}

Notes

extSubsetDecl is a component of the extPE, extSubset, and includeSect productions.

For more information, see the extSubset notes.

Example

The following example includes two lines from an XML source document and a defined element in an external parsed entity:

```
<?xml version="1.0" encoding="UTF-8"?>
<!DOCTYPE test SYSTEM "endstate.dtd">
<endstate>Goodbye, cruel world!</endstate>
<!ELEMENT endstate (#PCDATA)>
```

Related Productions

conditionalSect, extSubset, markupdecl, PEReference, TextDecl, S

GEDecl [71]   General Entity Declaration

Purpose

Identifies a general entity declaration.

EBNF Syntax

```
GEDecl ::= '<!ENTITY' S Name S EntityDef S? '>'
```

Standard Syntax

```
<!ENTITY[ ... ]Name[ ... ]EntityDef[ ... ]>
```

Where

- <!ENTITY marks the start of the general entity declaration.
- S represents one or more whitespace characters: spaces, carriage returns, line feeds, or tabs. (See the S production.) Syntax: {[#x20|#x9|#xD|#xA][#x20|#x9|#xD|#xA] ...[#x20|#x9|#xD|#xA]}
- Name specifies a valid XML name, starting with a letter or underscore character. (See the Name production.) Syntax: #xnnnn [#xnnnn][_][:][#xnnnn]|[0|1|2|3|4|5 |6|7|8|9][.]|[-][#xnnnn][#xnnnn]...[#xnnnn]

- EntityDef prepares a general entity definition. (See the EntityDef production.) Syntax: *EntityValue*| [*ExternalID*[*NDataDecl*]]
- > marks the end of the general entity declaration.

Notes

GEDecl is a component of the EntityDecl production.

An *unparsed entity* contains unparsed data, which may or may not be valid and has not been processed through an XML parser. An unparsed entity has a named notation, which the XML processor sends to the target application.

A *parsed entity* contains parsed data, which is replacement text and which has been processed through an XML parser. A parsed entity has a name and is called by an entity reference.

An *internal entity* has its content stored completely within the DTD. An internal entity is a parsed EntityValue. Its content is declared within the current XML document. Any other entity is an external entity.

An *external entity* has its content stored in a separate file that is completely outside the XML document. An unparsed external entity has an NDataDecl declaration. All other external entities are parsed.

A *general entity* is a variable named within the text of the document instance. In contrast, a *parameter entity* is a variable named within markup. A general entity is preceded by an ampersand symbol (&) and succeeded by a semicolon (;). Valid general entity categories are internal parsed general, external parsed general, and external unparsed general.

A document is well-formed if its internal general parsed entities are identical to their associated content productions and its external general parsed entities are identical to their associated extParsedEnt productions.

Because the greater-than symbol (>) is reserved as an end indicator, you should specify a greater-than symbol within character data by using the entity >.

Example

The following example shows a general entity declaration:

```
<!ENTITY copyright "This document is copyrighted by
    the Eddy Group, Inc.">
```

Related Productions

EntityDecl, EntityDef, EntityValue, ExternalID, markupdecl, Name, NDataDecl, PEDecl, PEDef, S

2

IanaCode [36]	IANA Language Code

Purpose

Names an IANA language code.

EBNF Syntax

IanaCode ::= ('i' | 'I') '-' ([a-z] | [A-Z])+

Standard Syntax

{i|I}-{[a-z]|[A-Z][[a-z]|[A-Z]]...[[a-z]|[A-Z]]}

Where

- i or I indicates that an IANA language code follows.
- - is a separator character.
- a-z and A-Z represent lowercase and uppercase letters of the current alphabet.

Notes

IanaCode is a component of the Langcode production.

To find an IANA language identifier, go to the Internet Assigned Numbers Authority (IANA) at http://www.iana.org.

Language codes and country codes are case-insensitive. Although not required, the language code is usually in lowercase and the country code is usually in uppercase.

For more information, see the Notes section under the LanguageID production.

Example

This example illustrates the xml:lang attribute and the IANA UK language code:

```
<para xml:lang="i-BS_4730">I'm speaking in
    proper English.</para>
```

Related Productions

ISO639Code, Langcode, LanguageID, Subcode, UserCode

ID	Identifier Attribute

Purpose

Specifies a valid XML identifier.

EBNF Syntax

See the TokenizedType production.

Standard Syntax

See the TokenizedType production.

Notes

ID is an uppercase-only reserved keyword indicating that the defined attribute is an identifier.

The ID attribute type enables complex linking and optional extended pointers. For more information, refer to Chapter 4, *XLink Language*, and Chapter 5, *XPointer Language*.

Some nonvalidating XML processors assume that the default attribute type is ID. This allows a well-formed document to use identifiers for complex linking.

For an XML document to be valid and compatible with SGML, each element type can have only one ID attribute type.

For an XML document to be valid, the ID attribute must conform to the Name production.

For an XML document to be valid, each ID name must be unique.

For an XML document to be valid, each ID must have a default value of #IMPLIED or #REQUIRED.

For more information, see the Notes section under the TokenizedType production. TokenizedType is a component of the AttType production.

Related Attributes

ENTITIES, ENTITY, IDREF, IDREFS, NMTOKEN, NMTOKENS

Related Productions

Name, Names, Nmtoken, Nmtokens, TokenizedType

2   Ideographic [86]   Ideographic Symbol

Purpose

Specifies an *ideogram*, a symbol or glyph that represents another character, a word, or other object.

EBNF Syntax

```
Ideographic ::= [#x4E00-#x9FA5] | #x3007
            | #x3021-#x3029]
```

Standard Syntax

```
#xnnnn
```

●—NOTE————————————————

For a list of supported base characters, see the preceding EBNF syntax.

Where

- #xnnnn represents an ideographic character supported by the Unicode Organization. For a complete list of supported ideographic characters, see Appendix A, *Unicode Characters and Character Sets*. For more information about Unicode characters, see Chapter 1, *Overview*, and the *Webliography*.

Note

Ideographic is a component of the Letter production.

Related Productions

BaseChar, Char, CharRef, CombiningChar, Digit, EntityRef, Extender, Letter, Name, PEReference, Reference

IDREF | Identifier Cross-Reference Attribute

Purpose
Specifies a valid XML identifier cross-reference.

EBNF Syntax
See the TokenizedType production.

Standard Syntax
See the TokenizedType production.

Notes
IDREF is an uppercase-only reserved keyword indicating that the defined attribute is an identifier cross-reference.

The IDREF attribute type enables complex linking and optional extended pointers. For more information, refer to Chapter 4, *XLink Language*, and Chapter 5, *XPointer Language*.

For an XML document to be valid, the IDREF attribute must conform to the Name production.

For an XML document to be valid, each IDREF name must match the value of an ID.

For more information, see the Notes section under the TokenizedType production. TokenizedType is a component of the AttType production.

Related Attributes
ENTITIES, ENTITY, ID, IDREFS, NMTOKEN, NMTOKENS

Related Productions
Name, Names, Nmtoken, Nmtokens, TokenizedType

IDREFS | Identifier Cross-Reference Attribute List

Purpose
Specifies a list of valid XML identifier cross-references.

EBNF Syntax

See the TokenizedType production.

Standard Syntax

See the TokenizedType production.

Notes

IDREFS is an uppercase-only reserved keyword indicating that a list of ID cross-references follows.

For an XML document to be valid, the IDREFS attribute must conform to the Names production.

For more information, see the Notes section under the TokenizedType production. TokenizedType is a component of the AttType production.

Related Attributes

ENTITIES, ENTITY, ID, IDREF, NMTOKEN, NMTOKENS

Related Productions

Name, Names, Nmtoken, Nmtokens, TokenizedType

Ignore [65]   Ignore

Purpose

Indicates the beginning and end of an included section nested in an ignored section.

EBNF Syntax

Ignore ::= Char* - (Char* ('<![' | ']]>') Char*)

Standard Syntax

[Char[Char]...[Char]]

Where

- Char specifies one legal character. (See the Char production.) Syntax: #xnnnn[n[n]]

Notes

Ignore is a component of the `ignoreSectContents` production.

Do not use the <, [, and] characters; combinations of those characters indicate the start and end of a character data section.

Because the greater-than symbol (>) is reserved as an end indicator, you should specify a greater-than symbol within character data by using the entity `&gt;`.

See the Notes section under the `conditionalSect` production.

Example

The following example from the XML specification shows two sections — one included and one ignored:

```
<!ENTITY % draft 'INCLUDE' >
<!ENTITY % final 'IGNORE' >
<![%draft;[
<!ELEMENT book (comments*, title, body, supplements?)>
]]><![%final;[
<!ELEMENT book (title, body, supplements?)>
]]>
```

Related Productions

Char, conditionalSect, extSubsetDecl, ignoreSect, ignoreSectContents, includeSect, S

ignoreSect [63]   Ignored Section

Purpose

Names a conditionally ignored section.

EBNF Syntax

```
ignoreSect ::= '<![' S? 'IGNORE' S?
    '[' ignoreSectContents* ']]>'
```

Standard Syntax

```
<![[ ... ]IGNORE[ ... ][[ignoreSectContents]
    [ignoreSectContents]...[ignoreSectContents]]]>
```

Where

- `<![` marks the start of the ignored character data section.
- `S` represents one or more whitespace characters: spaces, carriage returns, line feeds, or tabs. (See the `S` production.) Syntax: `{[#x20|#x9|#xD|#xA][#x20|#x9|#xD|#xA] ...[#x20|#x9|#xD|#xA]}`
- `IGNORE` is an uppercase-only reserved keyword indicating that the character data section should be ignored in XML processing.
- `[` marks the start of the contents of the ignored section.
- `ignoreSectContents` defines an ignored section's contents. (See the `ignoreSectContents` production.) Syntax: `Ignore [<![ignoreSectContents]]> Ignore] [<![ignoreSectContents]]> Ignore]... [<![ignoreSectContents]]> Ignore]`
- `]]>` marks the end of the ignored section.

Notes

`ignoreSect` is a component of the `conditionalSect` production. See the Notes section in the `conditionalSect` production.

Example

The following is a small ignored section:

```
<![ IGNORE [
<!ELEMENT byestate (#PCDATA)>
]]>
```

Related Productions

`conditionalSect`, `extSubsetDecl`, `Ignore`, `ignoreSectContents`, `includeSect`, `S`

ignoreSectContents [64]

Ignored Section Contents

Purpose

Defines an ignored section's contents.

EBNF Syntax

```
ignoreSectContents ::= Ignore
    ('<![' ignoreSectContents ']]>' Ignore)*
```

Standard Syntax

```
Ignore[<![ignoreSectContents]]>Ignore]
    [<![ignoreSectContents]]>Ignore]
    ...[<![ignoreSectContents]]>Ignore]
```

Where

- `<![` marks the start of the ignored section's contents.
- `Ignore` indicates the beginning and end of an included section nested in an ignored section. (See the `Ignore` production.) Syntax: `[Char[Char]...[Char]]`
- `ignoreSectContents` defines an ignored section's contents. (See the `ignoreSectContents` production.) Syntax: `Ignore [<![ignoreSectContents]]> Ignore] [<![ignoreSectContents]]> Ignore]... [<![ignoreSectContents]]> Ignore]`
- `]]>` marks the end of the ignored section's contents.

Notes

`ignoreSectContents` is a component of the `ignoreSect` and `ignoreSectContents` productions.

See the Notes section under `conditionalSect` production.

Example

The following example from the XML specification shows an included and ignored section with another included section nested in the ignored section:

```
<!ENTITY % draft 'INCLUDE' >
<!ENTITY % final 'IGNORE' >
<![%draft;[
<!ELEMENT book (comments*, title, body, supplements?)>
]]>
<![%final;[
<!ENTITY % glossary 'INCLUDE' >
<![%glossary;[
<!ELEMENT book (title, (term, def)?)>
]]>
<!ELEMENT book (title, body, supplements?)>
]]>
```

includeSect [62]   Included Section

Related Productions

conditionalSect, extSubsetDecl, Ignore, ignoreSect, includeSect, S

Purpose

Indicates an included section.

EBNF Syntax

```
includeSect ::= '<![' S? 'INCLUDE' S?
    '[' extSubsetDecl;* ']]>'
```

Standard Syntax

```
<![[ ... ]INCLUDE[ ... ][[extSubsetDecl;]
    [extSubsetDecl;]...[extSubsetDecl;]]]>
```

Where

- <![marks the start of the character data section.
- S represents one or more whitespace characters: spaces, carriage returns, line feeds, or tabs. (See the S production.)

Syntax: {[#x20|#x9|#xD|#xA][#x20|#x9|#xD|#xA]
...[#x20|#x9|#xD|#xA]}

- INCLUDE is an uppercase-only reserved keyword indicating that the character data section should be included in XML processing.
- [marks the start of the external subset declaration.
- ; marks the end of the external subset declaration.
- extSubsetDecl declares external subset markup and conditions. (See the extSubsetDecl production.)
  Syntax: [*markupdecl*|*conditionalSect*|*PEReference*
  |[...]][*markupdecl*|*conditionalSect*
  |*PEReference*|[...]]...[*markupdecl*
  |*conditionalSect*|*PEReference*|[...]]
-]]> marks the end of the character data section.

Notes

includeSect is a component of the conditionalSect production.

See the Notes section in the conditionalSect production.

You can include appropriate parts of the extSubsetDecl in the included section.

Example

The following is a small included section:

```
<![  INCLUDE [
<!ELEMENT histate (#PCDATA)>
]]>
```

Related Productions

conditionalSect, extSubsetDecl, Ignore, ignoreSect, ignoreSectContents, S

ISO639Code [35]   ISO639 Language Code

Purpose

Assigns an ISO639 language code.

EBNF Syntax

```
ISO639Code ::= ([a-z] | [A-Z]) ([a-z] | [A-Z])
```

Standard Syntax

```
{[a-z]|[A-Z]}{[a-z]|[A-Z]}
```

Where

- a-z and A-Z represent lowercase and uppercase letters of the current alphabet.

Notes

ISO639Code is a component of the Langcode production.

XML supports the ISO639: 1988 standard.

Language codes and country codes are case-insensitive. Although not required, the language code is usually in lowercase and the country code is usually in uppercase.

For more information, see the Notes section under the LanguageID production.

Example

This example illustrates the xml:lang attribute and the ISO639 en (English) language code:

```
<para xml:lang="en">I'm speaking in English.</para>
```

Related Productions

IanaCode, Langcode, LanguageID, Subcode, UserCode

Langcode [34]   Language Code

Purpose

Specifies a language code or identifier.

EBNF Syntax

```
Langcode ::= ISO639Code | IanaCode | UserCode
```

Standard Syntax

ISO639Code | *IanaCode* | *UserCode*

Where

- ISO639Code assigns a two-letter ISO639 language code. (See the ISO639Code production.) Syntax: {[a-z] |[A-Z]}{[a-z]|[A-Z]}

- IanaCode names an IANA language code preceded by an i or I prefix. (See the IanaCode production.) Syntax: {i|I}-{[a-z]|[A-Z][[a-z]|[A-Z]]...[[a-z] |[A-Z]]}

- UserCode identifies a user-assigned language preceded by an x or X prefix. (See the UserCode production.) Syntax: {x|X}-{[a-z]|[A-Z][[a-z]|[A-Z]]...[[a-z] |[A-Z]]}

Notes

Langcode is a component of the LanguageID production.

For more information, see the Notes section under the LanguageID production.

Example

This example illustrates the xml:lang attribute and the en (English) language code (using the international ISO639 standard):

```
<para xml:lang="en">I'm speaking in English.</para>
```

This example illustrates the xml:lang attribute with an added US subcode:

```
<para xml:lang="en-US">I'm speaking in English.</para>
```

Related Productions

IanaCode, ISO639Code, LanguageID, Subcode, UserCode

LanguageID [33]   Language Identifier

Purpose

Names a language identifier.

EBNF Syntax

```
LanguageID ::= Langcode ('-' Subcode)*
```

Standard Syntax

Langcode[-Subcode[-Subcode]...[-Subcode]]

Where

- Langcode specifies a language code or identifier. (See the Langcode production.) Syntax: ISO639Code|IanaCode|UserCode
- - is a separator character.
- Subcode specifies a language or country subcode. (See the Subcode production.) Syntax: {[a-z]|[A-Z]}[[a-z]| [A-Z]]...[[a-z]|[A-Z]]

Notes

Because of internationalization, declaring a language can be very important.

You can use the xml:lang attribute with any XML production to declare a language used as character data and attribute values in an XML document. IETF_RFC_1766 (ftp://ftp.isi. edu/in-notes/rfc1766.txt) lists supported values.

The language named in the xml:lang attribute is in effect until the next xml:lang attribute is declared.

To find ISO639 codes, go to http://www.sil.org/sgml/ iso639.html.

To find a language identifier, go to the Internet Assigned Numbers Authority (IANA), which is located at http://www. iana.org.

If the first subcode in a LanguageID element is comprised of two letters, it must be a country code listed in ISO 3166 (http:// sunsite.berkeley.edu/amher/iso_3166.html).

If the first subcode in a LanguageID element is comprised of more than two letters and is not a UserCode subcode, it must be a country code listed in IANA (http://www.iana.org/).

Language codes and country codes are case-insensitive. Although not required, the language code is usually in lowercase and the country code is usually in uppercase.

Examples

This example illustrates the xml:lang attribute and the ISO639 en (English) language code:

```
<para xml:lang="en">I'm speaking in English.</para>
```

This example illustrates the xml:lang attribute with an added US subcode:

```
<para xml:lang="en-US">I'm speaking in English.</para>
```

This example illustrates the xml:lang attribute and the IANA UK language code:

```
<para xml:lang="i-BS_4730">I'm speaking
    in proper English.</para>
```

This example illustrates the xml:lang attribute and a user-defined language code:

```
<para xml:lang="x-uk_eng">I'm speaking
    in proper English.</para>
```

Related Productions

IanaCode, ISO639Code, Langcode, Subcode, UserCode

Letter [84]   Letter

Purpose

Specifies a letter of the current alphabet.

EBNF Syntax

```
Letter ::= BaseChar | Ideographic
```

Standard Syntax

```
#xnnnn
```

Where

- BaseChar is an XML element representing an alphabetic character. (See the BaseChar production.) Syntax: #xnnnn

2

- Ideographic is an XML element representing an ideogram, a symbol that represents another character, a word, or other object. (See the Ideographic production.) Syntax: #x*nnnn*

Note

Letter is a component of the Name and NameChar productions.

Related Productions

BaseChar, Char, CharRef, CombiningChar, Digit, EntityRef, Extender, Ideographic, Name, PEReference, Reference

---

markupdecl [29]   Markup Declaration

Purpose

Declares markup of elements, attribute lists, entities, or notation within parameter entities.

EBNF Syntax

```
markupdecl ::= elementdecl | AttlistDecl
             | EntityDecl | NotationDecl | PI
             | Comment
```

Standard Syntax

elementdecl | *AttlistDecl* | *EntityDecl* | *NotationDecl*
  | *PI* | *Comment*

Where

- elementdecl constrains element content using an element type declaration. (See the elementdecl production.) Syntax: {<!ELEMENT[...]Name[...]contentspec}[...]{>}
- AttlistDecl declares an element's attribute list. (See the AttlistDecl production.) Syntax: <!ATTLIST [...]Name [AttDef[AttDef[...AttDef]]] [...]>

- `EntityDecl` writes an entity declaration. (See the `EntityDecl` production.) Syntax: `GEDecl|PEDecl`

- `NotationDecl` declares a notation name. (See the `NotationDecl` production.) Syntax: `<!NOTATION [ ... ]Name[ ... ]{ExternalID|PublicID}[ ... ]>`

- `PI` writes processing instructions. (See the `PI` production.) Syntax: `<?PITarget [[ ... ][Char[Char]...[Char]]?>`

- `Comment` inserts a nonprinting, nonparsed comment in the XML document. (See the `Comment` production.) Syntax: `<!--[[Char]|[-Char]][[Char]|[-Char]]... [[Char]|[-Char]]]-->`

Notes

`markupdecl` is a component of the `doctypedecl` and `extSubsetDecl` productions.

Use the `markupdecl` production only within document type definitions (DTDs).

Parameter entities are processed first, resulting in replacement text being placed in the markup declarations. Then the declarations are processed.

A parameter entity can contain an element type declaration, attribute list declaration, entity declaration, or notation declaration.

For an XML document to be valid, the complete markup declaration must be nested within the `PEReference` replacement text.

For an XML document to be well-formed, `PEReferences` can only be placed within the brackets ([and]) in the doctype declaration in the internal subset (the part of the DTD that is located within the source document). `PEReferences` cannot be placed within markup declarations in the internal subset.

`PEReferences` are allowed within markup declarations in external subsets (the part of a DTD that is stored in a separate document, completely outside the source document) and external parameter entities.

Nonvalidating XML processors can ignore `PEReferences`, because they are not required to process external subsets.

Internal subsets are higher in precedence than external subsets.

You can use conditional sections within external subsets but not within internal subsets.

Because the greater-than symbol (>) is reserved as an end indicator, you should specify a greater-than symbol within character data by using the entity >.

Do not include one dash (-) or two dashes in a comment; dashes are reserved for the start and end of the comment.

Examples

See the `AttlistDecl`, `Comment`, `elementdecl`, `EntityDecl`, `NotationDecl`, and `PI` productions.

Related Productions

`AttlistDecl`, `Comment`, `doctypedecl`, `elementdecl`, `EntityDecl`, `extSubsetDecl`, `markupdecl`, `NotationDecl`, `PI`

Misc [27]   Miscellaneous

Purpose

Inserts miscellaneous information in a prolog.

EBNF Syntax

```
Misc ::= Comment | PI | S
```

Standard Syntax

```
Comment | PI | [ ... ]
```

Where

- `Comment` inserts a nonprinting, nonparsed comment in the XML document. (See the `Comment` production.) Syntax: `<!--[[Char]|[-Char]][[Char]|[-Char]]...[[Char]|[-Char]]]-->`

* `PI` writes processing instructions. (See the `PI` production.) Syntax: `<?PITarget [[ ... ][Char[Char]...[Char]]?>`

* `S` represents one or more whitespace characters: spaces, carriage returns, line feeds, or tabs. (See the `S` production.)

Syntax: {[#x20|#x9|#xD|#xA][#x20|#x9|#xD|#xA]
...[#x20|#x9|#xD|#xA]}

Notes

Misc is a component of the document and prolog productions.

Because the greater-than symbol (>) is reserved as an end indicator, you should specify a greater-than symbol within character data by using the entity >.

Do not include one dash (-) or two dashes in a comment; dashes are reserved for the start and end of the comment.

This production helps to identify the current document, including the version of XML that was used to create it.

Although Misc enables you to add comments, processing instructions, and whitespace to the document and prolog production, do so carefully. Being careful helps links to work properly and XML processors to interpret XML statements correctly.

Examples

The following comment example marks the start of an element definition:

```
<!--defining <para> paragraph element and attributes-->
```

The following is probably the most commonly used processing instruction (PI):

```
<?xml version="1.0"?>
```

●─NOTE

The XML declaration is not within the Misc component. However, version="1.0" is.

These two examples show varying amounts of whitespace within the same comment line:

```
<!--defining <para> paragraph element-->
<!--defining      <para>      paragraph element-->
```

Related Productions

Comment, doctypedecl, document, EncodingDecl, Eq, PI, prolog, S, SDDecl, VersionInfo, VersionNum, XMLDecl

Mixed [51]   Mixed Element Content

Purpose

Defines mixed element content of character data and child elements.

EBNF Syntax

```
Mixed ::= '(' S? '#PCDATA' (S? '|' S? Name)*
          S? ')*'
        | '(' S? '#PCDATA' S? ')'
```

Standard Syntax

```
([ ... ]#PCDATA[[ ... ]|[ ... ]Name]
  [[ ... ]|[ ... ]Name][[ ... ]|[ ... ]Name]]
  [ ... ])*|([ ... ]#PCDATA[ ... ])
```

Where

- (marks the start of the names on the list.
- S represents one or more whitespace characters: spaces, carriage returns, line feeds, or tabs. (See the S production.) Syntax: {[#x20|#x9|#xD|#xA][#x20|#x9|#xD|#xA] ...[#x20|#x9|#xD|#xA]}
- #PCDATA is an uppercase-only reserved keyword indicating that parsed character data will follow.
- | is a character that separates one name from the next.
- Name specifies a valid XML name, starting with a letter or underscore character. (See the Name production.) Syntax: #xnnnn [#xnnnn][_][:][#xnnnn]|[0|1|2|3|4|5 |6|7|8|9][.]|[-][#xnnnn][#xnnnn]...[#xnnnn]
-) marks the end of the names on the list.

Notes

Mixed is a component of the contentspec production.

Mixed element content defines the content of an element as both element content and character data.

#PCDATA must be present as one of the elements; this distinguishes Mixed declarations from simple-choice declarations.

Mixed declarations allow elements to contain both character data and child elements, and enable a document to be valid.

For an XML document to be valid, any PEReference replacement text must be nested completely within its content particle in a choice, Mixed, or seq production.

For an XML document to be valid, any PEReference replacement text cannot be empty and its first or last nonblank characters should not be a pipe (|) or ,) character combination.

You cannot declare the same element type more than once in an XML document. However, you can declare attributes and entities more than once.

Mixed declarations cannot nest in other declarations.

Example

The following example shows an element with mixed content — an embedded element and character data:

```
<?xml version="1.0"?>
<DOCTYPE endstate[>
<!ELEMENT endstate (#PCDATA)>
<endstate>Goodbye, <bold>cruel</bold> world!</endstate>
```

Related Productions

contentspec, Name, S

Name [5]   Name

Purpose

Specifies a valid XML name, starting with a letter or underscore character.

EBNF Syntax

Name ::= (Letter | '_' | ':') (NameChar)*

Standard Syntax

[Letter|_|:] [[NameChar] [NameChar]...[NameChar]]

Where

- Letter is an XML element representing either an alphabetic character or an *ideogram*, a symbol that represents another character, a word, or other object. (See the Letter production.) Syntax: #xnnnn
- NameChar specifies one character in a name. (See the NameChar production.) Syntax: Letter|Digit|.|-|_|:|CombiningChar|Extender

Notes

Name is a data type used by the AttDef, AttlistDecl, Attr, Attribute, AttrTerm, cp, doctypedecl, elementdecl, EmptyElemTag, EntityRef, ETag, GEDecl, IdLoc, Locator, Mixed, Names, NDataDecl, NodeType, NotationDecl, NotationType, PEDecl, PEReference, PITarget, Query, STag, and Val productions.

A Name element must begin with a letter or underscore character (except the uppercase or lowercase letters X, M, or L, which are reserved).

Each Name must be unique.

Do not use a colon (:) in a name; the colon may be reserved in the future for namespaces, which is a method of making like names unique. Currently, namespaces use colons to differentiate names (for example, *oil:fluid* and *consume:fluid*, whereby the name *fluid* is no longer unique when the two documents are combined).

Example

Name can appear in almost any context in an XML document. For examples, look under the elements listed in the first paragraph under Notes.

Related Productions

AttDef, AttlistDecl, Attr, Attribute, AttrTerm, CombiningChar, cp, Digit, doctypedecl, elementdecl, EmptyElemTag, EntityRef, ETag, Extender, GEDecl, IdLoc, Letter, Locator, Mixed, Names, NDataDecl, Nmtoken, Nmtokens, NodeType, NotationDecl, NotationType, PEDecl, PEReference, PITarget, Query, S, STag, Val

NameChar [4]   Name Character

Purpose

Specifies one character in a name.

EBNF Syntax

```
NameChar ::= Letter | Digit | '.' | '-' | '_' | ':'
    | CombiningChar | Extender
```

Standard Syntax

Letter|*Digit*|.|-|_|:|*CombiningChar*|*Extender*

Where

- Letter is an XML element representing either an alphabetic character or an *ideogram*, a symbol that represents another character, a word, or other object. (See the Letter production.) Syntax: #xnnnn

- Digit is a number. (See the Digit production.) Valid values: 0, 1, 2, 3, 4, 5, 6, 7, 8, 9

- . -, _, and : are valid characters.

- CombiningChar specifies a character that combines with letters of the alphabet and other characters to denote special pronunciation or meaning. (See the CombiningChar production.) Syntax: #xnnnn

- Extender inserts an extender symbol. (See the Extender production.) Syntax: #xnnnn

Notes

NameChar is a component of the Name and Nmtoken productions.

A name character can be a letter, digit, or valid character, including a syllabic base character, combining character, or ideographic character.

A *syllabic base character* represents a syllable rather than a single letter.

A Name production must begin with a letter or underscore character (except the uppercase or lowercase letters X, M, or L, which are reserved).

A Nmtoken production can begin with any letter, digit, or valid character.

Do not use a colon (:) in a name; the colon may be reserved in the future for namespaces, which is a method of making like names unique. Currently, namespaces use colons to differentiate names (for example, *oil:fluid* and *consume:fluid*, whereby the name *fluid* is no longer unique when the two documents are combined).

Each Name or Nmtoken must be unique.

Related Productions

CombiningChar, Digit, Extender, Letter, Name, Names, Nmtoken, Nmtokens, S

Names [6]   Names

Purpose

Specifies one or more valid XML names, starting with a letter.

EBNF Syntax

Names ::= Name (S Name)*

Standard Syntax

Name[[...]*Name*][[...]*Name*]...[[...]*Name*]

Where

- Name specifies a valid XML name, starting with a letter or underscore character. (See the Name production.) Syntax: #xnnnn [#xnnnn][_][:][#xnnnn]|[0|1|2|3|4|5|6|7|8|9][.]|[-][#xnnnn][#xnnnn]...[#xnnnn]

- S represents one or more whitespace characters: spaces, carriage returns, line feeds, or tabs. (See the S production.) Syntax: {[#x20|#x9|#xD|#xA][#x20|#x9|#xD|#xA] ...[#x20|#x9|#xD|#xA]}

Notes

A Name production must begin with a letter or underscore character (except the uppercase or lowercase letters X, M, or L, which are reserved).

Each Name must be unique.

Do not use a colon (:) in a name; the colon may be reserved in the future for namespaces, which is a method of making like names unique. Currently, namespaces use colons to differentiate names (for example, *oil:fluid* and *consume:fluid*, whereby the name *fluid* is no longer unique when the two documents are combined).

Example

The following example presents a list of names:

```
COBOL  BASIC  RPG  ADA  C
```

Related Productions

AttDef, AttlistDecl, Attr, Attribute, AttrTerm, CombiningChar, cp, Digit, doctypedecl, elementdecl, EmptyElemTag, EntityRef, ETag, Extender, GEDecl, IdLoc, Letter, Locator, Mixed, Name, NDataDecl, Nmtoken, Nmtokens, NodeType, NotationDecl, NotationType, PEDecl, PEReference, PITarget, Query, S, STag, and Val

NDataDecl [76]   Unparsed External
                                     Entity Declaration

Purpose

Declares an unparsed external entity.

EBNF Syntax

```
NDataDecl ::= S 'NDATA' S Name
```

Standard Syntax

```
[ ... ]NDATA[ ... ]Name
```

Where

- S represents one or more whitespace characters: spaces, carriage returns, line feeds, or tabs. (See the S production.) Syntax: {[#x20|#x9|#xD|#xA][#x20|#x9|#xD|#xA] ...[#x20|#x9|#xD|#xA]}

2

- NDATA (notation data) is an uppercase-only reserved keyword that indicates that unparsed external nonmarkup data follows.
- Name specifies a valid XML name, starting with a letter or underscore character. (See the Name production.) Syntax: #xnnnn [#xnnnn][_][:][#xnnnn]|[0|1|2|3|4|5 |6|7|8|9][.]|[-][#xnnnn][#xnnnn]...[#xnnnn]

Notes

NDataDecl is a component of the EntityDef production.

An *unparsed entity* contains unparsed data (for example, GIF graphic files), which may or may not be valid and has not been processed through an XML parser. An unparsed entity has a named notation, which the XML processor sends to the target application.

An *external entity* has its content stored in a separate file, completely outside the XML document. An unparsed external entity has an NDataDecl declaration. All other external entities are parsed.

For an XML document to be valid, Name must match one of the declared names of the notation type.

Example

This example from the Extensible Markup Language recommendation includes an unparsed external entity declaration:

```
<!ENTITY hatch-pic
        SYSTEM "../grafix/OpenHatch.GIF"
        NDATA gif >
```

Related Productions

EntityDef, Name, S

Nmtoken [7]   Name Token

Purpose

Specifies a valid XML name token, starting with any character.

EBNF Syntax

```
Nmtoken ::= (NameChar)+
```

Standard Syntax

NameChar[[NameChar]...[NameChar]]

Where

- NameChar specifies one character in a name. (See the NameChar production.) Syntax: Letter|Digit|.|-|_|:|CombiningChar|Extender

Notes

Nmtoken is a component of the Enumeration and Nmtokens productions.

A Nmtoken production can begin with any letter, digit, or valid character.

The NMTOKEN attribute under the TokenizedType production must conform to the Nmtoken production.

Each Nmtoken must be unique.

Example

See the Nmtokens production:

Related Productions

CombiningChar, Digit, Enumeration, Extender, Letter, Name, Names, Nmtokens, S

Nmtokens [8]   Name Tokens

Purpose

Specifies one or more valid XML name tokens, starting with any character.

EBNF Syntax

```
Nmtokens ::= Nmtoken (S Nmtoken)*
```

Standard Syntax

Nmtoken[[...]Nmtoken][[...]Nmtoken]
...[[...]Nmtoken]]

Where

- Nmtoken specifies a valid XML name token, starting with any character. (See the Nmtoken production.) Syntax: NameChar[[NameChar]...[NameChar]]

- S represents one or more whitespace characters: spaces, carriage returns, line feeds, or tabs. (See the S production.) Syntax: {[#x20|#x9|#xD|#xA][#x20|#x9|#xD|#xA] ...[#x20|#x9|#xD|#xA]}

Notes

A Nmtoken production can begin with any letter, digit, or valid character.

The NMTOKENS attribute under the TokenizedType production must conform to the Nmtokens production.

Each Nmtoken must be unique.

Example

The following example is an enumerated list of name tokens:

(1st | 2nd | 3rd | 4th)

Related Productions

CombiningChar, Digit, Enumeration, Extender, Letter, Name, Names, Nmtoken, S

NotationDecl [82]   Notation Declaration

Purpose

Declares a notation name.

EBNF Syntax

NotationDecl ::= '<!NOTATION' S Name S (ExternalID
    | PublicID) S? '>'

Standard Syntax

```
<!NOTATION[ ... ]Name[ ... ]{ExternalID
|PublicID}[ ... ]>
```

Where

- `<!NOTATION` is an uppercase-only reserved keyword that marks the start of the notation declaration.
- `S` represents one or more whitespace characters: spaces, carriage returns, line feeds, or tabs. (See the `S` production.) Syntax: `{[#x20|#x9|#xD|#xA][#x20|#x9|#xD|#xA] ...[#x20|#x9|#xD|#xA]}`
- `Name` specifies a valid XML name, starting with a letter or underscore character. (See the `Name` production.) Syntax: `#xnnnn [#xnnnn][_][:][#xnnnn]|[0|1|2|3|4|5 |6|7|8|9][.]|[-][#xnnnn][#xnnnn]...[#xnnnn]`
- `ExternalID` names a parsed external entity. (See the `ExternalID` production.) Syntax: `SYSTEM[ ... ] SystemLiteral|PUBLIC[ ... ]PubidLiteral [ ... ]SystemLiteral`
- `PublicID` resolves an external identifier into a system identifier. (See the `PublicID` production.) Syntax: `PUBLIC[ ... ]PubidLiteral`
- `>` marks the end of the notation declaration.

Notes

`NotationDecl` is a component of the `markupdecl` production.

Notation defines the elements of a body of knowledge by using a formalized set of symbols or an alphabet. Braille, musical notes, and even computer file formats are types of notation. In XML, a notation names the format of an unparsed entity or an element that contains a notation attribute, or names the target application of a processing instruction.

A notation declaration names the notation itself, so that the notation can appear in entity declarations, attribute list declarations, attribute specifications, and some external identifiers.

Because the greater-than symbol (>) is reserved as an end indicator, you should specify a greater-than symbol within character data by using the entity >.

A notation name is always associated with a URI.

Example

This example declares a notation name for an `ExternalID`:

```
<!NOTATION  copyright  SYSTEM  "copyright.txt">
```

Related Productions

ExternalID, markupdecl, Name, PublicID, S

NotationType [58]   Notation Names

Purpose

Lists all the possible names of a notation type.

EBNF Syntax

```
NotationType ::= 'NOTATION' S '(' S? Name (S? '|'
                 S? Name)* S? ')'
```

Standard Syntax

```
NOTATION[ ... ]([ ... ]Name[[ ... ][ ... ]Name]
[[ ... ]|[ ... ]Name]...[[ ... ]|[ ... ]Name]]
[ ... ])
```

Where

- `NOTATION` is an uppercase-only reserved keyword indicating that a list of notation names follows.
- `S` represents one or more whitespace characters: spaces, carriage returns, line feeds, or tabs. (See the `S` production.) Syntax: `{[#x20|#x9|#xD|#xA][#x20|#x9|#xD|#xA] ...[#x20|#x9|#xD|#xA]}`
- `(` marks the start of the names on the list.
- `Name` specifies a valid XML name, starting with a letter or underscore character. (See the `Name` production.) Syntax: `#xnnnn [#xnnnn][_][:][#xnnnn]|[0|1|2|3|4|5 |6|7|8|9][.]|[-][#xnnnn][#xnnnn]...[#xnnnn]`
- `|` is a character that separates one name from the next.
- `)` marks the end of the names on the list.

Notes

NotationType is a component of the EnumeratedType production.

Notation defines the elements of a body of knowledge by using a formalized set of symbols or an alphabet. Braille, musical notes, and even computer file formats are types of notation. In XML, a notation names the format of an unparsed entity or an element that contains a notation attribute, or names the target application of a processing instruction.

A notation name is always associated with a URI.

For an XML document to be valid, each notation attribute type must match a declared notation name.

Example

The following example presents a list of name tokens:

```
NOTATION    (CGM  |  TIF  |  JPG  |  GIF)
```

Related Productions

EnumeratedType, Name, S

PEDecl [72]

Parameter-Entity Declaration

Purpose

Declares a parameter entity (PE).

EBNF Syntax

```
PEDecl ::= '<!ENTITY' S '%' S Name S PEDef S? '>'
```

Standard Syntax

```
<!ENTITY[ ... ]%[ ... ]Name[ ... ]PEDef[ ... ]>
```

Where

- <!ENTITY marks the beginning of a parameter-entity declaration.
- S represents one or more whitespace characters: spaces, carriage returns, line feeds, or tabs. (See the S production.)

Syntax: `{[#x20|#x9|#xD|#xA][#x20|#x9|#xD|#xA]`
`...[#x20|#x9|#xD|#xA]}`

- `%` indicates a parameter-entity reference.
- `Name` specifies a valid XML name, starting with a letter or underscore character. (See the `Name` production.) Syntax: `#xnnnn [#xnnnn][_][:][#xnnnn]|[0|1|2|3|4|5|6|7|8|9][.]|[-][#xnnnn][#xnnnn]...[#xnnnn]`
- `PEDef` prepares a parameter-entity definition. (See the `PEDef` production.) Syntax: `EntityValue|ExternalID`
- `>` marks the end of a parameter-entity declaration.

Notes

`PEDecl` is a component of the `EntityDecl` production.

A *parsed entity* contains parsed data, which is replacement text and which has been processed through an XML parser. A parsed entity has a name and is called by an entity reference.

An *internal entity* has its content stored completely within the DTD. An internal entity is a parsed `EntityValue`. Its content is declared within the current XML document. Any other entity is an external entity.

An *external entity* has its content stored in a separate file, completely outside the XML document. An unparsed external entity has an `NDataDecl` declaration. All other external entities are parsed.

A *parameter entity* (PE) is a variable that is named within markup in the prolog of a document, document type definition (DTD), or the document instance. A parameter entity is parsed, is preceded by a percent symbol (`%`), and is ended with a semicolon (`;`). Valid parameter-entity categories are internal parsed parameter and external parsed parameter. In other words, no unparsed parameter entities exist.

For a document to be well-formed, internal parsed parameter entities must be syntactically correct; external parameter entities must be syntactically correct and identical to their associated `extPE` productions.

Because the greater-than symbol (`>`) is reserved as an end indicator, you should specify a greater-than symbol within character data by using the entity `&gt;`.

Examples

The following example shows the parameter-entity declaration within the HTML INPUT element:

```
<!ENTITY % InputType
"(TEXT | PASSWORD | CHECKBOX |
  RADIO | SUBMIT | RESET |
  FILE | HIDDEN | IMAGE | BUTTON)"
>
```

The following example shows an external parameter entity for the Full Latin 1 character entity set and the related entity reference:

```
<!ENTITY % HTMLlat1 PUBLIC
"-//W3C//ENTITIES Full Latin 1//EN//HTML">
%HTMLlat1;
```

Related Productions

EntityDecl, EntityDef, EntityValue, ExternalID, GEDecl, markupdecl, Name, NDataDecl, PEDef, S

PEDef [74]	Parameter-Entity Definition

Purpose

Defines a parameter entity (PE).

EBNF Syntax

PEDef ::= EntityValue | ExternalID

Standard Syntax

EntityValue|ExternalID

Where

- EntityValue specifies an internal entity value. (See the EntityValue production.)

Syntax: `{"[^%&"]|'[^%&']}[|PEReference|Reference]`
`[|PEReference|Reference]...[|PEReference`
`|Reference]{"|'}`

- `ExternalID` names a parsed external entity. (See the `ExternalID` production.) Syntax: `SYSTEM[ ... ]` `SystemLiteral|PUBLIC[ ... ]PubidLiteral` `[ ... ]SystemLiteral`

Notes

`PEDef` is a component of the `PEDecl` production.

A *parsed entity* contains parsed data, which is replacement text and which has been processed through an XML parser. A parsed entity has a name and is called by an entity reference.

An *internal entity* has its content stored completely within the DTD. An internal entity is a parsed `EntityValue`. Its content is declared within the current XML document. Any other entity is an external entity.

An *external entity* has its content stored in a separate file, completely outside the XML document. An unparsed external entity has an `NDataDecl` declaration. All other external entities are parsed.

A *parameter entity* (PE) is a variable that is named within markup in the prolog of a document, document type definition (DTD), or the document instance. A parameter entity is parsed, is preceded by a percent symbol (%), and is ended with a semicolon (;). Valid parameter-entity categories are internal parsed parameter and external parsed parameter. In other words, no unparsed parameter entities exist.

For a document to be well-formed, internal parsed parameter entities must be syntactically correct; external parameter entities must be syntactically correct and identical to their associated `extPE` productions. The ampersand (&) is reserved; to specify an ampersand within character data, use the entity `&amp;`.

Examples

The following example shows the parameter-entity declaration within the HTML `INPUT` element:

```
<!ENTITY % InputType
"(TEXT | PASSWORD | CHECKBOX |
```

```
RADIO  |  SUBMIT  |  RESET  |
FILE  |  HIDDEN  |  IMAGE  |  BUTTON)"
>
```

The following example shows an external parameter entity for the Full Latin 1 character entity set and the related entity reference:

```
<!ENTITY % HTMLlat1 PUBLIC
"-//W3C//ENTITIES Full Latin 1//EN//HTML">
%HTMLlat1;
```

Related Productions

EntityDecl, EntityDef, EntityValue, ExternalID, GEDecl, markupdecl, Name, NDataDecl, PEDecl, S

PEReference [69]   Parameter-Entity Reference

Purpose

Identifies a parameter-entity reference.

EBNF Syntax

```
PEReference ::= '%' Name ';'
```

Standard Syntax

```
%Name;
```

Where

- % indicates a parameter-entity reference.
- Name specifies a valid XML name, starting with a letter or underscore character. (See the Name production.) Syntax: #xnnnn [#xnnnn][_][:][#xnnnn]|[0|1|2|3|4|5 |6|7|8|9][.]|[-][#xnnnn][#xnnnn]...[#xnnnn]
- ; indicates the end of the parameter-entity reference.

Notes

PEReference is a component of the doctypedecl, EntityValue, and extSubsetDecl productions.

An entity always has content, and most entities have a name.

Character references and entities begin with a variety of characters, but all end with a semicolon (;):

- Decimal character references start with the &# characters.
- Hexadecimal character references start with the &#x characters.
- Parsed general entities start with an ampersand (&).
- Parameter-entity references start with a percent sign (%).

For an XML document to be well-formed, if it has an internal DTD subset without any occurrence of the PEReference element, the entity reference name must match the same name in an entity declaration. In addition, the entity reference name does not need to declare amp, lt, gt, apos, or quot. You must declare the entity before you refer to it.

For an XML document to be well-formed, all PEReference occurrences must appear only in the DTD.

For a nonstandalone XML document with an external subset (the part of a DTD that is stored in a separate document, completely outside the source document) or external parameter entities to be compatible with SGML, it should declare amp with the && character reference, lt with &<, gt with >, apos with ', or quot with ".

For an XML document to be valid, the complete markup declaration must be nested within the PEReference replacement text.

PEReferences are allowed within markup declarations in external subsets and external parameter entities.

For an XML document to be well-formed, PEReferences can only be placed within the brackets ([and]) in the doctype declaration in the internal subset (the part of the DTD that is located within the source document). PEReferences cannot be placed within markup declarations.

Nonvalidating XML processors can ignore PEReferences, because they are not required to process external subsets.

Examples

The following example shows an external parameter entity for the Full Latin 1 character entity set and the related entity reference:

```
<!ENTITY % HTMLlat1 PUBLIC
"-//W3C//ENTITIES Full Latin 1//EN//HTML">
%HTMLlat1;
```

The following example declares the mixedtext element, which can contain both data and two parameter-entity references:

```
<!ELEMENT mixedtext (#PCDATA|%typeface;|%pointsize;)>
```

Related Productions

AttValue, BaseChar, Char, CharRef, CombiningChar, content, Digit, EntityRef, EntityValue, Extender, Ideographic, Letter, Name, Reference

---

PI [16]   Processing Instruction

Purpose

Instructs an XML processor.

EBNF Syntax

```
PI ::= '<?' PITarget (S (Char* - (Char* '?>' Char*)))?
'?>'
```

Standard Syntax

```
<?PITarget [[ ... ][Char[Char]...[Char]]?>
```

Where

- <? marks the start of a processing instruction.
- PITarget names a processing-instructions target application. (See the PITarget production). Syntax: Name
- S represents one or more whitespace characters: spaces, carriage returns, line feeds, or tabs. (See the S production.) Syntax: {[#x20|#x9|#xD|#xA][#x20|#x9|#xD|#xA] ...[#x20|#x9|#xD|#xA]}

- Char specifies one legal character. (See the Char production.) Syntax: #xnnnn[n[n]]
- ?> marks the end of a processing instruction.

Notes

PI is a component of the content, markupdecl, and Misc productions.

Processing instructions state how XML elements are processed.

A PI always starts with the name of an application associated with the instruction. When naming a target application, it's a good idea to use a notation name, which has an associated URI. The name is the PI target. (See the PITarget production.)

The XMLDecl production is a processing instruction.

When naming a target application, do not start the name with the uppercase or lowercase letters X, M, or L, which are reserved, except when you are declaring an XML document.

XML does not consider a PI to be character data; an XML processor sends the PI directly to the target application for processing.

For an XML document to be well-formed, all elements must be nested properly: All tags, elements, comments, processing instructions, character references, and entity references must be completely enclosed within one entity.

Do not use the ? > character combination within the processing instruction; the combination marks the end of the processing instruction.

Example

The following is probably the most commonly used processing instruction:

```
<?xml version="1.0"?>
```

Related Productions

Char, Name, PITarget, S

PITarget [17]

Processing-Instruction Target

2

Purpose

Names the target application for a processing instruction.

EBNF Syntax

```
PITarget ::= Name - (('X' | 'x') ('M' | 'm')
    ('L' | 'l'))
```

Standard Syntax

```
Name
```

Where

- Name specifies a valid XML name, starting with a letter or underscore character. (See the Name production.) Syntax:
  `#xnnnn [#xnnnn][_][:][#xnnnn]|[0|1|2|3|4|5`
  `|6|7|8|9][.]|[-][#xnnnn][#xnnnn]...[#xnnnn]`

Notes

PITarget is a component of the PI production.

When naming a target application, do not start the name with the uppercase or lowercase letters X, M, or L, which are reserved.

Example

The following is probably the most commonly used processing instruction:

```
<?xml version="1.0"?>
```

Related Productions

```
Char, Name, PI, S
```

prolog [22]   Prolog

2

Purpose

Describes an XML document.

EBNF Syntax

```
prolog ::= XMLDecl? Misc* (doctypedecl Misc*)?
```

Standard Syntax

[*XMLDecl*][[*Misc*][*Misc*]...[*Misc*]][*doctypedecl*[[*Misc*]
[*Misc*]...[*Misc*]]]

Where

- XMLDecl identifies an XML document as being XML and specifies version, encoding, and standalone information. (See the XMLDecl production.) Syntax: `<?xml VersionInfo [EncodingDecl][SDDecl][ ... ]?>`
- Misc inserts miscellaneous information in a prolog. (See the Misc production.) Syntax: `Comment|PI|[ ... ]`
- doctypedecl specifies an XML document type declaration. (See the doctypedecl production.) Syntax:
  `<!DOCTYPE[ ... ]Name[[ ... ]ExternalID]`
  `[ ... ][[markupdecl|PEReference|[ ... ] ]`
  `[[markupdecl|PEReference|[ ... ] ]...`
  `[[markupdecl|PEReference|[ ... ] ]][ ... ]>`

Notes

prolog is a component of the document production.

prolog is part of the XML declaration that defines an XML document.

prolog is the XML counterpart to the HTML <HEADER> element; the prolog describes the XML document very generally.

The XML declaration must occur first in the prolog, and the document type declaration must precede any start tags in an XML document.

Although Misc enables you to add comments, processing instructions, and whitespace to the prolog element, use good syntax. Being careful helps links to work properly and XML processors to interpret XML statements correctly.

Because the greater-than symbol (>) is reserved as an end indicator, you should specify a greater-than symbol within character data by using the entity >.

2

Examples

The following example is an entire self-contained XML document with a two-line prolog:

```
<?xml version="1.0"?>
<!DOCTYPE endstate[
<!ELEMENT endstate (#PCDATA)>
]>
<endstate>Goodbye, cruel world!</endstate>
```

The following example is an XML document with a two-line prolog that refers to an external DTD:

```
<?xml version="1.0"?>
<!DOCTYPE endstate SYSTEM "goodbye.dtd">
<endstate>Goodbye, cruel world!</endstate>
```

Related Productions

Comment, doctypedecl, document, EncodingDecl, Eq, Misc, PI, S, SDDecl, VersionInfo, VersionNum, XMLDecl

---

PubidChar [13]   Public Identifier Character

Purpose

Specifies a public identifier character within a public identifier literal.

EBNF Syntax

```
PubidChar ::= #x20 | #xD | #xA | [a-zA-Z0-9]
    | [-'()+,./:=?;!*#@$_%]
```

Standard Syntax

```
#x20 | #xD | #xA | [a-z | A-Z | 0-9] | [- | ' | ( | ) | +
   | , | . | / | : | = | ? | ; | ! | * | # | | $ | _ | % ]
```

Where

- #x20 (Unicode code #x0020) inserts a space, which is the equivalent of pressing the spacebar.
- #xD (Unicode code #x000D) inserts a carriage return (CR). This control character moves the cursor to the beginning of the next line.
- #xA (Unicode code #x000A) inserts a line feed (LF). This control character moves the cursor to the next line below its present position. For more information about Unicode characters, see Chapter 1, *Overview*, Appendix A, *Unicode Characters and Character Sets*, and the *Webliography*.
- a-z and A-Z represent lowercase and uppercase letters of the current alphabet.
- 0-9 are numbers from 0 to 9.
- -, ', (,), +, ,, ., /, :, =, ?, ;, !, *, #, @, $, _, and % are supported characters.

Notes

PubidChar is a component of the PubidLiteral production.

Related Productions

AttValue, EntityDef, EntityValue, PEDef, PEReference, PubidLiteral, Reference, SystemLiteral

---

PubidLiteral [12]   Public Identifier Literal

Purpose

Names a public identifier literal.

EBNF Syntax

```
PubidLiteral ::= '"' PubidChar* '"'
   | "'" (PubidChar - "'")* "'"
```

Standard Syntax

{ " | ' } [[*PubidChar*] [*PubidChar*] ... [*PubidChar*]] { " | ' }

Where

- PubidChar specifies public identifier characters. (See the PubidChar production.) Syntax: #x20 | #xD | #xA | [a-z | A-Z | 0-9] | [- | ' | (|) | + | , | . | / | : | = | ? | ; | ! | * | # | | $ | _ | %]

Notes

PubidLiteral is a component of the ExternalID and PublicID productions.

A literal such as PubidLiteral replaces the current value of an entity or attribute.

If you enclose a production, string, element, or other object within single quote marks, do not use single quote marks within the production, string, element, or other object; if you enclose a production, string, element, or other object within quotation marks, do not use quotation marks within the production, string, element, or other object.

Do not mix single quote marks and quotation marks; quotes at the beginning and end of a production, string, element, or other object must match.

Example

The following example shows an external parameter entity for the Full Latin 1 character entity set and the related general entity:

```
<!ENTITY % HTMLlat1 PUBLIC
"-//W3C//ENTITIES Full Latin 1//EN//HTML">
%HTMLlat1;
```

Related Productions

AttValue, EntityDef, EntityValue, ExternalID, PEDef, PEReference, PubidChar, PublicID, Reference, SystemLiteral

PublicID [83]   External Identifier

Purpose

Resolves an external identifier into a system identifier.

EBNF Syntax

```
PublicID ::= 'PUBLIC' S PubidLiteral
```

Standard Syntax

```
PUBLIC[ ... ]PubidLiteral
```

Where

- PUBLIC is an uppercase-only reserved keyword indicating that a public identifier follows.
- S represents one or more whitespace characters: spaces, carriage returns, line feeds, or tabs. (See the S production.) Syntax: {[#x20|#x9|#xD|#xA][#x20|#x9|#xD|#xA] ...[#x20|#x9|#xD|#xA]}
- PubidLiteral names a public identifier literal. (See the PubidLiteral production.) Syntax: {"|'} [[PubidChar][PubidChar]...[PubidChar]]{"|'}

Notes

PublicID is a component of the NotationDecl production.

All system identifiers are URIs.

Notation defines the elements of a body of knowledge by using a formalized set of symbols or an alphabet. Braille, musical notes, and even computer file formats are types of notation. In XML, a notation names the format of an unparsed entity or an element that contains a notation attribute, or names the target application of a processing instruction.

A notation declaration names the notation itself so that the notation can appear in entity declarations, attribute list declarations, attribute specifications, and in some external identifiers.

Example

The following example shows an external parameter entity for the Full Latin 1 character entity set and the related general entity:

```
<!ENTITY % HTMLlat1 PUBLIC
"-//W3C//ENTITIES Full Latin 1//EN//HTML">
%HTMLlat1;
```

Related Productions

ExternalID, markupdecl, NotationDecl, PublicID, S

2

Reference [67]   Reference

Purpose

Names an entity or parameter-entity reference.

EBNF Syntax

```
Reference ::= EntityRef | CharRef
```

Standard Syntax

EntityRef|CharRef

Where

- EntityRef identifies an entity reference. (See the EntityRef production.) Syntax: &Name;
- CharRef names a legal character from the ISO/IEC 10646 character set. (See the CharRef production.) Syntax: &#{dec_num[dec_num[...dec_num]]}; |&#x{hex_num[hex_num[...hex_num]]};

Notes

Reference is a component of the AttValue, content, and EntityValue productions.

An entity always has content, and most entities have a name.

Character references and entities begin with a variety of characters, but all end with a semicolon (;):

- Decimal character references start with the &# characters.
- Hexadecimal character references start with the &#x characters.

- Parsed general entities start with an ampersand (&).
- Parameter-entity references start with a percent sign (%).

Examples

The following are examples of entity references:

```
&copyright;
&editdate;
```

The following are examples of character references:

```
&#251;
&#x628;&#x631;&#x627;&#x64a;
```

Related Productions

AttValue, BaseChar, Char, CharRef, CombiningChar, content, Digit, EntityRef, EntityValue, Extender, Ideographic, Letter, Name, PEReference

---

S [3]   Whitespace

Purpose

Inserts whitespace in an XML document.

EBNF Syntax

```
S ::= (#x20 | #x9 | #xD | #xA)+
```

Standard Syntax

```
{[#x20|#x9|#xD|#xA][#x20|#x9|#xD|#xA]
   ...[#x20|#x9|#xD|#xA]}
```

Where

- #x20 (Unicode code #x0020) inserts a space, which is the equivalent of pressing the spacebar.
- #x9 (Unicode code #x0009) inserts a tab (HT). This control character moves the cursor to the next tab stop.

- #xD (Unicode code #x000D) inserts a carriage return (CR). This control character moves the cursor to the beginning of the next line.

- #xA (Unicode code #x000A) inserts a line feed (LF). This control character moves the cursor to the next line below its present position. For more information about Unicode characters, see Chapter 1, *Overview*, Appendix A, *Unicode Characters and Character Sets*, and the *Webliography*.

Notes

S is a component of the AttDef, AttlistDecl, choice, DefaultDecl, doctypedecl, elementdecl, EmptyElemTag, EncodingDecl, Enumeration, ETag, ExternalID, extSubsetDecl, GEDecl, ignoreSect, includeSect, Misc, Mixed, Names, NDataDecl, Nmtokens, NotationDecl, NotationType, PEDecl, PI, PublicID, SDDecl, seq, STag, TextDecl, VersionInfo, and XMLDecl productions.

The S production is a part of the XML specification. Do not use S in DTDs and XML documents. Instead, use xml:space or styles to add whitespace. Whitespace consists of one or more space characters, carriage returns, line feeds, or tabs — all regarded by XML as nonmarkup text.

An XML processor passes *all* nonmarkup characters to the target application. A validating XML processor passes the characters and also reports to the application on the whitespace characters within the content of elements.

A validating XML processor should differentiate whitespace from other element content and should disregard the amount of whitespace inserted between other objects in content.

Use whitespace to separate and align elements and attributes in a DTD and to format text in an output document.

Be aware that in some languages, whitespace separates some characters and words. However, in XML, this is not considered to be whitespace.

You can use the xml:space attribute, which is analogous to the HTML <PRE> element, to preserve all whitespace in the XML document. If you use the xml:space attribute and you want a valid document, you must declare xml:space as an enumerated type with a choice of only two values: default and preserve. The default value allows a target application to set its own whitespace values, and preserve keeps the whitespace values in the document, assuming that the application supports xml:space. For example:

```
<!ATTLIST PRE_TYPE    xml:space    (default|preserve)
    'preserve'>
```

xml:space applies to all the whitespace in a document, unless you insert another xml:space attribute.

The presence or absence of an xml:space attribute has no effect on the well-formedness or validity of an XML document.

By default, the root element does not address whitespace handling. However, you can specify a whitespace attribute in the root element.

Different computer platforms handle line ends differently. For example, Windows issues a carriage-return/line-feed combination at the end of a line, a Macintosh computer issues a carriage return, and a UNIX computer issues a line feed. To avoid this incompatibility, an XML processor issues one line-end control character, a #xA line-feed control character, at the end of a line.

Example

This example shows varying amounts of whitespace within the same line:

```
<!--defining <para> paragraph element-->
<!--defining    <para>    paragraph element-->
```

Related Productions

AttDef, AttlistDecl, choice, DefaultDecl, doctypedecl, elementdecl, EmptyElemTag, EncodingDecl, Enumeration, ETag, ExternalID, extSubsetDecl, GEDecl, ignoreSect, includeSect, Misc, Mixed, Names, NDataDecl, Nmtokens, NotationDecl, NotationType, PEDecl, PI, PublicID, SDDecl, seq, STag, TextDecl, VersionInfo, XMLDecl

SDDecl [32]

Standalone Document Declaration

2

Purpose

Declares a standalone document.

EBNF Syntax

```
SDDecl ::= S 'standalone' Eq (("'" ('yes' | 'no') "'")
           | '"' ('yes' | 'no') '"'))
```

Standard Syntax

```
[ ... ]standalone={"|'}yes|no{"|'}
```

Where

- S represents one or more whitespace characters: spaces, carriage returns, line feeds, or tabs. (See the S production.) Syntax: {[#x20|#x9|#xD|#xA][#x20|#x9|#xD|#xA] ...[#x20|#x9|#xD|#xA]}

- standalone is a string indicating that a standalone declaration follows.

- Eq represents an equal sign (=) preceded and succeeded by one or more spaces. (See the Eq production.) Syntax: =

- yes indicates that no external markup declarations are associated with the current XML document; that is, the document does not use a DTD or the DTD is included in the internal subset (the part of the DTD that is located within the source document).

- no indicates that external markup declarations may be associated with the current XML document. This is the default if any external markup declarations are associated with the document.

Notes

SDDecl is a component of the XMLDecl production.

A markup declaration referred to in a standalone declaration is located in either an external subset (the part of a DTD that is stored in a separate document, completely outside the source document), specified in the DTD or an external parameter entity specified in the internal subset (the part of the DTD that is located within the source document).

A standalone declaration refers to external declarations, not external entities.

The presence or absence of a standalone declaration has no effect on the well-formedness or validity of an XML document.

If no extSubsetDecls are associated with an XML document, an XML processor ignores the standalone declaration.

For an XML document to be valid, standalone must equal no if extSubsetDecls declare any of the following:

- Attributes with default values
- Entities (but not including &, ', >, <, and ")
- Attributes with values that can be *normalized* (that is, all markup is included rather than minimized) and, as a result, the values will change
- Element types have content, if whitespace occurs within the element

Do not mix single quote marks and quotation marks; quotes at the beginning and end of the standalone declaration's value must match.

Example

The following example declares a standalone document:

```
<?xml version="1.0" standalone="yes"?>
```

Related Productions

Eq, S, XMLDecl

seq [50]   Sequence List

Purpose

Specifies a sequence list of content particles.

EBNF Syntax

```
seq ::= '(' S? cp ( S? ',' S? cp )* S? ')'
```

Standard Syntax

```
([ ... ]cp[[ ... ],[ ... ]cp][[ ... ],[ ... ]cp]
...[[ ... ],[ ... ]cp][ ... ])
```

Where

- (marks the start of the names on the list.
- S represents one or more whitespace characters: spaces, carriage returns, line feeds, or tabs. (See the S production.) Syntax: {[#x20|#x9|#xD|#xA][#x20|#x9|#xD|#xA] ...[#x20|#x9|#xD|#xA]}
- cp includes a content particle grammar. (See the cp production.) Syntax: {Name|choice|seq}[?|*|+]
- , is a character that separates one name from the next.
-) marks the end of the names on the list.

Notes

seq is a component of the children and cp productions.

Content models consist of content particles (CPs), which are names of child element types, as well as choice lists and sequence lists, which are, in turn, other content particles. This allows you to write very complex element-type declarations, which must be matched exactly during processing. Of course, the more complex a declaration, the more chances for errors exist in processing an XML document.

For an XML document to be valid, any PEReference replacement text must be nested completely within its content particle in a choice, Mixed, or seq production.

For an XML document to be valid, any PEReference replacement text cannot be empty and its first or last nonblank characters should not be a pipe (|) or ,) character combination.

For more information, see the elementdecl and contentspec notes.

Example

The following example declares the longdoc element, which includes a sequence of three elements:

```
<!ELEMENT longdoc (intro, body, index)>
```

Related Productions

children, choice, contentspec, cp, Name, S

STag [40]	Start Tag

Purpose

Defines a start tag for a nonempty or empty XML element.

EBNF Syntax

```
STag ::= '<' Name (S Attribute)* S? '>'
```

Standard Syntax

```
<Name[[ ... ]Attribute][[ ... ]Attribute]
...[[ ... ]Attribute]]][ ... ]>
```

Where

- < marks the beginning of the start tag.
- Name specifies a valid XML name, starting with a letter or underscore character, for the element type. (See the Name production.) Syntax: #xnnnn [#xnnnn][_][:][#xnnnn] |[0|1|2|3|4|5|6|7|8|9][.]|[-][#xnnnn] [#xnnnn]...[#xnnnn]
- S represents one or more whitespace characters: spaces, carriage returns, line feeds, or tabs. (See the S production.) Syntax: {[#x20|#x9|#xD|#xA][#x20|#x9|#xD|#xA] ...[#x20|#x9|#xD|#xA]}
- Attribute names an attribute used to select an element. (See the Attribute production.) Syntax: Name[...]= [...]AttValue
- > marks the end of the start tag.

Notes

STag is a component of the element production.

An end tag (ETag) indicates the end of content.

The start of every element with content must be marked by a start tag. You can also mark the start of an empty element with a start tag.

The element type name for the start tag must match that for the end tag.

Each attribute contains two elements: a name and a value.

For an XML document to be well-formed, each attribute under an element, regardless of whether it has content, must be unique. However, the value of an attribute does not have to be unique.

For an XML document to be well-formed, all elements must be nested properly: All tags, elements, comments, processing instructions, character references, and entity references must be completely enclosed within one entity.

For an XML document to be valid, each of its attributes must have been declared and must match the declared type.

For an XML document to be well-formed, its attribute values must be within the internal subset (the part of the DTD that is located within the source document) and not refer to external entities.

A less-than symbol (<) is reserved; it indicates the start of markup, among other things. To specify a less-than symbol within character data, use the entity <.

Because the greater-than symbol (>) is reserved as an end indicator, you should specify a greater-than symbol within character data by using the entity >.

Examples

The following example is an entire self-contained XML document with one start tag:

```
<?xml version="1.0"?>
<!DOCTYPE endstate[
<!ELEMENT endstate (#PCDATA)>
]>
<endstate>Goodbye, cruel world!</endstate>
```

The following example is a start tag with two attributes:

```
<HITHERE ALIGN="left" ID="abc">
```

Related Productions

Attribute, content, element, EmptyElement, Eq, ETag

2

StringType [55]   String Type

Purpose

Specifies a character data string.

EBNF Syntax

StringType ::= 'CDATA'

Standard Syntax

CDATA

Where

- CDATA is an uppercase-only reserved keyword indicating that the attribute type is character data only.

Notes

StringType is a component of the AttType production.

Do not confuse CDATA with the CData production.

An attribute type allows you to ensure that proper and valid data is entered in an XML document.

Attributes are included within start tags and empty-element tags, not end tags.

For an XML document to be well-formed, you do not need to define any attribute types.

For an XML document to be valid, each of its elements' attributes must have been declared and must match the declared type.

An XML processor must normalize minimized attribute values before sending them to the target application.

Example

The following example shows a string attribute type:

       name   **CDATA** #IMPLIED

Related Productions

AttType, EnumeratedType, TokenizedType

Subcode [38]   Subcode

2

Purpose

Specifies a language or country subcode.

EBNF Syntax

Subcode ::= ([a-z] | [A-Z])+

Standard Syntax

{[a-z]|[A-Z]}[[a-z]|[A-Z]]...[[a-z]|[A-Z]]

Where

- a-z and A-Z represent lowercase and uppercase letters of the current alphabet.

Notes

Subcode is a component of the LanguageID production.

You can name more than one subcode.

For more information, see the "Notes" section under the LanguageID production.

Example

This example illustrates the xml:lang attribute with an added US (United States) subcode:

<para xml:lang="en-**US**">I'm speaking in English.</para>

Related Productions

IanaCode, ISO639Code, Langcode, LanguageID, UserCode

SystemLiteral [11]   System Literal

Purpose

Specifies a system literal, which is a system-identifier URI.

EBNF Syntax

```
SystemLiteral ::= ('"' [^"]* '"') | ("'" [^']* "'")
```

Standard Syntax

{ " | ' } URI { " | ' }

Where

- *URI* is a Uniform Resource Identifier, an Internet address, which is either an absolute Uniform Resource Locator (URL) or a Uniform Resource Name (URN), known as a system identifier.

Notes

SystemLiteral is a component of the ExternalID production.

A system literal is a URI, which identifies the content of an external entity. This is known as the *system identifier*.

A literal such as System Literal replaces the current value of an entity or attribute.

EntityValue supports entity references, which do not require a preceding # symbol. Each entity reference replaces one character.

If you enclose a production, string, element, or other object within single quote marks, do not use single quote marks within the production, string, element, or other object; if you enclose a production, string, element, or other object within quotation marks, do not use quotation marks within the production, string, element, or other object.

Within character data, you can use the apostrophe (') or quotation mark (") characters.

Do not mix single quote marks and quotation marks; quotes at the beginning and end of a production, string, element, or other object must match.

Example

The following example shows an external ID:

```
<!ENTITY copyright SYSTEM
   "http://www.myfiles.com/copyright.txt">
```

Related Productions

AttValue, EntityDef, EntityValue, ExternalID, PEDef,
PEReference, PubidChar, PubidLiteral, Reference

TextDecl [77]   Text Declaration

Purpose

Provides information about the version and encoding of an external parsed entity.

EBNF Syntax

```
TextDecl ::= '<?xml' VersionInfo? EncodingDecl S? '?>'
```

Standard Syntax

```
<?xml[VersionInfo] EncodingDecl[ ... ]?>
```

Where

- <?xml marks the start of the text declaration.
- VersionInfo names the XML version information. (See the VersionInfo production.) Syntax:
  [...]version={"|'}VersionNum{"|'}
- EncodingDecl defines an encoding declaration. (See the EncodingDecl production.) Syntax: [...]encoding = {"|'}EncName{"|'}
- S represents one or more whitespace characters: spaces, carriage returns, line feeds, or tabs. (See the S production.) Syntax: {[#x20|#x9|#xD|#xA][#x20|#x9|#xD|#xA] ...[#x20|#x9|#xD|#xA]}
- ?> marks the end of the text declaration.

Notes

TextDecl is a component of the extParsedEnt, extPE, and extSubset productions.

A text declaration is a literal and is *not* a reference to a parsed entity.

The text declaration is a stripped-down version of a document's opening XML declaration.

A text declaration appears only at the beginning of an external parsed entity.

If an external parsed entity uses an encoding that is *not* UTF-8 or UTF-16, it must contain an opening TextDecl that includes an EncodingDecl.

Example

The example shows a text declaration for an external parsed entity:

```
<?xml version="1.0" encoding="UTF-8"?>
```

Related Productions

EncodingDecl, extParsedEnt, extPE, extSubset, S, VersionInfo

TokenizedType [56]   Tokenized Type

Purpose

States that an element attribute is a tokenized set.

EBNF Syntax

```
TokenizedType ::= 'ID'   | 'IDREF'   | 'IDREFS'   | 'ENTITY'
                | 'ENTITIES'   | 'NMTOKEN'   | 'NMTOKENS'
```

Standard Syntax

```
ID | IDREF | IDREFS | ENTITY | ENTITIES | NMTOKEN | NMTOKENS
```

Where

- `ID` is an uppercase-only reserved keyword indicating that the defined attribute is an identifier. (See the `ID` entry in this chapter.)

- `IDREF` is an uppercase-only reserved keyword indicating that the defined attribute is an identifier cross-reference. (See the `IDREF` entry in this chapter.)

- `IDREFS` is an uppercase-only reserved keyword indicating that a list of `ID` cross-references follows. (See the `IDREFS` entry in this chapter.)

- `ENTITY` is an uppercase-only reserved keyword indicating that the defined attribute is an entity. (See the `ENTITY` entry in this chapter.)

- `ENTITIES` is an uppercase-only reserved keyword indicating that a list of `ENTITY`s follows. (See the `ENTITIES` entry in this chapter.)

- `NMTOKEN` is an uppercase-only reserved keyword indicating that the defined attribute is a name token. (See the `Nmtoken` production.)

- `NMTOKENS` is an uppercase-only reserved keyword indicating that a list of `NMTOKEN`s follows. (See the `Nmtokens` production.)

Notes

`TokenizedType` is a component of the `AttType` production.

An attribute type allows you to ensure that proper and valid data is entered in an XML document.

Attributes are included within start tags and empty-element tags, not end tags.

For an XML document to be well-formed, you do not need to define any attribute types.

For an XML document to be valid, each of its elements' attributes must have been declared and must match the declared type.

The `ID` and `IDREF` attribute types enable complex linking and optional extended pointers. For more information, refer to Chapter 4, *XLink Language*, and Chapter 5, *XPointer Language*.

Some nonvalidating XML processors assume that the default attribute type is `ID`. This allows a well-formed document to use identifiers for complex linking.

For an XML document to be valid and compatible with SGML, each element type can have only one ID attribute type.

For an XML document to be valid, the following attribute types must follow the rules and constraints controlling particular XML elements:

- ID, IDREF, and ENTITY must conform to the Name production.
- IDREFS and ENTITIES must conform to the Names production.
- NMTOKEN must conform to the Nmtoken production.
- NMTOKENS must conform to the Nmtokens production.

For an XML document to be valid, each ID name must be unique.

For an XML document to be valid, each ID must have a default value of #IMPLIED or #REQUIRED.

For an XML document to be valid, each IDREF name must match the value of an ID.

For an XML document to be valid, each ENTITY must be an unparsed entity declared in the DTD.

An XML processor must normalize minimized attribute values before sending them to the target application.

Example

The following example shows a tokenized type of attribute:

```
id      ID      #REQUIRED
```

Related Productions

AttType, EnumeratedType, StringType

UserCode [37]   User Language Code

Purpose

Identifies a user-assigned language.

EBNF Syntax

```
UserCode ::= ('x' | 'X') '-' ([a-z] | [A-Z])+
```

Standard Syntax

{x|X}-{[a-z]|[A-Z][[a-z]|[A-Z]]...[[a-z]|[A-Z]]}

Where

- x or X indicates that a user-assigned language follows.
- - is a separator character.
- a-z and A-Z represent lowercase and uppercase letters of the current alphabet.

Notes

UserCode is a component of the Langcode production.

Language codes and country codes are case-insensitive. Although not required, the language code is usually in lowercase and the country code is usually in uppercase.

For more information, see the "Notes" section under the LanguageID production.

Example

This example illustrates the xml:lang attribute and a user-defined language code:

```
<para xml:lang="x-uk_eng">I'm speaking in
    proper English.</para>
```

Related Productions

IanaCode, ISO639Code, Langcode, LanguageID, Subcode

VersionInfo [24] XML Version Information

Purpose

Specifies the XML version information.

EBNF Syntax

```
VersionInfo ::= S 'version' Eq ( "'" VersionNum "'"
    | '"' VersionNum '"' )
```

Standard Syntax

```
[ ... ]version = {"|'}VersionNum{"|'}
```

Where

- S represents one or more whitespace characters: spaces, carriage returns, line feeds, or tabs. (See the S production.) Syntax: {[#x20|#x9|#xD|#xA][#x20|#x9|#xD|#xA] ...[#x20|#x9|#xD|#xA]}
- version is a string indicating that the version number follows.
- Eq represents an equal sign (=) preceded and succeeded by one or more spaces. (See the Eq production.) Syntax: =
- VersionNum inserts an XML version number. (See the VersionNum production.) Syntax: {[a-z|A-Z|0-9|_ |.|:]|-[[a-z|A-Z|0-9|_|.|:]|-]...[[a-z |A-Z|0-9|_|.|:]|-]}

Notes

VersionInfo is a component of the TextDecl and XMLDecl productions.

The VersionInfo production states the version number for the XML specification supporting the current document.

Do not mix single quote marks and quotation marks; quotes at the beginning and end of a production, string, element, or other object must match.

For more information, see the "Notes" section under the XMLDecl production.

Examples

The following example declares an XML document:

```
<?xml version="1.0"?>
```

The following example declares a standalone document:

```
<?xml version="1.0" standalone="yes"?>
```

Related Productions

Comment, doctypedecl, document, EncodingDecl, Eq, Misc, PI, prolog, S, SDDecl, TextDecl, VersionNum, XMLDecl

VersionNum [26]

XML Version Number

Purpose

Specifies an XML version number.

EBNF Syntax

```
VersionNum ::= ([a-zA-Z0-9_.:] | '-')+
```

Standard Syntax

```
{[a-z|A-Z|0-9|_|.|:]|-[[a-z|A-Z|0-9|_|.|:]|-]
...[[a-z|A-Z|0-9|_|.|:]|-]}
```

Where

- a-z and A-Z represent lowercase and uppercase letters of the alphabet.
- 0-9 are numbers from 0 to 9.
- _, ., and : are supported characters.
- - is a trailing character.

Notes

VersionNum is a component of the VersionInfo production.

Inserting the version number in an XML document specifies that the document conforms to a particular XML standard.

Examples

The following example declares an XML document:

```
<?xml version="1.0"?>
```

The following example declares a standalone document:

```
<?xml version="1.0" standalone="yes"?>
```

Related Productions

Comment, doctypedecl, document, EncodingDecl, Eq, Misc, PI, prolog, S, SDDecl, VersionInfo, VersionNum, XMLDecl

xml:alternate style sheet	**Alternate Style Sheet**

Purpose

Instructs the XML processor to use the referred-to alternate style sheet.

Standard Syntax

```
<?xml:style sheet|alternate-style sheet
    href={"|'}stylename.css{"|'}
    type={"|'}text/css{"|'}[charset={"|'}
    charset{"|'}]
    [media={"|'}media{"|'}]
    [ title={"|'}doctitle{"|'}]?>
```

Where

- `style sheet` is a keyword indicating that the attached document is a style sheet.
- `alternate-style sheet` is a keyword indicating that the attached document is an alternate style sheet.
- `href` specifies a URI for a link to the external style sheet document.
- `type` specifies a type name of the link, for information within the current document.
- `charset` names the source of the character set of the data referred to by the `href` attribute.
- `media` indicates the type of destination.
- `title` specifies a title name of the external style sheet document.

Notes

You associate one or more style sheets with an XML document in the same way that you use the LINK element to associate an external style sheet document in an HTML document. Simply embed `xml:style sheet` or `xml:alternate-style sheet` processing instructions (PI) anywhere within the XML document prolog.

For more information about cascading style sheets, refer to Chapter 5, *Cascading Style Sheets*.

For information about DSSSL (Document Style Semantics and Specification Language) and DSSSL Online (DSSSL-O), refer to Chapter 6, *DSSSL-O*.

Example

The following example refers to the alternate styler1.css style sheet:

```
<?xml:alternate style sheet href="styler1.css"
type="text/css"?>
```

Related Processing Instruction

```
xml:style sheet
```

XMLDecl [23]   XML Declaration

Purpose

Identifies a document as XML and specifies the XML version, encoding, and standalone information.

EBNF Syntax

```
XMLDecl ::= '<?xml' VersionInfo EncodingDecl?
    SDDecl? S? '?>'
```

Standard Syntax

```
<?xml VersionInfo [EncodingDecl][SDDecl][ ... ]?>
```

Where

- <?xml marks the start of the XML document type declaration.
- VersionInfo names the XML version information. (See the VersionInfo production.) Syntax: [...]
  version={"|'}VersionNum{"|'}
- EncodingDecl defines an encoding declaration. (See the EncodingDecl production.) Syntax: [...]encoding =
  {"|'}EncName{"|'}

- SDDecl declares the standalone status of the current document. (See the SDDecl production.) Syntax: [...] standalone={"|'}yes|no{"|'}

- S represents one or more whitespace characters: spaces, carriage returns, line feeds, or tabs. (See the S production.) Syntax: {[#x20|#x9|#xD|#xA][#x20|#x9|#xD|#xA] ...[#x20|#x9|#xD|#xA]}

- ?> marks the end of the XML document type declaration.

Notes

XMLDecl is a component of the prolog production.

An XML declaration identifies an XML document, states the XML version that supports it, and can include the encoding declaration (using the EncodingDecl element) and standalone declaration (using the SDDecl production).

The XMLDecl element is a processing instruction.

Although an XML declaration is not required, you should begin an XML document with it.

If an XML declaration were required, SGML and HTML documents created before XML would not be well-formed. However, an optional XML declaration allows many of these documents to be well-formed without additional editing.

Examples

The following example declares an XML document:

```
<?xml version="1.0"?>
```

The following example declares a standalone document:

```
<?xml version="1.0" standalone="yes"?>
```

The following example declares an XML document and its encoding:

```
<?xml version="1.0" encoding='UTF-8'?>
```

Related Productions

Comment, doctypedecl, document, EncodingDecl, Eq, Misc, PI, prolog, S, SDDecl, VersionInfo, VersionNum

xml:lang   Language Code

Purpose

Instructs XML to process the referred-to XML language code.

Standard Syntax

```
<element xml:lang=code>language_text</element>
```

Where

- <element is the start tag containing the element type attributes, and start-tag delimiters.
- xml:lang is the processing instruction specifying that one or more language codes follows.
- code is the language code, country code, and/or subcode.
- > is the end of the start tag.
- language_text is the text output in the selected language.
- </element> is the end tag containing the element type and end-tag delimiters.

Notes

You can use the xml:lang attribute with any XML production to declare a language used as character data and attribute values in an XML document. IETF_RFC_1766 (ftp://ftp.isi. edu/ in-notes/rfc1766.txt) lists supported values.

The language named in the xml:lang attribute is in effect until the next xml:lang attribute is declared.

Language codes and country codes are case-insensitive. Although not required, the language code is usually in lowercase and the country code is usually in uppercase.

To find an IANA language identifier, go to the Internet Assigned Numbers Authority (IANA) at http://www.iana.org.

Examples

This example illustrates the xml:lang attribute and the IANA UK language code:

```
<para xml:lang="i-BS_4730">I'm speaking in
   proper English.</para>
```

This example illustrates the xml:lang attribute and the ISO639 en (English) language code:

```
<para xml:lang="en">I'm speaking in English.</para>
```

This example illustrates the xml:lang attribute with an added US subcode:

```
<para xml:lang="en-US">I'm speaking in English.</para>
```

This example illustrates the xml:lang attribute and a user-defined language code:

```
<para xml:lang="x-uk_eng">I'm speaking
   in proper English.</para>
```

Related Productions

IanaCode, ISO639Code, Langcode, LanguageID, Subcode, UserCode

xml:space   Whitespace

Purpose
Preserves the whitespace in an XML document.

Standard Syntax

```
xml:space   (default|preserve)
```

Where

- xml:space is the processing instruction specifying that a whitespace value follows.
- default allows a target application to set its own white-space values.
- preserve keeps the whitespace values in the document.

Notes

Use the xml:space attribute, which is analogous to the HTML <PRE> element, to preserve all whitespace in the XML document. An XML processor that does not support xml:space ignores the xml:space setting.

xml:space applies to all the whitespace in a document, unless you insert another xml:space attribute.

By default, the root element does not address whitespace handling. However, you can specify a whitespace attribute in the root element.

Different computer platforms handle line ends differently. For example, Windows issues a carriage-return/line-feed combination at the end of a line, a Macintosh computer issues a carriage return, and a UNIX computer issues a line feed. To avoid this incompatibility, an XML processor issues one line-end control character, a #xA line-feed control character, at the end of a line.

The S production is a part of the XML specification. Do not use S in DTDs and XML documents. Instead, use xml:space or styles to add whitespace.

The presence or absence of an xml:space attribute has no effect on the well-formedness or validity of an XML document.

Examples

The following example shows an attribute list with its element, choices, and default value:

```
<!ATTLIST PRE_TYPE   xml:space   (default|preserve)
    'preserve'>
```

Related Production

S

---

xml:style sheet   Style Sheet

Purpose

Instructs the XML processor to use the referred-to style sheet.

Standard Syntax

```
<?xml:style sheet|alternate-style sheet
    href={"|'}stylename.css{"|'}
    type={"|'}text/css{"|'}[charset={"|'}
    charset{"|'}]
    [media={"|'}media{"|'}]
    [ title={"|'}doctitle{"|'}]?>
```

Where

- style sheet is a keyword indicating that the attached document is a style sheet.
- alternate-style sheet is a keyword indicating that the attached document is an alternate style sheet.
- href specifies a URI for a link to the external style sheet document.
- type specifies a type name of the link, for information within the current document.
- charset names the source of the character set of the data referred to by the href attribute.
- media indicates the type of destination.
- title specifies a title name of the external style sheet document.

Notes

You associate one or more style sheets with an XML document in the same way that you use the LINK element to associate an external style sheet document in an HTML document. Simply embed xml:style sheet or xml:alternate-style sheet processing instructions (PI) anywhere within the XML document prolog.

For more information about cascading style sheets, refer to Chapter 5, *Cascading Style Sheets.*

For information about DSSSL (Document Style Semantics and Specification Language) and DSSSL Online (DSSSL-O), refer to Chapter 6, *DSSSL-O.*

Example

The following example refers to the styler.css style sheet:

```
<?xml:style sheet href="styler.css" type="text/css"?>
```

Related Processing Instruction

xml:alternate style sheet

XLink Language

The *productions* (that is, XML instructions or components comprising instructions) in this chapter enable
you to write XLinks, which in conjunction with XPointers
establish hyperlinks in XML documents. The XLink standard defines two types of links:

- *Simple links*, which are analogous to the A element in
  HTML. Simple links allow you to jump from a location in the current document to a destination in that
  current document or in another document. Simple
  links always move in one direction. For more information about simple links, see Section 4.2, "Simple
  Links," in the XLink working draft (`http://www.`
  `w3.org/TR/WD-xlink/`).

- *Extended links*, which enable you to define many
  links. Using extended links, you can jump from any
  link to another link. You can identify the content
  associated with a particular link so that if the content
  changes but the identifier remains the same, you can
  still access the link. Extended links can be inline or

out-of-line. An *inline link* is considered to be a local resource of the link. Child elements of inline links, however, are not part of the local resource; they are part of the link element. An *out-of-line* link specifies the location of the link. Because it's not a local resource, an application must be able to find it easily; out-of-line links are particularly useful for extended link groups, which are a particular type of extended link. (See the *group* entry in this chapter.) For more information about extended links, see Section 4.3, "Extended Links," in the XLink working draft (http://www.w3.org/TR/WD-xlink/).

Specifying a Simple Link in a DTD

To specify a simple link in a document type declaration (DTD), define an element using the following syntax:

```
<!ELEMENT simp_link ANY>
```

Define an attribute list and an xml:link attribute value:

```
<!ATTLIST simp_link
    xml:link           CDATA            #FIXED "simple"
```

You can list other attributes by using parameter entities (for example, %parmname1.ext;) and signal the end of the declaration by using a greater-than (>) symbol:

```
%parmname1.ext;
%parmname2.ext;
%parmname3.ext;
%parmname4.ext;
>
```

However, when you use parameter entities, editing the DTD in the future may be more difficult; the editor may have to jump to other parts of the DTD to understand your declarations and definitions.

For examples of simple link declarations, see Section 4, "Linking Elements," in the W3C's XML Linking Language (XLink) working draft at http://www.w3.org/TR/WD-xlink. In addition, you can find other examples throughout this chapter.

Specifying an Extended Link in a DTD

You can use extended links to access local, remote, or group resources.

Specifying an extended local link

To specify an extended local link in a DTD, define an element using the following syntax:

```
<!ELEMENT extend_link ANY>
```

Define an attribute list and an xml:link attribute value:

```
<!ATTLIST extend_link
     xml:link          CDATA          #FIXED "extended"
```

You can list other attributes by using parameter entities and signal the end of the declaration:

```
%parmname1.ext;
%parmname2.ext;
%parmname3.ext;
%parmname4.ext;
>
```

However, when you use parameter entities, editing the DTD in the future may be more difficult, because the editor may have to jump to other parts of the DTD to understand your declarations and definitions.

For examples of extended link declarations, see Section 4, "Linking Elements," in the W3C's XML Linking Language (XLink) working draft at http://www.w3.org/TR/WD-xlink. In addition, you can find other examples throughout this chapter.

Specifying an extended remote link

To specify an extended remote link in a DTD, define an element using the following syntax:

```
<!ELEMENT locator_link ANY>
```

Define an attribute list and an xml:link attribute value:

```
<!ATTLIST locator_link
    xml:link         CDATA            #FIXED "locator"
```

Then, list other attributes by using parameter entities and end the declaration.

Specifying an extended group link

To specify an extended group link in a DTD, define an element using the following syntax:

```
<!ELEMENT group_link (paper*)>
```

Define an attribute list, an xml:link attribute value, and a steps attribute (which allows extended linking to continue for a certain number of steps beyond the first containing resource):

```
<!ATTLIST group_link
    xml:link         CDATA            #FIXED "group"
    steps            CDATA            #IMPLIED
>
```

Specify an element for the document group:

```
<!ELEMENT paper EMPTY>
<!ATTLIST paper
    xml:link         CDATA            #FIXED "paper"
```

Then, list other attributes by using parameter entities and end the declaration.

For examples of simple, extended, and group link declarations, see Section 4, "Linking Elements," in the W3C's XML Linking Language (XLink) working draft at http://www.w3.org/TR/WD-xlink.

●—NOTE

In the command reference section on the remaining pages of this chapter, default values are underlined. In addition, boldface in examples highlights components of the current production. The superscript number that often appears on the right side of a production name refers you to the production as it appears in the XML specification.

actuate | Traversal Actuation

Purpose

Actuates link traversal with or without a request.

EBNF Syntax

```
"actuate        (auto|user)
```

Where

- auto retrieves the specified linking resource when any resources of that link are encountered.
- user does not retrieve the specified linking resource until the user explicitly asks for it.

Notes

Both the actuate and show attributes specify methods by which the link is traversed.

Link processing applications do not have to be programmed to implement actuate and show in a particular way.

The values of actuate and show can work in tandem.

If the value of actuate is auto, all auto resources must be retrieved and are retrieved in the order in which they were specified.

Example

This declaration, from the XLink working draft, is enclosed in the remote-resource-semantics.att parameter entity:

```
<!ENTITY % remote-resource-semantics.att
  "role        CDATA                #IMPLIED
   title       CDATA                #IMPLIED
   show        (embed|replace|new)  #IMPLIED
   actuate     (auto|user)          #IMPLIED
   behavior    CDATA                #IMPLIED"
>
```

Related Attributes

behavior, content-role, content-title, href, inline, role, show, steps, title, xml:attributes, xml:link

| **3** | **behavior** | **Link Behavior** |

Purpose

Specifies detailed link behavior.

EBNF Syntax

behavior   CDATA

Where

- CDATA represents *character data*; that is, any text that is not markup.

Notes

Use the behavior attribute as the location for instructions for link traversal.

Example

This declaration, from the XLink working draft, is enclosed in the remote-resource-semantics.att parameter entity:

```
<!ENTITY % remote-resource-semantics.att
  "role        CDATA                  #IMPLIED
   title       CDATA                  #IMPLIED
   show        (embed|replace|new)    #IMPLIED
   actuate     (auto|user)            #IMPLIED
   behavior    CDATA                  #IMPLIED"
>
```

Related Attributes

actuate, content-role, content-title, href, inline, role, show, steps, title, xml:attributes, xml:link

Connector [2]

Connector

Purpose

Enters a connector symbol to indicate the method by which a link is retrieved from the resource that contains it.

EBNF Syntax

```
Connector ::= '#' | '|'
```

Standard Syntax

\# | |

Where

- \# indicates that the resource containing the link is to be fetched in its entirety from the host on which it is located, and XPointer processing will take place on the client computer.

- | indicates that you are not giving retrieval or XPointer processing instructions.

Notes

Connector is a component of the Locator production.

Example

The following example uses the # connector to point to (using an ID XPointer) and fetch the complete ID(2489) resource, which is part of the test.xml document at the sample.com Web site:

```
<A xml:link="extended"
    href="http://www.sample.com/test.xml#ID(2489)">
Sample Document</A>
```

Related Productions

Locator, Name (see Chapter 2), URI, XPointer (see Chapter 4)

content-role   Local-Link-Resource Role

Purpose
Specifies the role of a local link resource.

EBNF Syntax

```
content-role   CDATA
```

Where

- CDATA represents *character data*; that is, any text that is not markup.

Notes
You can give a role to either a link resource or an entire link. If you assign a role to an entire link, use the content-role attribute; if you assign a role to a link resource, use the role attribute.

Examples
This example, from the XLink working draft, declares content-role and content-title attributes in a local-resource-semantics.att parameter entity:

```
<ENTITY % local-resource-semantics.att
 "content-role   CDATA           #IMPLIED
  content-title  CDATA           #IMPLIED"
```

This example shows a simple link:

```
<saylink xml:link="simple" title="Work"
    href="http://www.twain.com/xml/dog.xml" show="new"
    content-role="author">Mark Twain</saylink>
```

Related Attributes
actuate, behavior, content-title, href, inline, role, show, steps, title, xml:attributes, xml:link

content-title   Local-Link-Resource Title

Purpose
Specifies the title of a local link resource.

EBNF Syntax

```
content-title  CDATA
```

Where

* CDATA represents character data; that is, any text that is not markup.

Notes
The content-title is a displayed caption for the link.

The content-title attribute is optional.

XLink does not require an application to use a content-title in a particular way.

You can give a title to either a link resource or an entire link. If you give a title to an entire link, use the content-title attribute; if you give a title to a link resource, use the title attribute.

Example
This example, from the XLink working draft, declares content-role and content-title attributes in a local-resource-semantics.att parameter entity:

```
<ENTITY % local-resource-semantics.att
  "content-role   CDATA            #IMPLIED
   content-title  CDATA            #IMPLIED"
```

Related Attributes
actuate, behavior, content-role, href, inline, role, show, steps, title, xml:attributes, xml:link

| **href** | **Remote Resource Locator** |

Purpose

Names a remote resource locator.

EBNF Syntax

```
href     CDATA
```

Where

- CDATA represents character data; that is, any text that is not markup.

Notes

The href attribute shows the target URI and/or extended pointers of the link element.

Examples

This example shows a simple link from the XLink working draft:

```
<A xml:link="simple" href="http://www.w3.org/">The
W3C</A>
```

This example shows a link group and two link declarations:

```
<!ELEMENT GROUP (PAPERS*)>
<!ATTLIST GROUP
        xml:link CDATA #FIXED "GROUP"
        steps    CDATA #IMPLIED
<!ELEMENT PAPERS EMPTY>
<!ATTLIST PAPERS
        xml:link CDATA #FIXED "PAPERS"
        href     CDATA #REQUIRED
>
```

This example shows a simple link:

```
<saylink xml:link="simple" title="Work"
    href="http://www.twain.com/xml/dog.xml" show="new"
    content-role="author">Mark Twain</saylink>
```

This example shows several out-of-line extended links:

```
<tracings xml:link="extended" title="Trace"
  inline="false">
  <locator href="right_wing1.5" role="criticism"/>
  <locator href="left_wing3.1" role="counter"/>
  <locator href="professor8.3" role="analysis"/>
  <locator href="spin_doctor2.2" role="spin"/>
  <locator href="extremist10.12" role="distort"/>
  <locator href="talking_head7.7" role="summarize"/>
</tracings>
```

Related Attributes

actuate, behavior, content-role, content-title, inline,
role, show, steps, title, xml:attributes, xml:link

inline   Inline Link?

Purpose
Identifies an inline or out-of-line link.

EBNF Syntax

```
inline                  (true|false)"
```

Where

- true indicates that the current link is inline. This is the default.
- false indicates that the current link is out-of-line.

Notes
Extended links can be inline or out-of-line.

- An *inline link* is considered to be a local resource of the link. Child elements, however, are not part of the source link itself; they are part of the link.

- An *out-of-line* link specifies the location of the link so that an application can find it; out-of-line links are particularly useful for extended link groups.

Examples

This example, from the XLink working draft, is a declaration, enclosed in a `link-semantics.att` parameter entity:

```
<!ENTITY % link-semantics.att
    "inline          (true|false)        'true'
     role            CDATA               #IMPLIED"
```

This example shows several out-of-line extended links:

```
<tracings xml:link="extended" title="Trace"
  inline="false">
  <locator href="right_wing1.5" role="criticism"/>
  <locator href="left_wing3.1" role="counter"/>
  <locator href="professor8.3" role="analysis"/>
  <locator href="spin_doctor2.2" role="spin"/>
  <locator href="extremist10.12" role="distort"/>
  <locator href="talking_head7.7" role="summarize"/>
</tracings>
```

Related Attributes

actuate, behavior, content-role, content-title, href, role, show, steps, title, xml:attributes, xml:link

---

Locator [1]   Locator

Purpose

Aims a locator at a link resource.

EBNF Syntax

```
Locator ::= URI
          | Connector ( XPointer | Name)
          | URI Connector (XPointer | Name)
```

Standard Syntax

URI [#||[XPointer|[[#xnnnn|[_|:][NameChar]]]]]]

Where

- URI is the absolute or relative address of the resource that contains the link. (See the URI production.) Syntax: [[http:|file:|ftp:|mailto:][//hostname.dom [/filename.xml]]]

- # and | indicate the method by which a link is retrieved from the resource that contains it. (See the Connector production.) Syntax: #||

- XPointer locates partial sections, entire sections, or spans of sections in a containing resource. (See the XPointer production in Chapter 4.) Syntax: AbsTerm.OtherTerms|AbsTerm|OtherTerms

- Name specifies a valid XML name, starting with a letter or underscore character. (See the Name production in Chapter 2.) Syntax: #xnnnn [#xnnnn][_][:][#xnnnn] |[0|1|2|3|4|5|6|7|8|9][.]|[-][#xnnnn] [#xnnnn]...[#xnnnn]

Notes

The best way to locate an extended link is to use its identifier (ID). Then, if the link content changes and the ID does not, you can still locate the link.

If a link does not have an associated ID, you can try to find an ID associated with another section or element. Then, use a relative location term (for example, child or ancestor) to show the relationship between the found ID and the target link. For more information and examples, see the Keyword production in Chapter 4.

Examples

The following example of a simple link locates the test.xml document at the sample.com Web site.

```
<A xml:link="simple"
href="http://www.sample.com/test.xml">
Sample Document</A>
```

The following example of a simple link adds title and content-role attributes that would have been defined in the simple-link element's list of attributes:

```
<A xml:link="simple" title="Test Document"
   href="http://www.sample.com/test.xml"
   content-role="Test 1">
Sample Document</A>
```

The following example of an extended link locates the ID(2489) resource in the test.xml document:

```
<A xml:link="extended"
   href="http://www.sample.com/test.xml#ID(2489)">
   Sample Document</A>
```

Related Productions

Connector, Name (see Chapter 1), URI, XPointer (see Chapter 4)

Query [4]   Query

Purpose
Formulates a query to find an XPointer.

EBNF Syntax

```
Query ::= 'XML-XPTR=' ( XPointer | Name )
```

Standard Syntax

```
XML-XPTR=[XPointer|Name]
```

Where

- XML-XPTR= is a string that indicates that an XML query follows.
- *XPointer* locates partial sections, entire sections, or spans of sections in a containing resource. (See the XPointer production in Chapter 4). Syntax:
  AbsTerm.OtherTerms|AbsTerm|OtherTerms

- *Name* specifies a valid XML name, starting with a letter or underscore character. (See the Name production in Chapter 2.) Syntax: #x*nnnn* [#x*nnnn*][_][:][#x*nnnn*] | [0|1|2|3|4|5|6|7|8|9][.]|[-][#x*nnnn*] [#x*nnnn*]...[#x*nnnn*]

Note

The Query production replaces the ? connector.

Example

The following example of an extended link includes a query for the ID(2489) resource in the test.xml document:

```
<A xml:link="extended"
    href="http://www.sample.com/test.xml
    XML-XPTR=ID(2489)">Sample Document</A>
```

Related Productions

Name (see Chapter 2), URI, XPointer (see Chapter 4)

role	Remote-Link-Resource Role

Purpose

Specifies the role of a remote link resource.

EBNF Syntax

```
role        CDATA
```

Where

- CDATA represents character data; that is, any text that is not markup.

Notes

The role attribute is a string that specifies the meaning of a link — the author, creation or edit date, comments, and even documentation of the link, for those who will edit the link in the future.

You can give a role to either a link resource or an entire link. If you assign a role to an entire link, use the content-role attribute; if you assign a role to a link resource, use the role attribute.

Examples

This example, from the XLink working draft, is a declaration, enclosed in a link-semantics.att parameter entity:

```
<!ENTITY % link-semantics.att
  "inline        (true|false)      'true'
   role          CDATA             #IMPLIED"
```

This declaration, from the XLink working draft, is enclosed in the remote-resource-semantics.att parameter entity:

```
<!ENTITY % remote-resource-semantics.att
  "role      CDATA              #IMPLIED
   title     CDATA              #IMPLIED
   show      (embed|replace|new) #IMPLIED
   actuate   (auto|user)        #IMPLIED
   behavior  CDATA              #IMPLIED"
>
```

This example shows several out-of-line extended links:

```
<tracings xml:link="extended" title="Trace"
   inline="false">
   <locator href="right_wing1.5" role="criticism"/>
   <locator href="left_wing3.1" role="counter"/>
   <locator href="professor8.3" role="analysis"/>
   <locator href="spin_doctor2.2" role="spin"/>
   <locator href="extremist10.12" role="distort"/>
   <locator href="talking_head7.7" role="summarize"/>
</tracings>
```

Related Attributes

actuate, behavior, content-role, content-title, href, inline, show, steps, title, xml:attributes, xml:link

show	Show Link Resource?

Purpose

Shows whether a link resource is displayed or processed.

EBNF Syntax

```
show            (embed|replace|new)
```

Where

- embed embeds the new link resource in the current resource at the location at which traversal originated.
- replace replaces the current resource with the new link resource at the location at which traversal originated.
- new creates a new link resource without replacing the current resource.

Notes

Both the show and actuate attributes specify methods by which the link is traversed.

Link processing applications do not have to be programmed in a particular way to implement actuate and show.

The values of actuate and show can work in tandem.

Examples

This declaration, from the XLink working draft, is enclosed in the remote-resource-semantics.att parameter entity:

```
<!ENTITY % remote-resource-semantics.att
    "role       CDATA               #IMPLIED
    title       CDATA               #IMPLIED
    show        (embed|replace|new) #IMPLIED
    actuate     (auto|user)         #IMPLIED
    behavior    CDATA               #IMPLIED"
>
```

This example illustrates a simple link:

```
<saylink xml:link="simple" title="Work"
    href="http://www.twain.com/xml/dog.xml" show="new"
    content-role="author">Mark Twain</saylink>
```

3

Related Attributes

actuate, behavior, content-role, content-title, href,
inline, role, steps, title, xml:attributes, xml:link

steps	Extended Link Group Steps

Purpose

Specifies the number of steps that extended link group processing
continues through other groups.

EBNF Syntax

```
steps    CDATA
```

Where

- CDATA represents character data; that is, any text that is not
  markup.

Notes

Use the steps attribute to specify the number of extended
link groups to process before coming to an end. If you do not
specify a number of steps, too many extended link groups may
be processed — especially in the case of a large set of complex
XML documents.

Example

This example shows a link group and two link declarations:

```
<!ELEMENT GROUP (PAPERS*)>
<!ATTLIST GROUP
        xml:link CDATA #FIXED "GROUP"
```

```
                steps     CDATA #IMPLIED
<!ELEMENT PAPERS EMPTY>
<!ATTLIST PAPERS
            xml:link CDATA #FIXED "PAPERS"
            href     CDATA #REQUIRED
>
```

Related Attributes

actuate, behavior, content-role, content-title, href, inline, role, show, title, xml:attributes, xml:link

---

title	Remote-Link-Resource Title

Purpose

Specifies the title of a remote link resource.

EBNF Syntax

```
title         CDATA
```

Where

- CDATA represents character data; that is, any text that is not markup.

Notes

The title is a displayed caption for the link.

The title attribute is optional.

You can give a title to either a link resource or an entire link. If you give a title to an entire link, use the content-title attribute; if you give a title to a link resource, use the title attribute.

XLink does not require an application to use a title in a particular way.

Examples

This declaration, from the XLink working draft, is enclosed in the remote-resource-semantics.att parameter entity:

```
<!ENTITY % remote-resource-semantics.att
   "role           CDATA                    #IMPLIED
    title          CDATA                    #IMPLIED
    show           (embed|replace|new)      #IMPLIED
    actuate        (auto|user)              #IMPLIED
    behavior       CDATA                    #IMPLIED"
>
```

This example shows several out-of-line extended links:

```
<tracings xml:link="extended" title="Trace"
   inline="false">
   <locator href="right_wing1.5" role="criticism"/>
   <locator href="left_wing3.1" role="counter"/>
   <locator href="professor8.3" role="analysis"/>
   <locator href="spin_doctor2.2" role="spin"/>
   <locator href="extremist10.12" role="distort"/>
   <locator href="talking_head7.7" role="summarize"/>
</tracings>
```

Related Attributes

actuate, behavior, content-role, content-title, href, inline, role, show, steps, xml:attributes, xml:link

---

URI [3]   Uniform Resource
                                               Identifier

Purpose

Specifies the Uniform Resource Identifier (URI) of the resource that contains the link.

EBNF Syntax

```
URI ::= URIchar*
```

Standard Syntax

```
[URIchar][URIchar]...[URIchar]
```

Where

- *URIchar* represents the characters that make up an Internet address. Syntax: [[http:|file:|ftp: |mailto:][//*hostname.dom*[/*filename*.xml]]]

Notes

URI is a component of the Locator production.

A URI is the Internet address of a link.

The URI is either a URL (an absolute link) or a partial address (a relative link).

A Uniform Resource Locator (URL) is an Internet address composed of the protocol type (such as http:, ftp:, gopher:, mailto:, and so on), the name of the server to be contacted (such as www.w3.org), the folders or directories (such as /pub/WWW/Provider/), and the optional filename (for example, contents.xml or index.xml).

If the URI is not included, the document from which you are linking is considered to be the containing resource.

Examples

The following example of an extended link locates the ID(2489) resource in the test.xml document by using a URL:

```
<A xml:link="extended"
    href="http://www.sample.com/test.xml#ID(2489)">
Sample Document</A>
```

The following example of an extended link locates the ID(sect-01) resource in the test.xml document by using a partial address at the current site:

```
<A xml:link="extended" href="test.xml#ID(sect_01)">
Sample Document</A>
```

Related Productions

Connector, Locator, Name (see Chapter 2), XPointer (see Chapter 4)

xml:attributes	Attribute Names Map

3

Purpose

Maps user-chosen attribute names for a linking element.

EBNF Syntax

```
xml:attributes    CDATA
```

Where

- CDATA represents character data; that is, any text that is not markup.

Notes

Use xml:attributes to rename attributes (actuate, behavior, content-role, content-title, href, inline, role, show, steps, title) that are not unique.

The xml:attributes attribute must contain one or more pairs, each of which contains the original attribute name and the new name.

Example

This example, from the XLink working draft, shows a declaration that remaps title to xl-title and role to xl-role:

```
<!ATTLIST TEXT-BOOK
  xml:link        CDATA    #FIXED    "simple"
  xml:attributes  CDATA
                  #FIXED "title xl-title role xl-role"
```

Related Attributes

actuate, behavior, content-role, content-title, href, inline, role, show, steps, title, xml:link

xml:link   XLink Link Processing

Purpose

Processes one or more XLink linking elements that follow.

Standard Syntax

```
xml:link="simple" | "extended" | "locator" | "group"
    | "document"
```

Where

- simple indicates that a simple link follows.
- extended indicates that an extended link follows.
- locator indicates that a location term follows.
- group indicates that a linked group of documents follows.
- document indicates that an extended link document element follows.

Notes

Use xml:link to indicate that an XLink link follows.

A simple link has just one locator, included in the linking element.

An out-of-line simple link is valid; it is known as a *one-ended* link.

You can include any (use the ANY value) type of content in a link. However, the document must conform to its DTD.

Use an extended link group to accumulate a list of related links. Use an extended link document element to specify each document in the list.

To specify an extended link group, use the value group; to specify an extended link document element, use the value document.

You can express a link in two ways: either within a start tag and an end tag (see the first example) or as a declaration (see the second example).

Examples

The following example shows a simple link from the XLink working draft.

```
<A xml:link="simple" href="http://www.w3.org/">The
W3C</A>
```

This example shows a simple link declaration from the XLink working draft:

```
<!ATTLIST A xml:link CDATA #FIXED "simple">
```

This example shows a link group and two link declarations:

```
<!ELEMENT GROUP (PAPERS*)>
<!ATTLIST GROUP
          xml:link CDATA #FIXED "GROUP"
          steps    CDATA #IMPLIED
<!ELEMENT PAPERS EMPTY>
<!ATTLIST PAPERS
          xml:link CDATA #FIXED "PAPERS"
          href     CDATA #REQUIRED
>
```

This example shows a simple link:

```
<saylink xml:link="simple" title="Work"
   href="http://www.twain.com/xml/dog.xml" show="new"
   content-role="author">Mark Twain</saylink>
```

This example shows several out-of-line extended links:

```
<tracings xml:link="extended" title="Trace"
   inline="false">
   <locator href="right_wing1.5" role="criticism"/>
   <locator href="left_wing3.1" role="counter"/>
   <locator href="professor8.3" role="analysis"/>
   <locator href="spin_doctor2.2" role="spin"/>
   <locator href="extremist10.12" role="distort"/>
   <locator href="talking_head7.7" role="summarize"/>
</tracings>
```

Related Attributes

actuate, behavior, content-role, content-title, href, inline, role, show, steps, title, xml:attributes

XPointer Language

The *productions* (that is, XML instructions or components comprising instructions) in this chapter enable
you to create XPointers (extended pointers), which pinpoint
the location of XLink hyperlinks. XML supports two types
of links: *simple* and *extended*. Simple links are analogous to
HTML links, and extended links allow you to jump from
any link to any other link. Within extended links, you can
use XPointers to refine a location even further. For example,
you can find the seventh child of the third child of the fifth
element. XPointers use a series of location terms to point to
a particular link. A *location term* simply refers to a location
in a document. The first location term in an XPointer is usually absolute; then, you can follow with any combination of
absolute, relative, and string-match.

AbsTerm [4]   Absolute Location Term

4

Purpose

Specifies an absolute location term.

EBNF Syntax

```
AbsTerm ::= 'root()' | 'origin()' | IdLoc | HTMLAddr
```

Standard Syntax

root() | *origin()* | *IdLoc* | *HTMLAddr*

Where

- root() names the root folder or directory, the containing resource's highest level folder (analogous to the **c:** folder on a Windows computer). This is the default.

- origin() names the resource or document from which the link originated.

- IdLoc is a named identifier (ID) location within the containing resource. (See the IdLoc production.) Syntax: id(*Name*)

- HTMLAddr specifies an absolute HTML address for the containing resource. (See the HTMLAddr production.) Syntax: html([*SkipLit*])

Notes

The AbsTerm component is a subelement of the XPointer production.

An absolute location term allows you to set a specific starting point for a containing resource. Then, you can add relative and string-match location terms to further refine the link location.

If an XPointer does not start with an absolute location term (an `AbsTerm`), the root folder (`root()`) is the starting term.

If no location source exists, you can use an absolute location term and the `root`, `origin`, `id`, and `HTMLAddr` keywords to establish a location source.

The keywords `root()` and `origin()` have empty argument lists to set them apart from identifiers called `root` or `origin`.

In earlier versions of the XPointer language, the `origin()` location term was called `here()`.

Do not use the `origin()` location term in conjunction with a URI for a different containing resource.

You can use `origin()` to go to a particular page from the current document without using a formal name. For example, within an online book, you can go to "the following section," "the index," or "the title page."

You can use an XPointer to access an ID whose name remains the same but whose content has changed.

Examples

The following example uses an `ID` XPointer to fetch the complete `ID(2489)` resource, which is part of the `test.xml` document at the `sample.com` Web site:

```
<A xml:link="extended"
    href="http://www.sample.com/test.xml#ID(2489)">
Sample Document</A>
```

The following example of an extended link locates the `ID(sect-01)` resource in the `test.xml` document by using a partial address at the current site:

```
<A xml:link="extended" href="test.xml#ID(sect_01)">
Sample Document</A>
```

The following example starts at the root and traverses through subdirectories until it reaches the second instance of the `RECIPE` element:

```
root().descendant(2,"RECIPE")
```

The following example jumps to the Code section:

```
html(Code)
```

Related Productions

AttrTerm, HTMLAddr, IdLoc, OtherTerm, OtherTerms, RelTerm, SpanTerm, StringTerm, XPointer

<table><tr><td>**Arguments** [9]</td><td>**Arguments**</td></tr></table>

4

Purpose

Passes arguments to a keyword about the relative location of an element to be selected.

EBNF Syntax

```
Arguments ::= '(' InstanceOrAll
              (',' NodeType
              (',' Attr ',' Val)*)? ')'
```

Standard Syntax

```
(InstanceOrAll[,NodeType[,Attr,Val[,Attr,Val
   [,...Attr, Val]]]])
```

Where

- (marks the start of the arguments list.
- InstanceOrAll selects all instances or one instance of a targeted element or subelement. (See the InstanceOrAll production.) Syntax: all|Instance
- , is a character that separates arguments in locator terms.
- NodeType identifies a specific node type or number. (See the NodeType production.) Syntax: Name|#element|#pi|#comment|#text|#cdata|#all
- Attr names an attribute to control the selection of an element. (See the Attr production.) Syntax: *|Name
- Val specifies an attribute value on which to base an element selection. (See the Val production.) Syntax: #IMPLIED|*|Name|[SkipLit]
-) marks the end of the arguments list.

Notes

Arguments is a component of the RelTerm production.

All relative location terms operate using the same set of potential arguments.

Use the Attr production as an argument to select a particular attribute name within the location source.

Use the Val production as an argument to select a particular attribute value within the location source.

If you specify that NodeType be #all, matches may be contiguous or noncontiguous nodes.

Examples

The following examples choose the second child of an element for which the attribute BIRD has a value of 5:

```
child(2,#element,BIRD,5)
child(2,#element,"BIRD",5)
```

Related Productions

Attr, InstanceOrAll, NodeType, RelTerm, Val

Attr [13]   Attribute

Purpose

Names an attribute to control the selection of an element.

EBNF Syntax

```
Attr ::= '*'  |  Name
```

Standard Syntax

$*\ |\ [\ "\ |\ '\ ]\mathit{Name}[\ "\ |\ '\ ]$

Where

- * is a wildcard representing any attribute name.

- Name specifies a valid XML name, starting with a letter or underscore character. (See the Name production in Chapter 2.) Syntax: #x*nnnn* [#x*nnnn*][_][:][#x*nnnn*] |[0|1|2|3|4|5|6|7|8|9][.]|[-][#x*nnnn*] [#x*nnnn*]...[#x*nnnn*]

Notes

Attr is a component of the Arguments production.

The Attr production is not the same as the attr keyword.

Use the Attr production as an argument to find a particular attribute name within the location source.

If an attribute name is enclosed within quotes, Attr is case-sensitive; if an attribute name is not enclosed within quotes, Attr is case-insensitive.

Do not mix single quotes and double quotes; quotes at the beginning and end of a name must match.

A specific attribute name is preferable to the * wildcard. The wildcard is appropriate only when you are searching for a particular attribute value but not an attribute name.

If a particular node does not have an attribute name, no selection will be made.

Example

The following example chooses the second child of an element for which the attribute BIRD has a value of 5:

```
child(2,#element,BIRD,5)
```

Related Production

Arguments

AttrTerm [16]

Attribute-Match Location Term

Purpose

Defines an attribute-match location term.

EBNF Syntax

```
AttrTerm ::= 'attr(' Name ')'
```

Standard Syntax

```
attr(Name)
```

Where

- `attr(` is a string that marks the beginning of the location term.
- `Name` specifies a valid XML name, starting with a letter or underscore character. (See the `Name` production in Chapter 2.) Syntax: #x*nnnn* [#x*nnnn*][_][:][#x*nnnn*] |[0|1|2|3|4|5|6|7|8|9][.]|[-][#x*nnnn*] [#x*nnnn*]...[#x*nnnn*]
- `)` marks the end of the location term.

Notes

`AttrTerm` is a component of the `OtherTerm` production.

An attribute-match location term searches for an attribute name and returns the value of the attribute.

Example

The following example specifics the BIRD attribute:

```
attr(BIRD)
```

Related Productions

`AbsTerm`, `OtherTerm`, `OtherTerms`, `RelTerm`, `SpanTerm`, `StringTerm`, `XPointer`

HTMLAddr [6]   Absolute HTML Address

Purpose

Specifies an absolute HTML address.

EBNF Syntax

```
HTMLAddr ::= 'html(' SkipLit ')'
```

Standard Syntax

```
html([SkipLit])
```

Where

- html(is a string that marks the beginning of the location term.
- SkipLit is a string matching the NAME attribute of an HTML <A> element.
-) marks the end of the location term.

Notes

HTMLAddr is a component of the AbsTerm production.

HTMLAddr is analogous to HTML's # identifier (for example, <A HREF="#A">), which points to an anchor that is the target of a link.

Example

The following example looks for the first A-type element for which its NAME attribute has a value of WIDGET:

HTMLAddr(WIDGET)

Related Productions

AbsTerm, IdLoc, Name (see Chapter 2)

IdLoc [5]   Identifier Location

Purpose

Identifies an element by a particular identifier (ID).

EBNF Syntax

```
IdLoc ::= 'id(' Name ')'
```

Standard Syntax

```
id(Name)
```

Where

- id(is a string that marks the beginning of the location term.
- Name specifies a valid XML name, starting with a letter or underscore character. (See the Name production in Chapter 2.) Syntax: #x*nnnn* [#x*nnnn*][_][:][#x*nnnn*] |[0|1|2|3|4|5|6|7|8|9][.]|[-][#x*nnnn*] [#x*nnnn*]...[#x*nnnn*]
-) marks the end of the location term.

Notes

IdLoc is a component of the AbsTerm production.

IdLoc specifies an element with the ID type and with a particular name.

Examples

The following example fetches the complete ID(2489) resource, which is part of the test.xml document at the sample.com Web site:

```
<A xml:link="extended"
href="http://www.sample.com/test.xml#ID(2489)">
Sample Document</A>
```

The following example of an extended link locates the ID(sect-01) resource in the test.xml document:

```
<A xml:link="extended" href="test.xml#ID(sect_01)">
Sample Document</A>
```

Related Productions

AbsTerm, HTMLAddr, Name (see Chapter 2)

Instance [11]   Instance Number

Purpose

Inserts an instance, or occurrence, number.

EBNF Syntax

```
Instance ::= ('+' | '-')? [1-9] Digit*
```

Standard Syntax

[+|-][1-9]|[*Digit*[*Digit*[...*Digit*]]]

Where

- + is a character that indicates a positive number.
- - is a character that indicates a negative number.
- 1-9 represents a number from 1 to 9.
- Digit represents a digit supported by the Unicode Organization. (See the Digit production and Appendix A, *Unicode Characters and Character Sets.*) Syntax: #xnnnn

Notes

Instance is a component of the InstanceOrAll production.

Instance is a positive or negative occurrence number of an element or node. A positive instance number specifies a particular instance starting from the first time it occurs in the containing resource. A negative instance number specifies a particular instance starting from the last time it occurs in the containing resource.

Examples

The following example chooses the second child of an element for which the attribute BIRD has a value of 5:

```
child(2,#element,BIRD,5)
```

The following example selects the next-to-last following sibling of an element for which the attribute LAST has any value:

```
fsibling(-2,#element,"LAST",#IMPLIED)
```

Related Productions

Digit, InstanceOrAll

InstanceOrAll [10]

One Instance or All Instances

Purpose

Selects all instances or one instance of a targeted element or subelement.

EBNF Syntax

```
InstanceOrAll ::= 'all' | Instance
```

Standard Syntax

```
all | Instance
```

Where

- all selects all instances of the specified element or subelement.

- Instance specifies a relative or absolute instance, or occurrence, number of an element or subelement. (See the Instance production.) Syntax:
  `[+|-][1-9]|[Digit[Digit[...Digit]]]`

Notes

InstanceOrAll is a component of the Arguments and StringTerm productions.

The Instance production is a positive or negative occurrence number of an element or node. A positive instance number specifies a particular instance starting from the first time it occurs in the containing resource. A negative instance number specifies a particular instance starting from the last time it occurs in the containing resource.

If the value of Instance is less than or greater than the actual number of occurrences in the containing resource, the result is an error.

If you specify a value of All, matches may be contiguous or noncontiguous elements or nodes.

Example

The following example fetches all MIX elements that descend from the ID(2489) resource:

```
<A xml:link="extended"
href="http://www.sample.com/test.xml
#ID(2489).descendant(all,mix)">
Sample Document</A>
```

Related Productions

Arguments, Digit, Instance, Length, Position, StringTerm

4

Keyword [8]	Keyword

Purpose

Names a keyword indicating the relative location of an element to be selected.

EBNF Syntax

```
Keyword ::= 'child' | 'descendant' | 'ancestor'
          | 'preceding'| 'following' | 'psibling'
          | 'fsibling'
```

Standard Syntax

```
child|descendant|ancestor|preceding|following
    |psibling|fsibling
```

Where

- child is a successor to a particular location source.
- descendant is a child, grandchild, or other offspring of a particular location source.
- ancestor is a parent, grandparent, or other forebear of a particular location source.

- `preceding` is any element, related or not, processed properly before a particular location source is processed.

- `following` is any element, related or not, processed properly after a particular location source is processed.

- `psibling` is any element having the same parent as a particular location source and processed properly before the named location source is processed.

- `fsibling` is any element having the same parent as a particular location source and processed properly after the named location source is processed.

Notes

Keyword is a component of the `RelTerm` production.

If Keyword is not included in the `RelTerm` statement, the XPointer searches for the previously specified keyword. To avoid errors in XPointers, at least one Keyword must be included in an XML document having XPointers.

The ancestor of all other ancestors is known as the *outermost element* or *document element*.

When specifying a `child` keyword, naming an ID as well is a good idea. Using an ID allows the XPointer to start at a specific part of the location source whose content may or may not have been edited. If the ID name remains the same, the link will be valid; the content associated with the ID doesn't have an effect on the link.

The `descendant` keyword searches at a shallow level through all first-level offspring after the particular location source. This type of search is known as a *depth-first traversal*.

Use the `following` keyword to search through all elements following the particular location source, regardless of a parent relationship. Use the `fsibling` keyword to search through all elements following the particular location source and having the same parent.

Examples

The following example chooses the second child of an element for which the attribute BIRD has a value of 5:

```
child(2,#element,BIRD,5)
```

The following example selects the first text block within the first descendant:

```
descendant(2,#text)
```

The following example selects the next-to-last following sibling of an element for which the attribute LAST has any value:

```
fsibling(-2,#element,"LAST",#IMPLIED)
```

Related Productions

Arguments, RelTerm

Length [19]   Characters Length

Purpose

Sets the number of characters in a string to be selected.

EBNF Syntax

```
Length ::= [1-9] Digit*
```

Standard Syntax

```
[1-9][Digit[Digit[...Digit]]]
```

Where

- 1-9 represents a number from 1 to 9.
- Digit represents a digit supported by the Unicode Organization. (See the Digit production and Appendix A, *Unicode Characters and Character Sets*.) Syntax: #xnnnn

Notes

Length is a component of the StringTerm production.

If Length is equal to zero or is omitted altogether, the XPointer points to a location immediately preceding the character specified by the Position production.

Example

The following example selects the fourth dollar sign and five characters or spaces immediately following it:

```
id(chap1).string(4,'$',1,5)
```

Related Productions

```
Digit, InstanceOrAll, Position, StringTerm
```

NodeType [12]   Node Type   4

Purpose

Identifies a specific node type or number.

EBNF Syntax

```
NodeType ::= Name  |  '#element'  |  '#pi'  |  '#comment'
            |  '#text'  |  '#cdata'  |  '#all'
```

Standard Syntax

```
Name|#element|#pi|#comment|#text|#cdata|#all
```

Where

- Name specifies a valid XML name, starting with a letter or underscore character. (See the Name production in Chapter 2.) Syntax: #xnnnn [#xnnnn][_][:][#xnnnn] |[0|1|2|3|4|5|6|7|8|9][.]|[-][#xnnnn] [#xnnnn]...[#xnnnn]
- #element specifies an XML element. This is the default.
- #pi specifies XML processing instructions.
- #comment specifies XML comments.
- #text specifies text within the XML element or CDATA sections.

- #cdata specifies text within CDATA sections.
- #all allows you to specify all node types.

Notes

NodeType is a component of the Arguments production.

The #pi, #comment, #text, and #cdata node types are not affected by limitations (constraints) set within attributes. However, each of these node types allows the use of the StringTerm location term; that is, strings.

The #element node type allows attribute limitations. If attribute limitations are present, the #all node type is identical to the #element type.

The #element node type can contain all other node types.

If you specify #all, matches may be contiguous or noncontiguous nodes.

Examples

The following example chooses the second child of an element for which the attribute BIRD has a value of 5:

```
child(2,#element,BIRD,5)
```

The following example selects the first text block within the first descendant:

```
descendant(2,#text)
```

Related Productions

Arguments, Attr, InstanceOrAll, Val

OtherTerm [3]   Location Term Type

Purpose

Names a type of location term.

EBNF Syntax

```
OtherTerm ::= RelTerm | SpanTerm | AttrTerm |
StringTerm
```

Standard Syntax

`RelTerm | SpanTerm | AttrTerm | StringTerm`

Where

- `RelTerm` specifies a relative location term. (See the `RelTerm` production.) Syntax: `[Keyword] Arguments`
- `SpanTerm` finds a span of XPointers. (See the `SpanTerm` production.) Syntax: `span(XPointer,XPointer)`
- `AttrTerm` defines an attribute-match location term. (See the `AttrTerm` production.) Syntax: `attr(Name)`
- `StringTerm` defines a string-match location term. (See the `StringTerm` production.) Syntax: `string(InstanceOrAll,[SkipLit][,Position[,Length)`

Note

`OtherTerm` is a component of the `OtherTerms` production.

Examples

The following `RelTerm` example chooses the second child of an element for which the attribute `BIRD` has a value of 5:

```
child(2,#element,"BIRD",5)
```

The following `SpanTerm` example chooses a span beginning with the second child of an element for which the attribute `BIRD` has a value of 5 and ending with the next-to-last following sibling of an element for which the attribute `LAST` has any value:

```
span(child(2,#element,BIRD,5),fsibling(-2,#element,
"LAST",#IMPLIED))
```

The following `AttrTerm` example specifies the `BIRD` attribute:

```
attr(BIRD)
```

The following `StringTerm` example selects the fourth position in the second occurrence of the string `Hermione`:

```
root().string(2,"Hermione",4)
```

Related Productions

AbsTerm, AttrTerm, OtherTerms, RelTerm, SpanTerm, StringTerm, XPointer

OtherTerms [2]   Location Terms List

Purpose

Lists one or more other location terms.

EBNF Syntax

OtherTerm | OtherTerm '.' OtherTerm

Standard Syntax

OtherTerm | OtherTerm.OtherTerm

Where

- OtherTerm names a type of location term. (See the OtherTerm production.) Syntax:
  RelTerm | SpanTerm | AttrTerm | StringTerm
- . is a character that separates location terms.

Notes

OtherTerms is a component of the XPointer production.

If an XPointer does not start with an absolute location term (an AbsTerm), the root folder (root()) is the starting location term.

Examples

The following RelTerm example chooses the second child of an element for which the attribute BIRD has a value of 5:

```
child(2,#element,"BIRD",5)
```

The following SpanTerm example chooses a span beginning with the second child of an element for which the attribute BIRD has a value of 5. It ends with the next-to-last following sibling of an element for which the attribute LAST has any value.

```
span(child(2,#element,BIRD,5),fsibling(-2,#element,
"LAST",#IMPLIED)))
```

Related Productions

AbsTerm, AttrTerm, OtherTerm, RelTerm, SpanTerm, StringTerm, XPointer

---

Position [18]   Character Position

Purpose

Offsets a nonmarkup character from the start or end of a string.

EBNF Syntax

```
Position ::= ('+' | '-')? [1-9] Digit* | 'end'
```

Standard Syntax

[+|-][1-9][Digit[Digit[...Digit]]]|end

Where

- + is a character that indicates a positive number. The default is 1.
- - is a character that indicates a negative number.
- 1-9 represents a number from 1 to 9.
- Digit represents a digit supported by the Unicode Organization. (See the Digit production and Appendix A, *Unicode Characters and Character Sets*.) Syntax: #xnnnn
- end is a literal that selects the position following the last character in the match.

Notes

Position is a component of the StringTerm production.

Position cannot be equal to 0.

If Position has a positive value, the count starts to the right of the start of the string in the containing resource and its descendants. If Position has a negative value, the count starts to the left of the end of the string.

The value of Position counts characters and spaces but does not count markup characters or special characters.

Position is case-sensitive.

Examples

The following example selects the fourth position in the second occurrence of the string Hermione:

```
root().string(2,"Hermione",4)
```

The following example selects the fourth dollar sign and five characters or spaces immediately following it:

```
id(chap1).string(4,'$',1,5)
```

Related Productions

Digit, InstanceOrAll, Length, StringTerm

RelTerm [7]   Relative Location Term

Purpose

Specifies a relative location term.

EBNF Syntax

```
RelTerm ::= Keyword? Arguments
```

Standard Syntax

```
[Keyword] Arguments
```

Where

- Keyword names a keyword indicating the relative location of an element to be selected. (See the Keyword production.) Syntax: child|descendant|ancestor|preceding |following|psibling|fsibling

- Arguments passes arguments to a keyword about the relative location of an element to be selected. (See the Arguments production.) Syntax: (*InstanceOrAll*[,*NodeType*[,*Attr*,*Val*[,*Attr*,*Val* [,...*Attr*, *Val*]]]])

Notes

RelTerm is a component of the OtherTerm production.

If an XPointer does not start with an absolute location term (an AbsTerm), the root folder (root()) is the starting term.

Examples

The following example chooses the second child of an element for which the attribute BIRD has a value of 5:

```
child(2,#element,BIRD,5)
```

The following example selects the first text block within the first descendant:

```
descendant(2,#text)
```

The following example selects the next-to-last following sibling of an element for which the attribute LAST has any value:

```
fsibling(-2,#element,"LAST",#IMPLIED)
```

Related Productions

Arguments, Keyword, OtherTerm

SpanTerm [15]   Spanning Location Term

Purpose

Finds a span of XPointers.

EBNF Syntax

SpanTerm ::= 'span(' XPointer ',' XPointer ')'

Standard Syntax

span(*XPointer*,*XPointer*)

Where

- span(is a string that marks the beginning of the location term.
- XPointer locates partial sections, entire sections, or spans of sections in a containing resource. (See the XPointer production.) Syntax: *AbsTerm.OtherTerms* | *AbsTerm* | *OtherTerms*
- , is a character that separates the first and second XPointers.
-) marks the end of the location term.

Notes

SpanTerm is a component of the OtherTerm production.

SpanTerm locates a span from one XPointer to another. Depending on how an application is programmed, SpanTerm may or may not find complete elements. If SpanTerm finds incomplete elements, a document may not qualify as being well-formed.

StringTerm can also find part of a node. StringTerm selects one or more strings or locations between specified strings.

The range of the span starts at the first character of the data specified by the first XPointer and ends at the last character specified by the second XPointer.

Example

The following example chooses a span beginning with the second child of an element for which the attribute BIRD has a value of 5 and ending with the next-to-last following sibling of an element for which the attribute LAST has any value:

span(child(2,#element,BIRD,5),fsibling(-2,#element, "LAST",#IMPLIED)))

Related Productions

OtherTerm, XPointer

StringTerm [17]	**String-Match Location Term**

Purpose

Defines a string-match location term.

EBNF Syntax

```
StringTerm ::= 'string(' InstanceOrAll ','
    SkipLit (',' Position(',' Length)?)?)
```

Standard Syntax

string(*InstanceOrAll*,[*SkipLit*][,*Position*[,*Length*]])

Where

* string(is a string that marks the beginning of the location term.

* InstanceOrAll selects all instances or one instance of a targeted element or subelement. (See the InstanceOrAll production.) Syntax: all|*Instance*

* , is a character that separates arguments in locator terms.

* SkipLit is a string matching the NAME attribute of an HTML <A> element.

* Position is an optional component that offsets a non-markup character from the start or end of a string. (See the Position production.) Syntax:
[+|-][1-9][*Digit*[*Digit*[...*Digit*]]]|end

- Length is an optional component that sets the number of characters in a string. (See the Length production.) Syntax: [1-9][Digit[Digit[...Digit]]]

Notes

StringTerm is a component of the OtherTerm production.

StringTerm can find part of a node. StringTerm selects one or more strings or locations between specified strings.

SpanTerm also locates part of a node. Depending on how an application is programmed, SpanTerm may or may not find complete elements. If SpanTerm finds incomplete elements, a document may not qualify as being well-formed.

If you specify all, matches may be contiguous or noncontiguous nodes.

Examples

The following example selects the fourth position in the second occurrence of the string Hermione:

    root().string(2,"Hermione",4)

The following example selects the fourth dollar sign and five characters or spaces immediately following it:

    id(chap1).string(4,'$',1,5)

Related Productions

    Digit, InstanceOrAll, Length, Position

Val [14]   Attribute Value

Purpose

Specifies an attribute value on which to base an element selection.

EBNF Syntax

    Val ::= '#IMPLIED' | '*' | Name | SkipLit

Standard Syntax

#IMPLIED | * | Name | [SkipLit]

Where

- #IMPLIED indicates that the value is optional and that no default value exists.
- * indicates that any value is valid.
- Name specifies a valid XML name, starting with a letter or underscore character. (See the Name production in Chapter 2.) Syntax: #xnnnn [#xnnnn][_][:][#xnnnn] |[0|1|2|3|4|5|6|7|8|9][.]|[-][#xnnnn] [#xnnnn]...[#xnnnn]
- SkipLit is a string matching the NAME attribute of an HTML <A> element.

Notes

Val is a component of the Arguments production.

Use the Val production as an argument to select a particular attribute value within the location source.

If a particular node does not have an attribute value, no selection will be made.

Examples

The following example chooses the second child of an element for which the attribute BIRD has a value of 5:

child(2,#element,BIRD,5)

The following example selects the next-to-last following sibling of an element for which the attribute LAST has any value:

fsibling(-2,#element,"LAST",#IMPLIED)

Related Productions

Attr, Name (see Chapter 2)

XPointer [1]   XPointers

Purpose

Locates partial sections, entire sections, or spans of sections in a containing resource such as an XML document.

EBNF Syntax

```
XPointer ::= AbsTerm '.' OtherTerms | AbsTerm
                   | OtherTerms
```

Standard Syntax

AbsTerm.OtherTerms | *AbsTerm* | *OtherTerms*

Where

- `AbsTerm` specifies an absolute location term. (See the `AbsTerm` production.) Syntax: *root()* | *origin()* | *IdLoc* | *HTMLAddr*
- `.` is a character that separates location terms.
- `OtherTerms` lists one or more other location terms. (See the `OtherTerms` production.) Syntax: *OtherTerm.OtherTerm*

Notes

XPointer is a component of the `Locator`, `Query`, and `SpanTerm` productions.

An XPointer can search for an absolute or relative location, a span of locations, or one or more strings.

If an XPointer does not start with an absolute location term (an `AbsTerm`), the root folder (`root()`) is the starting term.

An XPointer is usually part of an XLink and is used to refine further a location within a document.

The first locator of a containing resource is usually a Uniform Resource Identifier (URI).

Each location term listed in an XPointer specifies a location by name or value, typically building on and further refining the previous location term in the list.

Example

The following example uses an ID XPointer to fetch the complete ID(2489) resource, which is part of the test.xml document at the sample.com Web site:

```
<A xml:link="extended"
    href="http://www.sample.com/test.xml#ID(2489)">
Sample Document</A>
```

● **NOTE**

You can find other XPointer examples throughout this chapter.

Related Productions

AbsTerm, AttrTerm, OtherTerm, OtherTerms, RelTerm, SpanTerm, StringTerm

Cascading Style Sheets

5

Those of us with long-standing personal computer experience — especially using word processors — are familiar with style sheets, which are used to define *rules* (formats and enhancements) for selected text, paragraphs, or entire documents. After attaching a style sheet, a user can apply a rule to selected text either by choosing that rule from a drop-down list box or pressing a shortcut key or key combination that represents the rule — a considerable shortcut from making several menu or dialog box selections. For example, without a style sheet, if a user wants to change selected text to a centered, 18-point boldface heading with the Helvetica typeface, he or she must make four separate selections from menus or toolbars or, at the very least, open a dialog box and make four choices. However, with a style sheet attached and a particular heading style defined, a user can make the same selections with the press of a single shortcut key or key combination.

● NOTE

All word processing programs have a default style sheet (in Microsoft Word for Windows, the default is called *Normal*), which automatically applies predefined formats to all new documents, their paragraphs, and text. For example, the Normal font in Word for Windows is Times New Roman, and the font size is 10 point. A default paragraph is left-aligned and single-spaced.

A rule is composed of two parts: The *selector* is the element to which the rule applies, and the *declaration* consists of the property and the value. In the example PARA { FONT: 12pt "Century Schoolbook" }, PARA is the selector, FONT is the property, and both 12pt and "Century Schoolbook" are values.

5

● NOTE

In this example, the font-size value is an approximation. For all headings, the font size probably depends on the editor in which you create the heading and the browser with which you view the heading. In fact, many experienced style sheet users recommend using relative, rather than absolute, font sizes. When a user sets an *absolute* font size, he or she specifies an actual size (for example, 12pt; however, when he or she sets a *relative* font size; he or she indicates how much larger or smaller the new size is from the current size.

In addition to text formatting and enhancements, you can use style sheets to set document-wide margins, add white space before and/or after a paragraph, align paragraphs, and much more. A user can instantly change the look of a document by attaching a different style sheet. Or, a user can make a single change in a style sheet to change one format for all the documents to which the style sheet is attached.

In May of 1996, the World Wide Web Consortium (W3C) announced the development of *cascading style sheets* (CSS), which are sets of document style sheets that enable XML (and HTML) developers to change a document's format and look — just as they would change a word processing document. You can attach multiple cascading style sheets to a single document and define several styles for a single element; in general, the style that is closest to a particular element affects that element. Currently, some browsers support style sheets — completely or partially — while many other browsers will support style sheets soon.

The era of cascading style sheets for XML (and HTML) documents is still at its very beginning. Two cascading style sheet standards exist: CSS1 and CSS2. CSS1 was the first standard for cascading style sheets; a simple set of rules to format and enhance text, paragraphs, and documents. CSS2, the current standard, adds to the CSS1 base a set of styles for visual browsers, aural devices, printers, Braille devices, and so on, as well as styles for table layout, internationalization features, and more. Because most browsers still do not support CSS2, using CSS1 presently is the best choice; this chapter features CSS1 properties. For information about the differences between CSS1 and CSS2, see Appendix B, *XML Editors and Utilities* in the Cascading Style Sheets, Level 2 CSS2 Specification (http://www.w3.org/TR/REC-CSS2/).

In this and the following chapters, you'll learn about two style sheet languages: CSS and DSSSL Online, which is a subset of the Document Style Semantics and Specification Language (DSSSL). Also currently under development is the XML Stylesheet Language (XSL), which uses XML-like documents and elements to style XML documents.

The *Webliography* to this book includes the section "Style Sheets," a list of online resources for a variety of style sheet languages: DSSSL, DSSSL-O, CSS1, CSS2, and XSL. In addition, you can find up-to-date reference material and links to other style sheet resources at the W3C site (http://www.w3c.org/).

The Advantages of Using Style Sheets

By attaching a single style sheet to all of its XML documents, a business can ensure an identical format for an entire document and its elements — using the same colors, fonts, font sizes, white space, indentations, line spacing, and margins. Professional page designers can distribute style sheet templates that include predefined table, heading, and body-text formats and alignments, text enhancements, and page background colors. Then, an XML developer can attach the template to a document and work only on the document's content — the formats and enhancements are already set by the template.

Viewers of this XML output can choose from alternative rules by clicking one of several links. For example, a visually impaired visitor can attach a style sheet that has large point sizes or, in a future CSS standard, attach a style sheet that has the capability to pronounce the document's words through a computer sound system. Or, visitors can attach style sheets that apply various colors to page and table backgrounds, as well as fonts, point sizes, and enhancements to text. Before printing a document, a user can choose a completely different "printing-optimization" style sheet. Users can design and create their own style sheets.

> Developers of XML documents should try to design style sheets that clash as little as possible with user-created style sheets and should realize that many browsers do not support style sheets. You should look at your documents with and without style sheets attached, to make sure that they look okay either way.

A style sheet enables an XML developer to define formats universally for all identical elements in a document. For example, all top-level headings should always look the same, and lower-level headings should vary so that each descending level has a gradually reduced point size and changed enhancements (such as using varying combinations of boldface, italics, and bold italics) to further differentiate among heading levels. Using a style sheet, a writer can change the font, font size, and color of all level-one headings by using a single style rule. Without a style sheet, a writer can either use the default styles or redefine the look of every instance of a level-one heading.

Specifying Styles

Specifying a style for an element is quite easy: Simply associate one or more rules with the element. An example of a paragraph (PARA) style follows:

```
PARA { color: red; font-family: Arial, "Century
Gothic", sans-serif;
font-style: italic }
```

or

```
PARA {
    color: red;
    font-family: Arial, "Century Gothic", sans-serif;
    font-style: italic
}
```

This set of properties specifies that all text in the paragraph is red, is either Arial, Century Gothic, or another sans serif typeface (depending on the fonts installed on the computer), and is italic. Because no point size (`font-size`) is specified, the browser uses the default size.

● **NOTE**

When a string consists of two words (for example, Century Gothic) or includes punctuation, enclose the string within quotation marks (for example, "Century Gothic").

If you want to use the same rules for several elements, you can list the elements and the rules that apply to them. Perhaps the most common use for this feature is to apply the same color to all heading levels in a document:

```
HEAD1, HEAD2, HEAD3, HEAD4 { color: red }
```

You can also define properties for elements that are embedded within other elements. The following example shows an HTML list item (LI) within an ordered list (OL):

```
OL LI { font-style: Arial; font-size: small }
```

● **NOTE**

Notice that similar elements, such as heading levels, are separated by commas, while dissimilar elements, such as OL and LI, are separated by a space.

If you want to add comments to a style sheet, enclose them within */; for example:

```
UL { font-weight: demi-bold } */ All unordered lists */
```

A cascading style sheet that is to be associated with an XML document is a document type declaration (DTD) with a special document type:

```
<!doctype style-sheet
    PUBLIC "-//A. Author//DTD  CSS Style Sheet//EN">
```

In the style sheet document, define elements and include rules to specify styles.

Associating a Cascading Style Sheet with an XML Document

You associate one or more style sheets with an XML document in the same way that you use the LINK element to associate an external style sheet document in an HTML document. Simply embed xml:style sheet or xml:alternate-style sheet processing instructions (PI) anywhere within the XML document prolog, using the following syntax:

```
<?xml:style sheet|alternate-style sheet
    href={"|'}stylename.css{"|'}
    type={"|'}text/css{"|'}[charset={"|'}charset{"|'}]
    [media={"|'}media{"|'}]
[ title={"|'}doctitle{"|'}]?>
```

where:

- style sheet is a keyword indicating that the attached document is a style sheet.
- alternate-style sheet is a keyword indicating that the attached document is an alternate style sheet.
- href spccifies a URI for a link to the external style sheet document.
- type specifies a type name of the link, for information within the current document.
- charset names the source of the character set of the data referred to by the href attribute.
- media indicates the type of destination.
- title specifies a title name of the external style sheet document.

For example:

```
<?xml:style sheet href="styler.css" type="text/css"?>
```

●—NOTE————————————————————————

For information about using xml:style sheet and xml:alternate style sheet, see their entries in Chapter 2, *XML Syntax*.

CSS in Plain English

Sometimes, connecting the name of a particular CSS property to its purpose is puzzling. So, Table 5-1 might help those of you who know the task that you want to perform but can't remember the property name. The left column of Table 5-1 is a list of tasks, alphabetized by italicized action words; the right column is a list of properties. Once you match a particular task with a property, you can apply the appropriate style.

Table 5-1   *CSS Properties*

If You Want to:	Use This Property:
set *all border colors*	border-color
set *all border properties*	border
set *all border styles*	border-style
control *all border widths*	border-width
set *all font properties*	font
set *all font styles*	font-style
control *all list properties*	list-style
control or size *all margins*	margin
control or size *all padding*	padding
attach or scroll the background image	background-attachment
specify the *background color*	background-color
specify a *background image*	background-image
set the *background image position*	background-position
specify *background properties*	background
set *bottom-border properties*	border-bottom
set the *bottom-border width*	border-bottom-width
control or size the *bottom margin*	margin-bottom
control or size the *bottom padding*	padding-bottom
change the *case of text*	text-transform
specify *character spacing*	letter-spacing

Continued

Continued

Table 5-1 *Continued*

If You Want to:	Use This Property:
decorate or blink text lines	text-decoration
display an element inline or in a box	display
style the *first letter* of a paragraph with a pseudo-element	first-letter
style the *first line* of a paragraph with a pseudo-element	first-line
float an element below an element	clear
float an element right or left	float
select a *font family* or name	font-family
set the *font size*	font-size
set a small-cap *font variant*	font-variant
set bold or light *font weight*	font-weight
specify the *foreground color*	color
specify element *height*	height
set *horizontal alignment* of text	text-align
identify an *important* statement	important
indent the first line	text-indent
set *left-border properties*	border-left
set *left-border width*	border-left-width
control or size the *left margin*	margin-left
control or size the *left padding*	padding-left
set *line height*	line-height
set a *list-item image* type	list-style-image
specify a *list's position*	list-style-position
set a *list number or bullet type*	list-style-type
repeat a background image	background-repeat
set *right-border properties*	border-right
set *right-border width*	border-right-width

If You Want to:	Use This Property:
control or size the *right margin*	margin-right
control or size the *right padding*	padding-right
set *spacing between words*	word-spacing
set *top-border properties*	border-top
set *top-border width*	border-top-width
control or size the *top margin*	margin-top
control or size the *top padding*	padding-top
set the *vertical alignment*	vertical-align
control *white space*	white-space
set an element's *width*	width

Style Sheet Properties

This section is comprised of properties that are currently documented for cascading style sheets. Each entry includes the syntax, a brief description, notes, and examples. To obtain up-to-date information from sites on the World Wide Web, refer to the resources in the "Style Sheets" section of the *Webliography*.

background   Background Properties

Purpose

Specifies up to five properties for the page background.

Syntax

```
background: { background-attachment_value
    | background-color_value
    | background-image_value| background-position_value
    | background-repeat_value }
```

Where

- *background-attachment_value* specifies the font size. For more information, see the background-attachment property.
- *background-color_value* specifies the font family. For more information, see the background-color property.
- *background-image_value* specifies the font style. For more information, see the background-image property.
- *background-position_value* specifies the font variant. For more information, see the background-position property.
- *background-repeat_value* specifies the font weight. For more information, see the background-repeat property.

Notes

This property specifies multiple properties for backgrounds in the same way that you can individually set rules for the background-attachment, background-color, background-image, background-position, and background-repeat properties.

You do not need to specify the property name. The browser should interpret the unique values for each property.

Table 5-2 contains selected hexadecimal color values.

The characteristics of this property are not inherited.

Example

```
P.image {background: url(pattern.gif) silver repeat
fixed }
```

Table 5-2 *Selected Colors and Their Hexadecimal Values*

Color	Hexadecimal Value
black	#000000
bright cyan	#00FFFF
bright fuchsia	#FF00FF
bright medium-yellow	#FFFF00
dark blue	#0000AA

Color	Hexadecimal Value
dark blue-green	#006666
dark gray	#808080
dark lime-green	#00AA00
dark purple	#880088
dark red	#AA0000
gray-white	#DDDDDD
light rose	#FFB6C1
medium blue	#0000CC
medium cyan	#00CCCC
medium fuchsia	#CC00CC
medium gold	#FFFFAA
medium gold-green	#CCCC00
medium gray	#999999
medium dull-green	#22AA22
medium lime-green	#00CC00
medium peach	#FAAAAC
medium red	#CC0000
medium rose	#FFADDA
navy blue	#0000FF
off-white 1	#F0F7F7
off-white 2	#FFFFF2
off-white 3	#F0F0F0
orange-red	#FF6347
pale blue	#AAADEA
pale cyan	#C0FFEE
pale gold	#FFFFCC
pale green	#ADEADA
pale green-gray	#AADEAD

Continued

Table 5-2 *Continued*

Color	Hexadecimal Value
pale purple	#ADAADA
pumpkin	#FF8127
reddish brown	#550000
strong blue	#0000FF
strong lime-green	#00FF00
strong red	#FF0000
white	#FFFFFF

5

background-attachment	Attach Background Image

Purpose

Specifies whether the background image is fixed or scrolls in the background of the page.

Syntax

```
background-attachment:{ scroll|fixed }
```

Where

- `scroll` scrolls a background image as a user scrolls up or down the current page. This is the default.
- `fixed` freezes the background image in place on the current page.

Note

The characteristics of this property are not inherited.

Example

```
BODY { background-image: url(pattern.gif);
       background-color: silver;
       background-attachment: fixed }
```

background-color	Background Color

Purpose

Specifies a background color for the current document or document part.

Syntax

```
background-color: { color-name | #rgb | #rrggbb
| rgb(rrr,ggg,bbb)
| rgb(rrr%, ggg%, bbb%) | transparent }
```

Where

- *color-name* specifies a foreground color by valid name (that is, red, maroon, yellow, green, lime, teal, olive, aqua, blue, navy, purple, fuchsia, black, gray, silver, or white).

- *#rgb* is a three-digit hexadecimal color code, where *r* represents the red attributes, from 0 to F; *g* represents the green attributes, from 0 to F; and *b* represents the blue attributes, from 0 to F, all in hexadecimal notation.

- *#rrggbb* is a six-digit hexadecimal color code, where *rr* represents the red attributes, from 00 to FF; *gg* represents the green attributes, from 00 to FF; and *bb* represents the blue attributes, from 00 to FF, all in hexadecimal notation.

- rgb(*rrr,ggg,bbb*) represents absolute red-green-blue values, each ranging from 000 to 255, in decimal notation.

- rgb(*rrr.d%, ggg.e%, bbb.f%*) represents the relative red-green-blue values, each ranging from 0.0% to 100.0%. Note that 0.0% is equivalent to an absolute value of 000, and 100.0% is equivalent to 255, in decimal notation.

- transparent represents no background color. This is the default.

Notes

The initial color value is set within the user's browser.

Table 5-2 contains selected hexadecimal color values. The characteristics of this property are not inherited.

Example

```
BODY { background-color: silver }
```

background-image	**Background Image**

Purpose

Specifies a background image for the current document or document part.

Syntax

```
background-image: { url(url_name)|none }
```

Where

- url_name names the URL of the image to be used for the background.
- none indicates no background image. This is the default.

Note

The characteristics of this property are not inherited.

Example

```
ONEPAGE { background-image: url(pattern.gif);
          background-color: silver }
```

background-position	**Background Image Position**

Purpose

Specifies a starting position for a background image.

Syntax

```
background-position:{ [+|-]percent%|[+|-]length|{1,2}
|[0%|[+|-]vert_pos]|[0%|[+|-]horiz_pos] }
```

Where

- *percent* is a positive value that is relative to the size of the image. Follow *percent* with a percentage sign (%).

- *length* is a positive value followed by a two-letter abbreviation representing the unit of measure.

- 1,2 represent the coordinates of the upper-left or lower-right corner of the image.

- *vert_pos* represents the vertical position of the image onscreen. Valid values are top, center, and bottom.

- *horiz_pos* represents the horizontal position of the image onscreen. Valid values are left, center, and right.

Notes

Valid relative units of measure are em (the height of the current font), ex (the height of the letter *x* in the current font), and px (pixels, relative to the size of the window). Valid absolute units of measure are in (inches), cm (centimeters), mm (millimeters), pt (points), and pc (picas).

If you specify one *percent* or *length*, it determines the horizontal position of the image.

The default value of 0% 0% is equivalent to the values of top-left and left-top.

The value of 0% 50% is equivalent to left, left-center, and center-left.

The value of 50% 0% is equivalent to top, top-center, and center-top.

The value of 100% 0% is equivalent to right-top and top-right.

The value of 0% 100% is equivalent to left-bottom and bottom-left.

The value of 100% 100% is equivalent to bottom-right and right-bottom.

The characteristics of this property are not inherited.

Example

```
ONEPAGE { background-image: url(pattern.gif);
          background-position: 50% 50%;
          background-color: silver }
```

background-repeat — Background Repeat

Purpose

Repeats a background image onscreen a particular number of times.

Syntax

```
background-repeat: { repeat | repeat-x | repeat-y
 | no-repeat }
```

Where

- repeat fills the page completely with the image. This is the default.
- repeat-x fills the page horizontally from the left edge to the right edge.
- repeat-y fills the page vertically from top to bottom.
- no-repeat does not repeat the image.

Note

The characteristics of this property are not inherited.

Example

```
BIGPAGE { background-image: url(pattern.gif);
  background-repeat: repeat-x; background-color: teal
}
```

border — Border Properties

Purpose

Specifies the color, style, and/or width of all four borders.

Syntax

```
border: {[ border-color_value] | [ border-style_value]
 [ border-width_value] }
```

Where

- *border-color_value* specifies the color of all four borders. For more information, see the border-color property.

- *border-style_value* specifies the style of all four borders. For more information, see the border-style property.

- *border-width_value* specifies the width of all four borders. For more information, see the border-top-width property.

Notes

This property specifies multiple properties for the four borders in the same way that you can individually set rules for the border-color, border-style, and border-width properties.

You do not need to specify the property name. The browser should interpret the unique values for each property.

Table 5-2 contains selected hexadecimal color values.

No initial value exists for this property.

The characteristics of this property are not inherited.

A border is outside the content of the page but within the page edges and within the top, left, right, and bottom margins.

Example

```
S { border: red double medium }
```

---

border-bottom   Bottom-Border Properties

Purpose

Specifies the color, style, and/or width of the bottom border.

Syntax

```
border-bottom: {[ border-color_value]
 |[ border-style_value]
 [ border-bottom-width_value] }
```

Where

- *border-color_value* specifies the border color. For more information, see the border-color property.
- *border-style_value* specifies the border style. For more information, see the border-style property.
- *border-bottom-width_value* specifies the border width. For more information, see the border-bottom-width property.

Notes

This property specifies multiple properties for a bottom border in the same way that you can individually set rules for the border-color, border-style, and border-bottom-width properties.

You do not need to specify the property name. The browser should interpret the unique values for each property.

Table 5-2 contains selected hexadecimal color values.

No initial value exists for this property.

The characteristics of this property are not inherited.

border-bottom accepts only one style, in contrast to border-style, which accepts as many as four.

A border is outside the content of the page but within the page edges and within the top, left, right, and bottom margins.

Example

```
IMG { border-bottom: black solid thick }
```

border-bottom-width	**Bottom-Border Width**

Purpose

Sets the width of the bottom border.

Syntax

```
border-bottom-width:{ thin|medium|thick|length }
```

Where

- thin is a narrower width than medium or thick.
- medium is wider than thin but narrower than thick. This is the default.
- thick is wider than thin or medium.
- *length* is a positive value followed by a two-letter abbreviation representing the unit of measure.

Notes

A border is outside the content of the page but within the page edges and within the top, left, right, and bottom margins.

The width of borders varies from browser to browser.

The characteristics of this property are not inherited.

Example

```
TEXT { border-bottom-width: thick }
```

border-color   Border Color

Purpose

Sets colors of one, two, three, or four borders.

Syntax

```
border-color: { [color-name_t|#rgb_t|#rrggbb_t
  |rgb(rrr_t,ggg_t,bbb_t)
  |rgb(rrr_t%, ggg_t%, bbb_t%)]
  [color-name_r|#rgb_r|#rrggbb_r
  |rgb(rrr_r,ggg_r,bbb_r)
  |rgb(rrr_r%, ggg_r%, bbb_r%)]
  [color-name_b|#rgb_b|#rrggbb_b
  |rgb(rrr_b,ggg_b,bbb_b)
  |rgb(rrr_b%, ggg_b%, bbb_b%)]
  [color-name_l|#rgb_l
```

```
|#rrggbb_l|rgb(rrr_l,ggg_l,bbb_l)
|rgb(rrr_l%, ggg_l%, bbb_l%)] }
```

Where

- *color-name_t*, *color-name_r*, *color-name_b*, and *color-name_l* specify border colors for the top, right, bottom, and left borders by valid name (that is, red, maroon, yellow, green, lime, teal, olive, aqua, blue, navy, purple, fuchsia, black, gray, silver, or white).

- *#rgb_t*, *#rgb_r*, *#rgb_b*, and *#rgb_l* each represent a three-digit hexadecimal color code for the top, right, bottom, and left borders, where *r* represents the red attributes, from 0 to F; *g* represents the green attributes, from 0 to F; and *b* represents the blue attributes, from 0 to F.

- *#rrggbb_t*, *#rrggbb_r*, *#rrggbb_b*, and *#rrggbb_l* each represent a six-digit hexadecimal color code for the top, right, bottom, and left borders, where *rr* represents the red attributes, from 00 to FF; *gg* represents the green attributes, from 00 to FF; and *bb* represents the blue attributes, from 00 to FF.

- rgb(*rrr_t,ggg_t,bbb_t*), rgb(*rrr_r,ggg_r,bbb_r*), rgb(*rrr_b,ggg_b,bbb_b*), and rgb(*rrr_l,ggg_l,bbb_l*) each represent absolute red-green-blue values for the top, right, bottom, and left borders. Each of the values ranges from 000 to 255, in decimal notation.

- rgb(*rrr.d_t%*, *ggg.e_t%*, *bbb.f_t%*), rgb(*rrr.d_r%*, *ggg.e_r%*, *bbb.f_r%*), rgb(*rrr.d_b%*, *ggg.e_b%*, *bbb.f_b%*), and rgb(*rrr.d_l%*, *ggg.e_l%*, *bbb.f_l%*) each represent the relative red-green-blue values, each ranging from 0.0% to 100.0%. Note that 0.0% is equivalent to an absolute value of 000, and 100.0% is equivalent to 255, both in decimal notation.

Notes

The initial border color value is set within the user's browser.

Table 5-2 contains selected hexadecimal color values.

The characteristics of this property are inherited.

A border is outside the content of the page but within the page edges and within the top, left, right, and bottom margins.

Example

```
HEAD4 { border-color: blue; border-width: thin }
```

border-left	Left-Border Properties

Purpose

Specifies the color, style, and/or width of the left border.

Syntax

```
border-left: {[ border-color_value]
 |[ border-style_value]
 [ border-left-width_value] }
```

Where

- *border-color_value* specifies the border color. For more information, see the border-color property.
- *border-style_value* specifies the border style. For more information, see the border-style property.
- *border-left-width_value* specifies the border width. For more information, see the border-left-width property.

Notes

This property specifies multiple properties for borders in the same way that you can individually set rules for the border-color, border-style, and border-left-width properties.

You do not need to specify the property name. The browser should interpret the unique values for each property.

Table 5-2 contains selected hexadecimal color values.

No initial value exists for this property.

The characteristics of this property are not inherited.

border-left accepts only one style, in contrast to border-style, which accepts as many as four.

A border is outside the content of the page but within the page edges and within the top, left, right, and bottom margins.

Example

```
INS { border-left: blue solid thin }
```

border-left-width   Left-Border Width

Purpose

Sets the width of the left border.

Syntax

```
border-left-width:{ thin|medium|thick|length }
```

Where

* thin is a narrower width than medium or thick.
* medium is wider than thin but narrower than thick. This is the default.
* thick is wider than thin or medium.
* length is a positive value followed by a two-letter abbreviation representing the unit of measure.

Notes

A border is outside the content of the page but within the page edges and within the top, left, right, and bottom margins.

The width of borders varies from browser to browser.

The characteristics of this property are not inherited.

Example

```
HEAD1 { border-left-width: 0.25in }
```

border-right

Right-Border Properties

Purpose

Specifies the color, style, and/or width of the right border.

Syntax

```
border-right: {[ border-color_value]
|[ border-style_value][ border-right-width_value] }
```

Where

- *border-color_value* specifies the border color. For more information, see the border-color property.
- *border-style_value* specifies the border style. For more information, see the border-style property.
- *border-right-width_value* specifies the border width. For more information, see the border-right-width property.

Notes

This property specifies multiple properties for borders in the same way that you can individually set rules for the border-color, border-style, and border-right-width properties.

You do not need to specify the property name. The browser should interpret the unique values for each property.

Table 5-2 contains selected hexadecimal color values.

No initial value exists for this property.

The characteristics of this property are not inherited.

border-right accepts only one style, in contrast to border-style, which accepts as many as four.

A border is outside the content of the page but within the page edges and within the top, left, right, and bottom margins.

Example

```
SPAN { border-right: teal dotted medium }
```

border-right-width   Right-Border Width

Purpose
Sets the width of the right border.

Syntax
```
border-right-width:{ thin|medium|thick|length }
```

Where
- thin is a narrower width than medium or thick.
- medium is wider than thin but narrower than thick. This is the default.
- thick is wider than thin or medium.
- length is a positive value followed by a two-letter abbreviation representing the unit of measure.

Notes
A border is outside the content of the page but within the page edges and within the top, left, right, and bottom margins.
The width of borders varies from browser to browser.
The characteristics of this property are not inherited.

Example
```
LONGQUOTE { border-right-width: 2pt }
```

border-style   Border Style

Purpose
Formats one, two, three, or four borders.

Syntax
```
border:{
[none|dotted|dashed|solid|double|groove|ridge
 |inset|outset][none|dotted|dashed|solid|double
 |groove|ridge|inset|outset][none
```

|dotted|dashed
|solid|double|groove|ridge|inset|outset][none
|dotted|dashed|solid|double|groove|ridge|inset
|outset] }

Where

- none omits a border. This overrides any border-width value.
- dotted draws a dotted-line border over the element background.
- dashed draws a dashed-line border over the element background.
- solid draws a solid-line border over the element background.
- double draws a double-solid-line border over the element background.
- groove draws a three-dimensional grooved border over the element background, using the border-color value.
- ridge draws a three-dimensional ridged border over the element background, using the border-color value.
- inset draws a three-dimensional inset over the element background, using the border-color value.
- outset draws a three-dimensional outset over the element background, using the border-color value.

Notes

Some browsers can't interpret most border-style values, so they draw a solid line instead.

The characteristics of this property are not inherited.

A border is outside the content of the page but within the page edges and within the top, left, right, and bottom margins.

If you supply one style, all borders are set to that style.

If you supply two or three styles, the browser supplies styles from the opposite side of the element. Elements are paired as follows: top and bottom, left and right.

Example

    HEAD1 { border-style: inset outset }

border-top   Top-Border Properties

Purpose

Specifies the color, style, and/or width of the top border.

Syntax

```
border-top: { border-color_value
  | border-style_value
  | border-top-width_value }
```

Where

- *border-color_value* specifies the border color. For more information, see the `border-color` property.

- *border-style_value* specifies the border style. For more information, see the `border-style` property.

- *border-top-width_value* specifies the border width. For more information, see the `border-top-width` property.

Notes

This property specifies multiple properties for borders in the same way that you can individually set rules for the `border-color`, `border-style`, and `border-top-width` properties.

You do not need to specify the property name. The browser should interpret the unique values for each property.

Table 5-2 contains selected hexadecimal color values.

No initial value exists for this property.

The characteristics of this property are not inherited.

`border-top` accepts only one style, in contrast to `border-style`, which accepts as many as four.

A border is outside the content of the page but within the page edges and within the top, left, right, and bottom margins.

Example

```
PARA.intro { border-top: red dotted thin }
```

border-top-width   Top-Border Width

Purpose
Sets the width of the top border.

Syntax
```
border-top-width:{ thin|medium|thick|length }
```

Where
- thin is a narrower width than medium or thick.
- medium is wider than thin but narrower than thick. This is the default.
- thick is wider than thin or medium.
- length is a positive value followed by a two-letter abbreviation representing the unit of measure.

Notes
A border is outside the content of the page but within the page edges and within the top, left, right, and bottom margins.
The width of borders varies from browser to browser.
The characteristics of this property are not inherited.

Example
```
BIGQUOTE { border-top-width: thin }
```

border-width   Border Width

Purpose
Sets the width of one, two, three, or four borders.

Syntax
```
border-width:{ [thin|medium|thick|length]
  [thin|medium|thick|length][thin|medium|thick|length]
  [thin|medium|thick|length] }
```

Where

- thin is a narrower width than medium or thick.
- medium is wider than thin but narrower than thick. This is the default.
- thick is wider than thin or medium.
- *length* is a positive value followed by a two-letter abbreviation representing the unit of measure.

Notes

A border is outside the content of the page but within the page edges and within the top, left, right, and bottom margins.

border-width is the equivalent of border-width-top, border-width-right, border-width-bottom, and/or border-width-left, in that order.

If you supply one width, all borders are set to that width.

If you supply two or three widths, the browser supplies widths from the opposite side of the element. Elements are paired as follows: top and bottom, left and right.

The width of borders varies from browser to browser.

The characteristics of this property are not inherited.

Example

```
UL { border-width: thin }
```

clear	Clear Element

Purpose

Displays a floating element next to or below the current element.

Syntax

```
clear: { none|left|right|both }
```

Where

- none does not wait for the margins to be clear; the element floats at the current alignment setting. This is the default.
- left floats an element after the left margin is clear.

- right floats an element after the right margin is clear.
- both floats an element after both the left and right margins are clear.

Note

The characteristics of this property are not inherited.

Example

```
IMG.clearex.gif { clear: left }
```

| **color** | **Foreground Color** |

Purpose

Specifies a foreground color for the current document or document part.

Syntax

```
color: { color-name | #rgb | #rrggbb | rgb(rrr,ggg,bbb)
  | rgb(rrr%, ggg%, bbb%) }
```

Where

- *color-name* specifies a foreground color by valid name (that is, red, maroon, yellow, green, lime, teal, olive, aqua, blue, navy, purple, fuchsia, black, gray, silver, or white).
- *#rgb* is a three-digit hexadecimal color code, where *r* represents the red attributes, from 0 to F; *g* represents the green attributes, from 0 to F; and *b* represents the blue attributes, from 0 to F.
- *#rrggbb* is a six-digit hexadecimal color code, where *rr* represents the red attributes, from 00 to FF; *gg* represents the green attributes, from 00 to FF; and *bb* represents the blue attributes, from 00 to FF.
- rgb(*rrr,ggg,bbb*) represents absolute red-green-blue values, each ranging from 000 to 255, in decimal notation.

- rgb(*rrr.d%*, *ggg.e%*, *bbb.f%*) represents the relative red-green-blue values, each ranging from 0.0% to 100.0%. Note that 0.0% is equivalent to an absolute value of 000, and 100.0% is equivalent to 255, in decimal notation.

Notes

The initial color value is set within the user's browser.
Table 5-2 contains selected hexadecimal color values.
The characteristics of this property are inherited.

Example

```
PARA.intro { color: teal; font-size: 10pt;
            font-style: italic }
```

5

display	Display Element

Purpose

Displays the current element in a particular way onscreen or in a printed format.

Syntax

```
display: { inline|block|list-item|none }
```

Where

- inline displays an inline box on the same line as the element that was most recently displayed.
- block creates a box in which to display the current element. This is the default.
- list-item creates a box in which to display the current element and adds a list-item marker.
- none does not display the element, its child elements, or the box.

Notes

An inline box is large enough to hold the content of the element. If the content is longer than one line, a new box is created for each line.

The characteristics of this property are not inherited.

You definitely should define this style for XML elements, because you might not always want to accept the default value of block.

The XML `xml:space` attribute also controls the display of elements in XML documents. For more information about `xml:space`, see its entry in Chapter 2, *XML Syntax.*

Example

```
Q { display: block }
```

float   Float Element   5

Purpose

Floats or inserts the element in the document.

Syntax

```
float: { left|right|none }
```

Where

- `left` floats the element on the left side and wraps text on its right side.
- `right` floats the element on the right side and wraps text on its left side.
- `none` displays the element as inserted on the page. This is the default.

Note

The characteristics of this property are not inherited.

Example

```
IMG.float.gif { float: left }
```

font | Font Properties

Purpose
Specifies up to six properties for fonts.

Syntax
```
font: { font-size_value |font-family_value|
  [[ font-style_value ]|[ font-variant_value ]
  |[ font-weight_value ]]|[ /line-height_value ]}
```

Where
- *font-size_value* specifies the font size. For more information, see the font-size property.
- *font-family_value* specifies the font family. For more information, see the font-family property.
- *font-style_value* specifies the font style. For more information, see the font-style property.
- *font-variant_value* specifies the font variant. For more information, see the font-variant property.
- *font-weight_value* specifies the font weight. For more information, see the font-weight property.
- *line-height_value* specifies the line height. For more information, see the line-height property.

Notes
This property specifies multiple properties for fonts in the same way that you can individually set rules for the font-size, font-style, font-variant, font-weight, and line-height properties.

You do not need to specify the property name. The browser should interpret the unique values for each property.

If you do not specify a particular value, the browser uses the initial value.

By default, the value of line-height is the height of one line of text.

No initial value exists for this property.

You can set percentage values for font-size and line-height only.

The characteristics of this property are inherited.

Example

```
PARA {FONT: small-caps/90% "times new roman", serif }
```

font-family   Font Family

Purpose

Specifies a font by name, font family, or both.

5

Syntax

```
font-family:{ ["]family_name_1["]| serif|sans-serif
|cursive|fantasy|monospace }[, ["]family_name_2["]
| serif|sans-serif|cursive|fantasy|monospace]
[..., ["]family_name_n["]| serif|sans-serif|cursive
|fantasy|monospace]}
```

Where

- *family-name* is the name of a specific typeface.
- serif, sans-serif, cursive, fantasy, and monospace are the names of generic typefaces that might match one or more family names on a particular computer.

Notes

This property specifies a font by name and/or font family.

You can specify multiple font families.

Ending a list of font families with at least one generic typeface is a good idea. This ensures that a font family will be defined.

The initial font-family value is set by the user's browser.

Use quotation marks to enclose family names of two or more words that are separated by spaces (for example, "Courier New" or "Bookman Old Style").

The characteristics of this property are inherited.

Example

```
BIGPAGE { FONT-FAMILY: "Times New Roman",
          "Book Antiqua",
          serif }
```

font-size	Font Size

Purpose

Specifies an absolute or relative font size.

Syntax

font-size: { *length* | *percent%* | *absolute_size*
| *relative_size* }

Where

- *length* is a positive value followed by a two-letter abbreviation representing the unit of measure.

- *percent* is a positive value that is relative to the font of the element immediately above the current element. Follow *percent* with a percentage sign (%).

- *absolute_size* is a set of font sizes that are determined by the user's browser. Valid values are xx-small, x-small, small, medium, large, x-large, xx-large.

- *relative_size* is larger than (larger) or smaller than (smaller) the font of the element immediately above the current element.

Notes

Valid relative units of measure are em (the height of the current font), ex (the height of the letter *x* in the current font), and px (pixels, relative to the size of the window). Valid absolute units of measure are in (inches), cm (centimeters), mm (millimeters), pt (points), and pc (picas).

The characteristics of this property are inherited.

Example

```
HEAD4 { FONT-SIZE: 14pt }
HEAD5 { FONT-SIZE: 125% }
HEAD6 { FONT-SIZE: larger }
```

font-style   Font Style

Purpose

Specifies one or more text enhancements.

Syntax

```
font-style: { normal|italic|oblique }
```

Where

- normal is unitalicized text. This is the default.
- italic is italicized text.
- oblique is usually slightly italicized text.

Notes

This property specifies the degree of slant for text.

If you choose italic and the current typeface does not offer italics, text may be oblique instead.

Synonyms for oblique include *slanted* and *incline*. A synonym for italic is *cursive*.

The characteristics of this property are inherited.

Example

```
HEAD2, HEAD4 { FONT-STYLE: italic; FONT-WEIGHT: bold}
```

font-variant   Font Variations

Purpose

Specifies one or more text variations.

Syntax

```
font-style: { normal | small-caps }
```

Where

- normal is any variation that is not small caps. This is the default.
- small-caps is a variation that is all uppercase characters that are smaller than the usual uppercase characters in a typeface.

Notes

This property specifies the case of text.

If a typeface does not include smaller uppercase characters, standard uppercase characters may be scaled down or may replace small caps.

The characteristics of this property are inherited.

Example

```
PARA.note { font-variant: small-caps;
    font-weight: bolder }
```

font-weight   Bold Font

Purpose

Specifies the degree of boldness or lightness of text.

Syntax

```
font-weight: { normal | bold | bolder | lighter
 | 100 | 200 | 300 | 400 | 500 | 600 | 700 | 800 | 900 }
```

Where

- normal is the standard, nonbold, nonlight text weight.
- bold is the standard boldface text.

- **bolder** is bolder than standard boldface. It can be the equivalent of ultrabold or heavy text. This is a relative value.
- **lighter** is the equivalent of light text. This is a relative value.
- **100** is the lightest weight.
- **200** and **300** are somewhere between light and normal weight.
- **400** is the equivalent of normal weight.
- **500** and **600** are somewhere between normal and bold weight. **500** is the equivalent of a medium weight.
- **700** is the equivalent of bold weight.
- **800** and **900** are bolder than bold weight.

Notes

This property specifies the boldness or lightness of the font, in an absolute or relative value.

The characteristics of this property are inherited.

Example

```
PARA.warning { font-weight: 800 }
```

height   Element Height

Purpose

Specifies the height of the selected element.

Syntax

```
height: { length | auto }
```

Where

- *length* is a positive value followed by a two-letter abbreviation representing the unit of measure.

- auto is a value automatically calculated by the user's browser. This is the default.

Notes

This property sets the height of the selected element, either in pixels or by calculating its height automatically, scaled proportionately with the width.

Valid relative units of measure are em (the height of the current font), ex (the height of the letter x in the current font), and px (pixels, relative to the size of the window). Valid absolute units of measure are in (inches), cm (centimeters), mm (millimeters), pt (points), and pc (picas).

If the height of the element is equal to auto, the aspect ratio (that is, the current proportions of the element) is maintained.

If both the height and width of the element are equal to auto, the browser does not change the element's dimensions.

The characteristics of this property are not inherited.

Example

```
IMG.bigpics { height: 400px; width: 250px }
```

Related Property

```
WIDTH
```

---

important	Important Declaration

Purpose

States that the current declaration is more important than others.

Syntax

```
! important;
```

Notes

Add ! important; to the end of a declaration to specify that the declaration overrides other declarations.

An author-defined declaration that is not important overrides a user-defined declaration that is not important.

An author-defined important declaration overrides a user-defined important declaration.

A user-defined important declaration overrides an author declaration that is not important.

letter-spacing   Character Spacing

Purpose

Sets spacing between characters.

Syntax

```
letter-spacing: { normal | [+|-]length }
```

Where

- normal represents the normal spacing between characters. This is the default.

- length is a positive value followed by a two-letter abbreviation representing the unit of measure. length is usually an increase in the spacing between characters, but can be a decrease (a negative value).

Notes

Valid relative units of measure are em (the height of the current font), ex (the height of the letter x in the current font), and px (pixels, relative to the size of the window). Valid absolute units of measure are in (inches), cm (centimeters), mm (millimeters), pt (points), and pc (picas).

The characteristics of this property are inherited.

Example

```
PARA.emphasis { letter-spacing: 4mm;
                font-weight: bolder }
```

Related Property

```
word-spacing
```

line-height

Baseline Height

Purpose

Specifies the height of the text line from baseline to baseline.

Syntax

`line-height: { normal | number | length | percent% }`

Where

- normal is the parent element's line height. The suggested numeric value for normal should range between 1.0 and 1.2. This is the default.
- number is a number by which the current font size is multiplied to result in a new line height.
- length is a positive value followed by a two-letter abbreviation representing the unit of measure.
- percent is a positive value that is relative to the size of the line height. Follow percent with a percentage sign (%).

Notes

This property specifies the height from baseline to baseline, in a number that is multiplied either by the present font size, the length (in the default unit of measure), or a percentage of the present font size.

Valid relative units of measure are em (the height of the current font), ex (the height of the letter x in the current font), and px (pixels, relative to the size of the window). Valid absolute units of measure are in (inches), cm (centimeters), mm (millimeters), pt (points), and pc (picas).

Negative values are not valid.

The initial line-height value is set by the user's browser.

The characteristics of this property are inherited.

Example

`SPAN { line-height: 110%; font-size: 12pt }`

list-style   List Style Properties

Purpose

Specifies up to three properties for lists.

Syntax

```
list-style: { list-style-image_value
  | list-style-position_value
  | list-style-type_value }
```

Where

- *list-style-image_value* specifies the image preceding list items. For more information, see the `list-style-image` property.

- *list-style-position_value* specifies the position of list items. For more information, see the `list-style-position` property.

- *list-style-type_value* specifies number or bullet type preceding list items. For more information, see the `list-style-type` property.

Notes

This property specifies multiple properties for list-item markers in the same way that you can individually set rules for the `list-style-image`, `list-style-position`, and `list-style-type` properties.

You do not need to specify the property name. The browser should interpret the unique values for each property.

Example

```
UL { list-style: url(button.gif) circle outside}
```

list-style-image   List-Style Image

Purpose
Specifies the image preceding items on an ordered or unordered list.

Syntax
```
list-style-image: { url(url_name)|none }
```

Where
- *url_name* names the URL of the image to be used for the list-item marker.
- none indicates no background image.

Note
The characteristics of this property are inherited.

Example
```
UL { list-style-image: url(button.gif) }
```

list-style-position   List-Style Position

Purpose
Specifies the position of the items on an ordered or unordered list.

Syntax
```
list-style-position: { inside|outside }
```

Where
- inside aligns the second line of the list-item text with the left margin (that is, under the list-item marker).
- outside displays the second line of the list-item text under the first line (that is, it creates a hanging indent). This is the default.

Note

The characteristics of this property are inherited.

Example

```
UL { list-style-position: outside }
```

list-style-type   List-Style Type

Purpose

Specifies the number or bullet type preceding items on an ordered
or unordered list.

Syntax

```
list-style-type: { disc|circle|square|decimal
  |lower-roman|upper-roman|lower-alpha|upper-alpha
  |none }
```

Where

- disc uses filled bullets. This is the default.
- circle uses unfilled circles.
- square uses filled square bullets.
- decimal uses Arabic numerals (1, 2, 3)
- lower-roman uses small Roman numerals (i, ii, iii).
- upper-roman uses large Roman numerals (I, II, III).
- lower-alpha uses lowercase alphabetic letters (a, b, c).
- upper-alpha uses uppercase alphabetic letters (A, B, C).
- none uses no bullets or numbers.

Note

The characteristics of this property are inherited.

Example

```
UL { list-style-type: square }
```

margin
Margin Characteristics

Purpose
Turns on or off one, two, three, or four margins or sets margin size.

Syntax
```
margin: { [length_top|percent_top%|auto]
  [length_right|percent_right%|auto]
  [length_bottom|percent_bottom%|auto]
  [length_left|percent_left%|auto] }
```

Where
- *length_top*, *length_right*, *length_bottom*, and *length_left* are positive or negative values followed by a two-letter abbreviation representing the unit of measure.

- *percent_top*, *percent_right*, *percent_bottom*, and *percent_left* are positive values that are relative to the parent element's selected margins. Follow *percent* with a percentage sign (%).

- auto represents top-margin, right-margin, bottom-margin, and left-margin values, automatically calculated by the user's browser.

Notes
This property turns on or off one, two, three, or four margins or sets margin size (in the default unit of measure) either as a percentage of the current width or automatically by calculating a minimum amount.

Valid relative units of measure are em (the height of the current font), ex (the height of the letter *x* in the current font), and px (pixels, relative to the size of the window). Valid absolute units of measure are in (inches), cm (centimeters), mm (millimeters), pt (points), and pc (picas).

If you supply one value, all margins are set to that value.

If you supply two or three values, the browser supplies values from the opposite side of the element. Elements are paired as follows: top and bottom, left and right.

A margin is above the content of the page, borders, and padding but within the page edges.

The characteristics of this property are not inherited.

Example

```
BIGPAGE {margin: 1in 1in 0.5in}
```

margin-bottom   Bottom Margin

Purpose

Turns on or off bottom margin and/or specifies bottom-margin size.

Syntax

```
margin-bottom: { 0|length|percent%|auto }
```

Where

- 0 represents the parent element's current bottom margin. This is the default.

- *length* is a positive or negative value followed by a two-letter abbreviation representing the unit of measure.

- *percent* is a positive value that is relative to the parent element's bottom margin. Follow *percent* with a percentage sign (%).

- auto is a value automatically calculated by the user's browser.

Notes

This property turns on or off bottom margins and/or sets a margin size (in the default unit of measure) either as a percentage of the current height or automatically by calculating a minimum amount.

Valid relative units of measure are em (the height of the current font), ex (the height of the letter *x* in the current font), and px (pixels, relative to the size of the window). Valid absolute units of measure are in (inches), cm (centimeters), mm (millimeters), pt (points), and pc (picas).

A margin is above the content of the page, borders, and padding but within the page edges.

The characteristics of this property are not inherited.

Example

```
BIGPAGE { margin-bottom: 18pt }
```

margin-left   Left Margin

Purpose

Turns on or off left margins and/or sets left-margin size.

Syntax

```
margin-left: { 0 | length | percent% | auto }
```

Where

- 0 represents the parent element's current left margin. This is the default.
- *percent* is a positive value that is relative to the parent element's left margin. Follow *percent* with a percentage sign (%).
- *length* is a positive or negative value followed by a two-letter abbreviation representing the unit of measure.
- auto is a value automatically calculated by the user's browser.

Notes

This property turns on or off the left margin and/or sets the left-margin size (in the default unit of measure) either as a percentage of the current width or automatically by calculating a minimum amount.

Valid relative units of measure are em (the width of the current font), ex (the width of the letter *x* in the current font), and px (pixels, relative to the size of the window). Valid absolute units of measure are in (inches), cm (centimeters), mm (millimeters), pt (points), and pc (picas).

A margin is above the content of the page, borders, and padding but within the page edges.

The characteristics of this property are not inherited.

Example

```
BIGPAGE { margin-right: 0.5in; margin-top: 1.0in;
margin-bottom: 1.0in; margin-left: 0.5in }
```

margin-right   Right Margin

Purpose

Turns on or off the right margin and/or sets the right-margin size.

Syntax

```
margin-right: { 0|length|percent%|auto }
```

Where

- 0 represents the parent element's current right margin. This is the default.

- *percent* is a positive value that is relative to the parent element's right margin. Follow *percent* with a percentage sign (%).

- *length* is a positive or negative value followed by a two-letter abbreviation representing the unit of measure.

- auto is a value automatically calculated by the user's browser.

Notes

This property turns on or off right margins and/or sets the right-margin size (in the default unit of measure) either as a percentage of the current width or automatically by calculating a minimum amount.

Valid relative units of measure are em (the width of the current font), ex (the width of the letter *x* in the current font), and px (pixels, relative to the size of the window). Valid absolute units of measure are in (inches), cm (centimeters), mm (millimeters), pt (points), and pc (picas).

A margin is above the content of the page, borders, and padding but within the page edges.

The characteristics of this property are not inherited.

Example

```
BODY { margin-right: 18pt; margin-top: 36pt;
  margin-bottom: 18pt; margin-left: 18pt }
```

margin-top   Top Margin

5

Purpose

Turns on or off top margins and/or sets top-margin size.

Syntax

```
margin-top: { 0|length|percent%|auto }
```

Where

- 0 represents the parent element's current top margin. This is the default.
- *percent* is a positive value that is relative to the parent element's top margin. Follow *percent* with a percentage sign (%).
- *length* is a positive or negative value followed by a two-letter abbreviation representing the unit of measure.
- auto is a value automatically calculated by the user's browser.

Notes

This property turns on or off top margins and/or sets a top-margin size (in the default unit of measure) either as a percentage of the current height or automatically by calculating a minimum amount.

Valid relative units of measure are em (the height of the current font), ex (the height of the letter *x* in the current font), and px

(pixels, relative to the size of the window). Valid absolute units of measure are in (inches), cm (centimeters), mm (millimeters), pt (points), and pc (picas).

A margin is above the content of the page, borders, and padding but within the page edges.

The characteristics of this property are not inherited.

Example

```
BODY { margin-top: 36pt }
```

padding   Padding Characteristics

5

Purpose

Turns on or off one, two, three, or four paddings and/or sets padding size.

Syntax

```
padding: { [length_top|percent_top%][length_right
|percent_right%][length_bottom|percent_bottom%]
[length_left|percent_left%] }
```

Where

- *length_top*, *length_right*, *length_bottom*, and *length_left* are positive or negative values followed by a two-letter abbreviation representing the unit of measure.

- *percent_top*, *percent_right*, *percent_bottom*, and *percent_left* are positive values that are relative to the parent element's selected paddings. Follow *percent* with a percentage sign (%).

Notes

This property turns on or off one, two, three, or four paddings and/or sets padding size (in the default unit of measure) either as a percentage of the current width or automatically by calculating a minimum amount.

Valid relative units of measure are em (the height of the current font), ex (the height of the letter x in the current font), and px

(pixels, relative to the size of the window). Valid absolute units of measure are in (inches), cm (centimeters), mm (millimeters), pt (points), and pc (picas).

If you supply one value, all paddings are set to that value.

If you supply two or three values, the browser supplies values from the opposite side of the element. Elements are paired as follows: top and bottom, left and right.

The characteristics of this property are not inherited.

Example

```
PARA.special { padding: 6pt 4pt }
```

padding-bottom   Bottom Padding

Purpose

Turns on or off bottom padding and/or specifies bottom-padding size.

Syntax

```
padding-bottom: { 0 | length | percent% }
```

Where

- 0 represents the parent element's current bottom padding. This is the default.

- *percent* is a positive value that is relative to the parent element's bottom padding. Follow *percent* with a percentage sign (%).

- *length* is a positive value followed by a two-letter abbreviation representing the unit of measure.

Notes

This property turns on or off bottom padding and/or sets a bottom-padding size (in the default unit of measure) either as a percentage of the current height or automatically by calculating a minimum amount.

Valid relative units of measure are em (the height of the current font), ex (the height of the letter *x* in the current font), and px

(pixels, relative to the size of the window). Valid absolute units of measure are in (inches), cm (centimeters), mm (millimeters), pt (points), and pc (picas).

Padding is above the content of the page, within the page edges, and below margins and borders.

The characteristics of this property are not inherited.

Example

```
BIGPAGE { padding-bottom: 8pt }
```

padding-left   Left Padding

Purpose

Turns on or off left padding and/or sets left-padding size.

Syntax

```
padding-left: { 0 | length | percent% }
```

Where

- 0 represents the parent element's current left padding. This is the default.

- *percent* is a positive value that is relative to the parent element's left padding. Follow *percent* with a percentage sign (%).

- *length* is a positive value followed by a two-letter abbreviation representing the unit of measure.

Notes

This property turns on or off the left padding and/or sets the left-padding size (in the default unit of measure) either as a percentage of the current width or automatically by calculating a minimum amount.

Valid relative units of measure are em (the width of the current font), ex (the width of the letter *x* in the current font), and px (pixels, relative to the size of the window). Valid absolute units of measure are in (inches), cm (centimeters), mm (millimeters), pt (points), and pc (picas).

Padding is above the content of the page, within the page edges, and below margins and borders.

The characteristics of this property are not inherited.

Example

```
BIGPAGE { padding-right: 0.5in; padding-top: 0.25in;
padding-bottom: 0.5in; padding-left: 0.5in }
```

padding-right   Right Padding

Purpose

Turns on or off the right padding and/or sets the right-padding size.

Syntax

```
padding-right: { 0|length|percent% }
```

Where

* 0 represents the parent element's current right padding. This is the default.

* *percent* is a positive value that is relative to the parent element's right padding. Follow *percent* with a percentage sign (%).

* *length* is a positive value followed by a two-letter abbreviation representing the unit of measure.

Notes

This property turns on or off right padding and/or sets the right-padding size (in the default unit of measure) either as a percentage of the current width or automatically by calculating a minimum amount.

Valid relative units of measure are em (the width of the current font), ex (the width of the letter *x* in the current font), and px (pixels, relative to the size of the window). Valid absolute units of measure are in (inches), cm (centimeters), mm (millimeters), pt (points), and pc (picas).

Padding is above the content of the page, within the page edges, and below margins and borders.

The characteristics of this property are not inherited.

Example

```
BIGPAGE { padding-right: 8pt; padding-top: 6pt;
padding-bottom: 4pt; padding-left: 8pt }
```

padding-top   Top Padding

Purpose

Turns on or off top padding and/or sets top-padding size.

Syntax

```
padding-top: { 0 | length | percent% }
```

Where

- 0 represents the parent element's current top padding. This is the default.

- *percent* is a positive value that is relative to the parent element's top padding. Follow *percent* with a percentage sign (%).

- *length* is a positive value followed by a two-letter abbreviation representing the unit of measure.

Notes

This property turns on or off top padding and/or sets a top-padding size (in the default unit of measure) either as a percentage of the current height or automatically by calculating a minimum amount.

Valid relative units of measure are em (the height of the current font), ex (the height of the letter *x* in the current font), and px (pixels, relative to the size of the window). Valid absolute units of measure are in (inches), cm (centimeters), mm (millimeters), pt (points), and pc (picas).

Padding is above the content of the page, within the page edges, and below margins and borders.

The characteristics of this property are not inherited.

Example

```
BIGPAGE { padding-top: 6pt }
```

text-align	**Horizontal Alignment**

Purpose

Sets horizontal alignment of selected text.

Syntax

```
text-align: { left|right|justify|center }
```

Where

- `left` aligns text within the element with the left margin. This is the default.
- `right` aligns text within the element with the right margin.
- `justify` aligns text within the element with both the left and right margins.
- `center` centers text within the element between the left and right margins.

Notes

This property specifies the alignment of text: with the left or right margin, with both left and right margins, or centered between the margins.

The initial alignment value depends on the user's browser and the direction in which the language is displayed.

The characteristics of this property are inherited.

Example

```
PARA.FORMAL { text-align: justify }
```

Related Property

```
vertical-align
```

text-decoration   Enhance Text

Purpose

Enhances text with either lines or blinking.

Syntax

```
text-decoration: { none|[underline|overline
|line-through|blink] }
```

Where

- none does not decorate the selected text. This is the default.
- underline underlines the selected text.
- overline draws a line over the selected text.
- line-through strikes through the selected text.
- blink turns on and off the display of selected text.

Notes

The characteristics of this property are not inherited. However, the children of the current elements should have the same text-decoration properties.

Although browsers should recognize blink, they may not "blink" the selected text.

Example

```
PARA.MESSAGE { TEXT-DECORATION: underline;
    TEXT-DECORATION: overline }
```

text-indent   First-Line Indention

Purpose

Indents the first line of text.

Syntax

```
text-indent: { length|percent% }
```

Where

- *length* is a positive value followed by a two-letter abbreviation representing the unit of measure.

- *percent* is a positive value that is relative to the width of the parent element. Follow *percent* with a percentage sign (%).

Notes

This property specifies the first-line indention of the text, measured from the left margin (in the default unit of measure) or as a percentage of change from the original indent.

Valid relative units of measure are em (the height of the current font), ex (the height of the letter *x* in the current font), and px (pixels, relative to the size of the window). Valid absolute units of measure are in (inches), cm (centimeters), mm (millimeters), pt (points), and pc (picas).

The characteristics of this property are inherited.

Example

```
PARA { text-indent: 0.5in }
```

text-transform	Change Case

Purpose

Changes case of the selected text.

Syntax

```
text-transform: { capitalize|uppercase|lowercase
|none }
```

Where

- capitalize applies initial uppercase to the selected text.
- uppercase applies all uppercase to the selected text.

- `lowercase` applies all lowercase to the selected text.
- `none` turns off the value inherited from the parent. This is the default.

Notes

This property transforms text to initial uppercase, all uppercase, or all lowercase, or turns off the case inherited from its parent.
The characteristics of this property are inherited.

Example

```
PARA.warning { text-transform: uppercase; font-weight:
900 }
```

5

vertical-align   Vertical Alignment

Purpose

Sets vertical alignment of the element.

Syntax

```
vertical-align: { baseline|sub|super|top|text-top
|middle|bottom|text-bottom|percent% }
```

Where

- `baseline` vertically aligns the element with the baseline of the current element or with the baseline of the parent element if the current element has no baseline. This is the default.
- `sub` makes the element a subscript.
- `super` makes the element a superscript.
- `top` vertically aligns the top of the element with the top of the highest element on the current line.
- `text-top` vertically aligns the element with the top of the parent element's typeface.

- middle vertically aligns the element with the middle of the element, computed by starting with the baseline and adding half the x-height of the parent element's typeface.
- bottom vertically aligns the bottom of the element with the lowest element on the current line.
- text-bottom vertically aligns the bottom of the element with the bottom of the parent element's typeface.
- *percent* is a positive value that is relative to the text's line height. Follow *percent* with a percentage sign (%).

Notes

This property specifies the vertical alignment of text with the baseline or font, or as a percentage above or below the baseline.

A percentage value is relative to the height of the affected element.

Using the top or bottom values may result in an inadvertent loop in the display of the element.

The characteristics of this property are not inherited.

Example

```
SUB { vertical-align: text-bottom; color: red }
```

Related Property

```
TEXT-ALIGN
```

white-space	White Space

Purpose

Turns on or off white space.

Syntax

```
white-space: { normal | pre | nowrap }
```

Where

- normal does not add white space to an element. This is the default.
- pre treats the element as preformatted content in the same way that the PRE element works in HTML documents.
- nowrap does not wrap text.

Notes

This property specifies whether white space is eliminated, as in normal HTML documents, or preformatted, as in the PRE element.

The characteristics of this property are inherited.

The XML xml:space processing instruction also controls white space in XML documents. For more information about xml:space, see its entry in Chapter 2, *XML Syntax*.

Example

```
HEAD1 { white-space: pre }
```

---

width   Element Width

Purpose

Specifies the width of the selected element.

Syntax

```
width: { length|percent%|auto }
```

Where

- *length* is a positive value followed by a two-letter abbreviation representing the unit of measure.
- *percent* is a positive value that is relative to the size of the image. Follow *percent* with a percentage sign (%).

- auto is a value automatically calculated by the user's browser. This is the default.

Notes

This property sets the width of the selected element, either in pixels, as a percentage of the original size, or by calculating its width automatically, scaled proportionately with the height.

Valid relative units of measure are em (the height of the current font), ex (the height of the letter x in the current font), and px (pixels, relative to the size of the window). Valid absolute units of measure are in (inches), cm (centimeters), mm (millimeters), pt (points), and pc (picas).

If the element is wider than the specified width, the browser will scale the element.

If the height of the element is equal to auto, the aspect ratio (proportions of the element) is maintained.

If both the height and width of the element are equal to auto, the browser does not change the element's dimensions.

The characteristics of this property are not inherited.

Example

```
IMG.bigpics { width: 250px }
```

Related Property

```
height
```

word-spacing   Word Spacing

Purpose

Sets spacing between words.

Syntax

```
word-spacing: { normal | [+|-]length }
```

Where

- normal represents the normal spacing between words. This is the default.

- *length* is a positive value followed by a two-letter abbreviation representing the unit of measure. *length* is usually an increase in the spacing between words, but can be a decrease (a negative value).

Notes

Valid relative units of measure are em (the height of the current font), ex (the height of the letter *x* in the current font), and px (pixels, relative to the size of the window). Valid absolute units of measure are in (inches), cm (centimeters), mm (millimeters), pt (points), and pc (picas).

The characteristics of this property are inherited.

Example

```
HEAD1 { word-spacing: 2pt }
```

Related Property

```
letter-spacing
```

Pseudo-Elements

Cascading style sheets allow you to specify particular styles for a first line or first letter of a paragraph.

first-line	First Line

Purpose

Style the first line of a paragraph.

Syntax

```
<PARA:first-line>first_line_text</PARA:first-line>
```

Where

- *first_line_text* represents the contents of the first line.

Notes

For first-line, you can use the following properties: background-attachment, background-color, background-image, background-position, background-repeat, clear, color, font, font-family, font-size, font-style, font-variant, font-weight, letter-spacing, line-height, text-decoration, text-transform, vertical-align, and word-spacing.

You can use the class attribute to specify first-line rules for all paragraphs in a particular class.

first-letter   First Letter

Purpose

Style the first letter of a paragraph.

Syntax

    <PARA:first-letter>first_character</PARA:first-letter>

Where

- *first_character* represents the first character in a paragraph.

Notes

For first-line, you can use the following properties: background-attachment, background-color, background-image, background-position, background-repeat, border, border-bottom, border-bottom-width, border-color, border-left, border-left-width, border-right, border-right-width, border-style, border-top, border-top-width, border-width, clear, color, float, font, font-family, font-size, font-style, font-variant, font-weight, line-height, margin, margin-bottom, margin-left, margin-right, margin-top, padding, padding-bottom, padding-left, padding-right, padding-top, text-decoration, text-transform, vertical-align (if the value of float is none), and word-spacing.

You can use the class attribute to specify first-letter rules for all paragraphs in a particular class.

·DSSSL-O

The Document Style Semantics and Specification Language (DSSSL) is a comprehensive and lengthy standard that is used to transform and style documents — the Standard Generalizcd Markup Language (SGML), and its subset, XML. The DSSSL standard, ISO/IEC 10179: 1996, documents both the transformation and styling languages that are used to specify document transformation and formatting in a platform- and vendor-neutral manner. DSSSL can be used with any document format for which a property set can be defined according to the Property Set Definition Requirements of ISO/IEC 10744. In particular, DSSSL can be used to specify the presentation of documents that are marked up according to ISO 8879: 1996, which is the SGML standard.

DSSSL Online (or DSSSL-O) comprises a subset of DSSSL characteristics that enable developers to style electronic documents so that they can be read by SGML, XML, and HTML browsers. This chapter introduces DSSSL-O and summarizes

its characteristics. For more information about DSSSL-O, go to
http://sunsite.unc.edu/pub/sun-info/standards/ dsssl/
dssslo/do980816.htm.

● — NOTE ———————————————————————————————

For information about incorporating styles into an XML document, see
the beginning of Chapter 5, *Cascading Style Sheets.*

DSSSL-O Flow-Objects Classes

DSSSL is made up of many elements, known as *characteristics,*
with which you can apply many types of styles to *flow objects* —
objects that fill a defined area in document output. Typical flow
objects include hyperlinks, characters, paragraphs, pages, groups
of adjacent pages, graphics, and tables. *Flow-objects classes,* which
are groups of related flow objects, include both named formatting
attributes and named *ports* — locations to which ordered lists of
flow objects are attached. This allows the organization of flow
objects as flow-objects trees, which demonstrate specific ancestor-
and-descendant relationships. When a flow-objects tree is created,
each flow object is associated with its own formatting characteristics. Formats of parent flow objects can control the formats of
child flow objects, or the child flow objects can have their own
formats.

The output of a formatted flow object "flows" into an *area,*
which is a rectangle with a set height and width. In many ways,
an area is analogous to a frame in a word processing document —
especially if you consider that a frame can include document
elements as diverse as text and graphics.

A *sosofo* (an acronym for **s**pecification **o**f a **s**equence **o**f **f**low
objects) specifies both the placement and formatting of particular
elements in a document. A sosofo allows you to nest one or more
child elements under a parent and specify particular formats for
all or particular elements. Under DSSSL, elements, attributes, and
other objects in a document are known as *nodes.*

As Chapter 5 explains, style sheets use *rules* to select a document element and apply formats and enhancements; and a cascading style sheet rule is composed of a *selector* (the element) and
a *declaration* (the property and value). DSSSL rules are also composed of two parts: A *query* "finds" one or more nodes, and a
make_expression forms a flow object from the node.

The DSSSL standard specifies categories of flow-objects classes, most of which are supported by DSSSL-O. DSSSL-O supports the following flow-object classes: `aligned-column`, `box`, `character`, `display-group`, `external-graphic`, `leader`, `line-field`, `link`, `marginalia`, `multi-mode`, `paragraph`, `paragraph-break`, `rule`, `score`, `scroll`, `sideline`, `simple-page-sequence`, `table`, `table-border`, `table-cell`, `table-column`, `table-part`, and `table-row`.

This section describes each of the flow-objects classes supported by DSSSL-O.

Aligned-Column

The aligned-column flow-objects class enables you to group paragraphs and control how they are displayed in a document. Characteristics in the aligned-column flow-objects class are `break-after`, `break-before`, `display-alignment`, `end-indent`, `keep`, `keep-with-next?`, `keep-with-previous?`, `may-violate-keep-after?`, `may-violate-keep-before?`, `space-after`, `space-before`, `start-indent`, and `writing-mode`.

Box

The box flow-objects class encloses one or more flow objects within a boxed border. You can display a box or *inline* it (embed it within a line). If a box is inlined, the direction of its border is perpendicular to the direction of the `writing-mode`. If the box is inlined, its size is the entire display area minus indents. Characteristics in the box flow-objects class are `background-color`, `background-layer`, `box-border-alignment`, `box-corner-"rounded`, `box-open-end?`, `box-size-after`, `box-size-before`, `box-type`, `break-after`, `break-before`, `color`, `display?`, `end-indent`, `inhibit-line-breaks?`, `keep`, `keep-with-next?`, `keep-with-previous?`, `layer`, `line-cap`, `line-dash`, `line-join`, `line-miter-limit`, `line-repeat`, `line-thickness`, `may-violate-keep-after?`, `may-violate-keep-before?`, `space-after`, `space-before`, `span`, `span-weak?`, `start-indent`, and `writing-mode`.

Character

The character flow-objects class includes characters and controls the behavior of characters in a document. Character flow objects are inlined; other flow objects cannot be nested under a character flow object. Characteristics in the character flow-objects class are allowed-ligatures, char, char-map, color, country, font-family-name, font-name, font-posture, font-proportionate-width, font-size, font-structure, font-weight, glyph-id, glyph-subst-method, glyph-subst-table, hyphenate?, hyphenation-method, inhibit-line-breaks?, input-tab?, input-whitespace-treatment, input-whitespace?, kern-mode, kern?, language, layer, ligature?, math-font-posture, position-point-shift, record-end?, space?, stretch-factor, and writing-mode.

Display-Group

The display-group flow-objects class *concatenates* (joins) the output of its child elements. The display-group and its children are all displayed. Because this is not an inline flow-objects class, all display-group flow objects cause a line break, whether or not they have any content. Characteristics in the display-group flow-objects class are break-after, break-before, keep, keep-with-next?, keep-with-previous?, may-violate-keep-after?, may-violate-keep-before?, space-after, and space-before.

External-Graphic

The external-graphic flow-objects class contains characteristics controlling external-entity graphics, which can be displayed or inlined. Other flow objects cannot be nested within an external-graphic flow object. Characteristics in the external-graphic flow-objects class are break-after, break-before, color, display-alignment, display?, end-indent, entity-system-id, escapement-direction, inhibit-line-breaks?, keep, keep-with-next?, keep-with- previous?, layer, max-height, max-width, may-violate-keep-after?, may-violate-keep-before?, notation-system-id, position-point-x, position-point-y, scale, space-after, space-before, span, span-weak?, start-indent, and writing-mode.

Leader

A leader is an inline series of dots joining one block of text with another. The most common use for leaders is in tables of contents —

between the chapter number and title on the left side of the page and the page number on the right side. Characteristics in the leader flow-objects class are `align-leader?`, `inhibit-line-breaks?`, `length`, `min-leader-repeat`, and `truncate-leader?`.

Line-Field

The line-field flow-objects class contains characteristics that control inline fields. Each line-field flow object is inlined. Characteristics in the line-field flow-objects class are `field-align`, `field-width`, `inhibit-line-breaks?`, and `writing-mode`.

Link

The link flow-objects class, which symbolizes a hypertext link, can be displayed or inlined. If link flow objects are nested, the most deeply nested object is active. The characteristic in the link flow-objects class is `destination`.

Marginalia

The marginalia flow-objects class symbolizes an *attachment area* (a defined and separate inline area attached to an object within, or sometimes outside, the area with which it is associated) on or near the margins. A marginalia flow object, which cannot contain nested flow objects itself, is nested within a paragraph flow object. Characteristics in the marginalia flow-objects class are `marginalia-keep-with-previous?`, `marginalia-sep`, and `marginalia-side`.

Multi-Mode

The multi-mode flow-objects class enables the presentation of two or more versions of a flow object. The ISO/IEC 10179: 1996 standard notes that a user might see a menu from which he or she can select a particular presentation mode. A multi-mode flow object can be displayed or inlined. Characteristics in the multi-mode flow-objects class are `multi-modes` and `principal-mode-simultaneous?`.

Paragraph

A paragraph flow object controls the behavior of paragraphs, including text formats, text enhancements, indention, and breaking from one area to another. Paragraph flow objects can be inlined or displayed. Characteristics in the paragraph flow-objects class are break-after, break-before, country, end-indent, expand-tabs?, first-line-start-indent, font-family-name, font-name, font-posture, font-proportionate-width, font-size, font-structure, font-weight, glyph-alignment-mode, hanging-punct?, hyphenation-exceptions, hyphenation-keep, hyphenation-ladder-count, hyphenation-method, ignore-record-end?, implicit-bidi-method, keep, keep-with-next?, keep-with-previous?, language, last-line-end-indent, last-line-quadding, line-breaking-method, line-composition-method, line-spacing, line-spacing-priority, lines, may-violate-keep-after?, may-violate-keep-before?, min-leading, min-post-line-spacing, min-pre-line-spacing, orphan-count, quadding, space-after, space-before, span, span-weak?, start-indent, widow-count, and writing-mode.

Paragraph-Break

The paragraph-break flow-objects class controls the display of multiple paragraphs, including whether they stay together and how they break. The paragraph-break flow-objects class includes all the characteristics of the paragraph flow object.

Rule

The rule flow-objects class symbolizes horizontal and vertical rule lines that are either displayed or inlined. Characteristics in the rule flow-objects class are break-after, break-before, color, display-alignment, end-indent, inhibit-line-breaks?, keep, keep-with-next?, keep-with-previous?, layer, length, line-cap, line-dash, line-repeat, line-thickness, may-violate-keep-after?, may-violate-keep-before?, orientation, position-point-shift, space-after, space-before, span, span-weak?, start-indent, and writing-mode.

Score

The score flow-objects class symbolizes inlined strikethrough lines drawn through characters and, optionally, through spaces. Use a score to indicate deleted text that you want to keep in a document, as documentation of the deletion. Scores and sidelines (revision marks) help workgroups show the editing progress of documents in development. Characteristics in the score flow-objects class are color, inhibit-line-breaks?, layer, line-cap, line-dash, line-repeat, line-thickness, score-spaces?, and type.

Scroll

The scroll flow-objects class displays a document from beginning to end. In other words, this flow-objects class does not allow for individual pages and page breaks. Characteristics in the scroll flow-objects class are background-color, background-layer, background-tile, end-margin, filling-direction, start-margin, and writing-mode.

Sideline

The sideline flow-objects class controls *sidelines*, or revision marks, which indicate additions, changes, or deletions in a document. Characteristics in the sideline flow-objects class are color, layer, line-cap, line-dash, line-repeat, line-thickness, sideline-rep, and sideline-side.

Simple-Page-Sequence

The characteristics in the simple-page-sequence flow-objects class produce entire pages that are formatted at an elementary level with a single header and a single footer. A particular document can contain several simple-page-sequence flow objects; this enables you to use different formats within a single document. Characteristics in the simple-page-sequence flow-objects class are bottom-margin, center-footer, center-header, footer-margin, header-margin, left-footer, left-header, left-margin, page-height, page-width, right-footer, right-header, right-margin, top-margin, and writing-mode.

Table

The table flow-objects class defines tables. Other table-related flow-objects classes that can be nested within the table flow-objects class are table-part, table-column, table-row, and table-cell. Characteristics in the table flow-objects class are after-column-border, after-row-border, before-column-border, before-row-border, break-after, break-before, display-alignment, end-indent, keep, keep-with-next?, keep-with-previous?, may-violate-keep-after?, may-violate-keep-before?, space-after, space-before, span, span-weak?, start-indent, table-auto-width-method, table-border, table-corner-rounded, table-width, and writing-mode.

Table-Border

The table-border flow-objects class specifies the attributes of table borders and table-cell borders. Characteristics in the table-border flow-objects class are border-alignment, border-omit-at-break?, border-present?, border-priority, color, layer, line-cap, line-dash, line-join, line-miter-limit, line-repeat, and line-thickness.

Table-Cell

The table-cell flow-objects class is the child of a table-row, table-part, or table flow object. Any displayed flow object can be nested within a table-cell flow object. Characteristics in the table-cell flow-objects class are background-color, background-layer, cell-after-column-border, cell-after-column-margin, cell-after-row-border, cell-after-row-margin, cell-background?, cell-before-column-border, cell-before-column-margin, cell-before-row-border, cell-before-row-margin, cell-crossed, cell-row-alignment, column-number, ends-row?, float-out-line-numbers?, float-out-marginalia?, float-out-sidelines?, line-cap, line-dash, line-repeat, line-thickness, n-columns-spanned, n-rows-spanned, and starts-row?.

Table-Column

The table-column flow object sets the attributes for *table columns*, which are groups of table cells stacked into same-width spans.

Characteristics in the table-column flow-objects class are column-number, `display-alignment`, `end-indent`, `n-columns-spanned`, `start-indent`, and width.

Table-Part

A table-part flow object can consist of three parts: the table body, the table header, and the table footer, all of which must have the same width. Table-column flow objects can occur only in the table body and have the highest precedence. Table-cell and table-row flow objects can occur in all three table parts. Characteristics in the table-part flow-objects class are break-after, break-before, keep, keep-with-next?, keep-with-previous?, may-violate-keep-after?, may-violate-keep-before?, space-after, space-before, table-part-omit-middle-footer?, table-part-omit-middle-header?.

Table-Row

The table-row flow object, which is the child of a table-part or table flow object, sets the attributes for table rows. Table-row flow object characteristics are ends-row? and starts-row?.

Specifying Styles

Styling in DSSSL-O is very similar to styling in CSS. For example, Chapter 5 includes this CSS example:

```
PARA {
    color: red;
    font-family: Arial, "Century Gothic", sans-serif;
    font-style: italic
}
```

A DSSSL-O example looks almost the same:

```
(element PARA_ONE
    (make paragraph
        color: red
        font-family-name: Arial, "Century Gothic", sans-
            serif
        font-posture: italic))
```

In DSSSL-O, you define a particular paragraph element (that is, PARA_ONE), use some different characters (()), and use DSSSL-O characteristics. Because DSSSL-O provides far more characteristics than CSS has properties, you can format and/or enhance elements in a wider variety of ways.

●—NOTE——————————————————————

For a comparison of CSS and DSSSL, see the electronic document "Is DSSSL Hard?" at http://itrc.uwaterloo.ca/~papresco/dsssl/hard.html.

DSSSL-O in Plain English

As you have learned, DSSSL-O includes many characteristics with which you can style a document. Some characteristics appear only once — in one flow-objects class; others appear often — in several flow-objects classes. Linking a particular characteristic name with its function isn't always easy. So, Table 6.1 might help you if you know that DSSSL-O can apply a specific format or enhancement, but can't remember the particular characteristic's name. The left column of Table 6.1 is a list of tasks, alphabetized by italicized action words; the right column is a list of characteristics. Match a task with a characteristic, and you're on your way.

Table 6-1 *DSSSL-O Flow-Objects Class Characteristics*

If You Want to:	Use This Characteristic
specify distance *after a box*	box-size-after
set *after-column margin* size	cell-after-column-margin
activate the table side *after the last column border*	after-column-border
activate the table side *after the last row border*	after-row-border
set *after-row margin* size	cell-after-row-margin
align a border line with a table border	border-alignment
align a box border line with a box border	box-border-alignment

If You Want to:	Use This Characteristic
align all but the last line in a paragraph	`quadding`
align cell contents with the row	`cell-row-alignment`
align flow object with writing mode	`display-alignment`
list all *allowed ligatures*	`allowed-ligatures`
set a *background color* for a flow object	`background-color`
specify the *background layer number* for a flow object	`background-layer`
specify distance *before a box*	`box-size-before`
set *before-column margin* size	`cell-before-column-margin`
set *before-row margin* size	`cell-before-row-margin`
turn on a *border after a column-aligned cell*	`cell-after-column-border`
turn on a *border after a row-aligned cell*	`cell-after-row-border`
turn on a *border before a column-aligned cell*	`cell-before-column-border`
turn on a *border before the first column*	`before-column-border`
turn on a *border before the first row*	`before-row-border`
turn on a *border before a row-aligned cell*	`cell-before-row-border`
name public identifier for *bidirectional processing method*	`implicit-bidi-method`
ask whether a table or cell *border exists*	`border-present?`
set *bottom margin*	`bottom-margin`
ask whether a broken *box has an open end*	`box-open-end?`
specify the bordered or background *box type*	`box-type`

Continued

Table 6-1   *Continued*

If You Want to:	Use This Characteristic
insert a *break after* a flow object	break-after
insert a *break before* a flow object	break-before
ask whether a *cell has a background*	cell-background?
center footer content	center-footer
center header content	center-header
specify a *character*	char
insert a *comment*	;
draw *cross line* in cell	cell-crossed
specify *destination URLs*	destination
display or inline a graphic	display?
set *end margin*	end-margin
end a record	record-end?
end a table row	ends-row?
set *ending edge indention*	end-indent
name *entity system identifier*	entity-system-id
specify *escapement direction*	escapement-direction
expand tab-position spacing	expand-tabs?
set *field alignment*	field-align
specify *field width*	field-width
set *filling direction*	filling-direction
set *first-line indention*	first-line-start-indent
float line-number areas to table	float-out-line-numbers?
float marginalia areas to table	float-out-marginalia?
float sideline attachment areas to table	float-out-sidelines?
keep *flow object and following one* on same page	may-violate-keep-after?

If You Want to:	Use This Characteristic
keep *flow object and preceding one* on same page	may-violate-keep-before?
specify a *font family name*	font-family-name
specify a *font name property*	font-name
specify the *font posture*	font-posture
set *font size*	font-size
set solid or outlined *font structure*	font-structure
set bold or light *font weight*	font-weight
set *font width* for proportional character	font-proportionate-width
set *footer margin*	footer-margin
set *foreground color*	color
specify *glyph alignment*	glyph-alignment-mode
provide *glyph identifier*	glyph-id
name the *glyph-reordering processing specification*	glyph-reorder-method
name the *glyph-substitution processing specification*	glyph-subst-method
identify *glyph-substitution tables* for the current glyph	glyph-subst-table
hang punctuation in margins and gutters	hanging-punct?
set *header margin*	header-margin
specify *hyphenated word segment locations*	hyphenation-keep
list *hyphenated words* and hyphen positions	hyphenation-exceptions
allow *hyphenation*	hyphenate?
specify number *hyphenation-ending lines*	hyphenation-ladder-count
name *hyphenation-method* public identifier	hyphenation-method

Continued

Table 6-1 *Continued*

If You Want to:	Use This Characteristic
ignore a record-end	`ignore-record-end?`
name the *ISO639 language code*	`language`
specify an *ISO3166 country code*	`country`
keep output together	`keep`
keep with the next flow object	`keep-with-next?`
keep with the previous flow object	`keep-with-previous?`
set loose or tight *kern spacing*	`kern-mode`
allow *kerning*	`kern?`
set *last-line alignment*	`last-line-quadding`
set *last-line indention*	`last-line-end-indent`
specify *layer number*	`layer`
repeat *leader pattern*	`min-leader-repeat`
set *left footer*	`left-footer`
set *left header*	`left-header`
set *left margin*	`left-margin`
allow *ligatures*	`ligature?`
name *line-break processing method*	`line-breaking-method`
inhibit *line breaks*	`inhibit-line-breaks?`
set *line cap* style	`line-cap`
name *line-composition processing method*	`line-composition-method`
specify *line dashes*	`line-dash`
specify *line-intersection look*	`line-join`
set *line-miter limit*	`line-miter-limit`
specify *line-repeats* in border	`line-repeat`
set *line-spacing distance*	`line-spacing`
set *line-spacing priority*	`line-spacing-priority`

If You Want to:	Use This Characteristic
specify *line thickness*	`line-thickness`
specify *lines formats*	`lines`
map a character	`char-map`
specify *marginalia attachment side* of flow-object area	`marginalia-side`
keep *marginalia with previous* flow-object area	`marginalia-keep-with-previous?`
specify a *math character's posture*	`math-font-posture`
specify *maximum graphic height*	`max-height`
specify *maximum graphic width*	`max-width`
set the *minimum leading* within the current paragraph flow object	`min-leading`
specify *minimum line spacing after* the current line	`min-post-line-spacing`
specify *minimum line spacing* before the current line	`min-pre-line-spacing`
list *multiple presentation modes*	`multi-modes`
identify the *notation system* containing an external graphic	`notation-system-id`
specify the *number of columns spanned*	`n-columns-spanned`
specify the *number of rows spanned*	`n-rows-spanned`
number a table column	`column-number`
offset the position point	`position-point-shift`
omit the footer table part	`table-part-omit-middle-footer?`
omit the header table part	`table-part-omit-middle-header?`
omit table border when there is a break	`border-omit-at-break`
orient a rule	`orientation`
specify the number of *orphan lines*	`orphan-count`

Continued

Table 6-1 *Continued*

If You Want to:	Use This Characteristic
set *page height*	page-height
set *page width*	page-width
specify a graphic's *position point x-coordinate*	position-point-x
specify a graphic's *position point y-coordinate*	position-point-y
display *principal mode presentation simultaneously* with other modes	principal-mode-simultaneous?
set *right footer*	right-footer
set *right header*	right-header
set *right margin*	right-margin
round the box corners	box-corner-rounded
round table corners	table-corner-rounded
set the *rule or leader length*	length
scale external graphic	scale
specify *score type* and attributes	type
separate a marginalia attachment and a flow-object area	marginalia-sep
separate a sideline attachment and a flow-object area	sideline-sep
specify *sideline attachment side* of flow-object area	sideline-side
ask whether to *snap a leader* to an invisible page grid	align-leader?
ask whether a character flow object is a *space*	space?
insert *space after* the flow-object area	space-after
insert *space before* the flow-object area	space-before
set a *span* of columns	span
start indent	start-indent

If You Want to:	Use This Characteristic
start *a table row*	starts-row?
set *starting margin*	start-margin
stretch a character	stretch-factor
strike through spaces	score-spaces?
specify a *strong or weak span*	span-weak?
input a *tab character*	input-tab?
identify the *table auto-width system*	table-auto-width-method
specify a *table border*	table-border
specify the *table-border priority*	border-priority
set *table-column width*	width
specify the *table width*	table-width
specify *text direction*	writing-mode
tile the scroll-area background until it is filled	background-tile
set *top margin*	top-margin
ask to *truncate a leader*	truncate-leader?
input *whitespace* flow object	input-whitespace?
specify *whitespace processing method*	input-whitespace-treatment
set the number of *widow lines*	widow-count

DSSSL-O Characteristics

This section is comprised of DSSSL-O characteristics. Each entry includes a brief description, the syntax, and notes. To make sure that you always have up-to-date information about DSSSL-O, periodically check the resources listed in the *Webliography*.

●—NOTE

In the command reference section on the remaining pages of this chapter, default values are underlined.

	Comment
;	

Purpose

Places a nonprinting comment in the style sheet document.

Syntax

> ; comment-text

Where

- ; indicates that a comment follows.
- *comment-text* is the text of the comment.

Notes

Use a comment to document a line or part of a style sheet. For example, you can state the reason for using a style or mark the beginning and end of related lines.

You can see the comment in the style sheet document but not in the published document.

	Last-Column Border
after-column-border	

Purpose

Activates the table border side that follows the last column.

Syntax

> after-column-border: #f | #t | *unlabeled_sosofo*

Where

- #f indicates that the Boolean value of this expression is false, or the expression is invalid or absent.
- #t indicates that the Boolean value of this expression is true.

- *unlabeled_sosofo* specifies a sequence of flow objects added to the flow-objects tree but not labeled with a symbol. The default is the value of the `table-border` characteristic.

Notes

The `after-column-border` characteristic is part of the table flow-objects class.

The default value of `after-column-border` is the value of the `table-border` characteristic.

An `after-column-border` value of #f or #t is the same as `border-present?` having a value of #f or #t, respectively.

If a table border exists, `after-column-border` inherits all other table characteristics.

The `after-column-border` characteristic is not inherited.

Related Characteristics

`after-row-border, before-column-border, before-row-border, border-present?, table-border`

after-row-border   Last-Row Border

Purpose

Activates the table border side that follows the last row.

Syntax

`after-row-border: #f|#t|`*unlabeled_sosofo*

Where

- #f indicates that the Boolean value of this expression is false, or the expression is invalid or absent.
- #t indicates that the Boolean value of this expression is true.
- *unlabeled_sosofo* specifies a sequence of flow objects added to the flow-objects tree but not labeled with a symbol. The default is the value of the `table-border` characteristic.

Notes

The `after-row-border` characteristic is part of the table flow-objects class.

The default value of `after-row-border` is the value of the `table-border` characteristic.

An `after-row-border` value of #f or #t is the same as `border-present?` having a value of #f or #t, respectively.

If a table border exists, `after-row-border` inherits all other table characteristics.

The `after-row-border` characteristic is not inherited.

Related Characteristics

`after-column-border, before-column-border, before-row-border, border-present?, table-border`

---

align-leader?   Align Leader?

Purpose

Indicates whether a leader is snapped to an invisible page grid.

Syntax

`align-leader?: #f|#t`

Where

- #f indicates that the Boolean value of this expression is false (that is, the leader is not snapped to the grid).
- #t indicates that the Boolean value of this expression is true (the leader is snapped to the grid). This is the default.

Notes

The `align-leader?` characteristic is part of the leader flow-objects class.

The `align-leader?` characteristic is inherited.

Related Characteristics

`inhibit-line-breaks?, length, min-leader-repeat, truncate-leader?`

allowed-ligatures   Allowed-Ligatures List

Purpose
Lists allowed ligatures.

Syntax
    allowed-ligatures: *glyph-ids-list* | *chars-list*

Where
- `glyph-ids-list` lists glyph identifiers. See the `glyph-id` characteristic.
- `chars-list` lists characters. See the `char` characteristic.

Notes
The `allowed-ligatures` characteristic is part of the character flow-objects class.

A *ligature* is a combination of two or more joined letters.

Only glyphs and characters on the `allowed-ligatures` list are recognized and can be used.

The default value of `allowed-ligatures` is an empty list.

The `allowed-ligatures` characteristic is inherited.

Related Characteristics
`char`, `glyph-id`, `glyph-reorder-method`, `glyph-subst-method`, `glyph-subst-table`, `ligature?`

background-color   Background Color

Purpose
Specifies a background color for the current flow object.

Syntax
    background-color: *color*

Where

- color represents one of several supported colors. The default is #f (no color).

Notes

The background-color characteristic is part of the box, scroll, and table-cell flow-objects classes.

The background-color characteristic cannot have a value if the value of border-type is border.

Supported color families include Device Gray, Device RGB, Device CMYK, Device KX, CIE LAB, CIE LUV, CIE Based ABC, and CIE Based A, all in the ISO/IEC 10179: 1996 standard. For more information, see section 12.5.9 in the ISO/IEC 10179: 1996 standard.

A cell-background? with a solid background has the color specified in the background-color characteristic.

The background-color characteristic is almost identical to the cascading style sheet background-color property.

The background-color characteristic is inherited.

Related Characteristics

background-layer, border-type, box-type, color

---

background-layer   Background Layer

Purpose

Specifies the layer number of the current background lines and marks for the flow object.

Syntax

background-layer: *integer*

Where

- *integer* is an integer. The default value is -1 (one layer below the foreground layer).

Notes

The background-layer characteristic is part of the box, scroll, and table-cell flow-objects classes.

The background-layer characteristic cannot have a value if the value of border-type is border.

The background-layer characteristic is inherited.

Related Characteristics

background-color, border-type, box-type, color, layer

---

background-tile   Background Tile

Purpose

Tiles the background of a scroll area until it is filled.

Syntax

background-tile: #f | external_graphic

Where

- #f indicates that the Boolean value of this expression is false, or the expression is invalid or absent. This is the default.

- external_graphic names the image used to tile the background.

Notes

The background-tile characteristic is part of the scroll flow-objects class.

Background tiling is similar to the tiling of wallpaper in Windows.

The background-tile characteristic is inherited.

Related Characteristic

background-layer

before-column-border

First-Column Border

Purpose
Activates the table border side that precedes the first column.

Syntax
```
before-column-border: #f | #t | unlabeled_sosofo
```

Where
- #f indicates that the Boolean value of this expression is false, or the expression is invalid or absent.
- #t indicates that the Boolean value of this expression is true.
- *unlabeled_sosofo* specifies a sequence of flow objects added to the flow-objects tree but not labeled with a symbol.

Notes
The before-column-border characteristic is part of the table flow-objects class.

The default value of before-column-border is the value of the table-border characteristic.

A before-column-border value of #f or #t is the same as border-present? having a value of #f or #t, respectively.

If a table border exists, before-column-border inherits all other table characteristics.

The before-column-border characteristic is not inherited.

Related Characteristics
after-column-border, after-row-border, before-row-border, border-present?, table-border

before-row-border

First-Row Border

Purpose
Activates the table border side that precedes the first row.

Syntax

```
before-row-border: #f|#t|unlabeled_sosofo
```

Where

- #f indicates that the Boolean value of this expression is false, or the expression is invalid or absent.
- #t indicates that the Boolean value of this expression is true.
- *unlabeled_sosofo* specifies a sequence of flow objects added to the flow-objects tree but not labeled with a symbol.

Notes

The before-row-border characteristic is part of the table flow-objects class.

The default value of before-row-border is the value of the table-border characteristic.

A before-row-border value of #f or #t is the same as border-present? having a value of #f or #t, respectively.

If a table border exists, before-row-border inherits all other table characteristics.

The before-row-border characteristic is not inherited.

Related Characteristics

```
after-column-border, after-row-border, before-column-
border, border-present?, table-border
```

border-alignment   Border Alignment

Purpose

Aligns the table border line with the actual location of the table border.

Syntax

```
border-alignment: center|start|end|outside|inside
```

Where

- center centers the table border line with the table border. This is the default.
- start aligns the table border line with the start of the writing-mode direction and adds space to the end.
- end aligns the table border line with the end of the writing-mode direction and adds space to the start.
- outside aligns the table border line with the outside edge of the table border.
- inside aligns the table border line with the inside edge of the table border.

Notes

The border-alignment characteristic is part of the table-border flow-objects class.

The border-alignment characteristic is inherited.

Related Characteristics

box-border-alignment, border-omit-at-break?, border-present?, border-priority

border-omit-at-break?	Omit Border at Break?

Purpose

Indicates whether the nearby border is present when there is a break in the table.

Syntax

border-omit-at-break?: #f|#t

Where

- #f indicates that the Boolean value of this expression is false (the border is present when there is a break). This is the default.
- #t indicates that the Boolean value of this expression is true (the border is erased when there is a break).

Notes

The border-omit-at-break characteristic is part of the
table-border flow-objects class.
  If the value of border-present? is #f, the border is erased.
  The border-omit-at-break characteristic is inherited.

Related Characteristics

border-present?, border-priority

border-present?   Border Present?

Purpose

Indicates whether a table border or cell border exists.

Syntax

border-present?: #f|#t

Where

- #f indicates that the Boolean value of this expression is
  false (the table border or cell border is not present).

- #t indicates that the Boolean value of this expression is
  true (the table border or cell border is present). This is the
  default.

Notes

The border-present? characteristic is part of the table-border
flow-objects class.
  A table-border value of #f or #t is the same as border-
present? having a value of #f or #t, respectively.
  If a table border exists, border-present? inherits all other
table characteristics.
  The border-present? characteristic is inherited.

Related Characteristics

after-column-border, after-row-border, before-column-
border, before-row-border, table-border

border-priority
Border Priority

Purpose
Sets the priority of the current table-border flow object.

Syntax
```
border-priority: integer
```

Where
- *integer* is an integer. The default value is 0.

Notes
The border-priority characteristic is part of the table-border flow-objects class.

The higher the value of the border-priority, the higher its priority.

If two table-border flow objects have the same assigned priority, processing stops and an error message appears.

The border-priority characteristic is inherited.

Related Characteristics
```
border-alignment, border-omit-at-break?, border-present
```

bottom-margin
Bottom Margin

Purpose
Specifies the distance from the bottom edge of the page to the bottom of the flow-object area.

Syntax
```
bottom-margin: length
```

Where
- *length* is an absolute length, in points. The default is 0pt.

Notes

The bottom-margin characteristic is part of the simple-page-sequence flow-objects class.

The bottom-margin characteristic is inherited.

Related Characteristics

footer-margin, header-margin, left-margin, right-margin, top-margin

box-border-alignment
Box Border Alignment

Purpose

Aligns the box border line with the actual location of the box border.

Syntax

box-border-alignment: center|outside|inside

Where

- center centers the box border line with the box border.
- outside aligns the box border line with the outside edge of the box border. This is the default.
- inside aligns the box border line with the inside edge of the box border.

Notes

The box-border-alignment characteristic is part of the box flow-objects class.

The box-border-alignment characteristic is inherited.

Related Characteristics

border-alignment, box-corner-rounded, box-open-end?, box-type

box-corner-rounded | Rounded Box Corners

Purpose

Specifies whether box corners are rounded or squared.

Syntax

box-corner-rounded: #f | #t | *x-y_pairs_list*

Where

- #f indicates that the Boolean value of this expression is false (box corners are squared). This is the default.
- #t indicates that the Boolean value of this expression is true (box corners are rounded).
- *x-y_pairs_list* indicates the location of particular rounded corners.

Notes

The box-corner-rounded characteristic is part of the box flow-objects class.

If the box is displayed, x indicates whether the target corner is before or after the writing-mode direction, and y indicates whether the target corner is before or after the placement direction, which is perpendicular to the writing-mode direction.

If the box is inline, x indicates whether the target corner is before or after the escapement-direction, and y indicates whether the target corner is before or after the line-progression direction, which is perpendicular to the escapement-direction.

The box-corner-rounded characteristic is inherited.

Related Characteristics

border-present?, table-corner-rounded

box-open-end? — Box Open End?

Purpose

Indicates whether a broken box should have a visible border.

Syntax

```
box-open-end?: #f | #t
```

Where

- #f indicates that the Boolean value of this expression is false (the box should have a visible border). This is the default.

- #t indicates that the Boolean value of this expression is true (the box should have an invisible border on one end).

Notes

The box-open-end? characteristic is part of the box flow-objects class.

The box-open-end? characteristic is inherited.

Related Characteristics

```
box-border-alignment, box-type
```

box-size-after — Box Size After

Purpose

Indicates the distance from the placement path (the baseline on which text rests) to the following edge of the box in the line-progression direction.

Syntax

```
box-size-after: length
```

Where

- *length* is an absolute length, in points. The default is 4pt.

Notes

The box-size-after characteristic is part of the box flow-objects class.

The box-size-after characteristic is inherited.

Related Characteristic

```
box-size-before
```

box-size-before — Box Size Before

Purpose

Indicates the distance from the placement path (the baseline on which text rests) to the preceding edge of the box in the line-progression direction.

Syntax

```
box-size-before: length
```

Where

- *length* is an absolute length, in points. The default is 8pt.

Notes

The box-size-before characteristic is part of the box flow-objects class.

The box-size-before characteristic is inherited.

Related Characteristic

```
box-size-after
```

box-type

Box Type

Purpose

Specifies the type of box — with a border, a background, or both.

Syntax

```
box-type: border | background | both
```

Where

- border indicates that the box will have a border. This is the default.
- background indicates that the box will have a background.
- both indicates that the box will have both a border and a background.

Notes

The box-type characteristic is part of the box flow-objects class. The box-type characteristic is inherited.

Related Characteristics

```
background-color, box-corner-rounded, color
```

break-after

Break After

Purpose

Indicates whether a page break is inserted after the current flow object appears.

Syntax

```
break-after: #f | page
```

Where

- #f indicates that the Boolean value of this expression is false (the current flow object does not cause a break after it appears). This is the default.

- page inserts a page break after the current flow object is displayed.

Notes

The break-after characteristic is part of the aligned-column, box, display-group, external-graphic, paragraph, rule, table, and table-part flow-objects classes.

The full version of DSSSL also supports the following values: page-region, column, and column-set.

The break-after characteristic is not inherited.

Related Characteristics

break-before, keep

6	**break-before**	Break Before

Purpose

Indicates whether a page break is inserted before the current flow object appears.

Syntax

break-before: #f | page

Where

- #f indicates that the Boolean value of this expression is false (the current flow object does not cause a break before it appears). This is the default.
- page inserts a page break before the current flow object is displayed.

Notes

The break-before characteristic is part of the aligned-column, box, display-group, external-graphic, paragraph, rule, table, and table-part flow-objects classes.

The full version of DSSSL also supports the following values: page-region, column, and column-set.

The break-before characteristic is not inherited.

Related Characteristics

```
break-after, keep
```

cell-after-column-border	Cell after Column Border

Purpose

Turns on a table border following the current cell in the direction in which the table columns fill the table.

Syntax

```
cell-after-column-border: #f | #t | unlabeled_sosofo
```

Where

- #f indicates that the Boolean value of this expression is false (the table border is not present). This is the default.
- #t indicates that the Boolean value of this expression is true (the table border is present).
- *unlabeled_sosofo* specifies a sequence of flow objects added to the flow-objects tree but not labeled with a symbol.

Notes

The cell-after-column-border characteristic is part of the table-cell flow-objects class.

The #f and #t values of the cell-before-row-border characteristic are equivalent to the respective #f and #t values of the border-present? characteristic.

The cell-after-column-border characteristic is inherited.

Related Characteristics

```
border-present?, cell-after-column-margin, cell-after-
row-border, cell-after-row-margin, cell-before-column-
border, cell-before-column-margin, cell-before-row-border,
cell-before-row-margin
```

cell-after-column-margin

Cell after Column Margin

Purpose

Specifies the size of the margin following the column in the direction in which the table columns fill the table.

Syntax

```
cell-after-column-margin: length
```

Where

- *length* is an absolute length, in points. The default is 0pt.

Notes

The cell-after-column-margin characteristic is part of the table-cell flow-objects class.

The cell-after-column-margin characteristic is inherited.

Related Characteristics

cell-after-column-border, cell-after-row-border, cell-after-row-margin, cell-before-column-border, cell-before-column-margin, cell-before-row-border, cell-before-row-margin

cell-after-row-border

Cell after Row Border

Purpose

Turns on a table border following the current cell in the direction in which the table rows fill the table.

Syntax

```
cell-after-row-border: #f|#t|unlabeled_sosofo
```

Where

- #f indicates that the Boolean value of this expression is false (the table border is not present). This is the default.
- #t indicates that the Boolean value of this expression is true (the table border is present).
- *unlabeled_sosofo* specifies a sequence of flow objects added to the flow-objects tree but not labeled with a symbol.

Notes

The `cell-after-row-border` characteristic is part of the table-cell flow-objects class.

The #f and #t values of the `cell-after-row-border` characteristic are equivalent to the respective #f and #t values of the border-present? characteristic.

The `cell-after-row-border` characteristic is inherited.

Related Characteristics

`cell-after-column-border`, `cell-after-column-margin`, `cell-after-row-margin`, `cell-before-column-border`, `cell-before-column-margin`, `cell-before-row-border`, `cell-before-row-margin`

cell-after-row-margin	Cell after Row Margin

Purpose

Specifies the size of the margin following the row in the direction in which the table rows fill the table.

Syntax

```
cell-after-row-margin: length
```

Where

- *length* is an absolute length, in points. The default is 0pt.

Notes

The cell-after-row-margin characteristic is part of the table-cell flow-objects class.

The cell-after-row-margin characteristic is inherited.

Related Characteristics

cell-after-column-border, cell-after-column-margin, cell-after-row-border, cell-before-column-border, cell-before-column-margin, cell-before-row-border, cell-before-row-margin

---

cell-background?	Cell Background?

Purpose

Indicates whether the current table cell has a solid background.

Syntax

cell-background?: #f | #t

Where

- #f indicates that the Boolean value of this expression is false (the table has a transparent background). This is the default.

- #t indicates that the Boolean value of this expression is true (the table has a solid background).

Notes

The cell-background? characteristic is part of the table-cell flow-objects class.

A cell-background? with a solid background has the color specified in the background-color characteristic.

The cell-background? characteristic is inherited.

Related Characteristic

background-color

cell-before-column-border	Cell before Column Border

Purpose

Turns on a table border preceding the current column in the direction in which the table columns fill the table.

Syntax

cell-before-column-border: #f | #t | *unlabeled_sosofo*

Where

- #f indicates that the Boolean value of this expression is false (the table border is not present). This is the default.
- #t indicates that the Boolean value of this expression is true (the table border is present).
- *unlabeled_sosofo* specifies a sequence of flow objects added to the flow-objects tree but not labeled with a symbol.

Notes

The cell-before-column-border characteristic is part of the table-cell flow-objects class.

The #f and #t values of the cell-before-row-border characteristic are equivalent to the respective #f and #t values of the border-present? characteristic.

The cell-before-column-border characteristic is inherited.

Related Characteristics

border-present?, cell-after-column-border, cell-after-column-margin, cell-after-row-border, cell-after-row-margin, cell-before-column-margin, cell-before-row-border, cell-before-row-margin

cell-before-column-margin
Cell before Column Margin

Purpose
Specifies the size of the margin prior to the column in the direction in which the table columns fill the table.

Syntax
```
cell-before-column-margin: length
```

Where
- *length* is an absolute length, in points. The default is 0pt.

Notes
The `cell-before-column-margin` characteristic is part of the table-cell flow-objects class.

The `cell-before-column-margin` characteristic is inherited.

Related Characteristics
`cell-after-column-border`, `cell-after-column-margin`, `cell-after-row-border`, `cell-after-row-margin`, `cell-before-column-border`, `cell-before-row-border`, `cell-before-row-margin`

cell-before-row-border
Cell before Row Border

Purpose
Turns on a table border preceding the current cell in the direction in which the table rows fill the table.

Syntax
```
cell-before-row-border: #f | #t | unlabeled_sosofo
```

Where

- #f indicates that the Boolean value of this expression is false (the table border is not present). This is the default.
- #t indicates that the Boolean value of this expression is true (the table border is present).
- *unlabeled_sosofo* specifies a sequence of flow objects added to the flow-objects tree but not labeled with a symbol.

Notes

The cell-before-row-border characteristic is part of the table-cell flow-objects class.

The #f and #t values of the cell-after-row-border characteristic are equivalent to the respective #f and #t values of the border-present? characteristic.

The cell-before-row-border characteristic is inherited.

Related Characteristics

border-present?, cell-after-column-border, cell-after-column-margin, cell-after-row-border, cell-after-row-margin, cell-before-column-border, cell-before-column-margin, cell-before-row-margin

cell-before-row-margin	Cell before Row Margin

Purpose

Specifies the size of the margin prior to the row in the direction in which the table rows fill the table.

Syntax

```
cell-before-row-margin: length
```

Where

- *length* is an absolute length, in points. The default is 0pt.

Notes

The cell-before-row-margin characteristic is part of the table-cell flow-objects class.

The cell-before-row-margin characteristic is inherited.

Related Characteristics

cell-after-column-border, cell-after-column-margin, cell-after-row-border, cell-after-row-margin, cell-before-column-border, cell-before-column-margin, cell-before-row-border

---

cell-crossed   Cross-Out Cell

Purpose

Draws one or two diagonal lines from cell corner to cell corner.

Syntax

cell-crossed: #f|with|across|both

Where

- #f indicates that the Boolean value of this expression is false (no diagonal lines are drawn within the current cell). This is the default.

- with draws a diagonal line from the first-row-and-first-column corner in the cell to the opposite corner.

- across draws a diagonal line from the first-row-and-last-column corner in the cell to the opposite corner.

- both draws two diagonal lines from both corners to the opposite corners.

Notes

The cell-crossed characteristic is part of the table-cell flow-objects class.

Use the line-cap, line-dash, line-repeat, and line-thickness characteristics to enhance diagonal lines.

The cell-crossed characteristic is inherited.

Related Characteristics

line-cap, line-dash, line-repeat, line-thickness

cell-row-alignment	Cell Row Alignment

Purpose

Sets the row-based alignment of the contents of the current cell.

Syntax

cell-row-alignment: <u>start</u>|end|center

Where

- start aligns the contents with the starting direction from which a table row is drawn. This is the default.
- end aligns the flow object in the ending direction in which a table row is drawn.
- center centers the flow object between the start and end of the direction in which a table row is drawn.

Notes

The cell-row-alignment characteristic is part of the table-cell flow-objects class.

The cell-row-alignment characteristic is inherited.

center-footer	Center Footer

Purpose

Contains inline flow objects centered between the left and right margins of the footer.

Syntax

center-footer: *unlabeled_sosofo*

Where

- *unlabeled_sosofo* specifies a sequence of flow objects added to the flow-objects tree but not labeled with a symbol. The default is an empty sosofo.

Notes

The center-footer characteristic is part of the simple-page-sequence flow-objects class.
The center-footer characteristic is not inherited.

Related Characteristics

center-header, footer-margin, header-margin, left-footer, left-header, right-footer, right-header

---

6

center-header   Center Header

Purpose

Contains inline flow objects centered between the left and right margins of the header.

Syntax

center-header: *unlabeled_sosofo*

Where

- *unlabeled_sosofo* specifies a sequence of flow objects added to the flow-objects tree but not labeled with a symbol. The default is an empty sosofo.

Notes

The center-header characteristic is part of the simple-page-sequence flow-objects class.
The center-header characteristic is not inherited.

Related Characteristics

center-footer, footer-margin, header-margin, left-footer, left-header, right-footer, right-header

char	Character

Purpose

Specifies a character.

Syntax

char: *character*

Where

- *character* is a character.

Notes

The char characteristic is part of the character flow-objects class.

If you do not specify a character and the current node has a char property, that character will be used for this characteristic.

If the value of char-map is *procedure*, *procedure* is applied to the value of char.

You can use this character as a glyph or as a hyphenation character, if the value of hyphenate? is #t.

The char characteristic is not inherited.

6

Related Characteristics

allowed-ligatures, char-map, color, font-name, font-posture, font-proportionate-width, font-structure, font-weight, glyph-id, hyphenate?, kern?, ligature?, math-font-posture, punct?

char-map	Character Map

Purpose

Maps the default char character.

Syntax

char-map: #f | *procedure*

Where

- #f indicates that the Boolean value of this expression is false (no associated character-mapping procedure exists). This is the default.
- *procedure* identifies a character-mapping procedure.

Notes

The char-map characteristic is part of the character flow-objects class.

The char-map characteristic is inherited.

Related Characteristic

char

color   Foreground Color

Purpose

Specifies a foreground color for the current flow object.

Syntax

color: *color*

Where

- color represents one of several supported colors. The default is the Device Gray color space.

Notes

The color characteristic is part of the box, character, external-graphic, rule, score, sideline, and table-border flow-objects classes.

Supported color families include Device Gray, Device RGB, Device CMYK, Device KX, CIE LAB, CIE LUV, CIE Based ABC, and CIE Based A, all in the ISO/IEC 10179: 1996 standard. For more information, see section 12.5.9 in the ISO/IEC 10179: 1996 standard.

The color characteristic is inherited.

Related Characteristic

background-color

column-number   Column Number

Purpose

Specifies the number of the first column in a table-cell span.

Syntax

column-number: *integer*

Where

* *integer* is a positive, non-zero integer.

Notes

The column-number characteristic is part of the table-cell and table column flow-objects classes.

The default column-number for a table column is equal to the value of the prior table-column flow object plus 1. If no prior table column flow object exists, the default column-number value is 1, which represents the first column in the table.

When a prior table row contains cells that span two or more rows, the table cells that follow use the column-number characteristic to clarify identification.

The default column-number for a table cell is the current table-column number.

The column-number characteristic is not inherited.

Related Characteristics

cell-after-column-margin, cell-before-column-margin, n-columns-spanned

| **country** | **Country Code** |

Purpose
Specifies the ISO 3166 country code.

Syntax

country: #f | *ISO_3166_country_code*

Where

- #f indicates that the Boolean value of this expression is false (no country code is specified). This is the default.
- *ISO_3166_country_code* is an uppercase country code, specified in the ISO 3166 standard.

Notes
The country characteristic is part of the character, paragraph, and paragraph-break flow-objects classes.

In DSSSL-O, language codes and country codes must be in uppercase characters.

In XML, language codes and country codes are case-insensitive. Although it is not required, the language code is usually in lowercase and the country code is usually in uppercase.

You can find a list of country codes at http://sunsite.berkeley.edu/amher/iso_3166.html.

Use the XML Subcode element to specify language and country codes within XML documents.

The country characteristic is inherited.

Related Characteristic
language

| **destination** | **Destination Link(s)** |

Purpose
Specifies one or more URLs on which a user can click to jump to a destination link.

Syntax

```
destination: #f | address | address_list
```

Where

- #f indicates that the Boolean value of this expression is false (that is, the named nested flow object is not considered to be part of the link and does not behave like a link).
- *address* specifies one URL to which a user can link.
- *address_list* lists two or more URLs to which a user can link.

Notes

The destination characteristic is part of the link flow-objects class.

For more information about Internet addresses, see section 12.5.8 of the ISO/IEC 10179: 1996 standard.

The destination characteristic is not inherited.

display-alignment   Display Alignment

Purpose

Aligns the current flow object based on the value of the current writing-mode characteristic.

Syntax

```
display-alignment: start | center | end
```

Where

- start aligns the flow object with the start of the writing-mode direction and adds space to the end. This is the default.
- center centers the flow object by adding space to the start and end of the writing-mode direction.
- end aligns the flow object with the end of the writing-mode direction and adds space to the start.

Notes

The display-alignment characteristic is part of the aligned-column, external-graphic, rule, table, and table-column flow-objects classes.

The full version of DSSSL also supports the following values: inside and outside.

The display-alignment characteristic is inherited.

Related Characteristics

end-indent, start-indent, writing-mode

---

display?   Display or Inline?

Purpose

Indicates whether a box or external graphic is displayed or inlined.

Syntax

display?: #f | #t

Where

- #f indicates that the Boolean value of this expression is false (the box or graphic is inlined). This is the default.
- #t indicates that the Boolean value of this expression is true (the box or graphic is displayed).

Notes

The display? characteristic is part of the box and external-graphic flow-objects classes.

The display? characteristic is not inherited.

---

end-indent   End Indent

Purpose

Specifies indention at the ending edge of the current writing-mode direction.

Syntax

```
end-indent: length-spec
```

Where

- *length-spec* is a relative or absolute length of the indention. The default is 0pt.

Notes

The end-indent characteristic is part of the aligned-column, box, external-graphic, paragraph, rule, table, and table-column flow-objects classes.
The end-indent characteristic is inherited.

Related Characteristics

```
start-indent, writing-mode
```

6

end-margin   Ending Margin

Purpose

Sets the distance from the edge of the last area in the writing-mode direction to the closest edge of the text area.

Syntax

```
end-margin: length-spec
```

Where

- *length-spec* is a relative or absolute length. The default is 0pt.

Notes

The end-margin characteristic is part of the scroll flow-objects class.
The end-margin characteristic is inherited.

Related Characteristics

```
start-margin, writing-mode
```

ends-row?   Ends Row?

Purpose

Indicates whether the current table cell ends a table row.

Syntax

```
ends-row?: #f|#t
```

Where

- #f indicates that the Boolean value of this expression is false (the current cell does not end a row). This is the default.
- #t indicates that the Boolean value of this expression is true (the current cell ends a row).

Notes

The ends-row? characteristic is part of the table-cell flow-objects class.

The only time that you can use the ends-row? characteristic is when a table cell is not in a table row; that is, no prior flow object exists or the prior flow object is not a table cell.

The ends-row? characteristic is not inherited.

Related Characteristic

```
starts-row?
```

entity-system-id   Entity System ID

Purpose

Identifies the system containing the external entity within which an external graphic resides.

Syntax

```
entity-system-id: #f|system_identifier
```

Where

- #f indicates that the Boolean value of this expression is false (no system identifier exists).

- *system_identifier* is a string that names the system containing the external entity within which the graphic resides.

Notes

The entity-system-id characteristic is part of the external-graphic flow-objects class.

An entity declaration statement within a document declares the system identifier.

The entity-system-id characteristic is not inherited.

Related Characteristic

notation-system-id

---

escapement-direction   Escapement Direction

Purpose

Specifies the direction in which a character displays or is inlined.

Syntax

escapement-direction: top-to-bottom | left-to-right | right-to-left

Where

- top-to-bottom indicates that a character prints or displays starting at the top and ending at the bottom.

- left-to-right indicates that a character prints or displays starting at the left and ending at the right.

- right-to-left indicates that a character prints or displays starting at the right and ending at the left.

Notes

The escapement-direction characteristic is part of the external-graphic flow-objects class.

The escapement point is located at the point at which the current character ends and the following character begins in an inline area.

The default value of escapement-direction is the same as that of the writing-mode characteristic.

Related Characteristic

writing-mode

---

expand-tabs?   Expand Tab Intervals?

6

Purpose

Indicates whether the spacing between tabs increases.

Syntax

expand-tabs?: #f | *integer*

Where

- #f indicates that the Boolean value of this expression is false, or the expression is invalid or absent.
- *integer* is a non-zero, positive number. The default value is 8.

Notes

The expand-tabs? characteristic is part of the paragraph flow-objects class.

The expand-tabs? characteristic allows you to set tab spacing, to align the contents of lines of monospace text.

The expand-tabs? characteristic is inherited.

Related Characteristics

input-tab?, lines

field-align

Field Align

Purpose

Aligns an inline field in the writing-mode direction.

Syntax

```
field-align: start|end|center
```

Where

- start aligns the field with the start of the writing-mode direction and adds space to the end. This is the default.
- end aligns the field with the end of the writing-mode direction and adds space to the start.
- center centers the field by adding space to the start and end of the writing-mode direction.

Notes

The field-align characteristic is part of the line-field flow-objects class.

The field-align characteristic is inherited.

Related Characteristics

```
field-width, inhibit-line-breaks?, writing-mode
```

field-width

Field Width

Purpose

Specifies the maximum width of an inline field.

Syntax

```
field-width: length-spec
```

Where

- *length-spec* is a relative or absolute length. The default is 0pt.

Notes

The `field-width` characteristic is part of the line-field flow-objects class.

If the inline field is wider than the value of the `field-width` characteristic, the width automatically increases to the width of the field.

If an inline field is located in a paragraph, a line break may be inserted before and after the field.

The `field-width` characteristic is inherited.

Related Characteristics

`field-align, inhibit-line-breaks?, writing-mode`

---

filling-direction   Filling Direction

6

Purpose

Specifies the direction in which the contents of a flow object fill the flow-object area.

Syntax

`filling-direction:` <u>`top-to-bottom`</u>`|left-to-right|right-to-left`

Where

- `top-to-bottom` indicates the direction in which text is printed or displayed, starting at the top and ending at the bottom. This is the default.

- `left-to-right` indicates the direction in which text is printed or displayed, starting at the left side and ending at the right side.

- `right-to-left` indicates the direction in which text is printed or displayed, starting at the right side and ending at the left side.

Notes

The `filling-direction` characteristic is part of the scroll flow-objects class.

Filling direction can be perpendicular to the placement direction.

The `filling-direction` characteristic is inherited.

Related Characteristics

`background-color`, `background-layer`, `background-tile`, `end-margin`, `start-margin`, `writing-mode`

first-line-start-indent   Indent First Line

Purpose

Sets the amount of starting indention for the first line of the current paragraph flow object.

Syntax

`first-line-start-indent:` *length-spec*

Where

- *length-spec* is a positive or negative relative or absolute length. The default is 0pt.

Notes

The `first-line-start-indent` characteristic is part of the paragraph flow-objects class.

The `first-line-start-indent` characteristic is inherited.

Related Characteristic

`last-line-end-indent`

float-out-line-numbers?

Float Line Numbers?

Purpose

Indicates whether line-number attachment areas should be associated with the parent table instead of the current table cell.

Syntax

```
float-out-line-numbers?: #f | #t
```

Where

- #f indicates that the Boolean value of this expression is false (the attachment should continue to be attached to the table cell). This is the default.
- #t indicates that the Boolean value of this expression is true (the attachment should be attached to the table.)

Notes

The `float-out-line-numbers?` characteristic is part of the table-cell flow-objects class.

The `float-out-line-numbers?` characteristic is inherited.

Related Characteristics

`float-out-marginalia?`, `float-out-sidelines?`

float-out-marginalia?

Float Marginalia?

Purpose

Indicates whether marginalia attachment areas should be associated with the parent table instead of the current table cell.

Syntax

```
float-out-marginalia?: #f | #t
```

Where

- #f indicates that the Boolean value of this expression is false (the attachment should continue to be attached to the table cell). This is the default.

- #t indicates that the Boolean value of this expression is true (the attachment should be attached to the table.)

Notes

The float-out-marginalia? characteristic is part of the table-cell flow-objects class.

The float-out-marginalia? characteristic is inherited.

Related Characteristics

float-out-line-numbers?, float-out-sidelines?

float-out-sidelines?   Float Sidelines?

Purpose

Indicates whether sideline attachment areas should be associated with the parent table instead of the current table cell.

Syntax

float-out-sidelines?: #f|#t

Where

- #f indicates that the Boolean value of this expression is false (the attachment should continue to be attached to the table cell). This is the default.

- #t indicates that the Boolean value of this expression is true (the attachment should be attached to the table.)

Notes

The float-out-sidelines? characteristic is part of the table-cell flow-objects class.

The float-out-sidelines? characteristic is inherited.

Related Characteristics

```
float-out-line-numbers?, float-out-marginalia?
```

font-family-name	Font Family Name

Purpose

Specifies the name of a font family.

Syntax

```
font-family-name: #f | string
```

Where

- #f indicates that the Boolean value of this expression is false, or the expression is invalid or absent.
- *string* is the name of a font family. The default value is iso-serif.

Notes

The font-family-name characteristic is part of the character, paragraph, and paragraph-break flow-objects classes.

The font-family-name characteristic is related to the cascading style sheet font-family property.

Related Characteristic

```
font-name
```

font-name	Font-Name Property

Purpose

Specifies the name of a font-name property.

Syntax

```
font-name: #f | public_identifier
```

Where

- #f indicates that the Boolean value of this expression is false (any font name is valid). This is the default.
- *public_identifier* is the name of a public identifier of a font property.

Notes

The font-name characteristic is part of the character, paragraph, and paragraph-break flow-objects classes.

When you specify a public identifier for the font-name characteristic, the values of the font-family-name, font-posture, font-proportionate-width, font-structure, and font-weight characteristics are ignored.

For the font-name characteristic to be valid, the value of glyph-alignment-mode must be font, or the value of both min-post-line-spacing and min-pre-line-spacing must be #f.

The font-name characteristic is related to the cascading style sheet font property.

The font-name characteristic is inherited.

Related Characteristics

font-family-name, font-posture, font-proportionate-width, font-structure, font-weight, glyph-alignment-mode, min-post-line-spacing, min-pre-line-spacing

font-posture   Font Posture

Purpose

Specifies the level of incline of flow object text.

Syntax

font-posture: #f | upright | oblique | italic | math

Where

- #f indicates that the Boolean value of this expression is false (any font posture is appropriate).

- upright indicates that each letter is completely vertical. This is the default.
- oblique indicates that each letter has a posture between upright and italic.
- italic indicates that each letter is slanted.
- math indicates that the slant level is the same as that of the math-font-posture characteristic.

Notes

The font-posture characteristic is part of the character, paragraph, and paragraph-break flow-objects classes.

For the font-posture characteristic to be valid, the value of glyph-alignment-mode must be font, or the value of both min-post-line-spacing and min-pre-line-spacing must be #f.

The full version of DSSSL also supports the following values: not-applicable, back-slanted-oblique, and back-slanted-italic.

The font-posture characteristic is related to the cascading style sheet font-style property.

The font-posture characteristic is inherited.

Related Characteristics

font-family-name, font-name, font-size, glyph-alignment-mode, math-font-posture, min-post-line-spacing, min-pre-line-spacing

---

font-proportionate-width	Font Proportionate Width

Purpose

Specifies a width setting for a proportional font.

Syntax

font-proportionate-width: #f | condensed | medium | expanded

Where

- #f indicates that the Boolean value of this expression is false (that any font width is appropriate).
- condensed indicates that the font width is reduced.
- medium indicates that the font width is the current width. This is the default.
- expanded indicates that the font width is increased.

Notes

The font-proportionate-width characteristic is part of the character, paragraph, and paragraph-break flow-objects classes.

For the font-proportionate-width characteristic to be valid, the value of glyph-alignment-mode must be font, or the value of both min-post-line-spacing and min-pre-line-spacing must be #f.

The full version of DSSSL also supports the following values: not-applicable, ultra-condensed, extra-condensed, semi-condensed, semi-expanded, extra-expanded, and ultra-expanded.

The font-proportionate-width characteristic is inherited.

Related Characteristics

font-family-name, font-name, font-size, glyph-alignment-mode, min-post-line-spacing, min-pre-line-spacing

font-size   Font Size

Purpose

Specifies an absolute font size in points.

Syntax

font-size: *length*

Where

- *length* is an absolute point size, in points. The default is 10pt.

Notes

The font-size characteristic is part of the character, paragraph, and paragraph-break flow-objects classes.

The font-size characteristic is almost identical to the cascading style sheet font-size property.

Related Characteristics

font-family-name, font-name, font-posture, font-proportionate-width, font-structure, font-weight

font-structure	Font Structure

Purpose

Specifies a solid, outlined, or other structure type for the current font.

Syntax

font-structure: #f | not-applicable | solid | outline

Where

- #f indicates that the Boolean value of this expression is false (any font structure is appropriate).
- not-applicable indicates that the current font does not offer font structure choices.
- solid indicates that each letter is completely solid. This is the default.
- outline indicates that each letter is outlined.

Notes

The font-structure characteristic is part of the character, paragraph, and paragraph-break flow-objects classes.

For the font-structure characteristic to be valid, the value of glyph-alignment-mode must be font, or the value of both min-post-line-spacing and min-pre-line-spacing must be #f.

The font-structure characteristic is inherited.

Related Characteristics

font-family-name, font-name, font-size, glyph-alignment-mode, min-post-line-spacing, min-pre-line-spacing

font-weight	Font Weight

Purpose

Specifies the degree of boldness or lightness of flow object text.

Syntax

font-weight: #f | light | <u>medium</u> | bold

Where

- #f indicates that the Boolean value of this expression is false, or the expression is invalid or absent.
- light is the equivalent of light text, which varies depending on the font selected.
- medium is the equivalent of normal text, which varies depending on the font selected. This is the default.
- bold is standard boldface.

Notes

The font-weight characteristic is part of the character, paragraph, and paragraph-break flow-objects classes.

The font-weight characteristic is similar to the cascading style sheet font-weight property.

The full version of DSSSL also supports the following values: not-applicable, ultra-light, extra-light, semi-light, semi-bold, extra-bold, and ultra-bold.

Related Characteristics

font-family-name, font-name, font-posture, font-proportionate-width, font-size, font-structure

footer-margin

Footer Margin

Purpose

Specifies the distance from the bottom edge of the page to the bottom of the footer area.

Syntax

```
footer-margin: length
```

Where

- *length* is an absolute length, in points. The default is 0pt.

Notes

The footer-margin characteristic is part of the simple-page-sequence flow-objects class.

The footer-margin characteristic is inherited.

Related Characteristics

```
center-footer, center-header, header margin,
left-footer, left-header, right-footer, right-header
```

glyph-alignment-mode

Glyph Alignment Mode

Purpose

Indicates the alignment of the current glyph within its paragraph flow object.

Syntax

```
glyph-alignment-mode: base|center|top|bottom|font
```

Where

- base aligns the glyph with the baseline of the current text line.
- center centers the glyph within the flow-object area.

- top aligns the glyph with the top of the flow-object area.
- bottom aligns the glyph with the bottom of the flow-object area.
- font uses the same alignment as the font used by the current writing-mode characteristic. This is the default.

Notes

The glyph-alignment-mode characteristic is part of the paragraph flow-objects class.

Related Characteristics

glyph-id, glyph-reorder-method, writing-mode

---

glyph-id   Glyph ID   6

Purpose

Identifies a glyph that will be inserted in the current flow-object area.

Syntax

glyph-id: #f | *glyph_id*

Where

- #f indicates that the Boolean value of this expression is false (no glyph identifier exists).
- *glyph_id* is a string naming the glyph to be inserted in the flow-object area.

Notes

The glyph-id characteristic is part of the character flow-objects class.

The glyph-id characteristic takes the value of the char characteristic.

The glyph-id characteristic is not inherited.

Related Characteristics

char, glyph-subst-table

glyph-reorder-method

Glyph-Reorder Method

Purpose

Names the glyph-reordering processing specification.

Syntax

```
glyph-reorder-method:
#f|public_identifier|public_identifier_list
```

Where

- #f indicates that the Boolean value of this expression is false (no glyph-reordering method exists). This is the default.
- *public_identifier* is the name of a public identifier.
- *public_identifier_list* is a list of public identifiers.

Notes

The glyph-reorder-method characteristic is part of the character flow-objects class.

Use the glyph-reorder-method characteristic to change the order of glyphs, if necessary, in particular languages.

The glyph-reorder-method characteristic is inherited.

Related Characteristics

glyph-id, glyph-reorder-method, glyph-subst-method, glyph-subst-table

glyph-subst-method

Glyph-Substitution Method

Purpose

Names the glyph-substitution processing specification.

Syntax

```
glyph-subst-method:
    #f | public_identifier | public_identifier_list
```

Where

- #f indicates that the Boolean value of this expression is false (no glyph-substitution method exists). This is the default.
- *public_identifier* is the name of a public identifier.
- *public_identifier_list* is a list of public identifiers.

Notes

The glyph-subst-method characteristic is part of the character flow-objects class.

Use the glyph-subst-method characteristic to substitute one or more glyphs for the current glyph.

The glyph-subst-method characteristic is inherited.

Related Characteristics

glyph-id, glyph-reorder-method, glyph-subst-table

---

glyph-subst-table — Glyph-Substitution Table

Purpose

Specifies one or more glyph-substitution tables for the current glyph.

Syntax

```
glyph-subst-table: #f | glyph_subst_table_list
```

Where

- #f indicates that the Boolean value of this expression is false (no glyph-substitution table exists). This is the default.
- *glyph_subst_table_list* represents one or more glyph-substitution tables listed in the order in which they should be accessed.

Notes

The glyph-subst-table characteristic is part of the character flow-objects class.

The glyph-subst-table characteristic is inherited.

Related Characteristics

glyph-id, glyph-reorder-method, glyph-subst-method

---

hanging-punct?   Hanging Punctuation?

Purpose

Indicates whether punctuation characters are allowed in column margins or gutters.

Syntax

hanging-punct?: #f | #t

Where

- #f indicates that the Boolean value of this expression is false (hanging punctuation is not allowed). This is the default.
- #t indicates that the Boolean value of this expression is true (hanging punctuation is allowed).

Notes

The hanging-punct? characteristic is part of the paragraph flow-objects class.

The hanging-punct? characteristic is inherited.

---

header-margin   Header Margin

Purpose

Specifies the distance from the top edge of the page to the top of the header area.

Syntax

```
header-margin: length
```

Where

- *length* is an absolute length, in points. The default is 0pt.

Notes

The header-margin characteristic is part of the simple-page-sequence flow-objects class.
The header-margin characteristic is inherited.

Related Characteristics

```
center-footer, center-header, footer-margin, left-footer,
left-header, right-footer, right-header
```

hyphenate?   Hyphenate?

Purpose

Indicates whether hyphenation is allowed.

Syntax

```
hyphenate?: #f | #t
```

Where

- #f indicates that the Boolean value of this expression is false (hyphenation is not allowed). This is the default.
- #t indicates that the Boolean value of this expression is true (hyphenation is allowed).

Notes

The hyphenate? characteristic is part of the character flow-objects class.
The hyphenate? characteristic is inherited.

Related Characteristics

```
hyphenation-exceptions, hypenation-keep, hyphenation-
ladder-count, hyphenation-method
```

hyphenation-exceptions	Explicit Hyphenation

Purpose

Lists words that can be hyphenated and shows the hyphen position in each entry.

Syntax

```
hyphenation-exceptions: strings_list
```

Where

- *strings_list* is a list of words that can be hyphenated. The default is an empty list.

Notes

The hyphenation-exceptions characteristic is part of the paragraph flow-objects class.

Insert #, \, or - to show the hyphenation location in a word.

The hyphenation-exceptions characteristic is inherited.

Related Characteristics

hyphenation-keep, hyphenation-ladder-count, hyphenation-method

hyphenation-keep	Hyphenated-Word Location

Purpose

Sets the location of both parts of a hyphenated word.

Syntax

```
hyphenation-keep: #f | spread | page | column
```

Where

- #f indicates that the Boolean value of this expression is false (no explicit hyphenation-keep setting exists). This is the default.
- spread keeps both parts of a hyphenated word within a two-page spread.
- page keeps both parts of a hyphenated word within one page.
- column keeps both parts of a hyphenated word within one column.

Notes

The hyphenation-keep characteristic is part of the paragraph flow-objects class.

The hyphenation-keep characteristic is inherited.

Related Characteristics

hyphenation-exceptions, hyphenation-ladder-count, hyphenation-method

hyphenation-ladder-count	Hyphenation Ladder Count

Purpose

Specifies the maximum number of lines in a row that can end with the hyphenation character.

Syntax

hyphenation-ladder-count: #f | *integer*

Where

- #f indicates that the Boolean value of this expression is false, or the expression is invalid or absent. This is the default.
- *integer* is a positive, non-zero integer.

Notes

The hyphenation-ladder-count characteristic is part of the paragraph flow-objects class.

The hyphenation-ladder-count characteristic is inherited.

Related Characteristics

hyphenation-exceptions, hyphenation-keep, hyphenation-method

hyphenation-method	Hyphenation Method ID

Purpose

6

Names the public identifier for the hyphenation-processing specification.

Syntax

hyphenation-method: #f | public_identifier

Where

- #f indicates that the Boolean value of this expression is false, or the expression is invalid or absent. This is the default.

- public_identifier is the name of a public identifier.

Notes

The hyphenation-method characteristic is part of the character, paragraph, and paragraph-break flow-objects classes.

The hyphenation-method characteristic is inherited.

Related Characteristics

hyphenation-exceptions, hyphenation-keep, hyphenation-ladder-count

ignore-record-end?   Ignore Record End?

Purpose

Indicates whether to ignore the occurrence of a true record-end? characteristic.

Syntax

```
ignore-record-end?: #f | #t
```

Where

- #f indicates that the Boolean value of this expression is false (recognizes an occurrence of a true record-end? characteristic). This is the default.

- #t indicates that the Boolean value of this expression is true (ignore an occurrence of a true record-end? characteristic).

Notes

The ignore-record-end? characteristic is part of the paragraph flow-objects class.

The ignore-record-end? characteristic is inherited.

Related Characteristics

```
lines, record-end?
```

implicit-bidi-method   Bidirectional ID

Purpose

Names the public identifier for the specification that determines the direction in which the contents of the current paragraph flow object are displayed.

Syntax

```
implicit-bidi-method: #f | public_identifier
```

Where

- #f indicates that the Boolean value of this expression is false, or the expression is invalid or absent. This is the default.
- *public_identifier* is the name of a public identifier.

Notes

The implicit-bidi-method characteristic is part of the paragraph flow-objects class.

The implicit-bidi-method characteristic includes the writing-mode characteristic settings for characters. However, the implicit-bidi-method specification may not recognize certain writing-mode characteristic settings.

The implicit-bidi-method characteristic is inherited.

Related Characteristic

writing-mode

---

inhibit-line-breaks?   Inhibit Line Breaks?

Purpose

Indicates whether line breaks can occur before and after the current flow object.

Syntax

inhibit-line-breaks?: #f | #t

Where

- #f indicates that the Boolean value of this expression is false (line breaks are allowed). This is the default.
- #t indicates that the Boolean value of this expression is true (line breaks are inhibited).

Notes

The inhibit-line-breaks? characteristic is part of the box, character, external-graphic, leader, line-field, rule, and score flow-objects classes.

The `inhibit-line-breaks?` characteristic applies only if the formatting program attempts to insert a line break when fitting the flow object into the flow-object area.

The `inhibit-line-breaks?` characteristic is inherited.

Related Characteristics

`align-leader?`, `field-width`, `length`, `min-leader-repeat`, `truncate-leader?`

input-tab?	Input Tab?

Purpose

Indicates whether the current flow object is a tab.

Syntax

`input-tab?: #f | #t`

Where

- `#f` indicates that the Boolean value of this expression is false (this character is not a tab).

- `#t` indicates that the Boolean value of this expression is true (this character is a tab).

Notes

The `input-tab?` characteristic is part of the character flow-objects class.

The default value is the `input-tab?` property of the `char` characteristic if `char` is not explicitly given a value. Otherwise, the default value is `#f`.

The `input-tab?` characteristic is not inherited.

Related Characteristics

`expand-tabs?`, `input-whitespace?`

input-whitespace-treatment

Whitespace Treatment

Purpose

Specifies the method for dealing with whitespace in a flow object.

Syntax

```
input-whitespace-treatment: preserve|collapse|ignore
```

Where

- preserve retains whitespace as it is input. This is the default.
- collapse reduces input whitespace to one space.
- ignore completely disregards input whitespace.

Notes

The input-whitespace-treatment characteristic is part of the character flow-objects class.

Whitespace, which is the nontext, nongraphical part of a document, separates page elements and improves page design.

If the input-whitespace-treatment characteristic has a value of collapse or ignore, the input-whitespace? characteristic must be #t.

The input-whitespace-treatment characteristic is inherited.

The XML xml:space attribute also controls the display of elements in XML documents. For more information about xml:space, see its entry in Chapter 2, *XML Syntax*.

Related Characteristic

input-whitespace?

input-whitespace?

Input Whitespace?

Purpose

Indicates whether the current flow object is whitespace.

Syntax

```
input-whitespace?: #f | #t
```

Where

- #f indicates that the Boolean value of this expression is false (this character is not whitespace).
- #t indicates that the Boolean value of this expression is true (this character is whitespace).

Notes

The input-whitespace? characteristic is part of the character flow-objects class.

Whitespace, which is the nontext, nongraphical part of a document, separates page elements and improves page design.

The default value is the input-whitespace? property of the char characteristic if char is not explicitly given a value. Otherwise, the default value is #f.

The input-whitespace? characteristic is not inherited.

The XML xml:space attribute also controls the display of elements in XML documents. For more information about xml:space, see its entry in Chapter 2, *XML Syntax*.

Related Characteristic

```
input-tab?, input-whitespace-treatment
```

---

keep   Keep Together

Purpose

Indicates whether output produced by the current flow object stays together.

Syntax

```
keep: #f | page
```

Where

- #f indicates that the Boolean value of this expression is false (the output produced by the flow object does not stay together on the same page). This is the default.
- page keeps the output on the same page.

Notes

The keep characteristic is part of the aligned-column, box, display-group, external-graphic, paragraph, rule, table, and table-part flow-objects classes.

If the keep characteristic has the value page, the flow object will have an ancestor that is a page-sequence flow-objects class.

The full version of DSSSL also supports the following values: column-set, column, and #t.

The keep characteristic is not inherited.

Related Characteristics

break-after, break-before, may-violate-keep-after?, may-violate-keep-before?

keep-with-next?   Keep with Next?

Purpose

Indicates whether to keep the current flow object with the following one.

Syntax

keep-with-next?: #f | #t

Where

- #f indicates that the Boolean value of this expression is false (do not explicitly keep the flow objects together). This is the default.
- #t indicates that the Boolean value of this expression is true (explicitly keep the flow objects together).

Notes

The keep-with-next? characteristic is part of the aligned-column, box, display-group, external-graphic, paragraph, rule, table, and table-part flow-objects classes.

The keep-with-next? characteristic is not inherited.

Related Characteristic

keep-with-previous?

keep-with-previous?	Keep with Previous?

Purpose

Indicates whether to keep the current flow object with the prior one.

6

Syntax

keep-with-previous?: #f | #t

Where

- #f indicates that the Boolean value of this expression is false (do not explicitly keep the flow objects together). This is the default.

- #t indicates that the Boolean value of this expression is true (explicitly keep the flow objects together).

Notes

The keep-with-previous? characteristic is part of the aligned-column, box, display-group, external-graphic, paragraph, rule, table, and table-part flow-objects classes.

The keep-with-next? characteristic is not inherited.

Related Characteristic

keep-with-next?

kern-mode
Kern Mode

Purpose
Specifies the looseness or tightness of spacing between characters.

Syntax
```
kern-mode: loose|normal|kern|tight|touch
```

Where
- `loose` spaces characters farther apart than `normal`.
- `normal` is standard spacing between characters. This varies depending on the selected typeface and point size. This is the default.
- `kern` spaces characters slightly closer together than `normal`.
- `tight` spaces characters more tightly together than `kern`.
- `touch` spaces characters together until they touch.

Notes
The `kern-mode` characteristic is part of the character flow-objects class.

The `kern-mode` characteristic is similar to the cascading style sheet `letter-spacing` property.

Kerning is also known as *escapement adjustment*.

For more information about kerning, see section 8.8.1.6 of ISO 9541-1.

The `kern-mode` characteristic is inherited.

Related Characteristic
```
kern?
```

kern?
Allow Kerning?

Purpose
Indicates whether kerning is allowed in the current flow object.

Syntax

```
kern?: #f | #t
```

Where

- #f indicates that the Boolean value of this expression is false (kerning is not allowed). This is the default.
- #t indicates that the Boolean value of this expression is true (kerning is allowed).

Notes

The kern? characteristic is part of the character flow-objects class. Kerning is also known as *escapement adjustment*.

For more information about kerning, see section 8.8.1.6 of ISO 9541-1.

The kern? characteristic is inherited.

Related Characteristic

```
kern-mode
```

language	Language Code

Purpose

Specifies the ISO639 language code.

Syntax

```
language: #f | ISO639_language_code
```

Where

- #f indicates that the Boolean value of this expression is false (no language code is specified). This is the default.
- *ISO_639_language code*

Notes

The language characteristic is part of the character, paragraph, and paragraph-break flow-objects classes.

In DSSSL-O, language codes and country codes must be in uppercase characters.

In DSSSL-O, language codes and country codes are case-insensitive. Although it is not required, the language code is usually in lowercase and the country code is usually in uppercase.

You can find a list of ISO 639 codes at `http://www.sil.org/sgml/iso639.html`.

Use the XML `ISO639Code` element to specify language codes within XML documents.

The `language` characteristic is inherited.

Related Characteristic

country

---

6   last-line-end-indent   Indent Last Line

Purpose

Sets the amount of ending indention for the last line of the current paragraph flow object.

Syntax

last-line-end-indent: *length-spec*

Where

- *length-spec* is a positive or negative relative or absolute length. The default is 0pt.

Notes

The `last-line-end-indent` characteristic is part of the paragraph flow-objects class.

The `last-line-end-indent` characteristic is inherited.

Related Characteristic

first-line-start-indent

last-line-quadding

Last-Line Quadding

Purpose

Sets the alignment for the last line either in the current paragraph or preceding a break.

Syntax

```
last-line-quadding: relative|start|end
   |spread-inside
   |spread-outside|page-inside|page-outside|center
|justify
```

Where

- relative aligns the flow object by using the value of the quadding characteristic. This is the default.
- start aligns the flow object with the start of the writing-mode direction and adds space to the end.
- end aligns the flow object with the end of the writing-mode direction and adds space to the start.
- spread-inside aligns the flow object with the next inside page of a two-page spread.
- spread-outside aligns the flow object with the next outside page of a two-page spread.
- page-inside aligns the flow object with the next inside column.
- page-outside aligns the flow object with the next outside column.
- center centers the flow object by adding space to the start and end of the writing-mode direction.
- justify aligns the flow object between the margins, based on the writing-mode direction.

Notes

The last-line-quadding characteristic is part of the paragraph flow-objects class.

If the value of last-line-quadding is either spread-inside or spread-outside, the current flow object must have a page-sequence flow-objects class ancestor.

If the value of last-line-quadding is either page-inside or page-outside, the current flow object must have a column-set-sequence flow-objects class ancestor.

The last-line-quadding characteristic is inherited.

Related Characteristics

quadding, writing-mode

layer	Foreground Layer

Purpose

Specifies the layer number of the current foreground lines and marks for the current flow object.

Syntax

layer: *integer*

Where

- *integer* is an integer. The default value is 0.

Notes

The layer characteristic is part of the box, character, external-graphic, rule, score, sideline, and table-border flow-objects classes.

Layers with higher values are closer to the top than layers with lower values.

Background layers have a default of -1.

The look of layers of objects depends on the application with which you view the objects. Results can vary.

The layer characteristic is inherited.

Related Characteristics

background-layer, background-color, border-type, box-type, color

left-footer   Left Footer

Purpose

Contains inline flow objects aligned with the left margin of the footer.

Syntax

```
left-footer: unlabeled_sosofo
```

Where

- *unlabeled_sosofo* specifies a sequence of flow objects added to the flow-objects tree but not labeled with a symbol. The default is an empty sosofo.

Notes

The left-footer characteristic is part of the simple-page-sequence flow-objects class.

The left-footer characteristic is not inherited.

Related Characteristics

center-footer, center-header, footer-margin, header-margin, left-header, right-footer, right-header

left-header   Left Header

Purpose

Contains inline flow objects aligned with the left margin of the header.

Syntax

```
left-header: unlabeled_sosofo
```

Where

- *unlabeled_sosofo* specifies a sequence of flow objects added to the flow-objects tree but not labeled with a symbol. The default is an empty sosofo.

Notes

The left-header characteristic is part of the simple-page-sequence flow-objects class.
The left-header characteristic is not inherited.

Related Characteristics

center-footer, center-header, footer-margin, header-margin, left-footer, right-footer, right-header

left-margin   Left Margin

Purpose

Specifies the distance from the left edge of the page to the left side of the flow-object area.

Syntax

left-margin: *length*

Where

- *length* is an absolute length, in points. The default is 0pt.

Notes

The left-margin characteristic is part of the simple-page-sequence flow-objects class.
The left-margin characteristic is inherited.

Related Characteristics

bottom-margin, footer-margin, header-margin, right-margin, top-margin

length | Object Length

Purpose
Sets the length of the rule or leader.

Syntax
```
length: length | length-spec
```

Where
- *length*, the value for characteristics of the rule flow-objects class, is an absolute length, in points.
- *length-spec*, the value for characteristics of the leader flow-objects class, is a relative or absolute length.

Notes
The length characteristic is part of the leader and rule flow-objects classes.

If you do not specify an explicit length for a leader or rule, it will be determined for you.

The min-leader-repeat characteristic is ignored if the length characteristic has a value.

If the leader occurs on the last line of a paragraph, the value of the leader length will be ignored.

The length characteristic is not inherited.

Related Characteristics
align-leader?, inhibit-line-breaks?, min-leader-repeat, truncate-leader?

ligature? | Allow Ligatures?

Purpose
Indicate whether ligatures are allowed in the current flow object.

Syntax
```
ligature?: #f | #t
```

Where

- #f indicates that the Boolean value of this expression is false (ligatures are not allowed). This is the default.
- #t indicates that the Boolean value of this expression is true (ligatures are allowed).

Notes

The ligature? characteristic is part of the character flow-objects class.

The ligature? characteristic is inherited.

Related Characteristic

allowed-ligatures

6

| **line-breaking-method** | **Line-Breaking ID** |

Purpose

Names the public identifier for the line-breaking specification for the current paragraph flow object.

Syntax

line-breaking-method: #f | *public_identifier*

Where

- #f indicates that the Boolean value of this expression is false, or the expression is invalid or absent. This is the default.
- *public_identifier* is the name of a public identifier.

Notes

The line-breaking-method characteristic is part of the paragraph flow-objects class.

The line-breaking-method characteristic is inherited.

Related Characteristics

    line-composition-method, lines

line-cap   Line Cap

Purpose

Specifies the cap style for the border line.

Syntax

    line-cap: butt | round | square

Where

- butt indicates the butt cap style. This is the default.
- round indicates the round cap style.
- square indicates the square cap style.

Notes

The line-cap characteristic is part of the box, rule, score, sideline, table-border, and table-cell flow-objects classes.
    The line-cap characteristic is inherited.

Related Characteristics

    line-dash, line-join, line-miter-limit, line-repeat, line-thickness

line-composition-method   Line-Composition ID

Purpose

Names the public identifier for the line-composition specification for the current paragraph flow object.

Syntax

line-composition-method: **#f**|*public_identifier*

Where

- **#f** indicates that the Boolean value of this expression is false, or the expression is invalid or absent. This is the default.
- *public_identifier* is the name of a public identifier.

Notes

The line-composition-method characteristic is part of the paragraph and paragraph-break flow-objects classes.

The line-composition specification defines both document and character properties.

The line-composition-method characteristic is inherited.

Related Characteristics

line-breaking-method, lines

line-dash   Line Dash

Purpose

Specifies the pattern of dashes for the border line.

Syntax

line-dash: *lengths_list*

Where

- *lengths_list* is a list of lengths making up the dash pattern. The default is 0pt (no length).

Notes

The line-dash characteristic is part of the box, rule, score, sideline, table-border, and table-cell flow-objects classes.

To obtain a list of line-dash patterns (CurrentDashPattern) and the numbers for each, refer to ISO/IEC 10180.

The line-dash characteristic is inherited.

Related Characteristics

line-cap, line-join, line-miter-limit, line-repeat, line-thickness

line-join   Line Join

Purpose

Specifies the look of the intersections of lines in a border.

Syntax

line-join: <u>miter</u> | round | bevel

Where

- miter indicates that the intersection is mitered. This is the default.
- round indicates that the intersection is rounded.
- bevel indicates that the intersection is beveled.

Notes

The line-join characteristic is part of the box and table-border flow-objects classes.

The line-join characteristic is inherited.

Related Characteristics

line-cap, line-dash, line-miter-limit, line-repeat, line-thickness

line-miter-limit   Line-Miter Limit

Purpose

Specifies the maximum number of miters for joined lines.

Syntax

line-miter-limit: *number*

Where

- *number* indicates the maximum number of miters. The default is 10.

Notes

The line-miter-limit characteristic is part of the box and table-border flow-objects classes.

The line-miter-limit characteristic is inherited.

Related Characteristics

line-cap, line-dash, line-join, line-repeat, line-thickness

6 | line-repeat   Line Repeat

Purpose

Specifies the number of lines making up the current border.

Syntax

line-repeat: *integer*

Where

- *integer* is an integer. The default value is 1.

Notes

The line-repeat characteristic is part of the box, rule, score, sideline, table-border, and table-cell flow-objects classes.

The line-repeat characteristic is inherited.

Related Characteristics

line-cap, line-dash, line-join, line-miter-limit, line-thickness

line-spacing   Line Spacing

Purpose
Sets the vertical spacing between text lines.

Syntax
```
line-spacing: length-spec
```

Where
* *length-spec* is a relative or absolute length. The default value is 12pt.

Notes
The line-spacing characteristic is part of the paragraph flow-objects class.

6

Line spacing might be adjusted between the prior line or non-line area until it matches the value of the line-spacing characteristic. If the previous area is not a line, the line-spacing value might be the value of the line-spacing characteristic minus the value of the min-post-line-spacing characteristic.

The line-spacing characteristic is inherited.

Related Characteristics
line-spacing-priority, lines, min-leading, min-post-line-spacing, min-pre-line-spacing

line-spacing-priority   Line-Spacing Priority

Purpose
Sets the line-spacing priority for the current paragraph flow object before the adjacent paragraph flow objects.

Syntax

```
line-spacing-priority: force | integer
```

Where

- force forces the highest line-spacing priority.
- *integer* is an integer indicating an absolute line-spacing priority. The default value is 0.

Notes

The line-spacing-priority characteristic is part of the paragraph flow-objects class.

The greater the value of *integer*, the higher the priority.

When two paragraph flow objects are adjacent, the one with the higher priority wins: its display values control the appearance of both flow objects. For more information, see section 12.5.4.1 of the ISO/IEC 10179: 1996 DSSSL standard.

The line-spacing-priority characteristic is inherited.

Related Characteristics

line-spacing, lines, min-leading, min-post-line-spacing, min-pre-line-spacing

---

line-thickness   Line Thickness

Purpose

Specifies the thickness of the border line.

Syntax

```
line-thickness: length
```

Where

- *length* is an absolute length, in points. The default is 1pt.

Notes

The line-thickness characteristic is part of the box, rule, score, sideline, table-border, and table-cell flow-objects classes.

The line-thickness characteristic is inherited.

Related Characteristics

line-cap, line-dash, line-join, line-miter-limit, line-repeat

lines	Lines Formats

Purpose

Specifies the format of lines within the current paragraph.

Syntax

lines: <u>wrap</u>|asis|none

Where

- wrap wraps lines within the defined flow-object area. This is the default.
- asis displays lines without wrapping them until a true record-end? characteristic is encountered.
- none displays lines without wrapping them at all.

Notes

The lines characteristic is part of the paragraph flow-objects class.

The full version of DSSSL also supports the following values: asis-wrap and asis-truncate.

The lines characteristic is inherited.

Related Characteristics

first-line-start-indent, ignore-record-end?, last-line-end-indent, record-end?

marginalia-keep-with-previous?	Marginalia Keep with Previous?

Purpose

Indicates whether the current marginalia area is allied with the previous or following flow-object area.

Syntax

```
marginalia-keep-with-previous?: #f | #t
```

Where

- #f indicates that the Boolean value of this expression is false (the marginalia area is allied with the following flow-object area). This is the default.
- #t indicates that the Boolean value of this expression is true (the marginalia area is allied with the previous flow-object area).

Notes

The marginalia-keep-with-previous? characteristic is part of the marginalia flow-objects class.

The marginalia-keep-with-previous? characteristic is inherited.

Related Characteristics

```
marginalia-sep, marginalia-side
```

marginalia-sep Marginalia Separation

Purpose

Specifies the amount of space between the flow-object area and the marginalia attachment.

Syntax

```
marginalia-sep: length-spec
```

Where

- *length-spec* is a relative or absolute length. The default value is 0pt.

Notes

The marginalia-sep characteristic is part of the marginalia flow-objects class.

If length-spec is a negative length, the separation is within the flow-object area.

The marginalia-sep characteristic is inherited.

Related Characteristics

marginalia-keep-with-previous?, marginalia-side, side-line-sep

marginalia-side   Marginalia Side

Purpose

Specifies the part of the flow-object area to which a marginalia flow object is attached.

Syntax

marginalia-side: <u>start</u>|end

Where

- start places the marginalia attachment on the starting side of the writing-mode direction. This is the default.
- end places the marginalia attachment on the ending side of the writing-mode direction.

Notes

The marginalia-side characteristic is part of the marginalia flow-objects class.

The marginalia-side characteristic is inherited.

Related Characteristics

marginalia-keep-with-previous?, marginalia-sep, side-line-side

math-font-posture   Math Font Posture

Purpose

Specifies the level of incline of flow object text identified as math.

Syntax

```
math-font-posture: #f|upright|oblique|italic
```

Where

- #f indicates that the Boolean value of this expression is false (any font posture is appropriate).
- upright indicates that each letter is completely vertical. This is the default.
- oblique indicates that each letter has a posture between upright and italic.
- italic indicates that each letter is slanted.

Notes

The math-font-posture characteristic is part of the character flow-objects class.

The full version of DSSSL also supports the following values: not-applicable, back-slanted-oblique, and back-slanted-italic.

The math-font-posture characteristic is not inherited.

Related Characteristics

char, font-family-name, font-name, font-posture, font-size, glyph-alignment-mode, min-post-line-spacing, min-pre-line-spacing

---

max-height   Maximum Height

Purpose

Specifies the maximum height of an external graphic.

Syntax

```
max-height: length-spec
```

Where

- *length-spec* is a relative or absolute length.

Notes

The max-height characteristic is part of the external-graphic flow-objects class.

The max-height characteristic is in effect only when the scale characteristic has a value of max or max-uniform.

The max-height characteristic is not inherited.

Related Characteristics

max-width, scale

---

max-width   Maximum Width   6

Purpose

Specifies the maximum width of an external graphic.

Syntax

max-width: *length-spec*

Where

- *length-spec* is a relative or absolute length.

Notes

The max-width characteristic is part of the external-graphic flow-objects class.

The max-width characteristic is in effect only when the scale characteristic has a value of max or max-uniform.

The max-width characteristic is not inherited.

Related Characteristics

max-height, scale

may-violate-keep-after?

Violate Keep After?

Purpose

Indicates whether the current flow object and the following one can remain on the same page although the value of the keep characteristic may disallow it.

Syntax

```
may-violate-keep-after?: #f | #t
```

Where

- #f indicates that the Boolean value of this expression is false (the behavior of the two flow objects must follow the value of the keep characteristic). This is the default.
- #t indicates that the Boolean value of this expression is true (the value of the keep characteristic can be ignored).

Notes

The may-violate-keep-after? characteristic is part of the aligned-column, box, display-group, external-graphic, paragraph, rule, table, and table-part flow-objects classes.

The may-violate-keep-after? characteristic is not inherited.

Related Characteristics

break-after, break-before, keep, may-violate-keep-before?

may-violate-keep-before?

Violate Keep Before?

Purpose

Indicates whether the current flow object and the preceding one can remain on the same page although the value of the keep characteristic may disallow it.

Syntax

```
may-violate-keep-before?: #f|#t
```

Where

- #f indicates that the Boolean value of this expression is false (the behavior of the two flow objects must follow the value of the keep characteristic). This is the default.
- #t indicates that the Boolean value of this expression is true (the value of the keep characteristic can be ignored).

Notes

The may-violate-keep-before? characteristic is part of the aligned-column, box, display-group, external-graphic, paragraph, rule, table, and table-part flow-objects classes.

The may-violate-keep-before? characteristic is not inherited.

Related Characteristics

```
break-after, break-before, keep, may-violate-keep-after?
```

min-leader-repeat	Minimum Leader Pattern Repeat

Purpose

Specifies the minimum number of times that a leader pattern (a character-space combination) appears.

Syntax

```
min-leader-repeat: integer
```

Where

- *integer* is a positive, non-zero number. The default value is 1.

Notes

The min-leader-repeat characteristic is part of the leader flow-objects class.

The min-leader-repeat characteristic is ignored if the length characteristic has a value.

If the value of min-leader-repeat is greater than the actual space available, the leader will not appear.

If a leader is in a paragraph, the start-indent, last-line-end-indent, and areas outside the leader are subtracted from the total flow-object area of the paragraph to compute the leader length.

The min-leader-repeat characteristic is inherited.

Related Characteristics

align-leader?, inhibit-line-breaks?, length, truncate-leader?

6   min-leading   Minimum Leading

Purpose

Specifies the minimum *leading* (space between the lines) for the lines within the current paragraph flow object.

Syntax

min-leading: #f | length-spec

Where

- #f indicates that the Boolean value of this expression is false, or the expression is invalid or absent. This is the default.
- *length-spec* is a relative or absolute length of minimum leading.

Notes

The min-leading characteristic is part of the paragraph flow-objects class.

The priority of the current line-spacing setting is determined by the line-spacing-priority characteristic.

If min-leading is not #f, the space between the prior area and the current area must be at least the value of the min-leading characteristic.

The `min-leading` characteristic is inherited.

Related Characteristics

`line-spacing`, `line-spacing-priority`, `lines`, `min-post-line-spacing`, `min-pre-line-spacing`

min-post-line-spacing	Minimum Line Spacing After

Purpose

Specifies the minimum line spacing after the current line.

Syntax

`min-post-line-spacing:` **#f** | *length-spec*

Where

- `#f` indicates that the Boolean value of this expression is false, or the expression is invalid or absent. This is the default.

- *length-spec* is a relative or absolute length of minimum line spacing.

Notes

The `min-post-line-spacing` characteristic is part of the paragraph flow-objects class.

The actual line spacing for the current line is determined by the `min-leading` characteristic.

Line-spacing might be adjusted between the prior line or nonline area until it matches the value of the `line-spacing` characteristic. If the previous area is not a line, the line-spacing value might be the value of the `line-spacing` characteristic minus the value of the `min-post-line-spacing` characteristic.

The priority of the current line-spacing setting is determined by the `line-spacing-priority` characteristic.

The `min-post-line-spacing` characteristic is inherited.

Related Characteristics

line-spacing, line-spacing-priority, lines, min-leading, min-pre-line-spacing

min-pre-line-spacing	Minimum Line Spacing Before

Purpose

Specifies the minimum line spacing before the current line.

Syntax

min-pre-line-spacing: #f | *length-spec*

Where

- #f indicates that the Boolean value of this expression is false, or the expression is invalid or absent. This is the default.
- *length-spec* is a relative or absolute length of minimum line spacing.

Notes

The min-pre-line-spacing characteristic is part of the paragraph flow-objects class.

The actual line spacing for the current line is determined by the min-leading characteristic.

The priority of the current line-spacing setting is determined by the line-spacing-priority characteristic.

The min-pre-line-spacing characteristic is inherited.

Related Characteristics

line-spacing, line-spacing-priority, lines, min-leading, min-post-line-spacing

multi-modes

Multiple Modes

Purpose

Lists two or more modes of presentation of a flow object.

Syntax

```
multi-modes: list
```

Where

* *list* lists at least two modes of presentation.

Notes

The `multi-modes` characteristic is part of the multi-mode flow-objects class.

A list item can specify a port name only or contain a port name and a description of the presentation mode.

The list must include the principal port, represented by `#f`.

Each entry on the list must be unique.

The `multi-modes` characteristic is not inherited.

Related Characteristic

```
principal-mode-simultaneous?
```

n-columns-spanned

Number of Columns Spanned

Purpose

Specifies the number of columns in the current span.

Syntax

```
n-columns-spanned: integer
```

Where

- *integer* is a positive, non-zero number. The default value is 1.

Notes

The n-columns-spanned characteristic is part of the table-cell and table-column flow-objects classes.

The n-columns-spanned characteristic is not inherited.

Related Characteristics

cell-after-column-margin, cell-before-column-margin, column-number, n-rows-spanned

---

6 | **notation-system-id** | **Notation System ID**

Purpose

Identifies the system containing the notation associated with an external graphic.

Syntax

notation-system-id: *system_identifier*

Where

- *system_identifier* is a string naming the notation associated with an external graphic.

Notes

The notation-system-id characteristic is part of the external-graphic flow-objects class.

A notation declaration within a document declares the system identifier.

The notation-system-id characteristic is not inherited.

Related Characteristic

entity-system-id

n-rows-spanned — Number of Rows Spanned

Purpose
Specifies the number of rows in the current span.

Syntax
```
n-rows-spanned: integer
```

Where
* *integer* is a positive, non-zero number. The default value is 1.

Notes
The n-rows-spanned characteristic is part of the table-cell flow-objects class.

The n-rows-spanned characteristic is not inherited.

Related Characteristics
cell-after-row-margin, cell-before-row-margin, column-number, n-columns-spanned

orientation — Rule Orientation

Purpose
Specifies the direction in which a rule is oriented and whether it is displayed or inlined.

Syntax
```
orientation: horizontal|vertical|escapement
|line-progression
```

Where
* horizontal indicates that the rule is displayed horizontally.
* vertical indicates that the rule is displayed vertically.

- escapement indicates that the rule is inlined and centered in the line-progression direction.
- line-progression indicates that the rule is inlined and oriented in the line-progression direction, and starts at the position point.

Notes

The orientation characteristic is part of the rule flow-objects class.

If the value of orientation is escapement, you can offset the rule by using the position-point-shift characteristic.

If the value of orientation is line-progression, the placement of the following flow objects is not affected by the placement of the rule.

The orientation characteristic is not inherited.

Related Characteristics

color, inhibit-line-breaks?, length, line-cap, line-dash, line-repeat, line-sep, line-thickness, position-point-shift

orphan-count   Orphan-Lines Count

Purpose

Specifies the number of orphan lines allowed at the end of a flow-object area.

Syntax

orphan-count: *integer*

Where

- *integer* is a positive, non-zero number. The default value is 2.

Notes

The orphan-count characteristic is part of the paragraph flow-objects class.

When a paragraph breaks from one page to the next, sometimes one or two lines are at the bottom of the first page or at the top of the next page. This is not always desirable. An *orphan* is a single line at the bottom of a page, and a *widow* is a single line at the top of a page. The orphan-count and widow-count characteristics correct orphans and widows, respectively.

The orphan-count characteristic is inherited.

Related Characteristics

```
widow-count
```

page-height   Page Height

Purpose

Specifies the page height, from the top edge to the bottom edge.

Syntax

```
page-height: length
```

Where

- *length* is an absolute length, in points. The default varies, depending on the computer system.

Notes

The page-height characteristic is part of the simple-page-sequence flow-objects class.

The page-height characteristic is inherited.

Related Characteristics

```
bottom-margin, footer-margin, header-margin, left-margin,
page-width, right-margin, top-margin
```

page-width   Page Width

Purpose

Specifies the page width, from the left edge to the right edge.

Syntax

```
page-width: length
```

Where

- *length* is an absolute length, in points. The default varies, depending on the computer system.

Notes

The `page-width` characteristic is part of the simple-page-sequence flow-objects class.

The `page-width` characteristic is inherited.

Related Characteristics

`bottom-margin`, `footer-margin`, `header-margin`, `left-margin`, `page-length`, `right-margin`, `top-margin`

---

position-point-shift   Position-Point Shift

Purpose

Offsets the position point in the direction of line-progression.

Syntax

```
position-point-shift: length-spec
```

Where

- *length-spec* is a relative or absolute length. The default value is 0pt.

Notes

The `position-point-shift` characteristic is part of the character and rule flow-objects classes.

If you offset the position point by a positive *length-spec*, the flow-object area shifts away from the line-progression direction.

The position-point-shift characteristic is valid only if the current flow object is inlined.

The position-point-shift characteristic is not inherited.

Related Characteristics

color, inhibit-line-breaks?, length, line-cap, line-dash, line-repeat, line-sep, line-thickness, orientation

position-point-x	Position-Point X-Coordinate

Purpose

Specifies the x coordinate for the position point of an external graphic.

Syntax

position-point-x: *length-spec*

Where

- *length-spec* is a relative or absolute length. The default is 0 if the value of the writing-mode characteristic is left-to-right or right-to-left.

Notes

The position-point-x characteristic is part of the external-graphic flow-objects class.

The position-point-x characteristic is valid only when the graphic is inlined.

If you do not specify the position-point-x characteristic, the default value is 0.

The position-point-x characteristic is not inherited.

Related Characteristics

end-indent, max-height, max-width, position-point-y, start-indent

position-point-y

Position-Point
Y-Coordinate

Purpose

Specifies the *y* coordinate for the position point of an external graphic.

Syntax

```
position-point-y: length-spec
```

Where

* *length-spec* is a relative or absolute length. The default is 0 if the value of the writing-mode characteristic is top-to-bottom.

Notes

The position-point-y characteristic is part of the external-graphic flow-objects class.

The position-point-y characteristic is valid only when the graphic is inlined.

If you do not specify the position-point-y characteristic, the default value is 0.

The position-point-y characteristic is not inherited.

Related Characteristics

```
position-point-x
```

principal-mode-simultaneous?

Principal-Mode
Simultaneous?

Purpose

Indicates whether the principal-mode presentation displays simultaneously with other presentation modes.

Syntax

```
principal-mode-simultaneous?: #f | #t
```

Where

- #f indicates that the Boolean value of this expression is false (the principal mode and other modes are not displayed simultaneously). This is the default.
- #t indicates that the Boolean value of this expression is true (the principal mode and other modes are displayed simultaneously).

Notes

The principal-mode-simultaneous? characteristic is part of the multi-mode flow-objects class.

The principal-mode-simultaneous? characteristic is inherited.

Related Characteristic

multi-modes

6

quadding   Quadding

Purpose

Sets the alignment for all but the last line in the current paragraph.

Syntax

quadding: <u>start</u> | end | center

Where

- start aligns the flow object with the start of the writing-mode direction and adds space to the end. This is the default.
- end aligns the flow object with the end of the writing-mode direction and adds space to the start.
- center centers the flow object by adding space to the start and end of the writing-mode direction.

Notes

The quadding characteristic is part of the paragraph flow-objects class.

The full version of DSSSL also supports the following values: spread-inside, spread-outside, page-inside, page-outside, and justify.

The quadding characteristic is inherited.

Related Characteristics

last-line-quadding, writing-mode

record-end?	Record End?

Purpose

Indicates whether the current flow object ends a record.

Syntax

record-end?: #f | #t

Where

- #f indicates that the Boolean value of this expression is false (the flow object is not a record-end).
- #t indicates that the Boolean value of this expression is true (the flow object is a record-end).

Notes

The record-end? characteristic is part of the character flow-objects class.

The default value of the record-end? characteristic is the value of the record-end? property of the char characteristic.

A record-end? characteristic signals the end of a line when the value of the lines characteristic is asis.

The record-end? characteristic is not inherited.

Related Characteristics

char, lines

right-footer   Right Footer

Purpose

Contains inline flow objects aligned with the right margin of the
footer.

Syntax

```
right-footer: unlabeled_sosofo
```

Where

- *unlabeled_sosofo* specifies a sequence of flow objects added
  to the flow-objects tree but not labeled with a symbol. The
  default is an empty sosofo.

Notes

The right-footer characteristic is part of the simple-page-
sequence flow-objects class.

The right-footer characteristic is not inherited.

Related Characteristics

center-footer, center-header, footer-margin, header-
margin, left-footer, left-header, right-header

right-header   Right Header

Purpose

Contains inline flow objects aligned with the right margin of the
header.

Syntax

```
right-header: unlabeled_sosofo
```

Where

- *unlabeled_sosofo* specifies a sequence of flow objects added to the flow-objects tree but not labeled with a symbol. The default is an empty sosofo.

Notes

The right-header characteristic is part of the simple-page-sequence flow-objects class.

The right-header characteristic is not inherited.

Related Characteristics

center-footer, center-header, footer-margin, header-margin, left-footer, left-header, right-footer

right-margin
Right Margin

Purpose

Specifies the distance from the right edge of the page to the right side of the flow-object area.

Syntax

right-margin: *length*

Where

- *length* is an absolute length, in points. The default is 0pt.

Notes

The right-margin characteristic is part of the simple-page-sequence flow-objects class.

The right-margin characteristic is inherited.

Related Characteristics

bottom-margin, footer-margin, header-margin, left-margin, top-margin

scale
Scale

Purpose

Sets scaling of an external graphic.

Syntax

    scale: number|two_number_list| max|max-uniform

Where

- *number* represents a single number by which both the horizontal and vertical dimensions of the graphic are scaled.

- *two_number_list* represents a two-number list by which the graphic is scaled. The first number scales the horizontal dimension, and the second number scales the vertical dimension.

- max scales both the horizontal and vertical dimensions of the graphic to fill the maximum available space without necessarily keeping the dimensions in their original proportions.

- max-uniform scales both the horizontal and vertical dimensions of the graphic to fill the maximum available space while keeping the dimensions in their original proportions. This is the default.

Notes

The scale characteristic is part of the external-graphic flow-objects class.

The scale characteristic is not inherited.

Related Characteristics

    max-height, max-width

score-spaces?   Score Spaces?

Purpose

Indicates whether strikethrough characters are drawn over spaces.

Syntax

```
score-spaces?: #f | #t
```

Where

- #f indicates that the Boolean value of this expression is false (strikethrough characters are drawn over characters only).
- #t indicates that the Boolean value of this expression is true (strikethrough characters are drawn over both characters and spaces). This is the default.

Notes

The score-spaces? characteristic is part of the score flow-objects class.

The score-spaces? characteristic is inherited.

Related Characteristics

color, layer, inhibit-line-breaks?, line-cap, line-dash, line-repeat, line-thickness

sideline-sep   Sideline Separation

Purpose

Specifies the amount of space between the flow-object area and the sideline attachment.

Syntax

```
sideline-sep: length-spec
```

Where

- *length-spec* is a positive or negative relative or absolute length.

Notes

The `sideline-sep` characteristic is part of the sideline flow-objects class.

If `length-spec` is a negative length, the separation is within the flow-object area.

The `sideline-sep` characteristic is inherited.

Related Characteristics

`marginalia-sep, sideline-side`

sideline-side   Sideline Side

Purpose

Specifies the part of the flow-object area to which a sideline flow object is attached.

Syntax

`sideline-side: start│end│both`

Where

- `start` places the sideline attachment on the starting side of the `writing-mode` direction.
- `end` places the sideline attachment on the ending side of the `writing-mode` direction.
- `both` places the sideline attachment to both sides.

Notes

The `sideline-side` characteristic is part of the sideline flow-objects class.

The `sideline-side` characteristic is inherited.

Related Characteristics

`marginalia-side, sideline-sep`

space-after — Space After Flow Object

Purpose

Inserts space after the flow-object area.

Syntax

```
space-after: display_space
```

Where

- *display_space* is the display space after the flow object. The default is no space after.

Notes

The `space-after` characteristic is part of the aligned-column, box, display-group, external-graphic, paragraph, rule, table, and table-part flow-objects classes.

The `space-after` characteristic is not inherited.

Related Characteristic

```
space-before
```

space-before — Space Before Flow Object

Purpose

Inserts space before the flow-object area.

Syntax

```
space-before: display_space
```

Where

- *display_space* is the display space prior to the flow object. The default is no space before.

Notes

The space-before characteristic is part of the aligned-column, box, display-group, external-graphic, paragraph, rule, table, and table-part flow-objects classes.

The space-before characteristic is not inherited.

Related Characteristic

space-after

space?   Space?

Purpose

Indicates whether the character flow object is a space.

Syntax

space?: #f | #t

Where

- #f indicates that the Boolean value of this expression is false (the flow object is not a space).

- #t indicates that the Boolean value of this expression is true (the flow object is a space).

Notes

The space? characteristic is part of the character flow-objects class.

The default value of the space? characteristic is the value of the char characteristic.

The space? characteristic is not inherited.

Related Characteristic

char

span
Column Span

Purpose
Sets the span of columns in which the current flow object is located.

Syntax
```
span: integer
```

Where
- *integer* is a positive, non-zero number. The default value is 1.

Notes
The span characteristic is part of the box, external-graphic, paragraph, rule, and table flow-objects classes.
The span characteristic is inherited.

Related Characteristic
```
span-weak?
```

span-weak?
Weak Span?

Purpose
Specifies whether the current span is strong or weak.

Syntax
```
span-weak?: #f | #t
```

Where
- #f indicates that the Boolean value of this expression is false (strong). This is the default.
- #t indicates that the Boolean value of this expression is true (weak).

Notes

The span-weak? characteristic is part of the box, external-graphic, paragraph, rule, and table flow-objects classes.

The span-weak? characteristic is in effect if a flow object spans more than one column.

A multicolumn span is strong if all the columns are within the same column subset and location. For more information, see section 12.6.5.1 in the DSSSL standard (ISO/IEC 10179: 1996).

The span-weak? characteristic is inherited.

Related Characteristic

span

start-indent   Start Indent

Purpose

Specifies indention at the starting edge of the current writing-mode direction.

Syntax

```
start-indent: lenqth-spec
```

Where

- *length-spec* is a relative or absolute length of the indention. The default value is 0pt.

Notes

The start-indent characteristic is part of the aligned-column, box, external-graphic, paragraph, rule, table, and table-column flow-objects classes.

The start-indent characteristic is inherited.

Related Characteristics

end-indent, writing-mode

start-margin
Starting Margin

Purpose

Sets the distance from the edge of the first area in the writing-mode direction to the closest edge of the text area.

Syntax

```
start-margin: length-spec
```

Where

- *length-spec* is a relative or absolute length. The default value is 0pt.

Notes

The start-margin characteristic is part of the scroll flow-objects class.

The start-margin characteristic is inherited.

Related Characteristics

```
end-margin, writing-mode
```

starts-row?
Starts Row?

Purpose

Indicates whether the current table cell starts a table row.

Syntax

```
starts-row?: #f| #t
```

Where

- #f indicates that the Boolean value of this expression is false (the current cell does not start a row). This is the default.
- #t indicates that the Boolean value of this expression is true (the current cell starts a row).

Notes

The `starts-row?` characteristic is part of the table-cell flow-objects class.

The only time that you can use the `starts-row?` characteristic is either when a table cell is not in a table row; that is, no prior flow object exists; if the prior flow object is not a table cell; or the prior flow object is a table cell with an `ends-row?` characteristic equal to #t.

The `starts-row?` characteristic is not inherited.

Related Characteristic

`ends-row?`

---

stretch-factor   Stretch Factor

6

Purpose

Specifies how far a character is stretched.

Syntax

`stretch-factor: number`

Where

- *number* (1) indicates the size of the stretch.

Notes

The `stretch-factor` characteristic is part of the character flow-objects class.

The `stretch-factor` characteristic stretches characters to enclose math formulae and math delimiters. The amount of stretch depends on the styling program, the particular glyph, the particular font, and font size.

The `stretch-factor` characteristic is not inherited.

Related Characteristics

`font-family-name, font-size, glyph-id`

table-auto-width-method | Automatic Table Width Method

Purpose
Names the public identifier for setting automatic table widths.

Syntax
```
table-auto-width-method: #f│public_identifier
```

Where
- #f indicates that the Boolean value of this expression is false, or the expression is invalid or absent. This is the default.
- *public_identifier* is the name of a public identifier.

Notes
The table-auto-width-method characteristic is part of the table flow-objects class.

The table-auto-width-method characteristic is inherited.

Related Characteristic
```
table-width
```

table-border | Table Border

Purpose
Specifies a table border.

Syntax
```
table-border: #f│#t│unlabeled_sosofo
```

Where
- #f indicates that the Boolean value of this expression is false, or the expression is invalid or absent. This is the default.

- #t indicates that the Boolean value of this expression is true.

- *unlabeled_sosofo* specifies a sequence of flow objects added to the flow-objects tree but not labeled with a symbol.

Notes

The table-border characteristic is part of the table flow-objects class.

A table-border value of #f or #t is the same as border-present? having a value of #f or #t, respectively.

Related Characteristics

after-column-border, after-row-border, before-column-border, before-row-border, border-present?

---

table-corner-rounded	Rounded Table Corners

Purpose

Specifies whether table corners are rounded or squared.

Syntax

table-corner-rounded: #f | #t | *x-y_pairs_list*

Where

- #f indicates that the Boolean value of this expression is false (table corners are squared). This is the default.

- #t indicates that the Boolean value of this expression is true (table corners are rounded).

- *x-y_pairs_list* enables particular rounded corners.

Notes

The table-corner-rounded characteristic is part of the table flow-objects class.

The *x* of the x-y pair indicates the before-or-after position of rounded corners in the column dimension, and *y* indicates the before-or-after position of rounded corners in the row dimension of the table.

The table-corner-rounded characteristic is inherited.

Related Characteristics

border-present?, box-corner-rounded, table-border

---

table-part-omit-middle-footer?	**Table-Part Omit Footer?**

Purpose

Indicates whether a table contains footer content.

Syntax

table-part-omit-middle-footer?: #f | #t

Where

- #f indicates that the Boolean value of this expression is false (the table contains footer content). This is the default.
- #t indicates that the Boolean value of this expression is true (the table does not contain footer content).

Notes

The table-part-omit-middle-footer? characteristic is part of the table-part flow-objects class.

The table-part-omit-middle-footer? characteristic is inherited.

Related Characteristic

table-part-omit-middle-header?

table-part-omit-middle-header?	Table-Part Omit Header?

Purpose

Indicates whether a table contains header content.

Syntax

```
table-part-omit-middle-header?: #f | #t
```

Where

- #f indicates that the Boolean value of this expression is false (the table contains header content). This is the default.

- #t indicates that the Boolean value of this expression is true (the table does not contain header content).

Notes

The `table-part-omit-middle-header?` characteristic is part of the table-part flow-objects class.

The `table-part-omit-middle-header?` characteristic is inherited.

Related Characteristic

```
table-part-omit-middle-footer?
```

table-width	Table Width

Purpose

Specifies the width of a table.

Syntax

```
table-width: #f | length-spec
```

Where

- #f indicates that the Boolean value of this expression is false, or the expression is invalid or absent.
- *length-spec* is a relative or absolute length. The default is the value of the *display size*, the container in which the current flow object resides, minus any indention values.

Notes

The table-width characteristic is part of the table flow-objects class.

The table-width characteristic is not inherited.

Related Characteristic

table-auto-width-method

6

top-margin	Top Margin

Purpose

Specifies the distance from the top edge of the page to the top of the flow-object area.

Syntax

top-margin: *length*

Where

- *length* is an absolute length, in points. The default is 0pt.

Notes

The top-margin characteristic is part of the simple-page-sequence flow-objects class.

The top-margin characteristic is inherited.

Related Characteristics

bottom-margin, footer-margin, header-margin, left-margin, right-margin

truncate-leader?

Truncate Leader?

Purpose

Indicates whether the last combination of characters and spaces in a leader is truncated.

Syntax

```
truncate-leader?: #f | #t
```

Where

- #f indicates that the Boolean value of this expression is false (the end of the leader is not truncated). This is the default.

- #t indicates that the Boolean value of this expression is true (the end of the leader is truncated).

Notes

The truncate-leader? characteristic is part of the leader flow-objects class.

The truncate-leader? characteristic is inherited.

Related Characteristics

align-leader?, inhibit-line-breaks?, length, min-leader-repeat

type

Score Type

Purpose

Specifies the type of score, its position, its length, and the character with which it is drawn.

Syntax

```
type: before | through | after | length-spec | character
```

Where

- before draws the score before the placement path in the line-progression direction.
- through draws the score through the characters of the flow object.
- after draws the score after the placement path in the line-progression direction.
- *length-spec* is the score's relative or absolute length.
- *character* specifies the character with which the score is drawn.

Notes

The type characteristic is part of the score flow-objects class. The type characteristic is not inherited.

Related Characteristics

color, inhibit-line-breaks?, layer

---

widow-count

Widow-Lines Count

Purpose

Specifies the number of widow lines allowed at the beginning of a flow-object area.

Syntax

widow-count: *integer*

Where

- *integer* is a positive, non-zero integer. The default value is 2.

Notes

The widow-count characteristic is part of the paragraph flow-objects class.

When a paragraph breaks from one page to the next, sometimes one or two lines are at the bottom of the first page or at the top of the next page. This is not always desirable. An *orphan* is a single line at the bottom of a page, and a *widow* is a single line at the top of a page. The orphan-count and widow-count characteristics correct orphans and widows, respectively.

The widow-count characteristic is inherited.

Related Characteristic

orphan-count

---

width   Table-Column Width

Purpose

Specifies the width of a table column.

Syntax

width: *length-spec*

Where

* *length-spec* is a relative or absolute length.

Notes

The width characteristic is part of the table-column flow-objects class.

The value of the table-auto-width characteristic overrides the value of width.

The width characteristic is not inherited.

Related Characteristics

column-number, table-auto-width

---

writing-mode   Writing Direction

Purpose

Sets th e direction in which text is displayed or inlined.

Syntax

writing mode: <u>left-to-right</u>, right-to-left,
top-to-bottom

Where

- left-to-right indicates the direction in which text is printed or displayed, starting at the left side and ending at the right side. This is the default.

- right-to-left indicates the direction in which text is printed or displayed, starting at the right side and ending at the left side.

- top-to-bottom indicates the direction in which text is printed or displayed, starting at the top and ending at the bottom.

Notes

The writing-mode characteristic is part of the aligned-column, box, character, external-graphic, line-field, paragraph, rule, scroll, simple-page-sequence, and table flow-objects classes.

The writing-mode characteristic is inherited.

Related Characteristics

border-alignment, box-corner-rounded, cell-row-alignment, display-alignment, end-indent, escapement-direction, field-align, filling-direction, glyph-alignment-mode, implicit-bidi-method, last-line-quadding, marginalia-side, position-point-x, position-point-y, quadding, sideline-side, start-indent

Unicode Characters and Character Sets

In the past, software and electronic-document developers used the ASCII and Latin-1 characters. Now, XML supports the entire Unicode character set. In addition to ASCII and Latin-1 characters, which are a small part of the Unicode character set, Unicode includes many other special characters and — to completely support the internationalization of XML documents — alphabets from many languages.

This appendix is made up of sections for each character-class element. Starting each section is one or more tables illustrating and describing characters from character sets commonly used by English-speaking individuals. The "Other Supported Character Sets" sections contain information about supported characters within non-English character sets. For more information about non-English character sets, refer to the Unicode 2.0 Charts Web page (http://www.unicode.org/Unicode.charts/normal/Unicode2.0.html). This page lists all currently supported Unicode character sets and provides links for each.

Legal or special characters enable you to embed alphabetic characters, symbols, and non-keyboard characters in a document. XML's character-class elements (that is, `BaseChar`, `CombiningChar`, `Digit`, `Extender`, `Ideographic`, and `Letter`) support the special characters listed in the following tables.

For more information about character-class elements, including the syntax and specific characters supported by each, see Chapter 2, *XML Syntax.*

●─**NOTE**─────────────────────────────

The `Char` element supports any Unicode character, including those documented in this part and excluding #xFFFE and #xFFFF.

Tables A-1 through A-21 have all, or some, of these column headings:

Char (Character)	A typed character.
Glyph	An image of the character or symbol, the counterpart to Char.
UTC Code	The code assigned by the Unicode Organization's Unicode Technical Committee.
Entity Name	The approved syntax for the characters. In most cases, you should use this syntax instead of the numeric entity reference.
Numeric Entry Reference	A numeric code counterpart to the entity name.
Description	A brief description of the character.

●─**NOTE**─────────────────────────────

In addition to the characters specified in this part, XML also supports four standard control characters:

#x9 (Unicode code #x0009), which inserts a tab (HT).
#xA (Unicode code #x000A), which inserts a line feed (LF).
#xD (Unicode code #x000D), which inserts a carriage return (CR).
#x20 (Unicode code #x0020), which inserts a space.

BaseChar Characters and Character Sets

This section covers the characters and character sets supported by the BaseChar element.

Latin 1 Uppercase and Lowercase

Table A-1 contains the alphabetic characters in the Special Characters — Latin 1 Uppercase and Lowercase set, in the BaseChar element.

Table A-1   *BaseChar Special Characters — Latin 1 Uppercase and Lowercase*

Char.	UTC Code	Char.	UTC Code	Char.	UTC Code	Char.	UTC Code
A	#x0041	N	#x004E	a	#x0061	n	#x006E
B	#x0042	O	#x004F	b	#x0062	o	#x006F
C	#x0043	P	#x0050	c	#x0063	p	#x0070
D	#x0044	Q	#x0051	d	#x0064	q	#x0071
E	#x0045	R	#x0052	e	#x0065	r	#x0072
F	#x0046	S	#x0053	f	#x0066	s	#x0073
G	#x0047	T	#x0054	g	#x0067	t	#x0074
H	#x0048	U	#x0055	h	#x0068	u	#x0075
I	#x0049	V	#x0056	i	#x0069	v	#x0076
J	#x004A	W	#x0057	j	#x006A	w	#x0077
K	#x004B	X	#x0058	k	#x006B	x	#x0078
L	#x004C	Y	#x0059	l	#x006C	y	#x0079
M	#x004D	Z	#x005A	m	#x006D	z	#x007A

Latin 1 Supplementary

Table A-2 contains the XML-supported characters in the Latin 1 Supplementary set, in the BaseChar element.

Table A-2 *BaseChar Special Characters — Latin 1 Supplementary*

Glyph	UTC Code	Entity Name	Numeric Entry Reference	Description
À	#x00C0	&Agrave;	&#192;	Grave Accent A
Á	#x00C1	&Aacute	&#193;	Acute Accent A
Â	#x00C2	&Acirc;	&#194;	Circumflex Above A
Ã	#x00C3	&Atilde;	&#195;	Tilde Above A
Ä	#x00C4	&Auml;	&#196;	Umlaut Above A
Å	#x00C5	&Aring;	&#197;	Ring Above A
Æ	#x00C6	&AElig;	&#198;	Ligature AE
Ç	#x00C7	&Ccedil;	&#199;	Cedilla C
È	#x00C8	&Egrave;	&#200;	Grave Accent E
É	#x00C9	&Eacute;	&#201;	Acute Accent E
Ê	#x00CA	&Ecirc;	&#202;	Circumflex Above E
Ë	#x00CB	&Euml;	&#203;	Umlaut Above E
Ì	#x00CC	&Igrave;	&#204:	Grave Accent I
Í	#x00CD	&Iacute;	&#205;	Acute Accent I
Î	#x00CE	&Icirc;	&#206;	Circumflex Above I
Ï	#x00CF	&Iuml;	&#207;	Umlaut Above I
Ð	#x00D0	&ETH;	&#208;	Icelandic ETH
Ñ	#x00D1	&Ntilde;	&#209;	Tilde Above N
Ò	#x00D2	&Ograve;	&#210;	Grave Accent O
Ó	#x00D3	&Oacute;	&#211;	Acute Accent O
Ô	#x00D4	&Ocirc;	&#212;	Circumflex Above O
Õ	#x00D5	&Otilde;	&#213;	Tilde Above O
Ö	#x00D6	&Ouml;	&#214;	Umlaut Above O
Ø	#x00D8	&Oslash;	&#216;	Stroke or Slash O

Glyph	UTC Code	Entity Name	Numeric Entry Reference	Description
Ù	#x00D9	Ù	Ù	Grave Accent U
Ú	#x00DA	Ú	Ú	Acute Accent U
Û	#x00DB	Û	Û	Circumflex Above U
Ü	#x00DC	Ü	Ü	Umlaut Above U
Ý	#x00DD	Ý	Ý	Acute Accent Y
Þ	#x00DE	Þ	Þ	Icelandic THORN
ß	#x00DF	ß	ß	Sharp s
à	#x00E0	à	à	Grave Accent a
á	#x00E1	á	á	Acute Accent a
â	#x00E2	â	â	Circumflex Above a
ã	#x00E3	ã	ã	Tilde Above a
ä	#x00E4	ä	ä	Umlaut Above a
å	#x00E5	å	å	Ring Above a
æ	#x00E6	æ	æ	Ligature ae
ç	#x00E7	ç	ç	Cedilla c
è	#x00E8	è	è	Grave Accent e
é	#x00E9	é	é	Acute Accent e
ê	#x00EA	ê	ê	Circumflex Above e
ë	#x00EB	ë	ë	Umlaut Above e
ì	#x00EC	ì	ì	Grave Accent i
í	#x00ED	í	í	Acute Accent i
î	#x00EE	î	î	Circumflex Above i
ï	#x00EF	ï	ï	Umlaut Above i
ð	#x00F0	ð	ð	Icelandic eth
ñ	#x00F1	ñ	ñ	Tilde Above n
ò	#x00F2	ò	ò	Grave Accent o
ó	#x00F3	ó	ó	Acute Accent o
ô	#x00F4	ô	ô	Circumflex Above o

Continued

Table A-2 *Continued*

Glyph	UTC Code	Entity Name	Numeric Entry Reference	Description
õ	#x00F5	õ	õ	Tilde Above o
ö	#x00F6	ö	ö	Umlaut Above o
ø	#x00F8	ø	ø	Stroke or Slash o
ù	#x00F9	ù	ù	Grave Accent u
ú	#x00FA	ú	ú	Acute Accent u
û	#x00FB	û	û	Circumflex Above u
ü	#x00FC	ü	ü	Umlaut Above u
ý	#x00FD	ý	ý	Acute Accent y
þ	#x00FE	þ	þ	Icelandic thorn
ÿ	#x00FF	ÿ	ÿ	Umlaut Above y

Extended Latin-A

Table A-3 contains the XML-supported characters in the Extended
Latin-A set, in the BaseChar element.

Table A-3 *BaseChar Special Characters — Extended Latin-A*

Glyph	UTC Code	Entity Name	Description
Ā	#x0100	Ā	Macron A
ā	#x0101	ā	Macron a
Ă	#x0102	Ă	Breve Above A
ă	#x0103	ă	Breve Above a
Ą	#x0104	Ą	Ogonek A
ą	#x0105	ą	Ogonek a
Ć	#x0106	Ć	Acute Accent C
ć	#x0107	ć	Acute Accent c
Ĉ	#x0108	Ĉ	Circumflex Above C
ĉ	#x0109	ĉ	Circumflex Above c

Glyph	UTC Code	Entity Name	Description
Ċ	#x010A	Ċ	Dot Above C
ċ	#x010B	ċ	Dot Above c
Č	#x010C	Č	Caron C
č	#x010D	č	Caron c
Ď	#x010E	Ď	Caron D
ď	#x010F	ď	Caron d
Đ	#x0110	Đ	Stroke D
đ	#x0111	đ	Stroke d
Ē	#x0112	Ē	Macron E
ē	#x0113	ē	Macron e
Ĕ	#x0114	n/a	Breve Above E
ĕ	#x0115	n/a	Breve Above e
Ė	#x0116	Ė	Dot Above E
ė	#x0117	ė	Dot Above e
Ę	#x0118	Ę	Ogonek E
ę	#x0119	ę	Ogonek e
Ě	#x011A	Ě	Caron E
ě	#x011B	ě	Caron e
Ĝ	#x011C	Ĝ	Circumflex Above G
ĝ	#x011D	ĝ	Circumflex Above g
Ğ	#x011E	Ğ	Breve Above G
ğ	#x011F	ğ	Breve Above g
Ġ	#x0120	Ġ	Dot Above G
ġ	#x0121	ġ	Dot Above g
Ģ	#x0122	Ģ	Cedilla G
ģ	#x0123	n/a	Cedilla g
Ĥ	#x0124	Ĥ	Circumflex Above H
ĥ	#x0125	ĥ	Circumflex Above h
Ħ	#x0126	Ħ	Stroke H

Continued

Table A-3 *Continued*

Glyph	UTC Code	Entity Name	Description
ħ	#x0127	ħ	Stroke h
Ĩ	#x0128	Ĩ	Tilde Above I
ĩ	#x0129	ĩ	Tilde Above i
Ī	#x012A	Ī	Macron I
ī	#x012B	ī	Macron i
Ĭ	#x012C	n/a	Breve Above I
ĭ	#x012D	n/a	Breve Above i
Į	#x012E	Į	Ogonek I
į	#x012F	į	Ogonek i
İ	#x0130	İ	Dot Above I
ı	#x0131	ı	Dotless i
Ĵ	#x0134	Ĵ	Circumflex Above J
ĵ	#x0135	ĵ	Circumflex Above j
Ķ	#x0136	Ķ	Cedilla K
ķ	#x0137	ķ	Cedilla k
ĸ	#x0138	n/a	kra
Ĺ	#x0139	Ĺ	Acute Accent L
ĺ	#x013A	ĺ	Acute Accent l
Ļ	#x013B	Ļ	Cedilla L
ļ	#x013C	ļ	Cedilla l
Ľ	#x013D	Ľ	Caron L
ľ	#x013E	ľ	Caron l
Ł	#x0141	Ł	Stroke L
ł	#x0142	ł	Stroke l
Ń	#x0143	Ń	Acute Accent N
ń	#x0144	ń	Acute Accent n
Ņ	#x0145	Ņ	Cedilla N
ņ	#x0146	ņ	Cedilla n

Glyph	UTC Code	Entity Name	Description
Ň	#x0147	Ň	Caron N
ň	#x0148	ň	Caron n
Ŋ	#x014A	Ŋ	ENG
ŋ	#x014B	ŋ	eng
Ō	#x014C	Ō	Macron O
ō	#x014D	ō	Macron o
Ŏ	#x014E	n/a	Breve Above O
ŏ	#x014F	n/a	Breve Above o
Ő	#x0150	Ő	Double Acute Accent O
ő	#x0151	ő	Double Acute Accent o
Œ	#x0152	Œ	Ligature OE
œ	#x0153	œ	Ligature oe
Ŕ	#x0154	Ŕ	Acute Accent R
ŕ	#x0155	ŕ	Acute Accent r
Ŗ	#x0156	Ŗ	Cedilla R
ŗ	#x0157	ŗ	Cedilla r
Ř	#x0158	Ř	Caron R
ř	#x0159	ř	Caron r
Ś	#x015A	Ś	Acute Accent S
ś	#x015B	ś	Acute Accent s
Ŝ	#x015C	Ŝ	Circumflex Above S
ŝ	#x015D	ŝ	Circumflex Above s
Ş	#x015E	Ş	Cedilla S
ş	#x015F	ş	Cedilla s
Š	#x0160	Š	Caron S
š	#x0161	š	Caron s
Ţ	#x0162	Ţ	Cedilla T
ţ	#x0163	ţ	Cedilla t
Ť	#x0164	Ť	Caron T

Continued

Table A-3 *Continued*

Glyph	UTC Code	Entity Name	Description
ť	#x0165	ť	Caron t
Ŧ	#x0166	Ŧ	Stroke T
ŧ	#x0167	ŧ	Stroke t
Ũ	#x0168	Ũ	Tilde Above U
ũ	#x0169	ũ	Tilde Above u
Ū	#x016A	Ū	Macron U
ū	#x016B	ū	Macron u
Ŭ	#x016C	Ŭ	Breve Above U
ŭ	#x016D	ŭ	Breve Above u
Ů	#x016E	Ů	Ring Above U
ů	#x016F	ů	Ring Above u
Ű	#x0170	Ű	Double Acute Accent U
ű	#x0171	ű	Double Acute Accent u
Ų	#x0172	Ų	Ogonek U
ų	#x0173	ų	Ogonek u
Ŵ	#x0174	Ŵ	Circumflex Above W
ŵ	#x0175	ŵ	Circumflex Above w
Ŷ	#x0176	Ŷ	Circumflex Above Y
ŷ	#x0177	ŷ	Circumflex Above y
Ÿ	#x0178	Ÿ	Umlaut Above Y
Ź	#x0179	Ź	Acute Accent Z
ź	#x017A	ź	Acute Accent z
Ż	#x017B	Ż	Dot Above Z
ż	#x017C	ż	Dot Above z
Ž	#x017D	Ž	Caron Z
ž	#x017E	ž	Caron z

Extended Latin-B

Table A-4 contains the XML-supported characters in the Extended Latin-B set, in the BaseChar element.

Table A-4   *BaseChar Special Characters — Extended Latin-B*

Glyph	UTC Code	Description
ƀ	#x0180	Stroke b
Ɓ	#x0181	Hook B
Ƃ	#x0182	Topbar B
ƃ	#x0183	Topbar b
Ƅ	#x0184	Tone SIX
ƅ	#x0185	Tone six
Ɔ	#x0186	Open O
Ƈ	#x0187	Hook C
ƈ	#x0188	Hook c
Ɖ	#x0189	African D
Ɗ	#x018A	Hook D
Ƌ	#x018B	Topbar D
ƌ	#x018C	Topbard d
ƍ	#x018D	Turned delta
Ǝ	#x018E	Reversed E
Ə	#x018F	SCHWA
Ɛ	#x0190	Open E
Ƒ	#x0191	Hook F
ƒ	#x0192	Hook f
Ɠ	#x0193	Hook G
Ɣ	#x0194	GAMMA
ƕ	#x0195	hv
ɩ	#x0196	IOTA
Ɨ	#x0197	Stroke I

Continued

Table A-4 *Continued*

Glyph	UTC Code	Description
Kʻ	#x0198	Hook K
ƙ	#x0199	Hook k
ɫ	#x019A	Bar l
ƛ	#x019B	Stroke lambda
ɯ	#x019C	Turned M
Ɲ	#x019D	Left Hook N
η	#x019E	Long Right Leg n
Ɵ	#x019F	Middle Tilde O
Ơ	#x01A0	Horn O
ơ	#x01A1	Horn o
Ƣ	#x01A2	OI
ƣ	#x01A3	oi
Ƥ	#x01A4	Hook P
ƥ	#x01A5	Hook p
Ʀ	#x01A6	YR
Ƨ	#x01A7	Tone TWO
ƨ	#x01A8	Tone two
Ʃ	#x01A9	ESH
ƪ	#x01AA	Reversed ESH Loop
ƫ	#x01AB	Palatal Hook t
Ƭ	#x01AC	Hook T
ƭ	#x01AD	Hook t
Ʈ	#x01AE	Retroflex Hook T
Ư	#x01AF	Horn U
ư	#x01B0	Horn u
Ʊ	#x01B1	UPSILON
Ʋ	#x01B2	Hook V
Ƴ	#x01B3	Hook Y

Glyph	UTC Code	Description
y̓	#x01B4	Hook y
Z̵	#x01B5	Stroke Z
z̵	#x01B6	Stroke z
ʒ	#x01B7	EZH
Ǯ	#x01B8	EZH Reversed
ǯ	#x01B9	ezh Reversed
ȝ	#x01BA	ezh Tail
2̵	#x01BB	Stroke 2
5	#x01BC	Tone FIVE
ƽ	#x01BD	Tone five
ƾ	#x01BE	Stroke Inverted Glottal Stop
ƿ	#x01BF	Wynn
ǀ	#x01C0	Dental Click
ǁ	#x01C1	Lateral Click
ǂ	#x01C2	Alveolar Click
!	#x01C3	Retroflex Click
Ǎ	#x01CD	Caron A
ǎ	#x01CE	Caron a
Ǐ	#x01CF	Caron I
ǐ	#x01D0	Caron i
Ǒ	#x01D1	Caron O
ǒ	#x01D2	Caron o
Ǔ	#x01D3	Caron U
ǔ	#x01D4	Caron u
Ǖ	#x01D5	Umlaut Above Macron U
ǖ	#x01D6	Umlaut Above Macron u
Ǘ	#x01D7	Umlaut Above Acute Accent U
ǘ	#x01D8	Umlaut Acute Accent u
Ǚ	#x01D9	Umlaut Above Caron U

Continued

Table A-4 *Continued*

Glyph	UTC Code	Description
ǔ	#x01DA	Umlaut Above Caron u
Ǜ	#x01DB	Umlaut Above Grave Accent U
ǜ	#x01DC	Umlaut Above Grave Accent u
ə	#x01DD	Turned e
Ǟ	#x01DE	Umlaut Above Macron A
ǟ	#x01DF	UmlautAbove Macron a
Ǡ	#x01E0	Dot Above Macron A
ǡ	#x01E1	Dot Above Macron a
Ǣ	#x01E2	Macron AE
ǣ	#x01E3	Macron ae
G	#x01E4	Stroke G
g	#x01E5	Stroke g
Ǧ	#x01E6	Caron G
ǧ	#x01E7	Caron g
Ǩ	#x01E8	Caron K
ǩ	#x01E9	Caron k
Ǫ	#x01EA	Ogonek O
ǫ	#x01EB	Ogonek o
Ǭ	#x01EC	Ogonek Macron O
ǭ	#x01ED	Ogonek Macron o
Ǯ	#x01EE	Caron EZH
ǯ	#x01EF	Caron ezh
ǰ	#x01F0	Caron j
Ǵ	#x01F4	Acute Accent G
ǵ	#x01F5	Acute Accent g
Ǻ	#x01FA	Ring Above Acute Accent A
ǻ	#x01FB	Ring Above Acute Accent a
Ǽ	#x01FC	Acute Accent AE

Glyph	UTC Code	Description
ǽ	#x01FD	Acute Accent ae
Ǿ	#x01FE	Stroke Acute Accent O
ǿ	#x01FF	Stroke Acute Accent o
Ȁ	#x0200	Double Grave Accent A
ȁ	#x0201	Double Grave Accent a
Ȃ	#x0202	Inverted Breve A
ȃ	#x0203	Inverted Breve a
Ȅ	#x0204	Double Grave Accent E
ȅ	#x0205	Double Grave Accent e
Ȇ	#x0206	Inverted Breve E
ȇ	#x0207	Inverted Breve e
Ȉ	#x0208	Double Grave Accent I
ȉ	#x0209	Double Grave Accent i
Ȋ	#x020A	Inverted Breve I
ȋ	#x020B	Inverted Breve i
Ȍ	#x020C	Double Grave Accent O
ȍ	#x020D	Double Grave Accent o
Ȏ	#x020E	Inverted Breve O
ȏ	#x020F	Inverted Breve o
Ȑ	#x0210	Double Grave Accent R
ȑ	#x0211	Double Grave Accent r
Ȓ	#x0212	Inverted Breve R
ȓ	#x0213	Inverted Breve r
Ȕ	#x0214	Double Grave Accent U
ȕ	#x0215	Double Grave Accent u
Ȗ	#x0216	Inverted Breve U
ȗ	#x0217	Inverted Breve u

IPA Extensions

Table A-5 contains the XML-supported characters in the IPA Extensions set, in the BaseChar element.

Table A-5 *BaseChar Special Characters — IPA Extensions*

Glyph	UTC Code	Description
ɐ	#x0250	Turned a
ɑ	#x0251	alpha
ɒ	#x0252	Turned alpha
ɓ	#x0253	Hook b
ɔ	#x0254	Open o
ɕ	#x0255	Curl c
ɖ	#x0256	Tail d
ɗ	#x0257	Hook d
ɘ	#x0258	Reversed e
ə	#x0259	schwa
ɚ	#x025A	Hook schwa
ɛ	#x025B	Open e
ɜ	#x025C	Reversed Open e
ɝ	#x025D	Hook Reversed Open e
ɞ	#x025E	Closed Reversed Open e
ɟ	#x025F	Dotless Stroke j
ɠ	#x0260	Hook g
ɡ	#x0261	Script g
ɢ	#x0262	Small G
ɣ	#x0263	gamma
ɤ	#x0264	Rams horn
ɥ	#x0265	Turned h
ɦ	#x0266	Hook h
ɧ	#x0267	Hook heng
ɨ	#x0268	Stroke i

Glyph	UTC Code	Description
ɩ	#x0269	iota
ɪ	#x026A	Small I
ɫ	#x026B	Middle Tilde l
ɬ	#x026C	Belt l
ɭ	#x026D	Retroflex Hook l
ɮ	#x026E	lezh
ɯ	#x026F	Turned m
ɰ	#x0270	Turned Long leg m
ɱ	#x0271	Hook m
ɲ	#x0272	Left Hook n
ɳ	#x0273	Retroflex Hook n
ɴ	#x0274	Small N
ɵ	#x0275	Barred o
ɶ	#x0276	Small OE
ɷ	#x0277	Closed omega
ɸ	#x0278	Small PHI
ɹ	#x0279	Turned r
ɺ	#x027A	Turned Long Leg r
ɻ	#x027B	Hook Turned r
ɼ	#x027C	Long Leg r
ɽ	#x027D	Tail r
ɾ	#x027E	Fishhook r
ɿ	#x027F	Reversed Fishhook r
ʀ	#x0280	Small R
ʁ	#x0281	Inverted Small R
ʂ	#x0282	Hook s
ʃ	#x0283	esh
ʄ	#x0284	Stroke Hook Dotless j
ʅ	#x0285	Squat Reversed esh

Continued

Table A-5 *Continued*

Glyph	UTC Code	Description
ʆ	#x0286	Curl esh
ʇ	#x0287	Turned t
ʈ	#x0288	Retroflex Hook t
ʉ	#x0289	Bar u
ʊ	#x028A	upsilon
ʋ	#x028B	Hook v
ʌ	#x028C	Turned v
ʍ	#x028D	Turned w
ʎ	#x028E	Turned y
ʏ	#x028F	Small Y
ʐ	#x0290	Retroflex Hook z
ʑ	#x0291	Curl z
ʒ	#x0292	ezh
ʓ	#x0293	Curl ezh
ʔ	#x0294	Glottal Stop
ʕ	#x0295	Pharyngeal Voiced Fricative
ʖ	#x0296	Inverted Glottal Stop
ʗ	#x0297	Stretched C
ʘ	#x0298	Bilabial Click
ʙ	#x0299	Small B
ʚ	#x029A	Closed Open e
ʛ	#x029B	Small Hook G
ʜ	#x029C	Small H
ʝ	#x029D	Crossed-Tail j
ʞ	#x029E	Turned k
ʟ	#x029F	Small L
ʠ	#x02A0	Hook q
ʡ	#x02A1	Stroke Glottal Stop

Glyph	UTC Code	Description
ʕ	#x02A2	Stroke Reversed Glottal Stop
ʣ	#x02A3	dz Digraph
ʤ	#x02A4	dezh Digraph
ʥ	#x02A5	Curl dz Digraph
ʦ	#x02A6	ts Digraph
ʧ	#x02A7	tesh Digraph
ʨ	#x02A8	Curl tc Digraph

Spacing Modifier Letters

Table A-6 contains the XML-supported characters in the Spacing Modifier Letters set, in the BaseChar element.

Table A-6 *BaseChar Special Characters — Spacing Modifier Letters*

Glyph	UTC Code	Description
ʻ	#x02BB	Prime
ʼ	#x02BC	Double Prime
ʽ	#x02BD	Reversed Comma
ʾ	#x02BE	Right Half Ring
ʿ	#x02BF	Left Half Ring
ˀ	#x02C0	Glottal Stop
ˁ	#x02C1	Reversed Glottal Stop

Greek and Coptic

Table A-7 contains the XML-supported characters in the Greek and Coptic set, in the BaseChar element.

Table A-7   *BaseChar Special Characters — Greek and Coptic*

Glyph	UTC Code	Entity Name	Description
Ά	#x0386	n/a	Tonos ALPHA
Έ	#x0388	n/a	Tonos EPSILON
Ή	#x0389	n/a	Tonos ETA
Ί	#x038A	n/a	Tonos IOTA
Ό	#x038C	n/a	Tonos OMICRON
Ύ	#x038E	n/a	Tonos UPSILON
Ώ	#x038F	n/a	Tonos OMEGA
ΐ	#x0390	n/a	Dialytika Tonos iota
A	#x0391	&Agr;	ALPHA
B	#x0392	&Bgr;	BETA
Γ	#x0393	&Ggr;	GAMMA
Δ	#x0394	&Dgr;	DELTA
E	#x0395	&Egr;	EPSILON
Z	#x0396	&Zgr;	ZETA
H	#x0397	&EEgr;	ETA
Θ	#x0398	&THgr;	THETA
I	#x0399	&Igr;	IOTA
K	#x039A	&Kgr;	KAPPA
Λ	#x039B	&Lgr;	LAMBDA
M	#x039C	&Mgr;	MU
N	#x039D	&Ngr;	NU
Ξ	#x039E	&Xgr;	XI
O	#x039F	&Ogr;	OMICRON
Π	#x03A0	&Pgr;	PI
P	#x03A1	&Rgr;	RHO

Glyph	UTC Code	Entity Name	Description
Σ	#x03A3	&Sgr;	SIGMA
Τ	#x03A4	&Tgr;	TAU
Υ	#x03A5	&Ugr;	UPSILON
Φ	#x03A6	&PHgr;	PHI
X	#x03A7	&KHgr;	CHI
Ψ	#x03A8	&PSgr;	PSI
Ω	#x03A9	&OHgr;	OMEGA
Ϊ	#x03AA	n/a	Dialytika IOTA
Ϋ	#x03AB	n/a	Dialytika UPSILON
ά	#x03AC	n/a	Tonos alpha
έ	#x03AD	n/a	Tonos epsilon
ή	#x03AE	n/a	Tonos eta
ί	#x03AF	n/a	Tonos iota
ΰ	#x03B0	n/a	Dialytika Tonos upsilon
α	#x03B1	&agr;	alpha
β	#x03B2	&bgr;	beta
γ	#x03B3	&ggr;	gamma
δ	#x03B4	&dgr;	delta
ε	#x03B5	&egr;	epsilon
ζ	#x03B6	&zgr;	zeta
η	#x03B7	&eegr;	eta
θ	#x03B8	&thgr;	theta
ι	#x03B9	&igr;	iota
κ	#x03BA	&kgr;	kappa
λ	#x03BB	&lgr;	lambda
μ	#x03BC	&mgr;	mu
ν	#x03BD	&ngr;	nu
ξ	#x03BE	&xgr;	xi
ο	#x03BF	&ogr;	omicron

Continued

Table A-7 *Continued*

Glyph	UTC Code	Entity Name	Description
π	#x03C0	&pgr;	pi
ρ	#x03C1	&rgr;	rho
ς	#x03C2	&sfgr;	final sigma
σ	#x03C3	&sgr;	sigma
τ	#x03C4	&tgr;	tau
υ	#x03C5	&ugr;	upsilon
φ	#x03C6	&phgr;	phi
χ	#x03C7	&khgr;	chi
ψ	#x03C8	&psgr;	psi
ω	#x03C9	&ohgr;	omega
ϊ	#x03CA	n/a	Dialytika iota
ϋ	#x03CB	n/a	Dialytika upsilon
ό	#x03CC	n/a	Tonos omicron
ύ	#x03CD	n/a	Tonos upsilon
ώ	#x03CE	n/a	Tonos omega
ϐ	#x03D0	n/a	Beta Symbol
ϑ	#x03D1	n/a	Theta Symbol
ϒ	#x03D2	n/a	Hook Upsilon
ϓ	#x03D3	n/a	Acute Accent Hook Upsilon
ϔ	#x03D4	n/a	Umlaut Above Hook Upsilon
ϕ	#x03D5	n/a	Phi Symbol
ϖ	#x03D6	n/a	Pi Symbol
Ϛ	#x03DA	n/a	Stigma
Ϝ	#x03DC	n/a	Digamma
Ϟ	#x03DE	n/a	Koppa
Ϡ	#x03E0	n/a	Sampi
Ш	#x03E2	n/a	SHEI
ш	#x03E3	n/a	shei

Glyph	UTC Code	Entity Name	Description
৭	#x03E4	n/a	FEI
৭	#x03E5	n/a	fei
৳	#x03E6	n/a	KHEI
৯	#x03E7	n/a	khei
৪	#x03E8	n/a	HORI
੨	#x03E9	n/a	hori
ⳤ	#x03EA	n/a	GANGIA
ⳡ	#x03EB	n/a	gangia
⳥	#x03EC	n/a	SHIMA
⳦	#x03ED	n/a	shima
⳨	#x03EE	n/a	DEI
⳩	#x03EF	n/a	dei
ϰ	#x03F0	n/a	Kappa Symbol
ϱ	#x03F1	n/a	Rho Symbol
ϲ	#x03F2	n/a	Lunate Sigma Symbol
ϳ	#x03F3	n/a	Yot

Additional Extended Latin

Table A-8 contains the XML-supported characters in the Additional Extended Latin set, in the BaseChar element.

Table A-8   *BaseChar Special Characters — Additional Extended Latin*

Glyph	UTC Code	Description
Ḁ	#x1E00	Ring Below A
ḁ	#x1E01	Ring Below a
Ḃ	#x1E02	Dot Above B
ḃ	#x1E03	Dot Above b
Ḅ	#x1E04	Dot Below B

Continued

Table A-8 *Continued*

Glyph	UTC Code	Description
ḅ	#x1E05	Dot Below b
B̲	#x1E06	Line Below B
b̲	#x1E07	Line Below b
Ḉ	#x1E08	Cedilla Acute Accent C
ḉ	#x1E09	Cedilla Acute Accent c
Ḋ	#x1E0A	Dot Above D
ḋ	#x1E0B	Dot Above d
Ḍ	#x1E0C	Dot Below D
ḍ	#x1E0D	Dot Below d
D̲	#x1E0E	Line Below D
d̲	#x1E0F	Line Below d
Ḑ	#x1E10	Cedilla D
ḑ	#x1E11	Cedilla d
Ḓ	#x1E12	Circumflex Below D
ḓ	#x1E13	Circumflex Below d
Ḕ	#x1E14	Macron Grave Accent E
ḕ	#x1E15	Macron Grave Accent e
Ḗ	#x1E16	Macron Acute Accent E
ḗ	#x1E17	Macron Acute Accent e
Ḙ	#x1E18	Circumflex Below E
ḙ	#x1E19	Circumflex Below e
Ḛ	#x1E1A	Tilde Below E
ḛ	#x1E1B	Tilde Below e
Ḝ	#x1E1C	Breve Above Cedilla E
ḝ	#x1E1D	Breve Above Cedilla e
Ḟ	#x1E1E	Dot Above F
ḟ	#x1E1F	Dot Above f
Ḡ	#x1E20	Macron G

Glyph	UTC Code	Description
ḡ	#x1E21	Macron g
Ḣ	#x1E22	Dot Above H
ḣ	#x1E23	Dot Above h
Ḥ	#x1E24	Dot Below H
ḥ	#x1E25	Dot Below h
Ḧ	#x1E26	Umlaut Above H
ḧ	#x1E27	Umlaut Above h
Ḩ	#x1E28	Cedilla H
ḩ	#x1E29	Cedilla h
Ḫ	#x1E2A	Breve Below H
ḫ	#x1E2B	Breve Below h
Ḭ	#x1E2C	Tilde Below I
ḭ	#x1E2D	Tilde Below i
Ḯ	#x1E2E	Umlaut Above Acute Accent I
ḯ	#x1E2F	Umlaut Above Acute Accent i
Ḱ	#x1E30	Acute Accent K
ḱ	#x1E31	Acute Accent k
Ḳ	#x1E32	Dot Below K
ḳ	#x1E33	Dot Below k
Ḵ	#x1E34	Line Below K
ḵ	#x1E35	Line Below k
Ḷ	#x1E36	Dot Below L
ḷ	#x1E37	Dot Below l
Ḹ	#x1E38	Macron Dot Below L
ḹ	#x1E39	Macron Dot Below l
Ḻ	#x1E3A	Line Below L
ḻ	#x1E3B	Line Below l
Ḽ	#x1E3C	Circumflex Below L
ḽ	#x1E3D	Circumflex Below l

Continued

Table A-8 *Continued*

Glyph	UTC Code	Description
Ḿ	#x1E3E	Acute Accent M
ḿ	#x1E3F	Acute Accent m
Ṁ	#x1E40	Dot Above M
ṁ	#x1E41	Dot Above m
Ṃ	#x1E42	Dot Below M
ṃ	#x1E43	Dot Below m
Ṅ	#x1E44	Dot Above N
ṅ	#x1E45	Dot Above n
Ṇ	#x1E46	Dot Below N
ṇ	#x1E47	Dot Below n
Ṉ	#x1E48	Line Below N
ṉ	#x1E49	Line Below n
Ṋ	#x1E4A	Circumflex Below N
ṋ	#x1E4B	Circumflex Below n
Ṍ	#x1E4C	Tilde Above Acute Accent O
ṍ	#x1E4D	Tilde Above Acute Accent o
Ṏ	#x1E4E	Umlaut Tilde Above O
ṏ	#x1E4F	Umlaut Tilde Above o
Ṑ	#x1E50	Macron Grave Accent O
ṑ	#x1E51	Macron Grave Accent o
Ṓ	#x1E52	Macron Acute Accent O
ṓ	#x1E53	Macron Acute Accent o
Ṕ	#x1E54	Acute Accent P
ṕ	#x1E55	Acute Accent p
Ṗ	#x1E56	Dot Above P
ṗ	#x1E57	Dot Above p
Ṙ	#x1E58	Dot Above R
ṙ	#x1E59	Dot Above r

Glyph	UTC Code	Description
Ṛ	#x1E5A	Dot Below R
ṛ	#x1E5B	Dot Below r
Ṝ	#x1E5C	Dot Below Macron R
ṝ	#x1E5D	Dot Below Macron r
Ṟ	#x1E5E	Line Below R
ṟ	#x1E5F	Line Below r
Ṡ	#x1E60	Dot Above S
ṡ	#x1E61	Dot Above s
Ṣ	#x1E62	Dot Below S
ṣ	#x1E63	Dot Below s
Ṥ	#x1E64	Acute Accent Dot Above S
ṥ	#x1E65	Acute Accent Dot Above s
Ṧ	#x1E66	Caron Dot Above S
ṧ	#x1E67	Caron Dot Above s
Ṩ	#x1E68	Dot Above Dot Below S
ṩ	#x1E69	Dot Above Dot Below s
Ṫ	#x1E6A	Dot Above T
ṫ	#x1E6B	Dot Above t
Ṭ	#x1E6C	Dot Below T
ṭ	#x1E6D	Dot Below t
Ṯ	#x1E6E	Line Below T
ṯ	#x1E6F	Line Below t
Ṱ	#x1E70	Circumflex Below T
ṱ	#x1E71	Circumflex Below t
Ṳ	#x1E72	Umlaut Below U
ṳ	#x1E73	Umlaut Below u
Ṵ	#x1E74	Tilde Below U
ṵ	#x1E75	Tilde Below u
Ṷ	#x1E76	Circumflex Below U

Continued

Table A-8 *Continued*

Glyph	UTC Code	Description
ṷ	#x1E77	Circumflex Below u
Ṹ	#x1E78	Tilde Above Acute Accent U
ṹ	#x1E79	Tilde Above Acute Accent u
Ṻ	#x1E7A	Macron Umlaut Above U
ṻ	#x1E7B	Macron Umlaut Above u
Ṽ	#x1E7C	Tilde Above V
ṽ	#x1E7D	Tilde Above v
Ṿ	#x1E7E	Dot Below V
ṿ	#x1E7F	Dot Below v
Ẁ	#x1E80	Grave Accent W
ẁ	#x1E81	Grave Accent w
Ẃ	#x1E82	Acute Accent W
ẃ	#x1E83	Acute Accent w
Ẅ	#x1E84	Umlaut Above W
ẅ	#x1E85	Umlaut Above w
Ẇ	#x1E86	Dot Above W
ẇ	#x1E87	Dot Above w
Ẉ	#x1E88	Dot Below W
ẉ	#x1E89	Dot Below w
Ẋ	#x1E8A	Dot Above X
ẋ	#x1E8B	Dot Above x
Ẍ	#x1E8C	Umlaut Above X
ẍ	#x1E8D	Umlaut Above x
Ẏ	#x1E8E	Dot Above Y
ẏ	#x1E8F	Dot Above y
Ẑ	#x1E90	Circumflex Above Z
ẑ	#x1E91	Circumflex Above z
Ẓ	#x1E92	Dot Below Z

Glyph	UTC Code	Description
ẓ	#x1E93	Dot Below z
Ẕ	#x1E94	Line Below Z
ẕ	#x1E95	Line Below z
ẖ	#x1E96	Line Below h
ẗ	#x1E97	Umlaut Above t
ẘ	#x1E98	Ring Above w
ẙ	#x1E99	Ring Above y
aʾ	#x1E9A	Right Half Ring Above a
ẛ	#x1E9B	Dot Above Long s
Ạ	#x1EA0	Dot Below A
ạ	#x1EA1	Dot Below a
Ả	#x1EA2	Hook Above A
ả	#x1EA3	Hook Above a
Ấ	#x1EA4	Circumflex Above Acute Accent A
ấ	#x1EA5	Circumflex Above Acute Accent a
Ầ	#x1EA6	Circumflex Above Grave Accent A
ầ	#x1EA7	Circumflex Above Grave Accent a
Ẩ	#x1EA8	Circumflex Hook Above A
ẩ	#x1EA9	Circumflex Hook Above a
Ẫ	#x1EAA	Circumflex Tilde Above A
ẫ	#x1EAB	Circumflex Tilde Above a
Ậ	#x1EAC	Circumflex Above Dot Below A
ậ	#x1EAD	Circumflex Above Dot Below a
Ắ	#x1EAE	Breve Above Acute Accent A
ắ	#x1EAF	Breve Above Acute Accent a
Ằ	#x1EB0	Breve Above Grave Accent A
ằ	#x1EB1	Breve Above Grave Accent a
Ẳ	#x1EB2	Breve Hook Above A
ẳ	#x1EB3	Breve Hook Above a

Continued

Table A-8   *Continued*

Glyph	UTC Code	Description
Ẫ	#x1EB4	Breve Tilde Above A
ẫ	#x1EB5	Breve Tilde Above a
Ẵ	#x1EB6	Breve Above Dot Below A
ặ	#x1EB7	Breve Above Dot Below a
Ẹ	#x1EB8	Dot Below E
ẹ	#x1EB9	Dot Below e
Ẻ	#x1EBA	Hook Above E
ẻ	#x1EBB	Hook Above e
Ẽ	#x1EBC	Tilde Above E
ẽ	#x1EBD	Tilde Above e
Ế	#x1EBE	Circumflex Above Acute Accent E
ế	#x1EBF	Circumflex Above Acute Accent e
Ề	#x1EC0	Circumflex Above Grave Accent E
ề	#x1EC1	Circumflex Above Grave Accent e
Ể	#x1EC2	Circumflex Hook Above E
ể	#x1EC3	Circumflex Hook Above e
Ễ	#x1EC4	Circumflex Tilde Above E
ễ	#x1EC5	Circumflex Tilde Above e
Ệ	#x1EC6	Circumflex Above Dot Below E
ệ	#x1EC7	Circumflex Above Dot Below e
Ỉ	#x1EC8	Hook Above I
ỉ	#x1EC9	Hook Above i
Ị	#x1ECA	Dot Below I
ị	#x1ECB	Dot Below i
Ọ	#x1ECC	Dot Below O
ọ	#x1ECD	Dot Below o
Ỏ	#x1ECE	Hook Above O
ỏ	#x1ECF	Hook Above o

Glyph	UTC Code	Description
Ố	#x1ED0	Circumflex Above Acute Accent O
ố	#x1ED1	Circumflex Above Acute Accent o
Ồ	#x1ED2	Circumflex Above Grave Accent O
ồ	#x1ED3	Circumflex Above Grave Accent o
Ổ	#x1ED4	Circumflex Hook Above O
ổ	#x1ED5	Circumflex Hook Above o
Ỗ	#x1ED6	Circumflex Tilde Above O
ỗ	#x1ED7	Circumflex Tilde Above o
Ộ	#x1ED8	Circumflex Above Dot Below O
ộ	#x1ED9	Circumflex Above Dot Below o
Ớ	#x1EDA	Horn Above Acute Accent O
ớ	#x1EDB	Horn Above Acute Accent o
Ờ	#x1EDC	Horn Above Grave Accent O
ờ	#x1EDD	Horn Above Grave Accent o
Ở	#x1EDE	Horn Hook Above O
ở	#x1EDF	Horn Hook Above o
Ỡ	#x1EE0	Horn Tilde Above O
ỡ	#x1EE1	Horn Tilde Above o
Ợ	#x1EE2	Horn Above Dot Below O
ợ	#x1EE3	Horn Above Dot Below O
Ụ	#x1EE4	Dot Below U
ụ	#x1EE5	Dot Below u
Ủ	#x1EE6	Hook Above U
ủ	#x1EE7	Hook Above u
Ứ	#x1EE8	Horn Above Acute Accent U
ứ	#x1EE9	Horn Above Acute Accent u
Ừ	#x1EEA	Horn Above Grave Accent U
ừ	#x1EEB	Horn Above Grave Accent u
Ử	#x1EEC	Horn Hook Above U

Continued

Table A-8 *Continued*

Glyph	UTC Code	Description
ủ	#x1EED	Horn Hook Above u
Ữ	#x1EEE	Horn Tilde Above U
ữ	#x1EEF	Horn Tilde Above u
Ự	#x1EF0	Horn Above Dot Below U
ự	#x1EF1	Horn Above Dot Below u
Ỳ	#x1EF2	Grave Accent Y
ỳ	#x1EF3	Grave Accent y
Ỵ	#x1EF4	Dot Below Y
ỵ	#x1EF5	Dot Below y
Ỷ	#x1EF6	Hook Above Y
ỷ	#x1EF7	Hook Above y
Ỹ	#x1EF8	Tilde Above Y
ỹ	#x1EF9	Tilde Above y

Letterlike Symbols

Table A-9 contains the XML-supported characters in the Letterlike Symbols set, in the BaseChar element.

Table A-9 *BaseChar Special Characters – Letter-like Symbols*

Glyph	UTC Code	Description
Ω	#x2126	Ohm Sign
K	#x212A	Kelvin Sign
Å	#x212B	Angstrom Sign
e	#x212E	Estimated Symbol

Number Forms

Table A-10 contains the XML-supported characters in the Number Forms set, in the BaseChar element.

Table A-10   *BaseChar Special Characters — Number Forms*

Glyph	UTC Code	Description
⅀	#x2180	Roman Numeral 1000
⅁	#x2181	Roman Numeral 5000
⅂	#x2182	Roman Numeral 10000

Other Character Sets

Table A-11 lists other BaseChar character sets and the XML-supported characters for each.

● **NOTE**

Because it is difficult to use American fonts to display non-English special characters, the following table does not contain illustrations of the glyphs. To view the characters in this table, go to the Unicode Consortium's Web site (http://www.unicode.org/).

Table A-11   *Other BaseChar Character Sets*

Character Set	Supported Characters
Arabic Presentation Forms	#xFB50 - #xFBB1, #xFBD3 - #xFD3D, #xFD50 - #xFD8F, #xFD92 - #xFDC7, #xFDF0 - #xFDFB, #xFE70 - #xFE72, #xFE74, #xFE76 - #xFEFC
Arabic	#x0621 - #x063A, #x0641 - #x064A, #x0671 - #x06B7, #x06BA - #x06BE, #x06C0 - #x06CE, #x06D0 - #x06D3, #x06D5, #x06E5, #x06E6
Armenian	#x0531 - #x0556, #x0559, #x0561 - #x0587

Continued

Table A-11 *Continued*

Character Set	Supported Characters
Bengali	#x0985 - #x098C, #x098F, #x0990, #x0993 - #x09A8, #x09AA - #x09B0, #x09B2, #x09B6 - #x09B9, #x09DC, #x09DD, #x09DF - #x09E1, #x09F0, #x09F1
Bopomofo	#x3105 - #x312C
Cyrillic	#x0401 - #x040C, #x040E - #x044F, #x0451 - #x045C, #x045E - #x0481, #x0490 - #x04C4, #x04C7 - #x04C8, #x04CB - #x04CC, #x04D0 - #x04EB, #x04EE - #x04F5, #x04F8, #x04F9
Devanagari	#x0905 - #x0939, #x093D, #x0958 - #x0961
Georgian	#x10A0 - #x10C5, #x10D0 - #x10F6
Greek Extensions	#x1F00 - #x1F15, #x1F18 - #x1F1D, #x1F20 - #x1F45, #x1F48 - #x1F4D, #x1F50 - #x1F57, #x1F59, #x1F5B, #x1F5D, #x1F5F - #x1F7D, #x1F80 - #x1FB4, #x1FB6 - #x1FBC, #x1FBE, #x1FC2 - #x1FC4, #x1FC6 - #x1FCC, #x1FD0 - #x1FD3, #x1FD6 - #x1FDB, #x1FE0 - #x1FEC, #x1FF2 - #x1FF4, #x1FF6 - #x1FFC
Gujarati	#x0A8F - #x0A91, #x0A93 - #x0AA8, #x0AAA - #x0AB0, #x0AB2, #x0AB3, #x0AB5 - #x0AB9, #x0ABD, #x0AE0
Gurmukhi	#x0A05 - #x0A0A, #x0A0F, #x0A10, #x0A13 - #x0A28, #x0A2A - #x0A30, #x0A32, #x0A33, #x0A35, #x0A36, #x0A38, #x0A39, #x0A59 - #x0A5C, #x0A5E, #x0A72 - #x0A74, #x0A85 - #x0A8B, #x0A8D
Hangul Jamo	#x1100 - #x1159, #x115F - #x11A2, #x11A8 - #x11F9
Hangul Jamo	#x3131 - #x318E
Hangul Syllables	#xAC00 - #xFB06
Hebrew	#x05D0 - #x05EA, #x05F0 - #x05F2
Hiragana	#x3041 - #x3094
Kannada	#x0C85 - #x0C8C, #x0C8E - #x0C90, #x0C92 - #x0CA8, #x0CAA - #x0CB3, #x0CB5 - #x0CB9, #x0CDE, #x0CE0, #x0CE1
Katakana	#x30A1 - #x30FA

Character Set	Supported Characters
Lao	#x0E81, #x0E82, #x0E84, #x0E87, #x0E88, #x0E8A, #x0E8D, #x0E94 - #x0E97, #x0E99 - #x0E9F, #x0EA1 - #x0EA3, #x0EA5, #x0EA7, #x0EAA, #x0EAB, #x0EAD, #x0EAE, #x0EB0, #x0EB2, #x0EB3, #x0EBD, #x0EC0 - #x0EC4, #x0EDC, #x0EDD
Malayalam	#x0D05 - #x0D0C, #x0D0E - #x0D10, #x0D12 - #x0D28, #x0D2A - #x0D39, #x0D60, #x0D61
Oriya	#x0B05 - #x0B0C, #x0B0F, #x0B10, #x0B13 - #x0B28, #x0B2A - #x0B30, #x0B32, #x0B33, #x0B36 - #x0B39, #x0B3D, #x0B5C, #x0B5D, #x0B5F - #x0B61
Tamil	#x0B85 - #x0B8A, #x0B8E - #x0B90, #x0B92 - #x0B95, #x0B99, #x0B9A, #x0B9C, #x0B9E, #x0B9F, #x0BA3, #x0BA4, #x0BA8 - #x0BAA, #x0BAE - #x0BB5, #x0BB7 - #x0BB9
Telugu	#x0C05 - #x0C0C, #x0C0E - #x0C10, #x0C12 - #x0C28, #x0C2A - #x0C33, #x0C35 - #x0C39, #x0C60, #x0C61
Thai	#x0E01 - #x0E2E, #x0E30, #x0E32, #x0E33, #x0E40 - #x0E45
Tibetan	#x0F40 - #x0F47, #x0F49 - #x0F69

CombiningChar Characters and Character Sets

This section covers the characters and character sets supported by the CombiningChar element.

Combining Diacritical Marks

Table A-12 contains the XML-supported characters in the Combining Diacritical Marks set, in the CombiningChar element.

Table A-12   *CombiningChar Special Characters — Combining Diacritical Marks*

Glyph	UTC Code	Description
à	#x0300	Grave Accent Above
á	#x0301	Acute Accent Above
â	#x0302	Circumflex Above
ã	#x0303	Tilde Above
ā	#x0304	Macron Above
ā	#x0305	Overline
ă	#x0306	Breve Above
ȧ	#x0307	Dot Above
ä	#x0308	Dieresis Above
ả	#x0309	Hook Above
å	#x030A	Ring Above
a̋	#x030B	Double Acute Accent
ǎ	#x030C	Caron Above
a̍	#x030D	Vertical Line Above
a̎	#x030E	Double Vertical Line Above
ȁ	#x030F	Double Grave Accent
a̐	#x0310	Candrabindu
ȃ	#x0311	Inverted Breve Above
a̒	#x0312	Turned Comma Above
a̓	#x0313	Comma Above
a̔	#x0314	Reversed Comma Above
a̕	#x0315	Comma Above Right
a̖	#x0316	Grave Accent Below
a̗	#x0317	Acute Accent Below
a̘	#x0318	Left Tack Below
a̙	#x0319	Right Tack Below
a̚	#x031A	Left Angle Above
a̛	#x031B	Horn

Glyph	UTC Code	Description
ą̹	#x031C	Left Half Ring Below
ą̞	#x031D	Up Tack Below
ą̟	#x031E	Down Tack Below
ą̟	#x031F	Plus Sign Below
ą̠	#x0320	Minus Sign Below
ą̡	#x0321	Palatalized Hook Below
ą̢	#x0322	Retroflex Hook Below
ą̣	#x0323	Dot Below
ą̤	#x0324	Dieresis Below
ą̥	#x0325	Ring Below
ą̦	#x0326	Comma Below
ą̧	#x0327	Cedilla
ą̨	#x0328	Ogonek
ą̩	#x0329	Vertical Line Below
ą̪	#x032A	Bridge Below
ą̫	#x032B	Inverted Double Arch Below
ą̬	#x032C	Caron Below
ą̭	#x032D	Circumflex Below
ą̮	#x032E	Breve Below
ą̯	#x032F	Inverted Breve Below
ą̰	#x0330	Tilde Below
ą̱	#x0331	Macron Below
ą̲	#x0332	Low Line
ą̳	#x0333	Double Low Line
a̴	#x0334	Tilde Overlay
a̵	#x0335	Short Stroke Overlay
a̶	#x0336	Long Stroke Overlay
a̷	#x0337	Short Solidus Overlay
a̸	#x0338	Long Solidus Overlay

Continued

Table A-12   *Continued*

Glyph	UTC Code	Description
ą	#x0339	Right Half Ring Below
ą	#x033A	Inverted Bridge Below
ą	#x033B	Square Below
ą	#x033C	Seagull Below
ẍ	#x033D	X Above
ấ	#x033E	Vertical Tilde
a̅	#x033F	Double Overline
à	#x0340	Grave Tone Mark
á	#x0341	Acute Tone Mark
ã	#x0342	Greek Perispomeni
a̓	#x0343	Greek Koronis
ä	#x0344	Greek Dialytika Tonos
ą	#x0345	Greek Ypogegrammeni
a͠	#x0360	Double Tilde
a͡	#x0361	Double Inverted Breve

Combining Diacritical Marks for Symbols

Table A-13 contains the XML-supported characters in the Combining Diacritical Marks for Symbols set, in the CombiningChar element.

Table A-13   *CombiningChar Special Characters — Combining Diacritical Marks for Symbols*

Glyph	UTC Code	Description
a̐	#x20D0	Left Harpoon Above
a̓	#x20D1	Right Harpoon Above
a̒	#x20D2	Long Vertical Line Overlay
a̓	#x20D3	Short Vertical Line Overlay

Glyph	UTC Code	Description
ẫ	#x20D4	Anticlockwise Arrow Above
ẫ	#x20D5	Clockwise Arrow Above
ẫ	#x20D6	Left Arrow Above
ẫ	#x20D7	Right Arrow Above
ẫ	#x20D8	Ring Overlay
ẫ	#x20D9	Clockwise Ring Overlay
ẫ	#x20DA	Anticlockwise Ring Overlay
ẫ	#x20DB	Three Dots Above
ẫ	#x20DC	Four Dots Above
ẫ	#x20E1	Left Right Arrow Above

CJK Symbols and Punctuation

Table A-14 contains the XML-supported characters in the CJK Symbols and Punctuation set, in the CombiningChar element.

●—NOTE

In this table, the lowercase *a* is in the background of each character to show the position of that character from the baseline.

Table A-14 *CombiningChar Special Characters — CJK Symbols and Punctuation*

Glyph	UTC Code	Description
ẚ	#x302A	Level Tone Mark
ẚ	#x302B	Rising Tone Mark
ẚ°	#x302C	Departing Tone Mark
ẚ	#x302D	Entering Tone Mark
·ẚ	#x302E	Hangul Single Dot Tone Mark
ːẚ	#x302F	Hangul Double Dot Tone Mark

Other Character Sets

Table A-15 lists other CombiningChar character sets and the XML-supported characters for each.

●—NOTE————————————————————————————

Because it is difficult to use American fonts to display non-English special characters, the following table does not contain illustrations of the glyphs. To view the characters in this table, go to the Unicode Consortium's Web site (http://www.unicode.org/).

Table A-15 *Other Combining Char Character Sets*

Character Set	Supported Characters
Cyrillic	#x0483 - #x0486
Hebrew	#x0591 - #x05A1, #x05A3 - #x05B9, #x05BB - #x05BD, #x05BF, #x05C1 - #x05C2, #x05C4
Arabic	#x064B - #x0652, #x0670, #x06D6 - #x06DC, #x06DD - #x06DF, #x06E0 - #x6E4, #x06E7 - #x06E8, #x06EA - #x06ED
Devanagari	#x0901 - #x0903, #x093C, #x093E - #x094C, #x094D, #x0951 - #x0954, #x0962 - #x963
Bengali	#x0981 - #x0983, #x09BC, #x09BE, #x09BF, #x09C0 - #x09C4, #x09C7 - #x09C8, #x09CB - #x09CD, #x09D7, #x09E2 - #x09E3
Gurmukhi	#x0A02, #x0A3C, #x0A3E, #x0A3F, #x0A40 - #x0A42, #x0A47 - #x0A48, #x0A4B - #x0A4D, #x0A70 - #x0A71
Gujarati	#x0A81 - #x0A83, #x0ABC, #x0ABE - #x0AC5, #x0AC7 - #x0AC9, #x0ACB - #x0ACD
Oriya	#x0B01 - #x0B03, #x0B3C, #x0B3E - #x0B43, #x0B47 - #x0B48, #x0B4B - #x0B4D, #x0B56 - #x0B57
Tamil	#x0B82 - #x0B83, #x0BBE - #x0BC2, #x0BC6 - #x0BC8, #x0BCA - #x0BCD, #x0BD7
Telugu	#x0C01 - #x0C03, #x0C3E - #x0C44, #x0C46 - #x0C48, #x0C4A - #x0C4D, #x0C55 - #x0C56
Kannada	#x0C82 - #x0C83, #x0CBE - #x0CC4, #x0CC6 - #x0CC8, #x0CCA - #x0CCD, #x0CD5 - #x0CD6
Malayalam	#x0D02 - #x0D03, #x0D3E - #x0D43, #x0D46 - #x0D48, #x0D4A - #x0D4D, #x0D57

Character Set	Supported Characters
Thai	#x0E34 - #x0E3A, #x0E47 - #x0E4E
Lao	#x0EB1, #x0EB4 - #x0EB9, #x0EBB - #x0EBC, #x0EC8 - #x0ECD
Tibetan	#x0F18 - #x0F19, #x0F35, #x0F37, #x0F39, #x0F3E, #x0F3F, #x0F71 - #x0F84, #x0F86 - #x0F8B, #x0F90 - #x0F95, #x0F97, #x0F99 - #x0FAD, #x0FB1 - #x0FB7, #x0FB9
Hiragama	#x3099, #x309A

Digit

This section covers the characters and character sets supported by the Digit element.

ISO 646 Digits

Table A-16 contains the XML-supported characters in the ISO 646 Digits set, in the Digit element.

Table A-16   *Digit Special Characters — ISO 646 Digits*

Glyph	UTC Code	Description
0	#x0030	Digit Zero
l	#x0031	Digit One
2	#x0032	Digit Two
3	#x0033	Digit Three
4	#x0034	Digit Four
5	#x0035	Digit Five
6	#x0036	Digit Six
7	#x0037	Digit Seven
8	#x0038	Digit Eight
9	#x0039	Digit Nine

Other Character Sets

Table A-17 lists other Digit character sets and the XML-supported characters for each.

●—NOTE

Because it is difficult to use American fonts to display non-English special characters, the following table does not contain illustrations of the glyphs. To view the characters in this table, go to the Unicode Consortium's Web site (http://www.unicode.org/).

Table A-17 *Other Digit Character Sets*

Character Set	Supported Characters
Arabic-Indic Digits	#x0660 - #x0669
Eastern Arabic-Indic Digits	#x06F0 - #x06F9
Devanagari Digits	#x0966 - #x096F
Bengali Digits	#x09E6 - #x09EF
Gurmukhi Digits	#x0A66 - #x0A6F
Gujarati Digits	#x0AE6 - #x0AEF
Oriya Digits	#x0B66 - #x0B6F
Tamil Digits (no zero)	#x0BE7 - #x0BEF
Telugu Digits	#x0C66 - #x0C6F
Kannada Digits	#x0CE6 - #x0CEF
Malayalam Digits	#x0D66 - #x0D6F
Thai Digits	#x0E50 - #x0E59
Lao Digits	#x0ED0 - #x0ED9
Tibetan Digits	#x0F20 - #x0F29

Extender

This section covers the characters and character sets supported by the `Extender` element.

Extender Special Characters

Table A-18 contains the XML-supported characters for the `Extender` element. The character sets in which the characters are located are within parentheses.

Table A-18 *Extender Special Characters*

Glyph	UTC Code	Description
.	#x00B7	Middle Dot (C1 Controls and Latin-1 Supplement)
:	#x02D0	Triangular Colon (Spacing Modifier Letters)
.	#x02D1	Half Triangular Colon (Spacing Modifier Letters)
々	#x3005	Ideographic Iteration Mark (CJK Symbols and Punctuation)
〱	#x3031	Vertical Kana Repeat Mark (CJK Symbols and Punctuation)
〲	#x3032	Vertical Kana Repeat with Voiced Sound Mark (CJK Symbols and Punctuation)
/	#x3033	Vertical Kana Repeat Mark Upper Half (CJK Symbols and Punctuation)
/〟	#x3034	Vertical Kana Repeat with Voiced Sound Mark Upper Half (CJK Symbols and Punctuation)
\	#x3035	Vertical Kana Repeat Mark Lower Half (CJK Symbols and Punctuation)

Other Character Sets

Table A-19 lists other Extender character sets and the XML-supported characters for each.

Table A-19 *Other Extender Character Sets*

Character Set	Supported Characters
Greek	#x0387
Arabic	#x0640
Thai	#x0E46
Lao	#x0EC6
Hiragana	#x309D - #x309E
Katakana	#x30FC - #x30FE

Ideographic

This section covers the characters and character sets supported by the Ideographic element.

CJK Symbols and Punctuation

Table A-20 contains the XML-supported characters for the Ideographic element.

Table A-20 *Ideographic Special Characters — CJK Symbols and Punctuation*

Glyph	UTC Code	Description
○	#x3007	Number Zero
〡	#x3021	Hangzhou Numeral One
〢	#x3022	Hangzhou Numeral Two
〣	#x3023	Hangzhou Numeral Three
✕	#x3024	Hangzhou Numeral Four
〥	#x3025	Hangzhou Numeral Five
〦	#x3026	Hangzhou Numeral Six

Glyph	UTC Code	Description
仒	#x3027	Hangzhou Numeral Seven
仚	#x3028	Hangzhou Numeral Eight
夊	#x3029	Hangzhou Numeral Nine

Additional Character Set

Table A-21 lists the additional Ideographic character set and its XML-supported characters.

● NOTE

Because it is difficult to use American fonts to display non-English special characters, the following table does not contain illustrations of the glyphs. To view the characters in this table, go to the Unicode Consortium's Web site (http://www.unicode.org/).

Table A-21 *Additional Ideographic Character Set*

Character Set	Supported Characters
CJK Unified Ideographs	#x4E00 - #x9FA5

XML Editors
and Utilities

The Internet contains an evergrowing number of
resources, including downloadable freeware, shareware, and trial versions of XML editors and utilities as well
as fact sheets about the programs:

- **Commercial programs:** These full-featured programs are the most expensive; however, the company
  developing the programs can often afford to add
  more "bells and whistles" and user friendliness. You
  can often download a trial or demonstration version
  so you can try before you buy.

- **Trial versions:** Many commercial software publishers provide these incomplete or limited programs,
  also known as *demonstration programs* (or demos),
  before buying. A trial version may be an older version of the program, may expire on a particular date,
  or may not include all the features of the commercial
  software.

- **Shareware programs:** These programs usually contain every feature and function: you are expected to

483

buy a license after you try the program for a set number of days. In return, the author may send you program disks, a license, manuals, and notices of problems, fixes, and new releases.

- **Freeware programs:** As you might imagine, these programs are available at no cost from an altruistic developer or as a first-rate marketing effort. Freeware programs, which can be "lite" versions of commercial or shareware programs, can be just as good as their commercial or shareware counterparts.

This appendix provides information about XML editors and utilities with which you can develop or parse XML documents or create DTDs. As you might imagine, the list grows as more developers jump on the XML bandwagon. The first section of the appendix lists directories from sites that track XML programs. The remaining pages list individual programs. Under each entry is a brief description along with a URL for the developer's or program's home page.

Directories of XML Software

This section provides directories that list XML software resources. Some sites also list SGML software. Note that many SGML developers are adding XML support to their programs.

The Whirlwind Guide to SGML & XML Tools and Vendors (http://www.infotek.no/sgmltool/guide.htm) is the home page of several pages of SGML and XML tools, including the following:

- **SGML & XML Tools — Parsers and Engines** (http://www.infotek.no/sgmltool/sdk.htm) provides lists of software development kits for creating and parsing SGML and XML documents. Each entry states whether the program is commercial or freeware and names the platform under which it runs.

- **SGML & XML Tools — By Tool Category** (http://www.infotek.no/sgmltool/products.htm) categorizes SGML and XML tools. Click on a link to jump to one of the following categories: Editing and Composition, Electronic Delivery, Conversion, Document Storage and Management,

Control Information Development, Parsers and Engines (see the previous entry), and Resources.

- **James Tauber's XML INFORMATION:Software** (http://www.xmlinfo.com/) lists software and associated links under the following categories: XML Processors, APIs, XML Software, and XML Support in Other Software. Also look for the XML Processors/Parsers Comparison Matrix on a separate page at this site. This excellent site is undergoing reorganization currently.

- **XML Tools** (http://www.microsoft.com/xml/xmltools. asp) lists primarily commercial programs. With each entry is a short product description.

- **Software** (http://www.megginson.com/Software/ software.html) is a short page of assorted programs, patches, utilities, and classes.

- **Parser Central** (http://www.finetuning.com/parse.html) is an extensive list of XML programs of all types: parsers, software development kits, projects, scripting engines, development tools, and browsers. Each entry contains a long description.

- **Public SGML/XML Software** (http://www.sil.org/ sgml/publicSW.html) is one of Robin Cover's well-known and comprehensive pages. The emphasis is on freeware and on SGML. However, remember that many SGML tools now support XML. Each entry at this site is thoroughly described.

Web Site Technology

This section lists XML-related Web-site applications.

Balise Software Development Kit (http://www.balise. com/hpbody.htm) is a commercial Web development application compatible with C and C++.

Interaction (http://interaction.in-progress.com/), which enables conferencing, displays real-time information about the current status of a Web site. This shareware program runs on the Macintosh platform.

Web Automation Toolkit (http://www.webmethods.com/ products/automation_toolkit.html) converts business systems to the Web, using XML as the data exchange. The Web Automation

Toolkit includes an HTML/XML parser. Once you have developed a Web application, post it to the Web Automation Server (http://www.webmethods.com/products/server/).

XML Browsers

This section lists browsers that currently support XML or will do so in the near future.

JUMBO (Java Universal Molecular or Markup Browser for Objects) (http://www.vsms.nottingham.ac.uk/vsms/java/jumbo), written in Java, is currently a freeware XML browser. You can use it as a standalone program or as a set of applets running under Netscape Navigator or Internet Explorer. You can use JUMBO as an XML parser. JUMBO supports XSL style sheets.

Microsoft Internet Explorer (http://www.microsoft.com/ie/) will support XML in version 5.0.

Netscape Navigator (http://home.Netscape.com/) will support XML in a future release.

XML Development Tools

With the tools listed in this section, you can develop or support XML applications.

DataChannel XML Development Kit (http://www.datachannel.com/products/xdk/xml_dk.html) is part of DataChannel RIO (in the "XML Suites" section). Included in the XML Development Kit are the DXP parser, the DataChannel XML Generator, and the DataChannel DOM Builder.

Dual Prism (http://www.balise.com/products/dualp/dualp.htm) is a suite of document-management system and development applications. Use Dual Prism to generate HTML and/or XML from XML or SGML documents.

Java™ Development Kit (http://www.javasoft.com:/products/jdk/1.1/) is a suite of products with which you can compile, debug, and run Java applets and applications. Some XML programs require that you install the Java™ Development Kit.

●—NOTE—————————————————————————

Java supports Unicode as does XML. A variety of Java parsers are freely available for use in further XML development.

Proto (http://www.pierlou.com/prototype/body.htm) reads a valid XML document and shows how it will look onscreen. Proto is a Java-based application that you can program using ECMAScript or Tcl.

Python (http://www.python.org/) is a scripting language used in XML development (for example, for XED, PyPointers, xmlproc, and the XML Toolkit — all of which are mentioned in this appendix).

SAX 1.0 (A Simple API for XML) (http://www.megginson. com/SAX/index.html or http://www.microstar.com/XML/Sax/ sax.html) is a freeware Java-based API used for writing applications that use XML parsers but do not have to rely on a particular parser.

SAX for Python (http://www.stud.ifi.uio.no/~larsga/ download/python/xml/index) is a Python version of SAX.

XML Toolkit (http://csmctmto.interpoint.net/didx/ xml.html) is a Python-based program that develops XML-based applications. The toolkit includes a client-server XML non-validating processor and an implementation of Web Interface Definition Language (WIDL). The developer states that the XML Toolkit will always be under development.

XPublish (http://interaction.in-progress.com/) is an XML publishing system for Macintosh systems.

XML DOM Toolkits and Applications

This section lists applications that use the World Wide Web Consortium's DOM (Document Object Model) interface.

●—NOTE————————————————

As of this writing, DOM is under development. To keep track of DOM, periodically go to http://www.w3.org/DOM/.

DataChannel DOM Builder (http://www.datachannel. com/products/xdk/DXP/dom_builder.html) is a commercial product that creates XML using DOM. A copy of the Java Virtual Machine Version 1.1 is required.

FREE-DOM (http://www.docuverse.com/personal/ freedom/index.html) is a Java library that transforms DOM objects into XML. FREE-DOM uses Simple API for XML (SAX) and an XML parser that supports SAX 1.0. You must download both before using FREE-DOM.

PyPointers (`http://www.stud.ifi.uio.no/~larsga/ download/python/xml/index`) is a Python-based XPointer implementation that finds particular XPointers in XML and HTML documents using a DOM locator. The program also includes a general parser.

XML DTD Authoring

The applications listed here enable you to write DTDs.

Document·Architect (`http://www.arbortext.com/docarch. html`) is a commercial SGML DTD and style sheet editor that works with ADEPT·Editor.

Near and Far Designer (`http://www.microstar.com/ Products-And-Technologies/products-and-technologies.html`) is a visual DTD tool for novices and others. Using Near and Far Designer, one can create a DTD or import and edit a DTD.

Visual XML (`http://www.pierlou.com/visxml/body.htm`) is Java-based DTD and XML editor. The author also developed Proto (see a previous entry).

XML Editors

In this section, XML editors are listed.

ADEPT·Editor (`http://www.arbortext.com/editor.html`) is a commercial, word processor-type XML and SGML editor with built-in authoring aids for the creation of long documents.

ADEPT·Publisher (`http://www.arbortext.com/ publisher.html`) is a commercial UNIX-based XML and SGML editor with built-in authoring aids as well as a composition engine for printing PostScript documents.

Astoria (`http://www.chrystal.com/products/astoria.htm`) is a commercial package that manages the content of structured documents — especially technical ones for individuals or workgroups — from creation to storage. Astoria supports both SGML and XML.

Balise (`http://www.balise.com/hpbody.htm`) is a commercial application that manages and transforms structured documents. An SGML application, Balise supports XML and Rich Text Format

(RTF) documents. Balise includes a non-validating XML parser with full Unicode support.

DynaText® Professional Publishing System (http://www.inso.com/dynatext/dtxtds.htm) is a commercial program that produces long documents that can be published on CD-ROM, over a LAN, on the Web, or on an intranet. Components include DynaText CD/LAN Browser, DynaWeb® Web Publisher, the DynaText Software Development Kit, and publishing and authoring tools.

Visual XML (See the prior section.)

XED (http://www.cogsci.ed.ac.uk/~ht/xed.html) edits small- to medium-size XML document instances, checking your document structure as you work. XED uses the LT XML toolkit, Python, and Tk.

XML Pro (http://www.vervet.com/release-pr.html) is an editor that you can use to create valid or well-formed XML documents. XML Pro includes wizards that can guide you through document creation.

XML Parsers and Processors

With the tools in this section, you can parse and process XML documents.

Ælfred (http://www.microstar.com/XML/Aelfred/aelfred.html) is validating freeware parser for Java programmers who want to add XML support to their applets. A SAX driver is bundled with Ælfred.

DataChannel XML Parser (DXP) (http://www.datachannel.com/products/xml/DXP/) is a commercial, validating, Java-based XML parser for existing server-side programs that now integrate XML. DXP is the descendant of NXP (see next entry).

expat (EXtensible markup language PArser Toolkit) (http://www.jclark.com/xml/expat.html) is a non-validating C-based XML browser, which will be the core of the Netscape Mozilla XML effort.

Lark (http://www.textuality.com/Lark/) is a non-validating XML parser. Written in Java, Lark is freeware that recognizes the DTD.

Larval (http://www.textuality.com/Lark/) is a validating XML parser that has the rest of the characteristics and features of Lark.

Microsoft XML Parser in Java (http://www.microsoft. com/xml/parser/jparser.asp) is a validating Java-based parser, which checks for well-formed documents and optionally checks for validity.

NXP (http://www.edu.uni-klu.ac.at/~nmikula/NXP/) is a validating Java-based parser in the public domain.

PaxSyntactica (http://208.204.84.117/XMLTree-Viewer/) is an Xapi-J compliant XML parser.

SAXON (http://home.iclweb.com/icl2/mhkay/saxon.html) is a Java class library used for processing XML documents to produce XML or HTML transformations.

SP (http://www.jclark.com/sp/), which is primarily an SGML parser, can parse well-formed XML documents. SP is C++-based freeware.

Tcl (Tool Command Language) Toolkit (http://tcltk. anu.edu.au/XML/) is a toolkit for parsing XML documents and DTDs. Tcl Toolkit requires Tcl 8.0b1 (or greater).

XAF (http://www.megginson.com/XAF/home.html) processes XML documents with an Java-based SAX-conformant XML parser. XAF processes architectural forms rather than XML. XAF uses SAX input to read a document from another parser and uses SAX output to pass the processed version to the application.

XML for Java (http://www.alphaworks.IBM.com/formula/ xml/) is a validating XML parser written in Java. According to its home page, this parser "contains classes and methods for parsing, generating, manipulating, and validating XML documents."

xmlproc (http://www.stud.ifi.uio.no/~larsga/download/ python/xml/index) is a Python-based validating XML parser. At the time of this writing, this program is under development.

XP (http://www.jclark.com/xml/xp/index.html) is a Java-based parser that tests for well-formed documents. XP, which works under the JDK 1.1 (or greater) version, supports UTF-8, UTF-16, and ISO-8859-1.

XParse (http://www.jeremie.com/Dev/XML/) is a JavaScript-based XML parser that tests for well-formedness.

XML Scripting Engine

This section lists a Java-based scripting engine.

FESI (free ECMAScript Interpreter) (http://home. worldcom.ch/~jmlugrin/fesi/index.html) is equivalent to

JavaScript. You can use ECMAScript as a macro language and as an interactive interpreter used to debug programs. Because FESI is integrated with Java, you can use it to test Java libraries.

XML Suites

The suites of applications and utilities listed in this section enable you to perform a variety of XML-related functions.

DataChannel RIO (http://www.datachannel.com/rio/display_entry.html) is a commercial intranet publisher that organizes and distributes corporate information. DataChannel RIO requires a relational database management server.

DynaBase (http://www.inso.com/dynabase/index.htm) is a commercial content management and dynamic Web publishing system. DynaBase includes DynaBase Web Manager, DynaBase Web Author, DynaBase Data Server, DynaBase Web Developer, DynaBase Web Server plug-in, and the DynaBase Web Tool.

Frontier (http://www.scripting.com/frontier5/default.html) is a commercial content management package for the Windows and Macintosh platforms. The package includes an XML parser, XML database, XML remote procedure calls, and a scripting language.

LT XML (http://www.ltg.ed.ac.uk/software/xml/) is comprised of XML tools and a toolkit, all for developers. Use LT XML to process well-formed XML documents. The suite includes an XML parser, a query language, and a C-based API.

ObjectStore PSE PRO (http://www.odi.com/content/products/pse/ppjds.html) is a database management system (DBMS) designed to run under Java and compatible with JDK 1.1 (or greater). ObjectStore PSE Pro includes a query interface, indexing, persistent garbage collection, and an enhanced transaction model.

OmniMark® Konstructor (http://www.omnimark.com/summary/konst-info.html) is a content management and delivery suite, which includes Konstructor Load Manager, Konstructor Developer Tools, Konstructor Connectivity, and OmniMark Programming Language. For more information about the OmniMark Programming Language, which can run as a standalone application, go to http://www.omnimark.com/summary/omni-info.html. Note that you can download OmniMark LE to evaluate OmniMark programs.

POET Content Management Suite (http://www.poet. com/wildflower.htm) is made up of the POET Object Server, an SGML parser, an interpreter tool, a navigator, and an object-oriented C++-based programmer's API. For an overview of XML and content management, refer to http://www.poet.com/ CMSoverview/.

Tango Enterprise (http://www.everyware.com/products/ Tango/WhatIsTango.html) is a visual programming tool that enables you or your workgroup to create layered, dynamic Web applications. Tango Enterprise includes the Tango Development Studio and the Tango Application Server.

Style Sheet Applications

This section lists style sheet editors and processors.

● **NOTE**

Be aware that the XSL standard is not complete.

Cascade (http://interaction.in-progress.com/cascade/ index?id=3PLNQ) is a commercial cascading-style-sheet editor for Macintosh computers. You can download a free copy of Cascade Light or buy the professional shareware version.

Jade (http://www.jclark.com/jade/) is a style engine that implements DSSSL. Jade uses SP (see the "XML Parsers" section) to parse the style sheet. Jade can produce the following output: RTF, TeX, and two forms of SGML.

Sparse (http://www.jeremie.com/Dev/XSL/index.phtml) is an XSL style sheet processor, which requires a JavaScript-compatible browser.

Spice (http://www.w3.org/TR/1998/NOTE-spice-19980123. html) styles XML documents using ECMAScript using CSS rules and scripted flow objects. Note that Spice is a work in progress and is not a W3C standard.

XML Styler (http://www.arbortext.com/xmlstyler/) is an XSL style sheet processor.

xslj (http://www.cogsci.ed.ac.uk/~ht/xslj.html) converts XSL styles to DSSSL.

Glossary

absolute link
A link to another document using the complete URL or address, including the transfer protocol, the computer or network name, the directory or folder, and a filename (for example, `http://www.widget.com/index.html`). *See* relative link.

address
An electronic location to which e-mail is sent; an electronic location on the Internet or on a network.

agent
Robot. A search index that finds information from all or part of the Internet or a network, sometimes at a regular time or date or when page content changes. Another definition of agent is anything (such as a browser) that processes user request. *See* search index and search tool.

American National Standards Institute
See ANSI.

American Standard Code for Information Interchange
See ASCII.

ancestor
A higher-level element, such as a parent, in a family tree of elements. *See* child and parent.

anchor
The starting link that refers to another location within the current document or within another document; the ending link to which a starting link refers; the target and/or source of a link.

Anonymous FTP
See FTP.

ANSI
American National Standards Institute. A United States affiliate of the International Standardization Organization (ISO), an organization that formulates many international standards for characters, numbers, and symbols; computing; telecommunicating; and so on. *See* ISO.

archive
A collection of information, usually from the past but sometimes from the present.

ASCII
American Standard Code for Information Interchange. A coding standard for characters, numbers, and symbols that is the same as the first 128 characters of the ASCII character set but differs from the remaining characters. *See also* ASCII file.

ASCII file
A text file or a text-only file. A file format that can be read by almost any word processor or text editor, allowing for transfer and viewing between individuals with dissimilar computers, operating systems, and programs. ASCII files contain characters, spaces, punctuation, end-of-line marks, and some formats. *See also* ASCII.

association
A query expression, a transform expression, and, optionally, a priority expression. To match a specific application with a specific filename extension. *See* expression, priority expression, query expression, and transform expression.

atomic
In DSSSL style sheets, a flow object that does not have any ports. Other flow objects cannot be nested within this flow object, and no list of flow objects can be attached. *See* flow object, principal port, and port.

attachment
In DSSSL style sheets, a defined and separate inline area attached to an object (such as a table cell or margin) usually within but occasionally outside the flow-object area.

ATTLIST
In a document type definition (DTD), a list of attributes (that is, options or characteristics) defined for an element. An ATTLIST can also contain default values for attributes. *See* DTD and element.

attribute
A term for an option, which is a setting that affects the behavior of and further defines an element. Attributes can change or specify formats, alignments, text enhancements, paragraphs, or other parts of an SGML, HTML, or XML document. In an SGML or XML document type definition (DTD), the value of an attribute is either #REQUIRED (that is, it must be entered) or #IMPLIED (that is, it does not have to be entered). *See* attribute value and attributeName.

attribute value
The value of a particular attribute. Attribute values should be enclosed within single or double quotes. If an attributeName and attribute value are missing for an element, a default value is assigned to the attribute. *See* attributeName and attributes.

attributeName
The name of a particular attribute. For each attributeName, there is a value. *See* attribute value and attributes.

AU
A UNIX-based sound file format.

AVI
Audio Video Interleave; a popular Windows-based video file format.

bandwidth
A measurement of the amount of data that can flow from one part of an internet or network to another. Typically, bandwidth is measured in cycles per second (hertz) or bits per second (bps). The higher the bandwidth, the faster the data transfer speed.

base
See absolute link.

bidi
Bidirectional; enabling printing of lines of text from a particular side of the page to the other, usually from left to right or right to left.

binary data
Nontext data. An XML processor does not parse binary data. *See* text. *See also* parse.

bit
Binary digit. The smallest unit of computer information, represented by a 1 (which represents yes or on) or 0 (representing no or off).

bit map
A graphic image made up of pixels (also known as pels in some circles). Bit map file formats include BMP, GIF, and JPEG.

bookmarks
Hot lists. URLs of sites you regularly visit and that you have had your browser save. When you want to visit a "bookmarked" site, just select it from your browser's bookmark list.

browser
A program (such as Netscape Navigator, Microsoft Internet Explorer, or Mosaic) with which you can "surf" the World Wide Web as well as Gopher and FTP sites. Some browsers also provide e-mail and Telnet utilities. Other browsers are part of suites of Internet access programs.

cascading style sheets
Sets of style sheets that enable Web developers to change documents' format and appearance. *See* CSS1 and CSS2. *See also* DSSSL and XSL.

CDATA
Character data; a string of characters, which is enclosed within delimiters. When parsed, CDATA is not interpreted; it is inserted as text. *See* delimiter and #PCDATA.

CDF
See Channel Definition Format.

CGI
Common Gateway Interface. A protocol that enables developers to write programs that create Web document code in response to user requests; frequently used to connect databases to the World Wide Web.

channel
A set of related pages or documents. A channel resembles a television channel. *See also* Channel Definition Format and server push.

Channel Definition Format
CDF. A Microsoft-defined formal format that enables authors to create XML-based content to be downloaded automatically, using push technology, to client computers. *See also* channel and server push.

character
A single unit of information; a letter, digit, or symbol. *See* character class, character data, and legal characters.

character class
Character set; a grouping of related letters, digits, and symbols.

character data
Any characters that are not markup. *See* CDATA, markup, and text.

child
An element or other object that is nested under a parent element or object; a subelement of an element. *See* ancestor, nested, and parent.

client
A program (such as a browser) that is programmed to communicate with, and ask for information from, a server program (such as a World Wide Web or Gopher server) usually on a remote computer. *See* browser and server.

client pull
The automatic loading or reloading of a document at a specific time or time interval by a browser. You can write a CGI program to incorporate client pull features. In HTML, you can also use the META element to perform client pull. *See also* server push.

combining character
A character, such as an accent or circumflex, that is added above or below a letter of an alphabet.

Common Gateway Interface
See CGI.

connector
An operator, such as a vertical bar (|), OR, comma (,), or AND, which shows the relationship between two parts of an expression or program statement.

constraint
Limitations that are specified in a computer program.

construction rules
A set of standards that specify how a styling application makes and formats an element.

containing resource
A document in which an external link is located. *See* designated resource.

content
The information between the start tag and end tag in a Web document, or all the information in a document.

content model

In a document type definition (DTD), the description of an element's content, including subelements, connectors, and character data.

content particle

One unit of the content of an element type. *See* content and content model.

CSS1

The first standard for cascading style sheets; a simple set of rules to format and enhance text, paragraphs, and documents. *See* cascading style sheets and CSS2.

CSS2

The second standard for cascading style sheets, which adds to the CSS1 base a set of styles for visual browsers, aural devices, printers, braille devices, and so on, as well as styles for table layout, internationalization features, and more. *See* cascading style sheets and CSS1.

data characters

Nonmarkup characters that comprise element content.

declaration

A statement that defines the elements and attributes in a document without telling the computer how to use them. In a cascading style sheet, a declaration specifies a property (such as text emphasis) and its value (italic). A declaration defines markup, constraints, and attributes. *See* attributes, constraints, document type declaration, markup, and selector.

declarative syntax

A formalized set of declarations. *See* declaration.

delimiter

A character that indicates the start and end of a string or other piece of information. For XML, the usual delimiters are quotation marks (") and single quotes ('). *See* string.

descendant

All the elements or other objects that are nested under a parent element or object; subelements of the element. *See* ancestor, child, nested, and parent.

descriptive markup

Semantic markup; the act of creating and using markup terms that both describe and mark up at the same time. Descriptive markup is an XML feature that differentiates XML from HTML.

designated resource

A document in which an external link is defined. *See* containing resource.

document entity
The entire XML document as it will be read by a non-validating XML processor. This is in contrast to a document module, which is a part of the document as it is distributed over a network.

document instance
The entire SGML or XML document.

Document Object Model
See DOM.

document prolog
The part of an SGML, XML, or related document that includes the introduction to the document, possibly including the document type definition (DTD). The prolog in an HTML document is enclosed within the <HEAD> and </HEAD> tags.

Document Style Semantics and Specification Language
See DSSSL.

document type declaration
A declaration within an XML document that points to an external or internal document type definition (DTD). A document type declaration is *never* known as a DTD.

Document Type Definition
See DTD.

DOM
Document Object Model. An interface, also known as dynamic HTML, that enables various style sheets, programs, and scripts to access and change Web documents created with XML or HTML. *See* dynamic HTML.

domain
The two- or three-character codes for organizations (COM, EDU, INT, NET, GOV, MIL, NET) and for regions or countries (for example, the United States is US) in which the organization is located. Currently, new domains are under consideration.

domain name
The name for a site (for example, psu, which represents Pennsylvania State University, or lotus, which represents Lotus Development Corporation) and its domain. A typical domain name is psu.edu or lotus.com.

Domain Name System
DNS. The system by which Internet sites are named; for example, www.lotus.com or eddygrp@sover.net.

download
The transfer of a file from a remote computer to your computer. The standard protocol for downloading files from the Internet is anonymous FTP (file transfer protocol). *See* FTP and upload.

DSSSL
Document Style Semantics and Specification Language; ISO 10179: 1996. An international style-sheet standard. *See also* cascading style sheets and XSL.

DTD
Document Type Definition. A document, written with a special syntax for declarations, that specifies the elements, attributes, entities (special or legal characters), and rules for creating one document or a set of documents using XML, HTML, or another SGML-related markup language. In an XML document, a DTD is required to parse a document and test for validity. An XML document can access an internal DTD, which is stored at the beginning of the document, or an external DTD, which is a separate document. Within an XML document, the pointer to the DTD is known as a document type declaration. A document type declaration is *never* known as a DTD. *See also* document type declaration, external DTD subset, and internal DTD subset.

dynamic HTML
A combination of programming and HTML that allows the appearance and content of an HTML document to change whenever a user interacts with it. Interactions that trigger changes include moving the mouse, clicking, double-clicking, and pressing keys.

ECMAScript
A JavaScript standard. An object-oriented language with which developers enhance the content of Web documents (for example, to enable a user to change the look of a document). JavaScript has been standardized as ECMA-262 by the European Computer Manufacturers Association.

electronic mail
See e-mail.

element
A label with which you define part of an XML document. An element usually starts with a start tag, `<tagname>`, includes an element name, may contain subelements and contents with which you vary the results of the element, and may end with an end tag, `</tagname>`. An XML element may include certain data types or be empty. *See* end tag, start tag, and subelement.

element declaration
In the document type definition (DTD), a statement that defines a particular element, attributes, and other characteristics. *See* declaration and element.

element tree
The element-and-attribute skeleton of an XML document. An element tree reduces the document to its underlying structure of elements and attributes so that you can visually check the document's logic and flow. *See* grove.

e-mail
Electronic mail. Messages (which may have files attached) sent from an individual to one or more individuals on a network or remote computer.

e-mail address
The electronic mailing address of an individual, group, or organization. For example, my e-mail address is `eddygrp@sover.net` (where `eddygrp` is the user ID, the `@` (at) sign is a separator symbol, and `sover.net` is the name of the computer to which my e-mail address is identified). My e-mail address is pronounced "Eddy Group at sover dot net."

empty element
An element that has no content between the start tag and the end tag but refers to an object such as an image or a line break. *See* element, end tag, and start tag.

encoding
The act of converting a letter, digit, character, or a set of characters to another character or set of characters. In programming, encoding refers to converting from one format to another (for example, decimal to hexadecimal or binary to decimal). In XML, encoding refers to converting letters, digits, or characters to the supported UTF-8 or UTF-16 format. *See* UTF-8 and UTF-16.

end tag
The part of an XML statement that indicates the end of an element and its contents. The format of an end tag is `</elementname>`, in contrast to the start tag format, `<elementname>`. An end tag does not include attributes. *See* element and start tag.

entity
A special character; a single unit, or item. Entity is an all-purpose term that can also refer to a specific text or graphic file. There are several categories of entities in XML: general and parameter, parsed and unparsed, and external and internal. *See* general entity, parameter entity, parsed entity, and unparsed entity.

entity set
A character set; a set of related or standard characters.

enumerate
List the possible valid values for a data type.

escapement direction
In DSSSL style sheets, a direction in which a flow object is displayed or inlined. The escapement direction is perpendicular to both the line-progression direction and the placement direction; it is sometimes the reverse of the writing mode. *See* escapement point, flow object, line-progression direction, placement direction, and writing-mode direction.

escapement point
In DSSSL style sheets, the escapement point is located at the point at which the current character ends and the following character begins in an inline area, and the display or inline starts there toward the next or prior character, depending on the value of the `writing-mode` characteristic. This is in contrast to the position point. *See* position point.

ESIS
Element Structure Information Set. A parsed and normalized list of all the elements, attributes, and entities in a language, whether or not they appear in the document being parsed. ISO/IEC 13673: 1995 is the standard that describes ESIS. *See* attribute, element, entity, normalization, parse, and parser.

expression
An equation made up of elements, subelements, attributes, operators, subexpressions, and connectors.

extended link
A link to one or more locations within the current document and/or to one or more locations in other documents. To specify an extended link, use the `xml:link` attribute with the `extended` or the `locator` value. *See* extended link group and simple link.

extended link group
An extended link that stores a list of links to other documents. An extended link group is also known as an interlinked group. To specify an extended link group, use the `xml:link` attribute with the `group` value. *See* extended link and simple link.

extensible
The ability of a user to add his or her own labels to the command set of a language, such as XML.

external DTD subset
The part of a DTD that is stored in a separate document completely outside the XML document in which it is referenced. An external DTD subset can be referred to by more than one XML document. *See* DTD, external entity, internal entity, and internal DTD subset.

external entity
An entity with its content stored in a separate file completely outside the XML document. *See* DTD and internal entity.

FAQ
Frequently Asked Questions. Documents that list commonly asked questions and their answers about almost any topic, including computing and the Internet. FAQs are designed to save those in the know the bother of responding to questions asked and answered many times before. First-time visitors to a newsgroup or a support site should always read the FAQ (if one is provided) before asking questions.

File Transfer Protocol
See FTP.

filling direction
In DSSSL style sheets, the direction in which the flow-object area is filled with flow object content. The filling direction can be perpendicular to the placement direction. *See* placement direction. *See also* escapement direction, flow object, line-progression direction, and writing-mode direction.

firewall
A combination of a security program and hardware that creates a virtual wall between unwanted visitors and specified parts of a network.

fixed-width typeface
See monospaced typeface.

flow object
In DSSSL style sheets, a styled object that fills a defined area. Flow objects include hyperlinks, characters, paragraphs, pages, groups of adjacent pages, graphics, and tables.

freeware
Public-domain programs. Programs you can download and use without making any payment to the software publisher. *See also* shareware.

Frequently Asked Questions
See FAQ.

FTP
File Transfer Protocol. A protocol, or set of rules, that allows the access, reading, and/or downloading of files from a remote computer. You can either log on to a remote computer using an assigned user identifier (ID) and password, or use anonymous FTP, which uses the word anonymous as the user ID, and the user's e-mail address as the password. With the growth of the World Wide Web, FTP login is becoming transparent to the user; that is, FTP login is automatically enabled by the user clicking a link in a Web document.

general entity
A variable named within the text of the document instance. In contrast, a parameter entity is a variable named within markup. A general entity is preceded by an ampersand symbol (&) and succeeded by a semicolon (;). *See* document instance, entity, and parameter entity, parsed entity, and unparsed entity.

GIF
Graphics Interchange Format. A format for graphics files used within World Wide Web documents. GIF files are larger than graphics files with the JPEG format. *See also* JPEG.

glyph
A graphic that represents a character, particularly in a typeface.

grammar
A set of rules governing the structure of a document that conforms to a language standard. A document type definition (DTD) specifies the grammar of a particular SGML or XML document.

granularity
In computing, the relative coarseness of an object or group of objects. In XML, granularity indicates the number of children of parent elements. The more children and other descendants, the higher the level of granularity.

grove
In a tree structure of documents, a complete set (or *forest*) of documents and nodes. *See* node.

home page
The top hypertext document at a World Wide Web site or the document to which a user first goes when visiting a site. Typically, the home page provides an introduction to the site as well as links to the site's other pages. Most browsers are programmed to automatically go to a particular home page after your computer connects to the Internet.

host
A server. A computer that "hosts" other computers and provides information and services to client programs. *See* client and server.

HTML
Hypertext Markup Language. A subset of SGML (Standard Generalized Markup Language); the language with which you typically mark up (or create) documents, with hypertext links, for the World Wide Web. HTML 4.0 is the current version. *See* hypertext, link, SGML, and World Wide Web.

HTML document
A document created using elements and attributes from HTML (Hypertext Markup Language).

HTTP
Hypertext Transport Protocol. The rules and standards that client programs use to read hypertext files on host computers. *See* client, host, hypertext, and World Wide Web.

hyperlink
See link.

hypermedia
See multimedia.

hypertext
A variety of media in a document. Hypertext includes links to other documents or sections of documents, text, graphics, audio, and video. *See* link, multimedia, and World Wide Web.

HyTime
Hypermedia/Time-Based Structuring Language, ISO/IEC 19744. Hytime describes the links among a set of hypermedia objects in an SGML document. XLink is based on the foundations provided by HyTime. *See* XLink.

icon
A small button or graphic you click or double-click to open a folder, document, or file, to start a program, or to perform an action or issue a command (usually avoiding multiple steps).

identifier
A unique name used to identify or label a variable, procedure, macro, or other object.

ideographic character
An ideogram; a symbol or glyph that represents another character, a word, or other object.

IETF
Internet Engineering Task Force. An organization that evaluates and sets most standards for the Internet.

inline
In DSSSL style sheets, a newly defined verb indicating that an object is embedded inline. *See also* inline image and inline link.

inline image
A graphic embedded within the content of a Web document. In contrast, a displayed image is preceded by and followed by line or paragraph breaks.

inline link
A link specified within a linking element. An inline link is one of its own resources. *See* linking element, out-of-line link, and resource.

instance
See document instance.

internal DTD subset
The part of a DTD that is located within its source document. An internal DTD subset can be used temporarily for testing a document for well-formedness or validity and then replaced later with an external DTD subset. *See* DTD, external DTD subset, external entity, and internal entity.

internal entity
An entity with its content stored completely within the DTD. *See* DTD and external entity.

International Standardization Organization
See ISO.

internet
Two or more networks connected into a single network.

Internet
The largest internet of all, comprised of networks connecting government agencies, private and public organizations, educational institutions, laboratories, and individuals.

Internet Engineering Task Force
See IETF.

Internet media type
IMEDIA. *See* media type.

Internet provider
An organization that provides user access to the Internet. Also known as *Internet access provider* and *Internet service provider*.

interoperability
The capability of computer programs, computers, or peripherals to operate without regard for differences in their environments or the way in which they communicate with each other. For example, according to the Extensible Markup Language working draft, XML has been designed for ease of implementation and for interoperability with both SGML and HTML.

ISO
International Standardization Organization. An international standards-setting organization. ISO sets standards for computing, telecommunicating, and so on. ANSI, the American National Standards Institute, is the U.S. affiliate. *See* ANSI.

ISO/IEC 10646
An international standard that defines the codes and characters that constitute XML textual information.

JavaScript
See EcmaScript.

JPEG
Joint Photographic Expert Group. A graphics file format commonly used on the Internet that compresses images using a discrete cosine transform; this achieves impressive compression ratios (variable, up to 100 to 1), but results in loss of original pixel data, more noticeable with greater compression. JPEG graphics are usually smaller than GIF graphics. *See also* GIF.

keyword
(1) A reserved word; a word or phrase that is a unique part of a language, such as XML, and therefore unavailable for other uses within the language. (2) A metadata word or phrase. Search indexes use keywords to compile and optionally rank lists of Web documents. *See* search index and search tool.

ligature
A combination of two or more joined letters (for example, Æ).

line-progression direction
In DSSSL style sheets, a direction in which a flow object is displayed or inlined. The line-progression direction is perpendicular to both the escapement direction and the writing-mode direction. *See* escapement direction, flow object, placement direction, and writing-mode direction.

link
A highlighted and/or underlined word or phrase or a graphic that when clicked jumps to one or more particular places in another document or one or more sections of the current document. *See* hypertext and World Wide Web.

linking element
An element that includes a link and a description of its behavior and attributes. *See* element, link, locator, and resource.

local resource
The information or content within an inline link. *See* inline link, link, and linking element. *See also* remote resource.

location source
For an XPointer, the absolute starting point for a link. After pinpointing the
location source, use relative or string-match location terms to further refine
the link.

location term
Part of an XPointer; the term that refers to a location in a document. XPointer
location terms are absolute, relative, or string-match.

locator
Within a linking element, a character string that provides information about
finding a resource to which the element can link. *See* linking element and
resource.

macro
In computer programs, a set of instructions or keystrokes saved under a single
name. When a user runs a macro, a computer performs the instructions one
at a time. Macros are typically created as shortcuts to perform commonly
performed commands (such as opening a word-processing document, inserting
today's date in the header, and zooming the document to a particular size
onscreen).

man
Manual pages. Documentation for a program, such as UNIX.

markup
Commands that define attributes, such as formats and enhancements, and
describe the document. In XML and HTML documents, the commands with
which the document is marked up are known as *elements*. In XML, markup
includes start tags, end tags, empty-element tags, DTDs, formal references to
entities or characters, processing instructions, XML comments, and indicators
at the start and end of CDATA sections. The term *markup* refers to the marks
that editors make on manuscripts to be revised. *See* CDATA, DTD, empty
element, end tag, entity, start tag, and text.

MCF
Meta Content Framework. A standard for identifying and creating a hierarchy of a
document's metadata. *See* metadata.

media type
The type of file and its contents, formatted as *file type/file format*. Examples
include text/HTML and video/mpeg.

Meta Content Framework
See MDF.

metadata
According to Netscape documentation, "information about information." To enable search tools to find a Web document, the developer must provide information about the content and history of the document. Metadata can include keywords, dates of creation and modification, and the developer's name.

metalanguage
A language used to define markup languages such as HTML. SGML and XML are both metalanguages. *See* markup.

MIDI
Musical Instrumental Digital Interface. An audio standard for communications among computers, musical instruments, and synthesizers. MIDI files are commonly used to transfer musical information in a compact format.

MIME
Multipurpose Internet Mail Extensions or Multiple Internet Mail Extensions. A standard for sending and receiving messages that contain text, graphics, audio files, video files, and other multimedia files.

minimization
Methods of removing normally required XML, HTML, or SGML markup (such as start tags or end tags) when its location would be apparent with or without being present. In contrast, a normalized document contains all required markup. *See* normalization.

model group
In the document type definition (DTD), one or more collections of element names, each of which specifying the hierarchy of an XML document and enclosed within single quotes.

monospaced typeface
A font in which every character is a fixed width. A letter as wide as *w* or as narrow as *i* is given the same width. Monospaced text, which often represents computer code and keyboard entries, is ideal for spacing table columns.

MPEG
Moving Pictures Experts Group. A standard for both video and audio files.

multidirectional link
A link that you can traverse from several of its resources. *See* extended link, extended link group, link, resource, simple link, and traversal.

multimedia
Multiple media. A file composed of text, links, graphics, video files, and/or audio components.

Multiple Internet Mail Extensions
See MIME.

Multipurpose Internet Mail Extensions
See MIME.

Musical Instrumental Digital Interface
See MIDI.

name
A valid XML name that must begin with a letter or underscore character, not including the uppercase or lowercase letters X, M, or L, which are reserved. A name can include letters, digits, periods (.), dashes (-), underscores (_), colons (:), combining characters, and extenders. *See* name character and name token.

name character
One valid character in a name or name token. *See* name and name token.

name token
A valid XML name that can begin with any character, including letters, digits, periods (.), dashes (-), underscores (_), colons (:), combining characters, and extenders. *See* name and name character.

nested
A command line (including attributes) that is inserted completely within another command line.

newsgroup
A group devoted to discussing a particular topic, using mailing lists and other messages.

node
A point of connection. In a tree structure of documents, a node connects a group of documents to the tree. *See* grove.

normalization
Methods of including all required XML, HTML, or SGML markup (such as start tags or end tags) in a document. In contrast, a minimized document eliminates some markup. For interoperability among markup languages, it's best to normalize all documents. *See* minimization.

notation
A system of defining a means of communication using a formalized set of symbols or an alphabet. For example, notation can identify Braille, musical notes, and even computer file formats. In XML, a notation names the format of an unparsed entity or an element that contains a notation attribute or names the target application of a processing instruction.

occurrence indicator
In XML syntax, a symbol specifying how often a subelement may occur within a particular element. For example, an asterisk (*) indicates that a subelement can occur from none to any number of times, a question mark (?) indicates that a subelement can occur none or one time, and a plus sign (+) indicates that a subelement can occur one or more times.

Open Software Description
See OSD.

options
See attributes.

OSD
Open Software Description. An XML format that describes software and its codes. OSD will allow software developers to automatically transfer programs to client computers using server push. *See* server push.

out-of-line link
A link specified outside a linking element, as part of a group of multidirectional links. An out-of-line link is not one of its own resources. *See* linking element, multidirectional link, out-of-line link, and resource.

padding
In a Web document, the white space that surrounds data in cells or text on pages. *See also* white space.

parameter entity
PE; a variable named within markup in the prolog of a document, document type definition (DTD), and the document instance. A parameter entity is parsed, is preceded by a percent symbol (%), and is ended with a semicolon (;). *See* document instance, entity, and general entity.

parent
An element or other object under which other elements or objects are nested. In XML, an element is a parent of a subelement. *See* ancestor, child, and nested. *See also* root.

parse
The process of translating binary or textual data into language that can be read by a particular computer program. In XML, a validating parser produces ESIS output, including error and warning messages. *See* ESIS.

parsed entity
An entity that contains parsed data, which is replacement text. A parsed entity has a name and is called by an entity reference. *See* general entity, parameter entity, parse, unparsed data, and unparsed entity.

parser
A program that parses data into computer-readable language.

password
A hidden combination of characters and special symbols that a user types or that is automatically entered to gain access to a secure file, computer, directory, folder, or network.

#PCDATA
Parsable Character Data or Parsed Character Data. Mixed content; character data that can include CDATA, entities, and valid subelements. #PCDATA is any non-markup data. *See* CDATA.

PI
See processing instructions.

pixel
Picture element; pel. A dot that represents the smallest part of an image displayed on a computer monitor or printed on paper.

placement direction
In DSSSL style sheets, the direction between the starting and ending edges of the flow-object area. The placement direction is perpendicular to both the writing-mode direction and the escapement direction. *See* escapement direction, flow object, line-progression direction, and writing-mode direction.

placement path
In DSSSL style sheets, the baseline on which text rests in a styled document.

pointer
An element that contains an attribute that refers to one or more other elements in the same or a different document.

port
In DSSSL style sheets, a location in a flow object to which an ordered list of flow objects is attached. *See* atomic, flow object, and principal port.

position point
In DSSSL style sheets, the point at which a flow-object area starts. This is in contrast to the escapement point. *See* escapement point.

post
Send a message electronically; add a Web document to a server.

PostScript
A page description language developed by Adobe Systems; a standard for some Internet and word processing documents. If a document has a PS extension, it is a PostScript document.

principal port
In DSSSL style sheets, the port to which other ports are attached; the root port. *See* flow object and port.

processing instructions
PI; in an XML document, part of the markup that tells the XML processor or browser how to handle the following statement. In XML, a PI is preceded by a <? delimiter and ended by a ?> delimiter. *See* document prolog.

protocol
Standards or rules that control the way in which a program and computer, two computers, a computer and network, or two networks, and so on, communicate.

provider
See Internet provider.

public identifier
An external entity that is not restricted by a particular system, thereby potentially being available to a wider audience. Because it is not restricted to a specific system, a public identifier might be registered and contain information about its origins.

pull
See client pull.

push
See server push.

quadding
In printing, the act of spacing characters in a line of text by inserting a piece or pieces of metal. Quadding is also a DSSSL characteristic.

rank
A score assigned to an entry in a list of results from a search index. A high rank indicates that several keywords or other criteria in a Web document closely fit the keywords and other criteria that you entered. A low rank indicates very few matches. *See* search index and search tool.

RDF
Resource Description Framework. A standard for describing metadata in XML. *See* metadata and MCF.

recursive
A repetitive operation that includes some or all of the results of previous operations.

relative link

A link to a resource within the current document, directory or folder, or computer or network, using a partial URL or address (for example, /subdoc.xml). If your browser reads a partial URL or address, it will attempt to go to a relative link. *See* absolute link.

reserved word

A word or term used by a program or language for its own statements, declarations, and so on. Those using XML must not use reserved words to name files, variables, elements, and attributes. A few examples of reserved words in XML are CDATA, PCDATA, DTD, ENTITY, AND, and OR.

resource

An object that is the target of a link; information that has a URI associated with it. Resources can include files of all types and applications. *See* linking element, locator, subresource, and URI.

Resource Description Framework

See RDF.

RFC

Request for Comments. Official standards developed by the Internet Engineering Task Force (IETF). *See* IETF.

root

The document element; the ultimate parent element; an XML element within which all other XML elements are nested. In other words, all non-root elements are child elements of the root. *See* valid document and well-formed document. *See also* parent.

rule

(1) A horizontal line that is inserted in a document to separate sections or highlight text. A statement that defines the behavior of an element, subelement, entity, or other object. (2) One standard in construction rules, which specifies how a styling application formats an element.

schema

The description of data, its logical organization, content, and behavior.

scoping

The degree or scope to which a program can refer to a particular identifier.

search index

Search engine. A fill-out form in which you type one or more keywords, select or click checkboxes and/or option buttons, optionally select other parameters for an Internet search, and click a button to start the search. Examples of search indexes are AltaVista, Excite, Lycos, and Savvy Search. *See* search tool.

search tool
A search index (such as Savvy Search, AltaVista, Excite, Lycos, and many more) with which you search for Internet sites that closely match one or more keywords and other attributes that you select. This can also be a master list or directory (such as Yahoo!, the InterNIC Directory of Directories, the Whole Internet Catalog, or one of the World Wide Web Virtual Libraries), through which you can browse for Internet sites you might want to visit. *See* search index.

selector
A string that identifies an element to which a declaration applies. An element that affects a specific font is a selector on which type size, text color, and typeface families can apply. *See* declaration.

semantic markup
See descriptive markup.

server
A program (such as a World Wide Web or Gopher server) or computer that is programmed to communicate with, and provide information to, a client program (such as a browser). *See* browser and client.

server push
The automatic loading or reloading of a document or data at a specific time or time interval by a server. You can write a CGI program to incorporate server push features. *See also* client pull.

SGML
Standard Generalized Markup Language. An internationally accepted text-processing language specified by the ISO standard 8879. XML and HTML are both subsets of SGML. *See* HTML and XML.

shareware
A complete or partial version of a program that you can download and try out before buying it for a small fee. If the downloaded program is not a complete version, the author will send you a complete version, a manual, and sometimes additional programs when you license it. *See* freeware.

simple link
A unidirectional link, usually in-line but sometimes out-of-line, to another location within the current document or to a location in another document. XML simple links are similar to HTML links, which use the `<A>` tag. To specify a simple link in XML, use the `xml:link` attribute with the `simple` value. *See* extended link and extended link group.

site
A home page and its linked pages, all of which are located at a particular Internet address. *See* home page and site index.

site index
A table of contents or outline of a particular site. *See* site.

smart pull
A technique for automatically downloading content to a client. *See* client pull.

sosofo
In DSSSL style sheets, specification of a sequence of flow objects; an acronym indicating that the current styling rule does not actually create a flow object, it just provides instructions on how to create one.

Standard Generalized Markup Language
See SGML.

start tag
The part of an XML statement that indicates the start of an element and its contents. The format of a start tag is `<elementname>`, in contrast to the end tag format, `</elementname>`. *See* element and end tag.

streaming
A constant flow of data being transferred from one computer or network to another.

string
A group of one or more characters, usually text, enclosed within delimiters and sometimes given a unique name as identification. *See* delimiter and identifier.

style
One property or instruction in a style sheet. *See* style sheet.

style sheet
A set of instructions with which a word-processing or Web document is laid out or formatted. Style sheets format characters, paragraphs, pages, documents, and sets of documents. *See* cascading style sheets, DSSSL, and XSL.

subelement
An element nested within another element. A subelement is part of the content of its parent element. *See* element.

subresource
A fragment of an object that further specifies the targeted link (for example, a section within a file). *See* linking element, locator, and resource.

tag
See element. *See also* end tag and start tag.

text
Data that consists of characters. *See* binary.

title
A heading that describes a resource and its importance to a link. *See* linking element and resource.

token
A basic unit that cannot be further broken down. In XML, a token is a reserved word, operator, entity, a symbol, punctuation mark, or variable name.

traversal
The process of linking to a resource by a user or by programming code. *See* linking element and resource.

Unicode
A standards organization that develops the Unicode Worldwide Character Standard, which supports characters comprising the principal written languages of the world (thereby supporting Internet internationalization) as well as symbols either within or outside character sets. XML supports the entire Unicode character set, including the Private Use Area with which you can define your own special characters. The Unicode standard is synonymous with ISO 10646.

Uniform Resource Identifier
See URI.

Uniform Resource Locator
See URL.

unparsed data
Data that may or may not be valid but has not been validated by being processed through a parser. *See* general entity, parameter entity, parse, parsed entity, and unparsed entity.

unparsed entity
An entity that contains unparsed data. An unparsed entity has a named notation, which the XML processor sends to the target application. *See* general entity, notation, parameter entity, parse, parsed entity, and unparsed data.

upload
The transfer of a file from your computer to a remote computer. The standard protocol for uploading files is anonymous FTP (file transfer protocol). *See* download and FTP.

URI
Uniform Resource Identifier. The Internet address of an anchor. A URI can either be a URL (absolute link) or a partial address (relative link), or a URN (Uniform Resource Name). *See* URL and URN.

URL

Uniform Resource Locator. An Internet address composed of the protocol type (such as `http:`, `ftp:`, `gopher:`, and so on), the name of the server to be contacted (such as `www.w3.org`), the directories or folders (such as `/pub/WWW/Provider/`), and the optional filename (for example, `homepage.xml`). *See* URI and URN.

URN

Uniform Resource Name. An identifier that can contain a variety of information, including one or more URLs. *See* URI and URL.

user agent

See agent.

UTF-8

An 8-bit character representation, or encoding form, supported by the XML specification and the Unicode organization. UTF-8 is an amendment of ISO/IEC 10646. UTF-8, which contains the entire US-ASCII character set and the universal coded character set (UCS), is documented in RFC 2044. *See* UTF-16.

UTF-16

A 16-bit character representation, or encoding form, supported by the XML specification and the Unicode organization. UTF-16, which is an amendment of ISO/IEC 10646, enables characters outside the Basic Multilingual Plane (BMP) of ISO/IEC 10646 to be encoded. *See* UTF-8.

valid document

An XML document that is associated with a recognized document type declaration and that complies with all the rules and constraints defined in the DTD. *See* root and well-formed document.

W3C

World Wide Web Consortium; the organization that develops standards for the World Wide Web and contributes to XML, HTML, and style sheet standards.

WAV

A Windows-supported sound file format.

well-formed document

An XML document that is created within XML standards but is not necessarily associated with a document type declaration (hence, a DTD within the document type declaration). A well-formed document must include at least one root XML element within which other XML elements are nested and must follow all the defined rules in the current XML specification. *See* root and valid document.

white space
The "empty" sections of a document that do not include text or graphics. Use style sheets to add white space to a document in order to highlight headings and particular text and graphics, to improve the look of the document, and to make its text easier to read. *See* cascading style sheets and style sheets. *See also* padding.

World Wide Web
WWW, W3, or the Web. A hypertext-based information system that supports the use of multimedia, including text, links, graphics, video files, and sound files. The Web was developed at the European Laboratory for Particle Physics (CERN) in Switzerland.

writing-mode direction
In DSSSL style sheets, the direction in which a flow object is displayed or inlined. The writing-mode direction is sometimes the reverse of the escapement direction and perpendicular to both the placement direction and the line-progression direction. *See* escapement direction, flow object, line-progression direction, and placement direction.

XLink
Extensible Linking Language; a set of elements and attributes that define the linking behavior of XML documents.

XML
Extensible Markup Language; a "child" or subset of SGML and a markup language that coexists with both SGML and HTML. XML enables complex hyperlinks, supports long documents, and allows users to define their own elements.

XML document
A file, a record, a set of bits and bytes, or another object enabled by the XML standard. *See* XML.

XPointer
XML Pointer Language; an extended pointer; an absolute, relative, or string-match location that, along with XLink, targets a specific location in a containing document. *See* XLink.

XSL
Extensible Style Language. A style sheet language based on DSSSL and designed specifically for XML, which is currently under development. *See* cascading style sheets and DSSSL.

Webliography

After you have perused this book, you may find that you want more information about XML and related technologies — in the form of a tutorial, an article, or a specification. You can find many Web sites — increasing all the time — dedicated to XML. During the writing of this book, I visited many XML Web sites (commercial, academic, and individual) all over the world. With every exploration, I found more resources. This Webliography lists and briefly describes many of the best XML sites on the World Wide Web.

SGML

SGML is the parent of XML, so learning from SGML Web sites can help you understand XML. In this section are resources covering SGML.

SGML at the World Wide Web Consortium

This section includes SGML information from the W3C.

Overview of SGML Resources (http://www.w3.org/MarkUp/ SGML/), by Dan Connolly of the World Wide Web Consortium (W3C) is a list of links organized under the following headings: "Learning and Using SGML," "Specs, Drafts, and Reports," "Groups and Discussion Forums," and "Research Notebook."

SGML, XML, and Structured Document Interchange (http://www.w3.org/XML/Activity), by Dan Connolly and Jon Bosak of the World Wide Web Consortium (W3C) is an activity report on SGML and its "child," XML. Links to new papers, standards, and organizations are included.

SGML Standards

This section lists SGML standards sites.

SGML: Related Standards (http://www.sil.org/sgml/ related.html), by Robin Cover, lists and discusses standards for SGML, DSSSL, XML, and other language standards.

Interoperability and Standards (http://www.pira.co.uk/ IE/top011.htm) is a master list of standards organizations and standards information.

SGML Overviews

Information on SGML (http://jschem.korea.ac.kr/ computer/sgml/1.html) is a brief description of SGML, its history, its structure, and presentation.

About SGML (http://etext.virginia.edu/sgml.html) describes SGML and provides links to other SGML resources.

What Is SGML and How Does It Help? (http://gopher. sil.org/sgml/burnardw25-index.html), by Lou Burnard, is a 14-page introduction to SGML.

SGML — Your Multi-Platform Publishing and Information Management Solution (http://www.sq.com/resources/sgml/) is an introduction to SGML by SoftQuad, a company that is a major player. Getting Started with SGML (http://commerce4.best.com/~sgml/html/getstart.htm) is a 12-page guide to SGML. Also included is a glossary of terms.

SGML Tutorials and Primers

In this section, you find a variety of tutorials and primers.

Tutorial — A Brief Introduction to SGML (http://www.efi.joensuu.fi/~i_dgreen/sql/sgml.html) is a short tutorial, which concludes with a bibliography, links to Usenet FAQs, and other SGML Web sites.

TEI Guidelines for Electronic Text Encoding and Interchange: A Gentle Introduction to SGML (http://etext.virginia.edu/bin/tei-tocs?div=DIV1&id=SG) is one detailed 24-page chapter from the TEI Guidelines for Electronic Text Encoding and Interchange online book. Note that other chapters from this book are also available and worth reading.

The SGML Primer (http://www.sq.com/sgmlinfo/primbody.html or http://www.softquad.com/resources/sgml/primbody.html) discusses declarations, the document instance, entities, and DTDs.

SGML Introduction — An Introduction to the Standard Generalized Markup Language (SGML) (http://itrc.uwaterloo.ca/~engl210e/BookShelf/Tutorials/SGML/sgmlint.htm) is the first in a series of an excellent introduction to SGML.

Introduction to SGML (http://www.w3.org/TR/1998/REC-html40-19980424/intro/sgmltut.html#h-3.1) introduces SGML, especially in the context of the HTML 4.0 specification.

SGML Declarations

This section lists sites that discuss SGML declarations.

SGML Declarations (http://www.sil.org/sgml/wlw11.html), by Robin Cover, discusses SGML declarations, including document character sets and concrete syntax.

Understanding the SGML Declaration (http://www. omnimark.com/white/dec/) is an online book providing information about SGML declarations.

Document Character Sets by Example (http://www. mulberrytech.com/papers/docchar.htm) discusses how to describe character sets in an SGML declaration.

SGML References

This section contains SGML reference resources, all created by Harvey Bingham.

SGML Syntax Summary, with Extended Naming Rules (http://www.tiac.net/users/bingham/sgmlsyn/sgmlsyn.htm)

SGML Syntax Summary Table of Contents, with Annexes (http://www.tiac.net/users/bingham/sgmlsyn/ contents.htm)

SGML Syntax Summary Introduction (http://www. tiac.net/users/bingham/sgmlsyn/intro.htm)

SGML Syntactic Variables (http://www.tiac.net/ users/bingham/sgmlsyn/variabls.htm)

SGML Reference Delimiter Roles (http://www.tiac. net/users/bingham/sgmlsyn/delimits.htm)

SGML Keyword Syntactic Literals (http://www.tiac. net/users/bingham/sgmlsyn/literals.htm)

SGML Terminal Variables (http://www.tiac.net/ users/bingham/sgmlsyn/termvars.htm)

SGML Directories

This section lists directories containing many links to SGML resources.

The SGML Web Page (http://www.sil.org/sgml/sgml. html), by Robin Cover, is perhaps the most extensive list of SGML resources.

A List of SGML Reference Sites (http://www.cdc.com/ DocSvc/sgmlref.htm) is a long, detailed list of many SGML, DSSSL, DTD, and other related resources.

SGML on the Web (http://www.NCSA.uiuc.edu/SDG/ Software/Mosaic/WebSGML.html) is an eclectic list of SGML and many other resources.

SGML, DSSSL, and HyTime (http://clover.slavic.
pitt.edu/~djb/sgml.html) contains links ranging from general
SGML information to FTP archives to lists of software.

SGML Resources (http://www.arbortext.com/sgmlresrc.
html) presents many SGML links, a long list of books to buy, and
discussion and users groups.

Standard Generalized Markup Language (SGML) — Table
of Contents (http://navycals.dt.navy.mil/sgml.html) is a short
list of U.S. Navy SGML pages, including a repository of DTDs.

ISO/IEC JTC1/WG4 Home Page (http://www.ornl.gov/
sgml/WG8/wg8home.htm) includes links to SGML, style sheet
resources, and other language resources. Also provided are links
to ISO standards and a registry of WG4 documents.

Characters and Character Sets

Use legal characters to enhance a document with symbols such as
trademarks, international characters and alphabets, mathematical
symbols, and so on. This section points to several documents that
list special characters (that is, entities) supported by XML.

The Unicode Consortium (http://www.unicode.org/) is
responsible for the Unicode standard: compiling character groups,
setting data standards, establishing character mappings, and so
on. From this home page, you can read the Unicode Standard,
learn about conferences, link to resources, and find out more
about the Consortium. Unicode has also compiled charts and
names of special characters at this site.

A Short Overview of ISO/IEC 10646 and Unicode
(http://www.nada.kth.se/i18n/ucs/unicode-iso10646-
oview.html) is a nine-page document discussing the ISO/IEC
10646 international character set standard.

i18n/l10n: Character Sets (http://www.w3.org/
International/O-charset.html) discusses character
sets on the Internet and provides links to charset resources for
internationalization (that is, i18n) and localization (that is, l10n).
Also look at the overview page, at http://www.w3.org/
International/Overview.html.

Minimum European Subset of ISO/IEC 10646-1 (http://
www.indigo.ie/egt/standards/mes.html) lists characters and
scripts of Europe.

Mathematica 3.0 Characters from Assigned Unicode Space (http://www.ams.org/html-math/wolframchartables/ assignedzone.html) is a table with the following columns: Unicode hex, Mathematica name, character glyph (an image), SGML aliases, TeX aliases, and Mathematica aliases.

ISO-8859 Briefing and Resources (http://ppewww.ph. gla.ac.uk/~flavell/iso8859/iso8859-pointers.html) is a 13-page document that discusses the ISO-8859-1 character codes, which represent the most common characters — particularly for HTML but also supported by SGML and XML.

RFC 2044: UTF-8, a Transformation Format of Unicode and ISO 10646 (http://display.InterNIC.net/rfc/rfc2044. txt) presents information and examples about the Unicode standard and various character sets: UTF-8, US-ASCII, UCS-2, and UCS-4.

RFC 2130: The Report of the IAB Character Set Workshop (http://display.InterNIC.net/rfc/rfc2130.txt) provides an overview of character sets on the Internet, the problems and the ways in which characters are currently handled. Also included are discussions of language-handling and bi-directionality as well as a list of acronyms, a glossary, and more.

Basic Principles (http://www.cm.spyglass.com/unicode/ standard/principles.html) discusses encoding forms, characters and display cells, characters and glyphs, and language tagging. This document includes links to several other documents, including the following:

- **Character/Glyph Model** (http://www.cm.spyglass. com/unicode/standard/cgmodel.html) is a long academic paper on characters and glyphs.

- **File System Safe UTF** (http://www.cm.spyglass.com/ unicode/standard/fss-utf.html) discusses the UTF-8 encoding form of Unicode.

- **UCS-2 Encoding Form** (http://www.cm.spyglass.com/ unicode/standard/ucs2.html) is a short paper about the UCS-2 encoding form.

- **UCS Transformation Format 8 (UTF-8)** (http://www. cm.spyglass.com/unicode/standard/wg2n1036.html) discusses UTF-8 and UCS-4. Included is information about converting from UTF-8 characters to UCS-4 and from UCS-4 characters to UTF-8.

- **UCS Transformation Format 16 (UTF-16)** (http://
  www.cm.spyglass.com/unicode/standard/wg2n1035.html)
  presents information about UTF-16, including conversion
  from UTF-16 characters to UCS and from UCS characters
  to UTF-16.
- **Extended UCS-2 Encoding Form (UTF-16)** (http://
  www.cm.spyglass.com/unicode/standard/utf16.html) continues the discussion of UTF-16 and presents an overview
  of UCS-2, and three forms of UTF-16.
- **Supported Scripts** (http://www.cm.spyglass.com/
  unicode/standard/supported.html) is a short paper that
  provides information about primary and secondary
  language scripts.

Earliest Uses of Symbols of Relation (http://members.
aol.com/jeff570/relation.html) is a very interesting illustrated
history of symbols.

Internationalization

One of the purposes of XML is to "internationalize" Web
documents. This section contains language and country resources.

xml:lang Resources (http://www.altheim.com/xml/specs/
xmllang.html) provides links to language, country, and charset
pages.

Tags for the Identification of Languages (RFC 1766)
(ftp://ftp.isi.edu/in-notes/rfc1766.txt) is a good
introduction to the expression of languages on the Internet.

Technical Contents of ISO 639:1988 (http://www.sil.
org/sgml/iso639.html) lists two-letter language codes.

ISO 3166 Country Codes (http://www.wwwsite.com/
mboxes/country.htm) is a list of two-letter country codes.

**ISO 3166: Code for the Representation of Names of
Countries** (http://sunsite.berkeley.edu/amher/iso_3166.html)
lists two- and three-letter and three-digit country codes.

XML

As the centerpiece of this book, XML deserves a full treatment in
this Webliography. The resources in the following sections should
answer most, if not all, your XML questions.

XML at the World Wide Web Consortium

As the home of XML, the World Wide Web Consortium (W3C) is the best resource for XML information, as shown in this section.
Extensible Markup Language (XML) (http://www.w3.org/XML/) is the official XML home page. Here you'll always find up-to-date links to other applicable pages at W3C and elsewhere.
Extensible Markup Language (XML) 1.0 (http://www.w3.org/TR/1998/REC-xml-19980210) is the official W3C recommendation at the time of this writing.
Known Errors in the XML 1.0 Specification (http://www.w3.org/XML/xml-19980210-errata) lists any errors in the official recommendation at the time of this writing.
XML Activity (http://www.w3.org/XML/Activity.html) lists activities associated with XML. Throughout this document, you'll find links to important documents and related technologies.
RFC 1738: Uniform Resource Locators (http://www.w3.org/Addressing/rfc1738.txt) is a 22-page paper discussing the syntax and semantics for uniform resource locators (URLs).
RFC 1808: Relative Uniform Resource Locators (http://www.w3.org/Addressing/rfc1808.txt) is a 14-page paper discussing the syntax and semantics for relative URLs.
SGML, XML, and Structured Document Interchange (http://www.w3.org/XML/Activity.html) discusses the activities related to using generic SGML in Web documents.
XML Hacking is Fun (http://www.w3.org/XML/9705/hacking.html), by Dan Connolly, is essentially an informal note about creating three XML parsers.

XML Overviews

This section introduces novices to XML.
Generally Markup XML Resources (http://www.csclub.uwaterloo.ca/u/relander/Academic/XML/xml_mw.html), by Richard Lander, is a 12-page investigation of XML, its history, its capabilities, and its limitations.
XML, Java, and the Future of the Web (http://sunsite.unc.edu/pub/sun-info/standards/xml/why/xmlapps.htm), by Jon Bosak, introduces XML, describes its effect on the Web, and provides examples.

XML: A Professional Alternative to HTML (http://www. heise.de/ix/artikel/E/1997/06/106/), by Ingo Macherius, is a series of pages introducing XML. Also included are discussions of SGML, style sheets, XML tools, and online XML links.

X Marks the Spot (http://www.cs.caltech.edu/~adam/ papers/xml/x-marks-the-spot.html), by Rohit Khare and Adam Rifkin, is a 16-page paper covering the history of markup languages and exploring XML.

The Evolution of Web Documents: The Ascent of XML (http://www.cs.caltech.edu/~adam/papers/xml/ascent-of-xml.html), by Dan Connolly, Rohit Khare, and Adam Rifkin, discusses markup languages, HTML, and XML.

Capturing the State of Distributed Systems with XML (http://www.cs.caltech.edu/~adam/papers/xml/xml-for-archiving.html), by Rohit Khare and Adam Rifkin, looks at XML as a solution for distributed systems.

The Case for XML (http://www.mcs.net/~dken/xmlcase.htm) discusses the use of SGML, HTML, and XML and offers some practical XML business examples.

Extensible Markup Language (XML) (http://www.qucis. queensu.ca/achallc97/papers/p050.html) is by C. M. Sperberg-McQueen and Tim Bray, both of whom have been working on XML from its inception. This states the reasons for developing XML and covers the history of the XML working group.

An Introduction to Structured Documents (http://www. venus.co.uk/omf/cml/doc/tutorial/xml.html), by Peter Murray-Rust, is a paper on markup languages, XML, and custom languages, such as the Chemical Markup Language (CML), written by the author. Peter Murray-Rust is also the developer of JUMBO, the first XML browser.

Introduction to XML (http://www.ifi.uio.no/~larsga/ download/xml/xml_eng.html), by Lars Marius Garshol, covers XML and its features in 10 pages.

An Introduction to XML (http://www.arbortext.com/ nwalsh.html), by Norman Walsh, provides a more technical introduction to XML, XLink (when it was known as XML Link), and XSL (when it was XML Style) for those who might have some HTML or SGML experience.

XML for Managers (http://www.arbortext.com/xmlwp.html) is an XML white paper directed at managers, executives, and others who are thinking of using XML or converting from SGML to XML.

XML Tutorials

The tutorial in this section can get you started with XML. **Basic XML** (http://www.hypermedic.com/style/xml/xmltut. txt) is a two-chapter tutorial. When you have completed the tutorial, you will be able to write a well-formed XML document, create a simple DTD, and display the finished document online. **XML Tutorials** (http://www.hypermedic.com/style/xml/ xmlindex.htm), by Frank Boumphrey, is a directory page of XML resources, including a tutorial, other tutorial pages and XML resources, and Jon Bosak's XML markups of Shakespeare plays, the Bible, and the Koran.

XML Directories

Directories are usually lists of links organized under a heading or by category. This section contains valuable directories of XML resources.

Extensible Markup Language (XML) (http://www.sil. org/sgml/xml.html), by Robin Cover, is the most extensive and one of the best-organized XML directories. If you can't find a resource here, it probably doesn't exist.

XML: The Extensible Markup Language (http://www. xmlinfo.com/), by James K. Tauber, is one of the best XML sites. In several pages, the author covers every thinkable aspect of XML. At the time of this writing, the author was reorganizing into three separate sites.

XML Resources (http://www.finetuning.com/xml.html) provides many pages of XML-related links. Each entry includes a one- or two-paragraph description.

XML.com (http://www.xml.com/) provides links to articles and news about XML. The best feature at this site is an annotated version of the official XML 1.0 specification. The annotations, written by Tim Bray, include comments about particular features and explanations of terms.

XML Links by Adam Rifkin (http://www.cs.caltech. edu/~adam/local/xml.html) lists many XML links, including papers and other articles, links for beginners, advanced topics, and XML-related issues and papers.

What is XML? (http://www.gca.org/conf/xml/xml_ what.htm) contains many links to XML resources, including articles, software, and XML-related standards.

Extensible Markup Language JumpStart (http://www.
jeremie.com/JS/XML/all.html) is a tabular page with several
links to XML sites. Each entry includes information about the
type, content, audience, importance, and keywords. Jeremie, the
author, provides other JumpStart pages at his site.

What the ?XML! Home Page (http://www.geocities.
com/SiliconValley/Peaks/5957/xml.html) is a nicely designed
site with several links to other XML resources.

Extensible Markup Language (http://www.microsoft.com/
workshop/c-frame.htm#/sml/default.asp) is a very busy site that
contains the following categories: General Information, Authoring
XML, Displaying XML, XML Support in IE 4.0, XML Support
in IE 5.0, XML Demos, and XML Scenarios. It is best to use the
Internet Explorer browser to view this site properly.

XML FAQ

The following list of frequently-asked questions can answer
almost all your XML questions.

Frequently Asked Questions about the Extensible
Markup Language (http://www.ucc.ie/xml/), compiled by Peter
Flynn and many others, groups questions as follows: General
questions, Users of SGML (including browsers of HTML), Authors
of SGML (including writers of HTML), and Developers and
Implementors (including WebMasters and server operators). The
FAQ contains many external and internal cross-reference links.

XML Namespaces

A namespace is a set of unique names, defined in the DTD or
elsewhere. In XML, a qualified name is comprised of two parts:
an identifier and either a URI or element name, depending on
whether it is external or internal, respectively. The three papers
in this section discuss XML namespaces.

Namespaces in XML (http://www.w3.org/TR/WD-xml-names)
is a working draft describing a method for associating names with
namespaces in XML documents.

Why We Need Namespaces (Modules) (http://itrc.
uwaterloo.ca/~papresco/sgml/namespaces.html), by Paul
Prescod, is a response to the "Namespaces in XML" document
(see above entry).

XML Namespaces (http://www.microsoft.com/xml/
authoring/namespaces/namespaces.htm) presents namespaces
in lay terms.

Extended Backus-Naur Form

Extended Backus-Naur Form is the syntax used in the W3C's
specifications and in DTDs. This section lists resources for this
syntax and its predecessor, Backus-Naur Form.

   Extended Backus-Naur Form (EBNF) (http://www.cs.upe.
ac.za/staff/csabhv/slim/ebnf.html) is a short page describing
the syntax.

   How Far Can EBNF Stretch? (http://www.cs.man.ac.
uk/~pjj/bnf/ebnf_rjb93a_xbnf.mth) is a 25-page document
discussing EBNF and other forms in great detail.

   Language Theory (http://www.cs.man.ac.uk/~pjj/
bnf/ebnf_j_alan.html) discusses Extended Backus-Naur Form
and another syntax, Chomsky Normal Form.

   Backus-Naur Form (BNF) (http://lem.stud.fh-heilbronn.
de/doc/ada/lovelace/bnf.html) briefly describes the syntax and
provides examples.

Document Type Declarations

Documentation type declarations for both SGML and XML are
strikingly similar. This section contains Web resources for SGML
and XML DTDs.

Creating DTDs

Most of the resources in this section on creating DTDs are
SGML-related.

   **TEI Guidelines for Electronic Text Encoding and
Interchange: Structure of the TEI Document Type Definition**
(http://etext.virginia.edu/bin/tei-tocs?div=DIV1&id=ST)
describes the structure of a SGML DTD in 41 pages. Many
examples are included.

   Document Type Definition Files (http://www.livepage.
com/lpdocs/sgmled/.node-6602) is an introduction to SGML
DTDs.

Defining SGML Document Structures: The Document Type Definition (`http://www.ua.ac.be/MAN/WP31/t14.html`) is the first page of a tutorial-like section on DTDs in an SGML manual.

How to Read the HTML DTD (`http://www.w3.org/TR/1998/REC-html40-19980424/intro/sgmltut.html#h-3.3`) is the part of the HTML 4.0 specification devoted to reading the DTD on which the markup language is based.

Snafu Document Type Declaration (`http://www.math.utah.edu/docs/info/snafu_7.html`) is a formal SGML syntax declaration for three types of technical papers.

Creating a DTD and an SGML Declaration (`http://booksrv2.raleigh.ibm.com:80/cgi-bin/BookMgr/bookmgr.cmd/BOOKS/EHMAMA00/CONTENTS#COVER`) is the start of a large online book.

A Document Type Declaration for Formal Metadata (`http://geology.usgs.gov/tools/metadata/tools/doc/dtd.html`) is a well-documented SGML DTD conforming to the Content Standards for Digital Geospatial Metadata of the Federal Geographic Data Committee.

SGML Exceptions and XML (`http://www.arbortext.com/sgmlxept.html`) is a white paper on SGML exceptions and why XML does not allow exceptions.

● **TIP** ─────────────────────────────────

When you use a SGML DTD as the basis for an XML DTD, be sure to edit out SGML-only elements.

Sample DTDs

This section lists sample DTDs for both XML and SGML.

XML-Tagged Religion Set (`http://sunsite.unc.edu/pub/sun-info/xml/eg/religion.1.10.xml.zip`), by Jon Bosak, is a zipped file containing religious works and a DTD. For more information about this and the following entry, go to `http://www.sil.org/sgml/bosakXMLExamples980131.html`.

XML-Tagged Shakespeare Set (`http://sunsite.unc.edu/pub/sun-info/xml/eg/shakespeare.1.10.xml.zip`), by Jon Bosak, is a zipped file containing plays by Shakespeare and a DTD.

Article DTD (`ftp://www.sgml.com/article.dtd`) is a three-page SGML DTD.

DTD (ftp://navycals.dt.navy.mil/pub/dtd/81927.dtd) is a sample of a well-documented 14-page U.S. Navy SGML DTD.

MIL-M-38784C (ftp://navycals.dt.navy.mil/pub/dtd/3878c.dtd) is an ArborText version of a 16-page U.S. Navy SGML DTD.

Official Navy Baseline Tagset Library (http://navycals.dt.navy.mil/dtdfosi/tag_library.html) is a library of tags used in U.S. Navy DTDs.

XLink and XPointer Languages

This section lists both XLink and XPointer resources.

XML Linking Language (XLink) (http://www.w3.org/TR/WD-xlink) is the official working draft for the linking language.

XML Pointer Language (XPointer) (http://www.w3.org/TR/WD-xptr) is the official working draft for the extended-pointer language.

XML Linking Language (XLink) Design Principles (http://www.w3.org/TR/NOTE-xlink-principles) discusses implementing XLink and XPointer in XML documents.

XLink and XPointer Overview (http://www.sil.org/sgml/xlinkMaler980402.html), by Eve Maler, one of the two editors of the XLink and XPointer standards, is a response to a message about XLink. The document is an overview of both XLink and XPointer.

XML and Broken Links (http://www.sil.org/sgml/maler980331.html), by Eve Maler, is a response to a question about how XML treats broken links. The author explains how you can address potential broken links using XLink and XPointer.

What is XLink? (http://www.stg.brown.edu/~sjd/xlinkintro.html), by Steven J. DeRose, one of the two editors of the XLink and XPointer standards, introduces both XLink and XPointer.

TEI Guidelines for Electronic Text Encoding and Intern-change: Linking, Segmentation, and Alignment (http://etext.virginia.edu/bin/tei-tocs?div=DIV1&id=SA) is a long document that discusses links from an SGML point of view.

TEI Extended Pointers: A Brief Tutorial (http://www.sil.org/sgml/burnardExtPoint.html), by Lou Burnard, discusses how the Text Encoding Initiative (TEI) organization deals with extended pointers in SGML.

Style Sheets

Style sheets are an integral part of XML document output. This section lists resources for cascading style sheets (CSS1 and CSS2), DSSSL, DSSSL-O, and XSL.

Cascading Style Sheets

Cascading style sheets are supported in XML and HTML 4.0. This section includes cascading-style-sheet resources.

Cascading Style Sheets, Level 2, CSS2 Specification (http://www.w3.org/TR/REC-CSS2/) is the official specification for cascading style sheets.

Associating Stylesheets with XML Documents (http://www.w3.org/TR/NOTE-xml-stylesheet) is a brief note with examples showing how stylesheets are referred to in XML documents. W3C notes are available for discussion but are not standards.

DSSSL

Document Style Semantics and Specification Language (DSSSL) is the international standard for SGML documents. This section lists DSSSL resources.

Obtaining the DSSSL Standard (http://www.w3.org/International/obtainDSSSL.html) is a short document introducing DSSSL and on obtaining the copyrighted DSSSL standard, ISO/IEC 10179:1996.

Introduction to DSSSL (http://itrc.uwaterloo.ca/~papresco/dsssl/tutorial.html), by Paul Prescod, is a detailed 24-page introductory paper on DSSSL.

DSSSL: An Introduction (http://www.mcs.net/~dken/dslintro.htm) introduces DSSSL and DSSSL Online.

An Introduction to DSSSL (http://csg.uwaterloo.ca/~dmg/dsssl/tutorial/tutorial.html), by Daniel M Germán, is an online tutorial. To run the tutorial, you must have basic SGML and Scheme language knowledge. In addition, you must have required materials on your computer or on hand.

DSSSL Digest (ftp://ftp.ornl.gov/pub/sgml/WG8/DSSSL/digest.htm), produced by Henry S. Thompson, is a long document "containing all the procedures and top-level expressions from the electronic version of the DSSSL standard document."

Each entry includes at least one link to another part of the document.

In addition to his SGML resources (see a previous section), Harvey Bingham has also created a series of DSSSL reference resources.

- **DSSSL Syntax Summary Index** (http://www.tiac. net/users/bingham/dssslsyn/)
- **DSSSL Syntax Summary** (http://www.tiac.net/ users/bingham/dssslsyn/dssslsyn.htm)
- **DSSSL Syntax Table of Contents** (http://www.tiac. net/users/bingham/dssslsyn/contents.htm)
- **DSSSL Terminal Variables in Productions** (http:// www.tiac.net/users/bingham/dssslsyn/termvars.htm)
- **DSSSL Terminal Constants in Productions** (http:// www.tiac.net/users/bingham/dssslsyn/termcons.htm)
- **DSSSL Syntactic Constants in Productions** (http:// www.tiac.net/users/bingham/dssslsyn/syncons.htm)
- **DSSSL Syntactic Variable Index** (http://www.tiac. net/users/bingham/dssslsyn/svindex.htm)
- **DSSSL Syntactic Productions Repeated** (http://www. tiac.net/users/bingham/dssslsyn/svrepeat.htm)
- **DSSSL Syntactic Variables Unused in Any Production Definitions** (http://www.tiac.net/users/bingham/ dssslsyn/svunused.htm)
- **DSSSL Flow Object Characteristics** (http://www.tiac. net/users/bingham/dssslsyn/flobchrs.htm/)
- **DSSSL Characteristic Use in Flow Objects** (http:// www.tiac.net/users/bingham/dssslsyn/chrflobs.htm)
- **DSSSL Prototype Procedure Index** (http://www. tiac.net/users/bingham/dssslsyn/protondx.htm)
- **DSSSL Prototype Procedure Summary** (http://www. tiac.net/users/bingham/dssslsyn/protosum.htm)

The DSSSL Cookbook (http://www.mulberrytech.com/ dsssl/dsssldoc/cookbook/index.html) is the introductory page to a series of DSSSL tutorial-like topics.

ISO/IEC 10179:1996 (http://www.jclark.com/dsssl/), by James Clark, is a one-page directory of DSSSL links.

What's the DIS on DSSSL? (http://www.sgmlu.com/ documents/iai/swickes.htm), by Simon Wickes, is a four-page paper on the current state of DSSSL in 1995.
DTD DSSSL Style Sheet (http://csgwww.uwaterloo.ca/ ~dmg/dsssl/tutorial/play.dsl) is a DSSSL DTD written for "DTD for Plays" by Jon Bosak.
SGML: DSSSL Style Sheet for HTML 3.2 Print Output (http://www.sil.org/sgml/dsssl-o-html32.html), by Jon Bosak, is a well-documented style sheet.
Sample DSSSL HTML Stylesheet (ftp://sunsite.unc. edu/pub/sun-info/standards/dsssl/stylesheets/html3_2/NOTES and http://www.sil.org/sgml/html32dsl-bosak-rme.txt), by Jon Bosak, are two notes documenting the DSSSL style sheet for HTML 3.2 output.

DSSSL-O

DSSSL-Online is a DSSSL subset for electronic documents. This section lists DSSSL resources.
DSSSL Online Application Profile (http://sunsite.unc. edu/pub/sun-info/standards/dsssl/dssslo/do960816.htm) is a comprehensive DSSSL Online reference. Also included is information about flow objects and flow object classes.
DSSSL-O Tutorials (http://www.hypermedic.com/ style/dsssl/dslindex.htm) is a short directory of DSSSL-O, DSSSL, and other tutorials and resources.
Introduction to DSSSL — Example (http://www.jclark. com/dsssl/bcs/xmp.htm) is a style sheet that uses DSSSL Online and some programming.

XSL

The Extensible Style Language (XSL) is a future styling language for XML. This section lists XSL resources.

● NOTE

At the time of this writing, XSL is in the process of development. Resources in this section will most likely change to reflect changes in XSL.

Extensible Style Language (XSL) (http://www.w3.org/Style/XSL/) is the W3C home page for XSL.

A Proposal for XSL (http://www.w3.org/TR/NOTE-xsl.html) is the current W3C note for XSL. W3C notes are available for discussion but are not standards.

XSL Requirements Summary (http://www.w3.org/TR/WD-XSLReq) is a 22-page working draft that defines the scope of the XSL language.

An Introduction to XSL (http://www.ltg.ed.ac.uk/~ht/swindon.html), by Henry S. Thompson, is a five-page paper on XSL and its features.

XSL — A Proposed Stylesheet for XML (http://www.arbortext.com/xslwp.html), by Paul Grosso, discusses XSL, its history, background, and future. Also included is information about how XSL is related to DSSSL, HTML, and CSS.

XSL Tutorial (http://www.microsoft.com/xml/xsl/tutorial/tutorial.htm) is an extensive and complete 34-page tutorial on using XSL.

Basic XSL Style Sheets (http://www.hypermedic.com/style/xsl/xsl_tut1.txt) and **XSL: Beyond the Basics** (http://www.hypermedic.com/style/xsl/xsl_tut1.txt) is a two-part XSL tutorial.

Extensible Style Language (XSL) (http://www.sil.org/sgml/xsl.html), by Robin Cover, is a comprehensive directory of XSL links.

Style Sheet Resources DSSSL, XSL, XML (http://www.finetuning.com/xsl.html) is a directory of style sheet links. Each entry includes a lengthy description.

Extensible Style Sheets JumpStart (http://www.jeremie.com/JS/XSL/all.html) is a directory of XSL articles, software, and resources.

Other Standards and Specifications

XML does not stand alone; other technologies play a part in XML documents and other electronic documents. This section lists other standards and specifications.

Web and Web-Like Technology 1 (http://www.pira.co.uk/IE/top015.htm) is a directory of information and links to many technologies and standards.

World Wide Web Specifications — Related Standards
(http://www.ccs.org/validate/wwwspec.html) is a directory of
standards documents related to HTML and, hence, to XML. Many
links are included.

W3C Data Formats (http://www.w3.org/TR/NOTE-rdfarch),
by Tim Berners-Lee, discusses some W3C data format specifications and their relationships to each other.

Channel Definition Format (CDF) (http://www.microsoft.
com/standards/cdf.htm) defines content "push" technology for
many types of outputs.

Document Object Model Specification (http://www.
w3.org/TR/WD-DOM/) "allows programs and scripts to dynamically
access and update the content, structure, and style of documents."
This document is the official W3C specification.

Document Object Model (DOM) (http://www.w3.org/DOM/)
is the Document Object Model (DOM) home page.

Document Object Model Requirements (http://www.
w3.org/MarkUp/DOM/drafts/requirements.html) specifies the
scope of the DOM specification. Note that this document was
written before the specification was finalized.

EDI and XML (http://www.pira.co.uk/IE/top032.htm) discusses Electronic Data Interchange (EDI) and XML documents.
Also included are links to Electronic Commerce (EC)/EDI
resources.

Meta Content Framework Using XML (http://developer.
Netscape.com/one/metadata/submit.html) discusses a "data
model for describing information organization structures
(metadata) for collections of networked information." This is a
W3C note.

Deploying Metadata Representations of Web Content
(http://developer.Netscape.com/library/technote/metadata.
html) is an introduction to metadata. Several examples are
provided.

Open Software Description (OSD) (http://www.
microsoft.com/standards/osd/osdintro.htm) is an introduction
and home page for OSD, which describes software components
and platforms.

**Specification for the Open Software Description (OSD)
Format** (http://www.microsoft.com/standards/osd/osdspec.
htm) is an initial proposal for OSD.

Frequently Asked Questions about Open Software Description (OSD) (http://www.microsoft.com/standards/osd/osdfaq.htm) are answers to several frequently-asked questions about OSD.

Platform for Internet Content Selection (PICS) (http://www.w3.org/PICS/) is the W3C specification for the PICS standard and its use for labeling metadata to be associated with Internet content, especially for privacy and creating filtering mechanisms to prevent children from viewing inappropriate data.

Resource Description Framework (RDF) Model and Syntax (http://www.w3.org/TR/WD-rdf-syntax/) is a specification on RDF, "a foundation for processing metadata," providing "interoperability between applications that exchange machine-understandable information on the Web." W3C considers RDF to be a work in progress.

The World Wide Web Consortium Issues SMIL 1.0 as a W3C Recommendation (http://www.w3.org/Press/1998/SMIL-REC) is a press release announcing support for Synchronized Multimedia Integration Language (SMIL). According to the document, "SMIL enables authors to bring television-like content to the Web, avoiding the limitations for traditional television and lowering the bandwidth requirements for transmitting this type of content over the Internet."

XML-Data (http://www.w3.org/TR/1998/NOTE-XML-data-0105/) "describes an XML vocabulary for schemas, that is, for defining and documenting object classes." This document is a W3C note.

Specification for XML-Data (http://www.microsoft.com/standards/xml/xmldata.htm) is the document on which the XML-Data note (see the prior entry) is based.

Web Collections using XML (http://www.w3.org/TR/NOTE-XMLsubmit.html) discusses Web Collections, a metadata syntax and XML application that "describes the properties of an object." This document is a W3C note.

Glossaries

Markup languages, such as XML and SGML, use their own terminology — a combination of programming, engineering, and even printing. This section lists some useful glossaries.

Glossary (http://www.sgml.saic.com/html/glossary.html) is
a short SGML, XML, and HTML glossary.
Glossary (http://www.livepage.com/lpdocs/sgmled/
ancestorel) lists many SGML terms and thoroughly defines them.
Definitions of SGML-Related Terms (http://csgrad.cs.
vt.edu/~fdrake/cs5704/definitions.html) is an abbreviated list
of terms. Each definition, however, is quite long.
SGML Assessment: SGML Acronyms Explained (http://
www.sil.org/sgml/exetacro.html) is a lengthy list of SGML-
related acronyms.
Unicode Glossary (http://www.stonehand.com/unicode/
glosscnt.html) lists many terms related to characters, character
sets, and internationalization.
DSSSL Documentation Project Glossary (http://www.
mulberrytech.com/dsssl/dsssldoc/glossary.html) lists term
definitions contributed by members of the DSSSList subscribers.
HTML Glossary (http://www.willcam.com/cmat/html/
glossary.html) contains many terms related to HTML and
electronic publishing.
Glossary (http://booksrv2.raleigh.ibm.com/cgi-bin/
bookmgr/bookmgr.cmd/BOOKS/BLD05M00/GLOSSARY) is a 15-page
glossary, which is based on the *IBM Dictionary of Computing* and
which includes computing and SGML terms.
Hypertext Terms (http://www.w3.org/Terms) is a glossary of
computing and hyptertext terms.
Printing Terms (http://cmsmailserv.ucsc.edu/printing/
Custerms/custermsab.html) is a glossary of printing terms, broken
into 12 sections. Click on a range of letters to jump to a particular
section.

Index

(continued)

(continued)